3/4/77

DIRECTIONS IN PACIFIC TRADITIONAL LITERATURE

PHOTO BY SADIE J. DOYLE

KATHARINE LUOMALA

DIRECTIONS IN PACIFIC TRADITIONAL LITERATURE

Essays in Honor of Katharine Luomala

EDITED BY
Adrienne L. Kaeppler
H. Arlo Nimmo

Bernice P. Bishop Museum Special Publication 62

BISHOP MUSEUM PRESS
HONOLULU, HAWAII

PRINTING OF THIS BOOK was made possible by
partial financial support from the Wenner-Gren
Foundation for Anthropological Research, the National
Geographic Society, and Mrs. Helen Goo Carter. To
each of these the Trustees of Bishop Museum wish to
express their appreciation.

Library of Congress Catalog Card No. 75-41950
International Standard Book No. 0-910240-20-5

Dr. Roland W. Force, Director
Genevieve A. Highland, Editor
Sadie J. Doyle, Associate Editor

K ATHARINE LUOMALA received her bachelor's, master's, and doctoral degrees from the University of California at Berkeley and spent nine years there in their pursuit. Her association with Bishop Museum has been more than four times as long.

In preparation for a testimonial dinner held in her honor on April 18, 1973, I had occasion to consult Museum records and correspondence files and in this way learned some highly interesting things about Dr. Luomala. This volume is ample testimony of the high regard in which her students and colleagues hold her. But what of her mentors, those "ancestor figures" of past generations at Berkeley? What did they think of her? Coming of age in Berkeley — in Katharine Luomala's generation at least — was never easy. Graduate students in anthropology were tempered by a regimen of austere instruction in which quality of performance was not just expected, it was demanded. There were no frills and very little money to support students. More than one aspiring ethnologist was dispatched to a California Indian tribal remnant in the southern desert with $50 to last the summer. A thesis or dissertation was supposed to result. Out of this crucible of stern scholarly discipline whose ultimately benign philosophy had to be assumed because it was never very explicit, there emerged a cadre of professionals whose credentials were absolutely fine, a group whose productivity and quality of workmanship over the years proved that something surely was right about their training, however much it may have inclined them to be assessed rather generally as a fairly sober bunch. Katharine Luomala was one of these.

Throughout her career Dr. Luomala has maintained an interest in California Indians (her first field research dealt with the Diegueño

Indians) and in Pacific island peoples. It was after she had completed her doctoral dissertation on the Polynesian culture hero, Maui, that Professor E. W. Gifford wrote to the Director of Bishop Museum, recommending her. Given Professor Gifford's customary reserve and conservative approach to life, his characterization of Katharine Luomala as having "unusual qualifications for Polynesian library and museum work" and his noting that he had "a high respect for her honesty, perseverance, and intelligence" were downright eloquent.

A. L. Kroeber also wrote on her behalf, remarking that she was "very definitely a person of character, marked by self-reliance. Her personality," he went on to say, "is steady and even." Demonstrating his keen perception (as all who know her will attest), Kroeber added that, "She is sometimes taciturn, like many hard workers, but when the occasion demands it she opens up, and then is definitely amiable." As for her academic ability, Professor Kroeber remarked that Katharine Luomala "definitely ranks in the upper bracket of students who have received their anthropological training with us."

Dr. Luomala's principal appointment was always with the University of Hawaii, but she also, from 1938 onward, always held an affiliate appointment at Bishop Museum (as she does still) and always has identified with the Museum as well as the University. Certainly partly because of the recommendations she received from her professors she was appointed a Yale-Bishop Museum Fellow for 1938-39 and has been an Honorary Associate in Anthropology since 1941.

Even as a member of the Berkeley anthropology faculty that generally was not precisely noted for its unbridled praise of students, Professor Lowie probably established some sort of record as to reserve when he wrote in 1938 recommending Katharine Luomala to Dr. Peter Buck, saying that she had always impressed him "as a young woman of unimpeachable probity and rare steadfastness of purpose." Without risking the use of the superlative in the least he concluded, "Her presence is acceptable." And as with so many things Robert Lowie said, he was right.

To me Katharine Luomala has always seemed to provide paradoxes; some amusing and others that have earned respect for her. Of Finnish ancestry, she began her life in the chill surroundings of Minnesota, but moved on to spend most of her career in the sunny world of Polynesia and Micronesia. Her fair complexion and blonde hair have often confused those who thought her Polynesian because of the abundance of vowels in her surname.

Quiet, reserved, even shy at times, Katharine Luomala has another side — the side Alfred Kroeber saw. She can be surprisingly outgoing when inspired by her research interests. Some years back I invited Dr. Luomala to appear with me as a guest on a television program called "Bishop Museum Presents." The format was one which featured dialogue with various scientists in a 30-minute time slot. At first she was reluctant to appear, but my importuning prevailed and she relented. After some initial stiffness, our conversation grew quite animated and she obviously began to enjoy herself. She recalled field experiences, recounted anecdotes, shared some of her rich store of knowledge. The minutes sped by and I had hardly to say a word. She was magnificent! Totally immersed in our discussion, she continued for an hour or more as we adjourned from the studio to a nearby ice cream parlor.

I was always sorry the audience was unable to experience the full extent of her enthusiasm and the wealth of her personality as she spoke, without self-consciousness or reticence, of the things that mattered to her as an anthropologist. The depth of her dedication and her talent was revealed, showing her not only as a highly capable scholar and teacher, but as a charming and warm human being as well.

Katharine Luomala is richly deserving of the tribute paid her both by her professors nearly forty years ago and by those who studied with and under her in later years, and who, together, have created this encomium

ROLAND W. FORCE

B. P. Bishop Museum, Honolulu
April, 1976

PREFACE

> *If I give a mat it will rot,*
> *If I give cloth it will be torn,*
> *The poem is but bad, yet take it,*
> *That it be to thee boat and house,*
> *For thou art skilled in its taking,*
> *And ever have I joyed*
> *When the ignorant of heart have carried a poem*
> *In companionship with the wise.*
> —Voices on the Wind

CRAWFORD HALL at the University of Hawaii, at appointed hours in certain rooms, became a lively place. Gods and heroes appeared upon the stage in an ever-changing mélange—from Finland to Polynesia, from prehistoric times to the 20th century. Ibsen, the Grimm Brothers, Schehcrazade, Rangda and Barong, Hiawatha, Tahaki the handsome, Rama and Sita, and Maui the trickster played their parts alternately with Paul Radin, Clark Wissler, Robert Lowie, Stith Thompson, and Archer Taylor. These mythical personages, writers, collectors and theorizers were all equally remote to the novice folklore student in Anthropology 269, but through the presentation of Katharine Luomala they became old friends. And if one reads through one's notes taken during Dr. Luomala's folklore class, one finds an organized historical and theoretical presentation that is still as relevant and useful today as it was when the notes were taken—ten, twenty or more years ago. As students we learned not only about motif indices, definitions, narrative elements, and genres, but we also learned that folklore is an exciting, living phenomenon—that not only can we collect folktales of the past, but that folklore is constantly being created and used in everyday life in our own urban setting as well as in the nonliterate worlds. Katharine Luomala admonished us to collect in order to preserve the oral narrative arts of other peoples as well as to use the data for ethnographic and linguistic analysis and ultimately for theoretical contributions. This volume shows that Dr. Luomala's students have paid heed to her direction, for, although the student contributors cannot be classed as "folklorists," they have indeed collected and used folklore for many purposes. The seeds of this book were planted in 1968 during conversations among the two editors and Richard Stone about the influence of Dr. Luomala on her students. Many of us had taken her folklore classes and, owing to her influence, had collected oral literature in the field. Some of us had used this material in our theses and papers, yet we did not consider ourselves folklorists. We wondered, in fact, if she considered herself a folklorist—or if she, like the students she influenced, considered herself an anthropologist who used folklore as data. We hope we have not done violence to her teachings and that she will approve of her varied influence in our uses of traditional literature.

Her colleagues, too, are a diverse group. She and many of the famous names in Pacific studies, American studies, linguistics and folklore have had reciprocal influences on one another. In fact, so wide is her sphere that it became immediately apparent that we could only treat one small section of her interests in order to have a manageable book. We chose that aspect of Katharine Luomala's research interests that has made her famous throughout the anthropological world, that is, Pacific traditional literature. Only a few of her many colleagues fit into this small segment of her far-ranging interests and we hope others were not offended by not being asked to contribute. Two other papers by respected senior folklore scholars were written for this volume but were not included because they did not focus on the Pacific area—"The Study of the Folktale and Its Definitions" by Archer Taylor, and "The Migration of Folktales: Four Channels to the Americas" by Francis Lee Utley (published subsequently in *Current Anthropology,* 1974, Vol. 15, No. 1, pp. 5 - 27). Within the limitation of the subject matter we have tried to include a wide range of contributors including informants, students, and colleagues. In selecting contributors from among her many students, we invited only those who were directly influenced by her folklore interests, who conducted field research in the Pacific, and who have worked toward a degree under her.

At the outset, in good Luomala tradition, it is appropriate to define our terminology before we proceed to the essays themselves. "Pacific" here is used in a broad sense to include Polynesia, Melanesia, Micronesia,

Indonesia, the Philippines, and Japan. "Traditional literature" is used
rather than "folklore" because most of the contributors are not folklorists
and use their data with different emphases. Everyone knows and many
have pointed out that folklore, myths, and oral traditions can be bent
to any purpose and it is not the point of this book to say so once again.
Instead we wish to illustrate various "directions" of research in traditional
literature that can be traced to the influence of Katharine Luomala.
The influence on her students is obvious and it is probably correct to
assert that few of the ten contributors who were her students would
have collected and used this information if it had not been for her.
In fact the article by Eleanor Williamson was written originally as a
paper for Dr. Luomala's class. Katharine Luomala's long friendship with
Kenneth Emory and Samuel Elbert when they all taught together at
the University of Hawaii no doubt influenced them to collect such
information and to use productively the materials that they had already
collected. She encouraged Bacil Kirtley to prepare his Polynesian motif
index and he has now gone on to use his and Thompson's index in
comparative studies. She encouraged her informants to write up their
own information from their own cultural point of view and Mary Kawena
Pukui's contribution shows that inspiration. For many years Katharine
Luomala and William H. Lessa have been among the outstanding users
of oral tradition in the Pacific and their long friendship along with the
more recent one with Hiroko Ikeda have no doubt been mutually
stimulating. Thus each of the contributors can trace part of his "direction"
back to Katharine Luomala.

    This collection presents directions in Pacific traditional literature that
are in vogue in the 1970's and perhaps will point out directions that
future research may profitably take. The reader will note that the
contributors represented in the following pages are little interested in
"theory in folklore." Although they were asked for "contributions which
were analytical, theoretical, comparative, or which presented basic data,"
most contributions are essentially pragmatic or comparative in orientation. The contributors would seem to reject theory for its own sake,
but instead use ethnographic and historical oral traditions to weave their
conceptual frameworks. One wonders if perhaps this lack of interest
in theory is because of a reorientation on the part of many researchers
to make their information available for use by people of the culture
in which it was created and collected. UNESCO recognized the need
for such study and dissemination of oral tradition in the Pacific as the
first priority in the projected UNESCO study of Oceanic cultures. Indeed,
in a 1971 UNESCO meeting of experts on the study of Oceanic cultures
which included Pacific islanders it was recommended that practical

support be given to the training of indigenous scholars for the purpose of collecting oral traditions and that:

anthropologists, linguists, and historians be requested to consider as one of their responsibilities the recording of oral literature, in a form that may lead to publication in full of the authentic text in the local languages, accompanied by a faithful translation and all the appropriate scholarly commentary from the culture itself as well as from the theories of the disciplines concerned.

In much early folklore research in the Pacific the textual material was published either in the vernacular or in a European language, but seldom in both, and Pacific islanders have rightfully pointed out that this is not adequate in the scientific world of the 1970's. A few of the contributors here (notably Kenneth Emory, Adrienne Kaeppler, and Jack Ward) have included both vernacular and English texts and such articles will have uses which transcend the immediate purposes of this book. A related criticism by Hawaiians is that researchers do not publish basic Hawaiian data but just use them for theoretical constructs. The contributions of Mary Kawena Pukui, Eleanor Williamson, Samuel Elbert, William Kikuchi, and Adrienne Kaeppler will make a considerable amount of previously unpublished Hawaiian material available to the public. Another paper in this collection, that of Ben Finney, underscores another of the aims of the UNESCO program, in his urging of Pacific islanders to collect and write their own traditional literature. Accordingly we are especially pleased that Mary Kawena Pukui consented to publish her traditional material on Hawaiian leis. Most field workers today are not so fortunate as to have informants such as she, who not only fully answer the interrogator's questions, but pose questions he did not think to ask, and who point out further culturally relevant lines of inquiry. The UNESCO program of recording oral tradition in the Pacific will be carried out from 1973 to 1976 and is expected to generate substantial basic data. We can only hope for informants and collaborators such as Mary Kawena Pukui.

Another direction represented here is the comparative, in which a specific or areal traditional literature is placed in a wider context, as found in Bacil Kirtley with Polynesian narratives, William Kikuchi with fireball motifs, and Adrienne Kaeppler with dance interpretation. Contributions with theoretical or methodological implications or clarification will be found in an exposition of the myth-ritual controversy by William H. Lessa and in the functional interpretation of songs by H. Arlo Nimmo. Most contributions are based on the authors' own field work and add much new information to the realm of the oral literature of the Pacific area. On the other hand, David Eyde has convincingly reinterpreted

Malinowski. Samuel Elbert has expanded on one of Katharine Luomala's favorite themes, the use of place names in traditional literature. His demonstration of the secondary meaning of place names overshadowing their geographic importance is also exemplified by Kenneth Emory and Adrienne Kaeppler for the Tuamotu Islands and Tonga and suggests a pan-Polynesian literary device.

Another theme which emerges in this volume is the reflection of social organization in the traditional literature of the Pacific. Although social structure is never spelled out as such, the discerning anthropologist will find useful insights on values that reinforce sociopolitical structures. Nancy Pollock, for example, demonstrates the importance of traditional accounts of clan origin for understanding the hierarchy of clans in the Marshall Islands, and Jean Treloggen Peterson's essay on interethnic relations in northeast Luzon reveals how supernatural belief systems reflect and regulate the realities of social organization. This latter essay also suggests a model for examining schismogenesis which may be useful for examining similar phenomena elsewhere.

Richard L. Stone in his examination of the role of gossip in the political oligarchies of the Philippines demonstrates that gossip is a significant but little examined aspect of the social importance of contemporary oral tradition. The use of songs in political campaigns as presented by Eleanor Williamson is a superb example of appealing to ethnic oral traditions for calculated emotional responses in advancing political status—Western style. Ben Finney's essay on New Guinea stories of the Horatio Alger type adds another contemporary dimension to the uses of oral literature. He suggests that success stories of New Guineans who have excelled in Western enterprise may be used as an enculturative device in school textbooks to provide models to instill values that lead to success in present-day New Guinea and thereby may be used to further economic development.

Such diversity within this relatively narrow areal and subject matter points to the viability of the discipline and the flexibility of Katharine Luomala. The volume is far from uniform in the sophistication of writing style or orientation, which reflects the range of people touched by this woman. Some essays are descriptive accounts of particular oral literary traditions, transferring to the printed page what was formerly oral—an exercise which Katharine Luomala encouraged in all her students. Other essays apply traditional theoretical approaches to new bodies of data, while still others explore terrain less commonly trodden by students of oral literature. In addition, the essays reflect a genuine fondness for Katharine Luomala as a human being and a tremendous respect for her as teacher, colleague, and scholar. There is an old proverb that says that the greatest honor for a teacher is the recognition of her students. Perhaps the contributions made here will be a rung on her ladder of honor.

A.L.K.
H.A.N.

B. P. Bishop Museum, Honolulu
California State University, Hayward
September 1, 1972

CONTENTS

A TALE OF THREE CITIES

LEONARD MASON
University of Hawaii, Honolulu

I T MAY HAVE BEEN A MEETING of the Anthropological Society of Hawaii in the fall of 1946 when I first met Katharine Luomala. But of that I cannot be entirely certain. She had come to Hawaii that semester to join the University of Hawaii faculty in anthropology. I was just passing through Honolulu on my way back to the mainland from a research assignment in Micronesia.

Neither of us could then foresee that within six months Katharine and I would become colleagues at the University with adjoining offices in old Crawford Hall. By then I had returned to Hawaii to fill in for John Embree who was off to Southeast Asia on a United States government assignment. For three years, Katharine and I were the only anthropologists in the joint Department of Anthropology and Sociology. In the years since, anthropology at Hawaii has grown from a modest program of undergraduate studies to one that offers both master's and doctoral degrees. And the University's Manoa campus enrollment has climbed from 2,500 students to nearly 25,000.

Through the years, Katharine and I saw anthropology become established as an independent discipline at the University. As alternating chairmen of the new department, we learned to deal with the necessary but annoying "administrivia." Together we resisted the red tape and bureaucratic pressures of an expanding university which at times seemed to threaten our strong personal commitments to the promotion of quality rather than quantity among students choosing to major in anthropology and to the development of an active research program in Pacific Islands anthropology.

When Adrienne Kaeppler and Harry Nimmo asked me to prepare

a biographical sketch and a bibliography to be included in a *festschrift* for Katharine Luomala, I was of two minds about how to answer. Certainly I wanted to contribute to this volume in her honor on the occasion of her retirement from university service. We have shared experiences too many years at the University of Hawaii for me to feel otherwise. But I am no folklorist and I have conducted no research that could conceivably fall within the scope of the proposed collection. Preparation of the bibliography would certainly present no great difficulty. Katharine has compiled from time to time a listing of her many writings for distribution to interested parties. As for the biography, however, I did feel that it would be presumptuous of me to write in this vein about someone as accomplished as she is. Finally, I was persuaded that I was probably as well qualified as any other to undertake this means of honoring her. So I accepted the invitation.

It is with a deep sense of humility that I endeavor to do justice here to the image of one whom I regard most highly as friend, researcher, writer, and fellow teacher. But I do wish to share with others some of what I have learned, and come to cherish, about the person I have known now for a quarter century. Many who have had but brief or official dealings with Katharine Luomala perceive only a single dimension of her total character. Some, in the context of an initial formality, encounter what they imagine to be a resistance or barrier to further communication, for she is rarely casual in academic discourse. Yet with time and her acceptance of them, her students and her colleagues have found that she gives warmly and without reservation from her rich experience and her personal enthusiasm. It is the appreciation of that quality as much as the recognition of professional accomplishment which, I suspect, motivates those who have conceived and contributed to this collection of essays in her name.

This biographical statement is a distillation of countless items of information gleaned from Katharine Luomala's writings, from public records that report her professional activities, and from my own recollections and those of others who have been close to her over the years. An important feature of the *festschrift* has been to present it to her as a surprise. Of necessity, therefore, my research has had to be carried on covertly. I could not enlist the cooperation of her spouse, for she never married. Frequently I wanted to pick up the telephone and ask her for clarification of some incident in the past, but perforce I could not. In the course of my searching, as I explored those aspects of her long career less well known to me, I discovered new facets of her character and grew to understand her as a complete person more than ever before. My hope is that others who may read what I have written here will also experience some of that joy of discovery about our mutual friend and colleague.

The person to whom this *festschrift* is being dedicated, after reading what is written about her, may possibly view portions of the biographical essay as needlessly personal or private. I hope not. My only defense will be to remind her, as a fellow anthropologist, that one of the hallmarks of our profession is the objective inquiry and reporting about people, whether the subject be an anthropologist in Hawaii or, let us say, a community of Gilbert islanders. It happens that the focus of inquiry, here and now, is directed at the anthropologist. For once, the tables are turned. Peace to you, Katharine Luomala!

OVERVIEW

Contemplation of Katharine Luomala's career caused me to realize one thing at the very outset. This was the significant degree to which her life has been shaped by her residence and activities in each of three distinctly different communities. The impact of each of these, though different, has been remarkably complementary in the total effect. They are not all cities in the same sense, but their significance here makes them comparable. For that reason I have entitled this biographical review "A Tale of Three Cities," with apologies to Charles Dickens and acknowledgment of Katharine's lifelong commitment to the folktale.

The first of the three communities is Cloquet, a small town in northern Minnesota. This was Katharine's birthplace and where she grew up in rural Finnish-American surroundings and completed her primary and secondary education. The second is Berkeley, where she studied at the University of California, first as an undergraduate and later as a graduate student. This marked her exposure to a variant of Boasian anthropology and the start of a career in Oceanic mythology and folklore. The third is Honolulu, her residence for nearly half of her years. Here she was associated with the Bernice Pauahi Bishop Museum prior to World War II and also with the University of Hawaii from 1946 on.

Most of the war years in the early 1940's she spent in the nation's capital carrying on government research in a kind of applied anthropology. But in Washington, she seems to have been marking time. That period in my view represents something of a hiatus which fails to mesh meaningfully with her major interests either before or following the war.

Again the magic number three appears in recounting the communities where Katharine Luomala undertook her field researches. First, there was the Diegueño. While still a graduate student at Berkeley in 1934, she and a classmate did salvage ethnography with a male Diegueño informant on the Campo Indian Reservation in southernmost California.

Twenty-eight years after, the two women returned to their interest at Campo only to find that their sole informant had passed away. Second, as part of her research for a government agency in 1945 she interviewed townspeople in the Central Valley of California about their attitudes toward the Japanese-Americans who were soon to return to California after years of internment in wartime relocation centers. Her last field work was her most extensive undertaking of this sort. For five months in 1948-1949 she lived among the traditional Gilbert islanders of Tabi-teuea Atoll in eastern Micronesia. There she gave her attention primarily to collecting folklore and ethnographic data. This experience lent her a fine grasp of the dynamics of island living and has added depth to her interpretations of Oceanic folk-narratives, which were otherwise dependent upon documentary research.

Within the discipline of anthropology, Katherine Luomala is first a folklorist. She is also an ethnographer seriously interested in hard-core material culture, ethnoscience, and ethnohistory. Another way to describe her academic commitment would be to label her a cultural anthropologist whose primary data are folkloristic. She has a great capacity for synthesis. Her published works are a blend of the rigorous methodology displayed in her analysis of both field and documentary materials and her evident concern for the aesthetic impact of her written work. Her class lectures are painstakingly prepared and elegantly organized. Brilliantly creative, she focuses that creative talent on the literary quality of her writing. Her frequent talks to lay groups are light and witty, pleasurable as well as informative.

Her primary commitment in life is to serious scholarship. This is most evident in the extent of her own research and publication, in her interest in training undergraduates as well as graduate students in independent work, in her continuing support of local Sigma Xi and Phi Beta Kappa chapters, and in her stringent demands upon others for editorial competence in their written work, whether it be a term paper or an article submitted for publication. Her organizational ties have been stronger in the field of folklore than in anthropology, especially through her great contribution of time and effort to the American Folklore Society. More recently she has expanded the arena of her scholarly presence by participating in a number of international congresses convened in Europe and elsewhere which place priority upon ethnographic and folklore research.

One final comment in this overview. Katharine heartily dislikes waste of any kind—in her home, in her office, or in her professional work. Time, money, and energy are all very precious to her. She finds the routine demands of administration to be distasteful. She quickly becomes impatient with long-winded committee or other faculty meetings. Her world traveling, her holidays, even her leisure reading and avocations seem to lead ultimately into academically productive results. When she gives a talk, whether it be to a laymen's group or to a professional gathering, you can safely wager that the talk (or an expanded version of it, more likely) will turn up before long in some journal or proceedings somewhere in the world. When you think about it a moment, this is really a special kind of recycling. Katharine has been doing this for years before the concept became fashionable recently among advocates of environmental quality control. No doubt about it, she is a pro from the word "go." She is truly a scholar's scholar.

CLOQUET—YEARS OF NURTURE AND GROWTH

Katharine Luomala was born on September 10, 1907, in the little town of Cloquet in Carlton County in northeastern Minnesota. Her parents were John Erland and Eliina Forsness Luomala, both naturalized citizens who had come to Minnesota from Finland in their youth. Named Ellen Catarine Luomala at birth, she was the tenth of thirteen children. Some of her close friends and members of the family affectionately call her Kai (or Kaisa), but she is best known to others as Katharine. In Hawaii her surname causes occasional confusion about her ancestry because "Luomala" has a Polynesian ring to it, and she is known as an authority on Polynesian folklore and mythology. Once people see her in person, however, the sight of her blond hair quickly dispels that illusion.

Cloquet in the period of Katharine's childhood numbered only 5,000 residents more or less. The town lies about twenty miles west of Duluth, which is today the westernmost terminus of the St. Lawrence Seaway with a harbor that serves the exporting of iron ore from the famed Mesabi and Vermilion Ranges. A major part of Cloquet's population in the early years of this century labored in the manufacture of paper and wood products from timber cut in the Arrowhead region of northeastern Minnesota. Much of the land surrounding Cloquet supported farming and dairying. At the time of Katharine's birth, the Luomala family lived in town where her father worked as a clerk, store owner, and sawmill employee. Her mother contributed to the family income by operating a boarding house. Several years later they moved to the large farm which they owned about three miles north of Cloquet.

The immigration of Scandinavians into Minnesota had peaked by 1890. There followed a new migration of Finns and Slavs brought over from the Old Country to work in the iron mines. Many of these immigrants later settled on the land or took up residence in nearby towns. The small Finnish community of Esko, about five miles east of Cloquet, probably represented the cultural environment shared by the Luomalas at that time. It has been quaintly described in another place, as follows:

> The Finns are a clannish people who cling to their Old World manners and customs, and to a stranger may sometimes seem unfriendly. At one time a suspicious farmer accused them of practicing magic and of worshipping pagan deities. Entire families, he claimed, wrapped themselves in white sheets and retreated to a small square building set apart from the dwellings and worshipped their gods, calling upon them to bring rain and good harvests to Finns, and wrath upon their neighbors. On investigation, however, it was discovered that although they did wrap themselves in sheets and visit these "shrines" almost daily, it was not in the zeal of religion but for the purpose of taking baths. The Finns here are almost fanatical advocates of cleanliness, and each has his own "sauna" or steam bath-house (Federal Writers Project, 1938, p. 292).

The Luomalas, too, had a sauna on their farm. As a child Katharine was exposed to still other features of this powerful folk culture, including the Finnish language and the relating of Old World stories and folktales, to name but two examples.

The years of her childhood and youth must have presented a disturbing conflict of environments, when one contrasts the rigors of living year-round on a northern Minnesota farm with the warmth and security of belonging to a close-knit Old Country family. The dairy farm on which the Luomalas toiled daily was not a prosperous one. It required that every member of the household adhere to the Spartan virtues of hard work, denial, and faith in the future. Northern Minnesota winters are long and they can be bitter cold. Deep snow and the shortened hours of daylight made the miles traversed each day to and from school by Katharine and the other children an ordeal which at best could be frightening and at worst even dangerous, whether they walked or rode on a sled or in a bus.

On the afternoon and night of October 12, 1918, when Katharine was barely eleven years old, one of Minnesota's most devastating forest fires swept over the northeastern part of the state.

> Fifty to seventy-five separate fires merged and were fanned to huge proportions by a seventy-mile wind. The flames advanced over a vast area with incredible speed. More than 8,000 square miles were in the path of the flames and approximately 2,000 square miles, mainly in a radius of 50 to 100 miles of Duluth, were completely burned over. Nearly 400 persons lost their lives, 2,000 suffered burns, and about 13,000 were left homeless. Property loss, including standing timber, was approximately 25 million dollars. Cloquet suffered the heaviest loss, its residential and business sections being almost entirely destroyed. Quick action on the part of railroad officials and citizens saved the lives of all

but five. Residents who fled from the fire returned and built a new city (Federal Writers Project, 1938, p.292).

Katharine still recalls that awful day and night. In her freshman composition class at the University of California, under Professor Robert Palfrey Utter, an important influence in her career, she described her personal memories of the disastrous fire in an essay she entered, during her final year of graduate study, in a contest sponsored by the Cloquet Women's Friday Club and judged by a panel of experts from the Minnesota Historical Society. Her entry took the first prize of $25. Her vivid account of the famous holocaust was reprinted in Minnesota newspapers, and portions of it have been quoted by writers on forest conservation.

The following excerpts from her essay, as printed in *The Pine Knot*, Cloquet's daily paper, not only depict the tragedy of the fire itself but also provide us with fleeting glimpses of Katharine's perceptions of family and farm in the Finnish-American setting of her childhood (1936b).

"Even though it was Saturday, it hadn't been much of a day after all because it was wash day and potato picking time. Besides that, we children had been told to clean up the front lawn if we wanted to go to see Marguerite Clark in 'Seven Little Swans' that night .... Life was not simple for an eleven year old even in 1918."

As the afternoon wore on, the air grew smokier and the sky redder from the encroaching fires. Katharine's nineteen-year-old sister Mamie returned from town with stories that Cloquet might burn that night. Their father and the hired man had not returned from fighting fires in the back pasture. Their mother, on the advice of neighbors who had already been burned out, decided to abandon the farm. Sister Mamie and their eldest brother hitched the horses to a long, heavy potato truck.

"Even when we had left the yard, there had not been much fire about us, but now it suddenly swept about us until the whole world was on fire. Every tree on both sides of the road, every fence post, every stump, and every blade of grass was ablaze. Red flashes of flame skimmed up the trees and jumped across the branches which fell crashing to earth. The fence posts were rows of burning torches. The thick underbrush of the roadside was burning fiercely, and brands of fire fell into the road. The terrified horses dodged around them and galloped on. I expected any minute to be swept heavenward in a blazing wagon drawn by two snorting horses."

They soon discovered that Cloquet town was afire. They turned and drove back into the flames on the road they had already traveled.

"I was not afraid, though the sparks were flying into our laps and we had to put our hands over our heads to keep the fire out of our hair. Mamie had the reins .... I felt that no fire could hurt us while she was driving. She died the next year after the flu epidemic, and my most vivid memory of her still is as she was that night. She was like a goddess of some mythical, thundering chariot in Hades. The wind had torn away her hairpins, so that her long, heavy brown hair streamed in the wind. She drove the horses relentlessly over the fire in the road. Sometimes she would straighten and turn to look down at us as we huddled like frightened chickens in the truck box. It was her night."

They came then to a sheltered cove and a log cabin where many wagons and weeping people from the ravaged countryside had gathered. "The women rocked back and forth, back and forth, against each other. All that any of them could say was the Finnish phrase for 'Everything is gone.' "

While Katharine's mother took charge and plastered up burns with flour and corn syrup, the people related their experiences to the assembly. Then, suddenly, a man stomped into the cabin and told Mrs. Luomala that only ashes remained of the family home and that her husband and the hired man were gone, too. "I tried to figure it out, but nothing made sense .... We had nothing left. And who was going to melt tin at New Year to tell our fortunes when we had no father? No one else could do it right. I was hungry and wanted food. We had none now. Nothing was left but ashes."

Just then a large black horse came tearing up to the cabin. Through the door Katharine and the others saw that the man who jumped off the horse was Father. "His worried face and red rimmed, half closed eyes broke into smiles when he saw us. But he was very casual. 'Well, you are a runaway family,' he said. 'You never stay home. Everything's all right. Nothing burned. The wind turned in time to save the place. The hayshed roof blew off. The house is full of hungry people so you'd all better hurry home and do some cooking.' "

Whenever Katharine talks about her family from those early years in Cloquet, her recollections are replete with the reciprocal rewards of kinship and the personal security inherent in a setting of affection and love. There is also a quiet but unmistakable pride in the folk culture her family and neighbors maintained which enveloped her as she moved through childhood and early youth. Her mother's own strength of character seems to have been an important influence in shaping Katharine's outlook on the world. Her brothers and sisters and, later on, their spouses and children and grandchildren have provided Katharine over the years with the comfort of extended family relationships validated by the family's retention of holdings in the Cloquet farmland. As Katharine herself did not marry, these kin ties provide her with a family and incidentally enable her to pursue her teaching and research activities unhampered by demands of an immediate family.

In truth, the membership of that farm household near Cloquet was even more extended, if we acknowledge the close relationship between the Luomalas as farmers and the animals they tended and cared for night and day. Farm animals were well represented in the folk celebrations which complemented the more formal Finnish Lutheran observance of Christmas and other religious holidays. And antics of the animals always made up an important component of the Old World *märchen* whose narration was a regular feature of the Luomala family custom.

The mood of that Finnish-American dairy farm in the early 1900's is probably well captured in a 1952 news reporter's interview with Katharine about her folklore studies interests. After noting that Katharine's mother and an uncle had been famous story tellers at home, the news story concludes, "Their tales encompassed the early days of Minnesota, their neighbors and families, folklore of Finland and America told in a dramatic way to fill the child with a yearning for more and more stories of that type" (Stewart, 1952). It is scarcely surprising, then, that Katharine would translate her childhood fascination with legends and folktales into a lifetime profession, even though she did shift her regional focus from the Old World to Oceania.

She finished both elementary and high school in Cloquet. Of her work at this stage of her education, I know very little other than that she was a good student and took part successfully in high school debating contests. In her *Ethnobotany of the Gilbert Islands,* published many years later, she acknowledges a lifelong obligation to her high school botany teacher, Jane Nordquist, who "taught me to observe and first opened the door of science to me" (1953a, p. 2). Following her graduation from Cloquet High School she worked for a Cloquet public utilities company and, after her savings were lost in a local bank failure, obtained a better paying position at the Cloquet Lumber Company. This enabled her to earn and save enough money to join her older sister Signe in California and to enroll at the University of California at Berkeley.

BERKELEY–YEARS OF EXPECTATION AND PROMISE

UNDERGRADUATE STUDY

In the fall of 1927, Katharine Luomala began her freshman year at the University of California at Berkeley. Her older sister Signe had preceded her to the West Coast from Minnesota and was changing careers and attending the California School of Gardening in Hayward when she obtained a summer position as manager of a 900-acre asparagus ranch in Suisun, some thirty-five miles north of the Bay area. The owner of that farm was Miss Annie Montague Alexander, member of a *kama'aina* family in the Hawaiian Islands. It was through her sister Signe that Katharine first met Miss Alexander, who was well known at the University of California "for her sponsorship and support of research in zoology, paleontology, botany, and other fields" (Luomala, 1962b, pp. 341-342; compare Grinnell, 1958). Their meeting in 1927 was an auspicious one, for Miss Alexander gave much encouragement and financial assistance to Katharine's start in Polynesian studies after she had entered graduate school at the University. Meanwhile, a friendship was begun that would last until the older woman's death many years later.

Katharine in her freshman year was "already set to become an ethnographer and folklorist" (1962b, p. 342). With her preference for the study of oral narratives, she might as well have majored in English or in literature. She apparently anticipated more flexibility in anthropology for nourishing this interest of hers. There is no indication that she came into anthropology by way of American Indian studies, a major focus in the Berkeley department at that time. Such a motivation might have been expected because Katharine, while growing up in northern Minnesota, lived only a few miles from the Chippewa Indian Reservation at Fond du Lac. As an undergraduate she also took some work in botany and paleontology. She later credited Professor Charles Lipman of the Botany Department at Berkeley as one "who swung the door [of science] open wider to show the interrelations of several different disciplines" (1953a, p. 2).

Anthropology on the Berkeley campus was still very much an infant in the late 1920's. Professors Alfred L. Kroeber and Robert H. Lowie then comprised the principal teaching staff and shared responsibility for the introductory course. Kroeber's *Anthropology*, the first book written as a beginning text in the subject, was published in 1923. Full-time graduate students aiming at professional careers in the discipline began to enroll at Berkeley in the mid-1920's (Kroeber, 1957, p. 2). Just the year before Katharine began her freshman studies, the Berkeley department awarded its third doctorate in anthropology, to William Duncan Strong in 1926. The only Pacific Islands specialist on the staff was Professor Edward W. Gifford. He worked mainly at the Museum of Anthropology, then located in San Francisco. He came across the Bay to Berkeley three afternoons a week to conduct an upper division course in his specialty (McCown, 1969, pp. 88-89).

The year 1927 was still part of that excitingly prosperous period of "The Twenties" in the United States. However, the stock market crash in 1929 and the subsequent decline of the nation's economy were to take place before Katharine would graduate from the University. She, of course, was not at all prosperous when she arrived in California from the farm in far-off Minnesota. She managed to continue her studies only by working at various part-time jobs in the Berkeley area. Fortunately she received some added assistance from a Fred L. Lowengart Scholarship as a sophomore, and she held an Irene Purington Scholarship during her junior and senior years. When a senior she became a Reader in Anthropology. At that time she also made Phi Beta Kappa and was enrolled as an Associate Member in Sigma Xi. These awards testify that she was recognized as a good student, serious in her commitment to scholarship.

Her ties with the Berkeley campus have continued strong to this day. Some measure of her feeling about her adoption of Berkeley and California is suggested in these two sentences she would write many years later. "A memory shared by many of us who have lived under the Golden Bear banner of California is the hush which falls over the students seated in the sunshine and eucalyptus-laden air of the outdoor Greek Theatre in Berkeley before the words of the President of the University ring out and echo back from the brown hills, 'Fellow Californians!' It is a greeting known and felt in every corner of the state" (1946c, p. 208).

MASTER OF ARTS

After completing work for the A.B. degree in anthropology in 1931, Katharine Luomala enrolled in graduate work in the same department at Berkeley. In that same year, the Museum of Anthropology was returned to the Berkeley campus from San Francisco where it had been located since 1903. This move made the extensive anthropological collections of the Museum more immediately available for use in the teaching program at Berkeley. Also in 1931, Professor Ronald L. Olson was added to the anthropology faculty. He had completed his doctorate at Berkeley while Katharine was still in the midst of her undergraduate preparation. An extraordinarily gifted teacher, Olson during the 1930's presented both semesters of the introductory course to several hundred students with the help of two to four teaching assistants (McCown, 1969, p. 89). Professors Kroeber and Lowie were thereby enabled to devote more of their time to conducting upper division courses and graduate seminars. This, in brief, was the academic setting in which Katharine began her professional training as an anthropologist.

She continued her assignment as a Reader in Anthropology, while

the Great Depression gripped the entire country. Banks had failed by
the hundreds, mills and factories were shutting down, one worker in
four was unemployed, and many of those who were employed were
working for barely subsistence wages. A quarter of the nation's farmers
had lost their farms. To say the least, it was a most discouraging time
for everybody. In the election campaign of 1932, Democrat Franklin
Delano Roosevelt toured the country, promising aid to farmers, businessmen, and the unemployed. His "New Deal" in government was launched
shortly after he took office as the new President of the United States
in 1933. In that same year, Katharine completed her Master of Arts
degree in anthropology.

Her Master's thesis was entitled "Turtle's War Party: A Study in
Comparative Mythology" (1933). A widespread American Indian tale,
the legendary Turtle recruits a war party of animals, birds, and strange
objects (knife, brush, awl). When each of these in turn encounters trouble
in the enemy camp, Turtle goes in alone. He is captured and threatened
with various kinds of punishment. He begs his captors, above all, not
to throw him into the water, and thereby tricks them into sending him
back alive and safe to his natural environment. Katharine approached
her subject as an example of the secondary reinterpretation of familiar
Old World motifs into a burlesque of war parties, which were a favorite
American Indian preoccupation. Her documentation of Old and New
World variants of the tale, coupled with an examination of literary and
psychological aspects of the Indian versions, led to her own interpretation
of how New World story tellers reworked the Old World materials in
order to achieve their integration into Indian cultures. Years later, Katharine declared that Big Turtle had always been her favorite American
Indian character (1966a, p. 157).

Her Master's thesis committee was headed by Professor Lowie. Re-
calling his attention to parallels in cultural phenomena and their significance for reconstructing prehistory, there can be little doubt that Katharine's expressed interest in the comparative method received his hearty
approval. Although the Master's degree was a regular offering at Berkeley, it had never been closely integrated with the rest of the graduate
program (McCown, 1969, p. 90). Presumably, therefore, Katharine had
a good deal of leeway in developing this portion of her graduate experience. In 1937 she presented a summary of her thesis at a joint meeting
of the American Folklore Society and the American Anthropological
Association in New Haven. I believe this was her first formal presentation
of a research topic before a national professional group. To my knowledge she never published that paper nor any other version of her Master's
research.

DOCTOR OF PHILOSOPHY

The Master's degree behind her, Katharine Luomala immediately began work on the doctorate in anthropology at the Berkeley institution. She continued to assist Professor Kroeber as a reader for his undergraduate courses. The knowledge of Swedish and Finnish from family associations in Minnesota and of German and French acquired in school enabled her to secure additional part-time employment translating and abstracting technical articles for professors in botany and paleontology.

An unexpected happening in 1934 launched Katharine on serious pursuit of her major academic interest. Years later in a news interview (Stewart, 1952) she would recall how Miss Annie Alexander, impressed with Katharine's research on the mythological Turtle's war party, brought the completed thesis and its young authoress to the attention of Martha Warren Beckwith, Research Professor of Folklore at Vassar College. Dr. Beckwith was then in the process of completing a manuscript on Hawaiian mythology. This resulted in the folklorist asking Katharine to join her in Hawaii that summer to assist in checking references. Miss Alexander's financial assistance made it possible for Katharine to spend four months at Bishop Museum in Honolulu working alongside Mary Kawena Pukui, who was translating Hawaiian material for Dr. Beckwith. In the course of the summer employment, the young graduate student came to a decision to write her doctoral dissertation on Maui, the famed Polynesian demigod and culture hero.

Katharine would regard Dr. Beckwith as close friend and mentor until the latter's passing in 1959. In an essay written in her memory for the *Journal of American Folklore* (1962b), Katharine describes the close relationship between Dr. Beckwith and Miss Alexander, the two women who exerted such a prominent influence on her development at this stage of her professional career. As a young girl, Martha Beckwith had moved to Hawaii with her parents who were both school teachers. They also developed a plantation at Haiku on the island of Maui. It was there on Maui that Martha Beckwith and Annie Alexander forged the firm bonds of their lifelong friendship. The close ties between the two *kama'aina* families led the Alexanders in later years to provide financially for the creation of the Research Professorship in Folklore at Vassar College for the sole use of Dr. Beckwith. The latter had meanwhile studied under the anthropologist Franz Boas at Columbia University, earning her M.A. degree in 1906 and her Ph.D. in 1918 at that institution. Dr. Beckwith's most significant research in the opinion of many, *The Kumulipo: A Hawaiian Creation Chant*, was dedicated by her in 1951 to the memory of Annie M. Alexander, her "Lifelong friend and comrade from early days in Hawaii, whose generous sponsorship has made the author's research possible" (quoted in Luomala, 1962b, p. 341).

In the same essay Katharine tells how the Misses Beckwith and Alexander, in that summer of 1934, "deflected me into Polynesian study with the suggestion, already well-plotted by both of them secretly without my knowledge, that I immediately join Miss Beckwith ... to help her with her manuscript on *Hawaiian Mythology*." She adds, "I left four days later on the *Malolo*" for Honolulu (p. 342). She acknowledges her indebtedness through the years to the older woman's example which gave her "rigorous training and discipline in the standards of sound scholarship" (p. 343). In many respects the model provided by Dr. Beckwith's career as folklorist and anthropologist is reflected in Katharine's own development as a scholar. Thus, as she concludes in eulogizing her cicerone, "Despite the training the students of Boas got in folklore and the work many of them have done with it, Martha Beckwith was one of the few to become better known as folklorist than anthropologist" (p. 345).

Katharine's first attempt at field research followed closely on her return to California from Hawaii. It seems that some field work experience was required in the doctoral program at Berkeley, although in those days the Department could offer candidates no financial support nor did it prepare them for investigations in the field. Gertrude D. Toffelmier, a very close friend of Katharine's who was one year behind Katharine in the graduate program, shared in this initiation to field work. Many years later Mrs. Toffelmier told me about that experience. She happened to be traveling in southern California while Katharine was yet in Hawaii and she came upon the Campo Indian Reservation near the Mexican border. Upon inquiry she learned that the sheriff at Campo, a 58-year-old Diegueño Indian, would be willing to talk about traditional Diegueño culture if the two women could find themselves a place to live. Back in Berkeley, Professor Kroeber agreed to the proposal to conduct their research at Campo. He acknowledged that Indian groups in the northern part of the state had been overresearched by anthropologists and that more attention might well be given to the southern tribes. Neither Katharine nor her fellow graduate student cared much for compiling the culture element lists which were then in vogue in the Berkeley department as a topic for anthropological field inquiry. However, at Dr. Kroeber's suggestion, they agreed to look for some items to add to his lists.

Once again aided by her benefactor, Miss Alexander, Katharine joined Mrs. Toffelmier in the late summer of 1934 at the little town of Jacumba, some fifteen miles from the Campo Reservation, where they had arranged to stay in a small hotel. For two months they labored with their Diegueño informant. Apparently Katharine found very little in Diegueño mythology to feed her then current interest. Both women were getting a bit discouraged when they happened to ask about dreams and dreaming. Their informant proved to be a witch doctor, and the only one still practicing among the southern Diegueño. From then on he talked so volubly that they easily filled several notebooks on the subject.

Katharine and Gertrude Toffelmier (who had majored in psychology at Columbia University before coming to Berkeley) co-authored a lengthy article on dreams and dream interpretation based on their field interviews with the Diegueño witch doctor. It was published in the *Psychoanalytic Quarterly* (1936c). In 1962, with renewed interest in working up unused material from the 1934 field work, Katharine prepared and read a paper on individual changes in Diegueño sib membership at the Thirty-fifth International Congress of Americanists in Mexico City. A revised version of that paper was published in *Ethnology* (1963a). Also in 1962, Katharine returned with her old friend, Gertrude Toffelmier, to the Campo Indian Reservation for a week-long visit, only to learn that their witch doctor informant had passed away. Members of the family, still remembering the anthropologists and their research on the reservation twenty-eight years before, permitted them to place flowers on the grave of the deceased Indian practitioner.

Katharine's first year or so at Berkeley after completing her Master's degree can hardly be said to have been well integrated, considering such diverting activities as her excursion into Hawaiian mythology and her field contact with the Diegueño. However, from the end of 1934 until mid-1936, when she was awarded the doctorate in anthropology, she was deeply into her dissertation research. She took required seminars and research courses from Professors Lowie, Kroeber, Olson, and Gifford, who then comprised the nucleus of the anthropology faculty. She continued to assist as a Reader in the Department of Anthropology. In 1935 Sigma Xi admitted her to full membership in that honorary scientific society.

Occasionally Katharine remarks that she really educated herself at Berkeley, especially in her chosen field of folklore study. Among the faculty, Robert H. Lowie undoubtedly was the most helpful to her, and he served as chairman on the committees for both advanced degrees. Nevertheless she was working in an atmosphere of Boasian anthropology and was certainly subject to that impact. Kroeber and Lowie, central pillars of the program at Berkeley, had each earned his doctorate under Franz Boas in the latter's earlier years at Columbia University, as had

Martha Beckwith, the folklorist. The central significance of research based on field investigations coupled with an emphasis on empirical methodology constituted a direct heritage which Katharine brought away with her upon completion of her graduate study at the University of California. While she has continued to build on that heritage, she has not conformed rigidly to the entire model by any means.

One of her younger colleagues at the University of Hawaii who in recent years worked closely with her in a graduate seminar has given this impression of Katharine's value to the academic community (letter from David B. Eyde, July 23, 1971).

> She is firmly rooted in the Boasian tradition and understands it better than anyone I have ever run into. She makes it a meaningful approach for students, and certainly reinfluenced me in the direction of the Boasians during the last couple of years in Hawaii. At the same time, she knows what is going on in other schools of thought and makes it available to her students, especially in the form of the carefully chosen supplementary readings in all her courses. (At the same time, it is puzzling how little influenced she has been by the development of other schools of thought.)

The anthropology program at Berkeley varied but little between 1931 and 1938, according to Theodore D. McCown (1969), who was both doctoral candidate and a faculty member in the late 1930's. Graduate students were expected to be prepared on a variety of subjects for the Ph.D. qualifying exams, including world ethnography, the history and theory of anthropology, and three special fields within the discipline. World ethnography meant the language, culture history, and ethnology of the peoples of the world. It was first learned in undergraduate courses taught by Lowie and others and later by concentrated reading as a graduate student. Guidance in knowing the history and theory of anthropology was provided in a 30-page reading list, mostly articles considered to be important. Written examinations, five long days of them, were read by Professors Kroeber, Lowie, and Olson. Satisfactory work on these was followed with an oral examination by at least five professors from the Department and outside. The pattern or format appears generally familiar but, as McCown concludes, "The kind of anthropology that developed and flourished between the wars no longer exists" (p. 92). How closely did Katharine fit into this pattern as a graduate student? Notes on file with her dissertation (1936a) indicate that she had taken seminars in "History and Theory of Anthropology" from Lowie and in "Primitive Literature" from Paul Radin, plus research credits earned under Professors Lowie, Kroeber, and Olson, and folklorist Martha Beckwith (for the work done at Bishop Museum).

Katharine's dissertation topic was "Maui the Demigod: Factors in the Development of a Polynesian Hero Cycle." It was 88 pages long and was signed "Ellen Katharine Luomala." Her description of the approach she used in the study is informative about the way in which she had achieved an independence of method and purpose, yet continued to adhere to the basic imperatives of the Berkeley research tradition.

"The purpose of this study is not to use the tales as a key to Polynesian history, although a survey of the material is enough to convince one of the truth of Westervelt's statement that it constitutes one of the strongest links in the mythological chain of evidence binding the scattered islands of Polynesia into one nation. The approach is rather that of a mythologist, who, while appreciating the often observed uniformity of the cycle, has nevertheless been most impressed by the multitudinous local differences between the variants, and wishes to discover the processes involved in the obviously vital re-interpretation made of these myths in each archipelago. It is with the diversity of form in the literary and psychological re-creations of the character and deeds of Maui that this study is concerned. Specific historical facts have played their part, as have the social and religious influences which were current in each local culture. These will be taken into account" (p. 10).

The Doctor of Philosophy degree in anthropology was conferred upon Katharine Luomala in the company of three other recipients in that year of 1936, namely, George Devereux, Harold F. Driver, and Waldo R. Wedel. In the following year, Philip Drucker and Katharine's close friend Gertrude D. Toffelmier were similarly honored, and in 1938 Homer Barnett's name was added to the Berkeley roster of graduating anthropologists. These are names which characterize the period of Katharine's emergence from graduate preparation to possession of the discipline's union card, and to those who know the later works of these graduates they demonstrate the individual achievement by each Berkeley product as each fashioned his or her own kind of anthropology—just as Katharine Luomala did.

POSTGRADUATE ACTIVITIES

To have earned a Ph.D. in anthropology in the 1930's did not insure prompt advancement to membership on a university faculty, as would become the custom during the more prosperous years of the discipline, for example, in the 1960's. Though the annual production of new doctorates in the United States remained remarkably low during that earlier period, the teaching positions available in anthropology numbered even less. In the year after Katharine's receipt of the professional degree, not unlike others of her academic generation, she found much needed employment in activities that were related only indirectly to her primary anthropological interest.

The fledgling anthropologist continued to live in Berkeley. During the summer and early fall of 1936 she substituted for an absent staff member as assistant preparator in the University's Museum of Anthropology. Here, working under the Oceanic specialist E. W. Gifford, she was assigned to reorganize certain aspects of the museum library, accessions catalog, and lantern slide classification. Later, Gifford recommended Katharine to Bishop Museum as one who "possesses high qualifications for a dual position of museum work and anthropology research worker," adding that in the eight or nine years he had known her as a student at Berkeley he had gained "high respect for her honesty, perseverance, and intelligence" (letter to Dr. Peter Buck, Director, Bishop Museum, August 31, 1936). Although work in the Hawaii institution was not available to her just then, she had moved another step closer to an enduring association with Bishop Museum.

The next job, which would carry Katharine well into 1937, was with the National Park Service's Western Museums Laboratories in Berkeley. For that agency she produced a 115-page compendium on *Navaho Life of Yesterday and Today* (1938a), drawing upon the mass of already published materials and some unpublished notes provided by willing specialists on Navaho culture. The book, written to meet the demands of the Park Service, was a competent synthesis of the prehistory, history, and ethnography of the Navaho Indians of Arizona and New Mexico. Twenty years later Katharine would surprise a *Honolulu Advertiser* reporter when she admitted, "I once wrote a book on the Navaho, and believe it or not, I have never seen one before .... it was a library research book" (King, 1958). Her firsthand introduction to the subjects of her 1938 monograph finally took place in 1958 on her way home to Hawaii following a summer conference of folklorists at Indiana University. She had accepted an invitation to visit a friend and former social worker from Hawaii who was then employed in the same capacity in Arizona on the Navaho Reservation. Katharine's brief stay with her friend, Miss Inez Taylor, gave her the opportunity to meet Navaho Indians at tribal headquarters in Window Rock and to enjoy the spectacular Navaho Tribal Fair. The experience must have evoked a strange feeling of *déjà vu* despite the many changes in Navaho custom since the 1930's.

Publication of the Navaho study by the National Park Service merited a review in the *American Anthropologist* by Clyde Kluckhohn, acknowledged authority on the Navaho people (1939). Noting that "we have lacked a satisfactory general account" of the Navaho, he recommended the Luomala compilation as "useful to the general student of anthropology who wishes to get within a brief space a reasonably accurate picture of the Navaho." He went on, however, in a more critical vein: "There are numerous turns of phrase which seem to me unprofessional and misleading ... as 'The religious geniuses who conduct the nine-day chants' ... " (p. 312). Here he was referring to the Navaho "singers" who specialize in medicine and ritual. His criticism is noteworthy in view of Katharine's own aspirations and a recognized talent (in later years) to combine a literary flair with rigorously objective reporting. What is more significant about this early work is the evidence of her ability, even then, to sift through a great accumulation of materials and compress it into a concise statement. This she has demonstrated time and again in her major treatises on Polynesian folklore. No doubt this very quality appealed to editors Irwin T. Sanders and Richard B. Woodbury when they chose to reprint two sections from the National Park Service publication, under the titles "The Navajo Country" and "Clan Origins," in summarizing those aspects of Navaho life in their two-volume work on *Societies Around the World* (1953, Vol. 1, pp. 205-206, 264-265).

Resumption of work under the driving desire to immerse herself in Polynesian folklore research became possible during 1937-1938 when she won an award from the American Association of University Women, the Dorothy Bridgman Atkinson Fellowship. The grant amounted to $1,500 for the year, which seems awfully small nowadays, but that sum went a great deal farther to keep body, mind, and soul together in 1937 than it would in 1973. This support allowed Katharine to pursue independent postdoctoral studies at the University of Chicago and with anthropologist Ruth Benedict and others in New York City. She gave her primary attention to examining methodologies used in research on Old World epics and their applicability to the analysis of Polynesian traditions. At the same time she focused her effort on a comparison of legends about a prominent mythological family in Polynesian genealogies which included the red-skinned Tahaki (Tawhaki), regarded throughout the islands as a chief's chief of great virtue, and his grandson Rata the wanderer, who defied the "little people" (Menehunes) and then won them over to work with him. This concern with the Tahaki hero cycle complemented her earlier choice of the demigod Maui for her dissertation research and would lead in time to production of several short papers (1940c; 1940d; 1940e) and two chapters in her popular *Voices on the Wind* (1955a).

While yet studying research methodologies in Chicago, the persistent young woman, now entering her thirties, applied for a joint Bishop Museum—Yale University Fellowship to continue her folklore investigations

at the Museum in Hawaii. She solicited a supporting letter from Professor
A. L. Kroeber, who recommended her as "a high-grade scholar with
an independent mind." Describing her personality as "steady and even
. . . definitely a person of character, marked by self-reliance," he went
on to say, "she is sometimes taciturn, like many hard workers, but when
the occasion demands it she opens up, and then is definitely amiable."
Her preoccupation with folklore studies within the anthropological discipline he interpreted as evidently representing "the conversion of literary
proclivities into scientific-scholarly channels" (letter of recommendation,
January 18, 1938). Professor Robert H. Lowie, who had been her dissertation adviser, wrote in similar vein, "her scholarship as a comparative
folklorist is of high grade." He recalled that "as a student she tended
to avoid certain aspects of ethnology that were not congenial to her,
but she has always displayed exemplary independence in the fields she
has consistently cultivated since her early undergraduate days." Her research in folklore and mythology, he ventured, would be likely "to differ
advantageously from the somewhat compilatory labors of certain folklorists precisely because she sees the problems from a wider anthropological perspective" (letter of recommendation, January 17, 1938).

Successful in obtaining the coveted fellowship which paid her $2,000
for each of two years from 1938 to 1940, Katharine departed her Berkeley
base for that period to enjoy the unparalleled opportunity of integrating
her own research with the more comprehensive program of Polynesian
studies then underway at Bishop Museum, of poring through the Museum
library's extensive holdings in Polynesian literature and the collections
of unpublished manuscripts, and of working closely with the Museum
staff of recognized specialists in Polynesian anthropology.

She now had ample time to apply the comparative research methods
and procedures explored during the term of her AAUW Fellowship.
Named an Associate in Anthropology at Bishop Museum, she continued
to study the interrelationships of Polynesian heroic traditions, tracing
the diffusion of motifs in the legends, and clarifying cultural affinities
between the various Polynesian regions. While not disputing the oft expressed observation about Polynesian homogeneity in language, culture,
and mythology, she directed her attention rather to the rigorous explica-
tion of local differences which she discerned in the traditions. By this
approach she contributed to a better understanding of the cultural divisions within Polynesia and their differentiation in the course of Polynesian culture history. As she had pointed out in her application for fellowship aid, traditions may be regarded "as so much raw data, which can
be defined and compared as concretely and objectively as any elements
of material culture—axes, houses, etc." In this conviction she reflected

the methodological biases associated with both European researches on Old World epics and Boasian anthropology as she had encountered it at Berkeley. "To a specialist in mythology," she reiterated, "a myth incident or episode is as objective a unit as an axe, and the differences and similarities of these units can be observed equally clearly and scientifically" (1938e).

Committed to this intensive and controlled approach to the comparative study of Polynesian mythology, Katharine waded into a long neglected field of research, and began to separate the grain from the chaff contained in earlier publications by theorists who had utilized Polynesian traditions as a direct source of history in tracing the migrations of Oceanic peoples. Director Peter H. Buck of Bishop Museum, in *An Introduction to Polynesian Anthropology* (1945), took note of Katharine's folklore research in the late 1930's as a Bishop Museum Fellow (p. 46) and associated her with other comparativists in Polynesian mythology whose works had succeeded those of such well known authorities as Sir James Frazer of England and Professor Roland Dixon of Harvard (p. 47). In the summer of 1939 she took advantage of the meeting of the Sixth Pacific Science Congress in the San Francisco Bay Area to return briefly to Berkeley, where she delivered a paper on some of her research on the development of Polynesian hero-cycles (later published, 1940e).

During Katharine's sojourn in Hawaii, Bishop Museum published her comprehensive study of Oceanic, American Indian, and African myths of snaring-the-sun (1940a) which evolved from her preoccupation with the Maui myth-cycle. In a Polynesian version of this tale, Maui captures the capricious sun god with a rope of his sister's pubic hair and clubs him with his grandmother's jawbone, magically laming the sun so that now he moves more slowly through the sky prolonging the dusk before dark. From the discontinuous distribution of the tale and without evidence of loss in intervening areas, Katharine concluded that "each [major world] area had independently developed its own myth-complex about the theme" and that in each instance development was along different lines (p. 52). However, within the Pacific region, she found to the contrary that "geographic and historic connections overrule the possibility ... that the theme might have been independently invented in each Oceanic area" (p. 53). Stith Thompson, dean of American folklorists and author of *The Folktale*, has cited her comparative research on the sun-catcher story as "very thorough" (1946, p. 314). Twenty-four years later, Katharine supplemented her monograph by an article on the same theme (Motif A728, according to Thompson's motif-index) with additional material she had overlooked before or which had been published since by others, and also with Gilbertese variants of the myth collected by her personally during field work in 1947-1948 (1964a).

During the time that Katharine was in Hawaii she actively participated in the community of anthropologists and others affiliated with Bishop Museum and the University of Hawaii. Archaeology and Polynesia tended to be preserves of the Museum, while the University inclined toward acculturation and applied anthropology, but some anthropologists bridged the division of labor by joint appointment in both institutions. Differences between "pure" and "applied" science and research were not really important in this academic community. Informal interaction was regularized to some extent by weekly luncheon meetings held at a restaurant in the Kewalo district of Honolulu adjacent to the wharf from which the tuna fishing fleet operated.

Concerning this casual though tightly knit grouping, Katharine later recalled: "For a couple of years before the end of 1941, Gordon Bowles, John de Young, and Jack Porteus spent Thursday at the Museum working on Mokapu bones, and then would go with some of the staff, usually [Kenneth P.] Emory, [Margaret] Titcomb, and myself, to Kewalo for lunch. Converging from the [University at the] opposite end of town would be [Felix M.] Keesing, [John] Embree, and [Denzel] Carr. Other 'regulars' were Edwin G. Burrows and Laura Thompson. Psychology was sometimes represented by Colin Herrick, Geology by Chester Wentworth, Botany by Harold St. John, Oriental Languages by Edward Schafer, and Geography by John W. Coulter. Then there were at times visitors, just going out on expeditions to the south Pacific or returning home. As anyone, regardless of previous interests, becomes a scientist on marrying one, spouses were often present too, and our Kewalo table was often a very long and noisy one" (1970c, p. 30).

A grant of funds from her benefactor, Miss Annie Alexander, made it possible for Katharine to extend her stay in Hawaii an extra six months. In 1941 she returned to Berkeley. During the University's spring term she assisted Professor Kroeber in research on the Indian arts of North and South America. In the summer she undertook her first teaching assignment when she offered a course on American Indian cultures as Lecturer in Anthropology at the University of California at Berkeley.

Until this time, the closing year of her Berkeley association, Katharine fortunately had been able to focus her efforts, within anthropology, almost exclusively in folklore research. Occasional forays away from Berkeley had brought her into closer touch with scholarly resources required to develop her commitment to Polynesian folklore studies. Disciplinary training and, of necessity from time to time, gainful employment were dependent primarily upon facilities available in the Berkeley area, especially at the University of California. In that environment, she found herself inevitably involved to some extent in American Indian ethnology. Any anthropologist who concentrates his major investigative effort in a particular region will recognize the advantage that occasional work in another region allows to broaden one's analytic perspective and thus to enhance the quality of the research conducted in the region of one's primary interest. The complementary relationship between Polynesian and American Indian studies during Katharine's Berkeley years undoubtedly contributed much to her maturation as a researcher and extended her foundation of experience for use in future course offerings as a teacher. Regardless of her contribution to American Indian anthropology, Katharine had by this time unquestionably demonstrated her promise and her commitment as a scholar in the field of Oceanic studies.

And then the events of World War II touched her career, as they did for so many of us in that generation. New opportunities opened up for the practical application of scholarly experience. Unfamiliar assignments in other regions and other subject areas of anthropology invited new commitments by those who became thus involved.

MARKING TIME DURING WORLD WAR II

The years associated with America's participation in World War II saw Katharine Luomala shift her base of operations from Berkeley to Washington, D.C. She worked in the latter city for several government agencies, from 1942 to 1946, as interviewer and analyst in surveys of public opinion on various topics of domestic significance. She traveled frequently and extensively about the country in pursuit of these labors, always working out of the nation's capital. This was a kind of applied anthropology, utilizing the techniques of interviewing, analyzing, and reporting which are fundamental to the academic discipline. Now these same techniques and experiences were being turned to meet the more immediate and practical demands of a nation at war.

According to all accounts, Katharine performed well in the new role, even though at times she found aspects of the employment distasteful, as when she encountered attitudes among local populations reflecting prejudice and bigotry incompatible with the open-mindedness and objectivity implicit in her practice of anthropology. That she did not continue on in government service following the termination of some agencies after the war is perhaps indicative of her basic reaction to the whole experience. Nonetheless, as Katharine has demonstrated again and again, though a task be not entirely to her liking she is not one to avoid responsibility. In those war years, she dug in and gave her best

effort, no matter what the assignment. Once she had decided to return
to academe, however, she appears to have put the entire engagement
of the past four years behind her, except to tidy up some observations
for publication. She came back to the university campus culture with
a fresh enthusiasm in the scholarly role she had set aside for the duration
of the war.

By what means Katharine accomplished the transition from Berkeley
to Washington in 1942 I do not know. In the first two years she served
as Social Science Analyst, and Study Director, in the Division of Program
Surveys, Bureau of Agricultural Economics, U.S. Department of Agriculture. There she showed an adeptness at applying sampling techniques
in relation to public opinion surveys. Her acknowledged talent in drawing out reluctant interviewees during her visits to various parts of the
country may have been related as much to the experience of her earlier
years in a northern Minnesota farming community as to any technical
ability gained from her anthropological training.

In her bibliography for this first half of her wartime employment,
there is only a reference to "Restricted reports, mimeographed, on attitudinal surveys on various subjects" (1942-1943). For many of us old-timers
who similarly served in a federal agency during World War II, the story
is much the same—a gap in the personal publication record resulting
from an officially expressed need to classify reports in graded degrees
of secrecy, often with seemingly little relation to the contents. For many
of us, and possibly it is the same for Katharine, we find it difficult
now to recall the details, or even the titles, of some of those reports
which at the time so completely demanded our attention.

WAR RELOCATION AUTHORITY

In 1944 Katharine changed jobs, moving to the Community Analysis
Section of the War Relocation Authority. In the early months of 1942
the United States government had created the War Relocation Authority
(WRA), within the Department of the Interior, to supervise the internment of more than one hundred thousand Japanese-Americans evacuated from West Coast states as a wartime emergency measure. Evacuees
were transferred to ten Relocation Centers located in Colorado, Wyoming, Arizona, California, Idaho, Utah, and Arkansas. Open conflict pro-
voked by dissidents disrupted several of the center communities toward
the end of 1942. WRA administrators belatedly recognized that they
lacked adequate understanding of community trends within the centers.
So the Community Analysis Section was set up within WRA and community analysts were recruited to serve in all relocation centers and at

headquarters in Washington, D.C. For the most part, these analysts had a background in social anthropology. Within the centers, they "reported on evacuee attitudes, predicted probable reaction to proposed administrative programs, and, in general, studied the social organization of the relocation center community and its functioning from day to day, but most of all during crises." Analysts in Washington "coordinated the work in the centers and synthesized center reports" for use by WRA officials in Washington (Luomala, 1948, p. 30).

As a social science analyst assigned to Section headquarters in the capital city, Katharine was able to apply much of the experience gained while working in the Department of Agriculture. One of her co-workers in the Community Analysis Section told me many years later that she still recalled Katharine's impressive ability to pick out things from the multitudinous reports received, sifting all kinds of material, and her insistence that all writing for administrators' eyes be done clearly and colorfully. In the main office of the Community Analysis Section, Katharine helped to produce the great variety of reports which aimed at interpreting administrative problems in the centers in the light of the cultural background and current orientations of the Japanese-American evacuees. As Assistant Head of the Section, she worked closely with anthropologist Edward H. Spicer, then section chief after a term as community analyst in one of the Arizona relocation centers. When she was not in Washington, she was out visiting the relocation communities or sampling attitudes in other parts of the country where the evacuees were gradually being relocated upon their release from the centers.

Once when reminiscing about those wartime years in Washington, Katharine remarked, "Sometimes it seemed to me that the best place to come across [old friends and former acquaintances in anthropology] was in the middle of the street at 14th and Pennsylvania, Washington, D.C., and since it was wartime one did not ask but hoped to be told where they were coming from and where they were going" (1970c, p. 31). Like Katharine, many American anthropologists had offered their services during the national crisis, applying their technical skills and knowledge within countless government agencies both civilian and military. Among anthropologists whom Katharine either knew or worked with in the Community Analysis Section of WRA, at headquarters or in the centers, were (besides Edward Spicer), John Embree, John Provinse, Margaret Lantis, Morris Opler, Weston LaBarre, Marvin Opler, E. Adamson Hoebel, Rachel Reese Sady, and G. Gordon Brown, to name only some of them.

The Community Analysis Section adopted a policy of reproducing its several series of reports in mimeographed form without any security classification. These were open to use by other government agencies, social scientists, and others who might wish to learn from the WRA experience of managing migrants en masse. Katharine assisted in the compilation of a 200-page bibliographic guide to these materials listing a total of 2,356 items (1945-1946). After the war she published an article in the journal *Applied Anthropology*, with details about the availability of WRA records, and particularly those of the Community Analysis Section, for research by interested scholars (1948). She urged there that these materials not be forgotten after their immediate usefulness to the WRA program had ended: "It is to be hoped that no agency of the United States Government ever has to administer again a program in which many innocent American citizens are kept behind barbed wire by their own government . . . . Continued research alone can glean the lessons to be gained from the experiences of administering ten relocation centers . . . and returning their residents to normal, independent life. Continued research alone can serve to keep alive our awareness of the lapse into hysteria in World War II in regard to our residents, citizens, and aliens, of Japanese origin, though we all tried hard not to fall into hysteria about persons of German descent, citizens or aliens, as in World War I. Must we Americans learn our lesson, one nationality at a time?" (p. 32). In one of these Community Analysis Reports she contributed to a general description of Buddhism in Japan and in the United States and its relation to the Japanese-American evacuee experience (1944a). She also co-authored two studies on the problems of relocation encountered by evacuees after leaving the Rohwer Center in Arkansas (1944b, 1944c).

As the Community Analysis Program developed, moving toward a closing out of the relocation centers, Katharine participated in a survey of the attitudes and mood of West Coast communities where evacuees were scheduled to return. Working out of San Francisco for ten weeks beginning in December, 1944, she sampled public opinion in central California by means of intensive interviews throughout the Sacramento and San Joaquin Valleys. Selected were ten communities from which large numbers of Japanese-Americans had been evacuated in early 1942. These included such towns as Yuba City, Sacramento, Stockton, Merced, Fresno, and Bakersfield. She directed her principal line of questioning at key men and women—leaders in agriculture, business, education, religion, and government—about problems of housing, jobs, sentiment, and the like which might be expected to develop in each community when Japanese-American evacuees started to return "home." As time allowed, she supplemented these data with background material from newspaper files, government archives, and Chamber of Commerce records. The explosion of public sentiment against the prospect of the evacuees' return did not materialize, and the West Coast surveys were terminated after three months.

Katharine's official reports on the attitudinal survey in California (1945a, 1945b) were followed up after the war with two technical accounts for anthropologists. One of these was reprinted in the *Pacific Citizen,* official publication of the Japanese American Citizens League (1946d). The other was a revised version of a paper given in May, 1946, at a Society for Applied Anthropology symposium on the WRA Community Analysis Program as an example of applied anthropology in the United States government (1947a). Here she discussed some of the field problems she and others encountered in their investigations in the "world beyond the fences of the centers" (p. 25). She noted the strain and anxiety which pressed upon them constantly, "The analysts tried to cover as much territory as possible and as quickly and thoroughly as possible to get both the details and the general outline of community sentiment .... They had the dual problem, first, of getting ... the information, and, secondly, of writing it up at once and getting it to the ... office quickly." In a more philosophical vein, she added, "The realization that good information and quick action might prevent tension leading to evacuee loss of life and property frequently frayed the disposition and patience of a staff eager to bring about the peaceful acceptance of the Japanese by West Coast people" (p. 30).

She wrote a more popularized review of her California experience, directed at a lay audience, in which she discussed the forces that develop intolerance and those that operate to counteract it, and concluded with a qualified optimism, "The battle for tolerance is not yet won, but fellow Californians are teaching the rest of us Americans many practical ways of making the Bill of Rights and the Golden Rule apply to everybody in America" (1946c).

Katharine Luomala along with Marvin K. Opler and Asael T. Hansen were selected to assist Edward H. Spicer in preparing the final report on the relocation program as experienced by Japanese-American evacuees and the United States government and viewed from the perspective of the Community Analysis Section of WRA. Both Hansen and Opler had served as community analysts in the relocation centers, Hansen at Heart Mountain, Wyoming, and Opler at Tule Lake, California. Katharine wrote the Prologue to this monograph, working with the others in Washington during the final six months when WRA was closing down. The study was issued in 1946 by WRA under the title of *Impounded People: Japanese-Americans in the Relocation Centers* (Spicer and Others, 1946). It was characterized by the authors as "a report concerning a group of people during a crucial period in their experience; it is not a report on the policy or operation of the government agency which played a considerable role in the crucial experience" (p. 1). The University of Arizona Press reissued the publication in 1969.

Katharine and her three colleagues, like many others who had worked in the Community Analysis Section of WRA, have since returned to full-time participation in anthropological teaching, writing, and research as professors of anthropology. Their brief wartime careers as community analysts in the employ of a government agency are now but the remembrance of a generation past.

HONOLULU—YEARS OF REALIZATION AND FULFILLMENT

Already I have described Katharine Luomala's two earlier sojourns in Honolulu, at Bishop Museum in the summer of 1934 and again for more than two years in 1938-1940. However, I have decided to begin this portion of my "Tale of Three Cities" with her return to Honolulu in 1946. Since then she has maintained a permanent residence in this city.

In writing Katharine's biography to this point, I have followed a chronological sequence, moving with her from year to year. From here on, I intend to dispense with that format. Her activities since 1946 have been so many and so interrelated through time that it will be easier and more economical for me to write about them in a topical rather than chronological order. With this consideration in mind, I have chosen to touch upon seven aspects of this latest stage in her career. These are seven areas in each of which she has made an important contribution, as teacher, researcher, field worker, writer, administrator, editor, and traveler.

Another biographer might have arranged his observations with more (or fewer) categories and dealt with them in another order. My own selection and sequence I have determined quite arbitrarily. Admittedly the categories overlap in many respects. I will meet that problem in my own way as it arises. I start here with Katharine's role as Teacher because that was the primary status she assumed upon joining the University of Hawaii faculty in 1946. I will conclude with her role as Traveler because this is what impresses me most about her activities during the past few years.

TEACHER

John Embree, who had been the first to head the Community Analysis Section of WRA, returned in 1945 to the University of Hawaii teaching post from which he had taken leave at the beginning of World War II. Planning the postwar development of anthropology at the Hawaii institution, he invited his onetime colleague from WRA to join him. He and Katharine had already known each other in the closing years of prewar Honolulu when both of them had met weekly for lunch at the Kewalo restaurant for friendly interchange with other anthropologists from the Museum and the University.

On August 15, 1946, Katharine arrived in Honolulu for the third time in her life, having made the trip across the water from San Francisco on the old *Matsonia*. When she first came to Hawaii in 1934, she had also booked passage aboard ship. It had been the *Malolo* then, two years before Pan American Airways would establish regular trans-Pacific clipper flights between the West Coast and Hawaii. In 1946 she once again made the crossing by water, even though by that date air travel to Honolulu had become fairly routine. Her reason was simply that she could take more baggage with her that way than if she came by air.

Katharine's first appointment to the University faculty in anthropology was with the rank of Assistant Professor. In 1948 she was promoted to an Associate Professorship, and in 1952 she advanced to the status of full Professor. Over the years, Katharine has probably taught about every course offered in anthropology at the University of Hawaii. It was only in the early 1960's, when the Department began to offer the Ph.D. degree, that expansion of the faculty to provide a wider range of courses relieved some of the pressure on us oldtimers. During most of the earlier years, Katharine and Saul H. Riesenberg and I were the only full-time staffers in anthropology, although Kenneth Emory from Bishop Museum helped out on a part-time basis. After 1957 Robert Jay replaced Saul Riesenberg when the latter moved to the Smithsonian Institution. I remember that the full-time members of the faculty took turns teaching the very large introductory classes, whose enrollments persuaded University administrators to approve upper-division anthropology courses with only very small registrations. For a decade or so, after Katharine joined the faculty, there were only a few undergraduate majors in anthropology and almost no graduate students except the one or two recruited each year as teaching assistants for the introductory course.

In those earlier years, Katharine generally taught the courses on Polynesia, Oceania, American Indian, "primitive" religion (as we called it then), the history of anthropological theory for our few advanced students, and, of course, folklore. Later she organized a two-semester offering on Asian cultures. When we could afford greater variety in the 1960's she developed a course on the folk cultures of Europe expressing her

longtime interest in the folk art and oral literature of Old World Europeans. With inauguration of the doctoral program, she assumed a major
responsibility in the pro-seminar on social and cultural anthropology
required of all graduate students. In both the lean years of the Department and the richer ones that followed, Katharine was the "anchor man"
without whom the Department could never have progressed as it did.
In recent years she has found it possible to concentrate pretty much
on her favorite offerings—oral art, comparative religion, and the history
of anthropology, with an occasional sharing of the departmental obligation for a beginning course in cultural anthropology.

For the sake of teaching, Katharine has given of her summers only
sparingly. She prefers to reserve those months for her own research and
for professional travel. Once or twice she helped out in Hawaii when
the Department was unable to support visiting professors from the mainland. However, she did teach in summer at the University of California
at Berkeley (in 1949 and 1966; she had first lectured there in the summer
of 1941), at the University of Minnesota (in 1962), and at Indiana University (in 1958). Each of these mainland institutions holds a special
attraction for Katharine which no doubt explains her willingness to
spend a valued summertime in teaching there. To undertake a summer
session in Berkeley returned her to familiar academic ground and to
the rich library resources of that campus. To teach in Minnesota gave
her opportunity to renew old family ties in the land of her childhood
and youth. To take part in a summer institute at Indiana University
carried with it the pleasure of mingling with other specialists like herself
at one of the truly outstanding centers for folklore studies.

Katharine's unquestioned dedication to the researching and organizing of course lectures and her very special relationship with her students,
both graduate and undergraduate, have often been remarked. In themselves they are sufficient reason for the idea of this *festschrift* to have
originated among former students who, in appreciation of the richness
and warmth of her tutelage, wish to bear witness more publicly to her
influence in the classroom and in academic counseling.

It is a pleasure to report here the substance of comments related
to me by some of those who studied under Katharine in prior years
to document her contribution to this aspect of the socializing process
within anthropology. Her course on folklore, for example, introduces
the class to the subject in a well organized historical and theoretical
presentation of the material. Not only do the students learn in detail
about motif-indexes, narrative elements, genres, and the like, but they
are also made aware that the pursuit of folklore research can be an
exciting adventure. Folklore, they are told, is not at all confined to tradi-

tional cultures long dead or now dying. It continues to live in the present, adapting to the changing circumstances and new requirements of a people who preserve its viability by spontaneous creation and constant replenishment.

The rigor and exactitude she demands of students in their preparation of class reports or graduate theses are recognized by them to be no more than what she requires of herself. She sets a high standard by her own example, and thereby motivates students to levels of achievement which they very likely would not attain otherwise. Well do they realize the time and care she devotes to reviewing their term papers and dissertations when they read the detailed penciled comments on grammatical style as well as content. She edits their reports not just once-over-lightly but frequently four or five times before handing them back. Such personal attention to each individual's development in the program and the thought which goes into her evaluation of student performance are the sort of thing that has prompted at least one student to say, "She is not only a professor but she is also a warm human being."

Some students feel that Katharine is not an easy person to approach or to talk with outside the classroom, particularly when the relationship is a new one. But, again and again, many of those same students have noted that once they measure up to Katharine's standards of commitment they can rest assured of her full support. Some students report a lack of enthusiasm for her classroom delivery as she reads from typed notes on assorted pieces of paper. But in time they come to appreciate the immense amount of labor and thought she obviously puts into her lectures, each one usually a gem of organization and genuinely original and thought-provoking.

In the context of these student reactions, I must add a footnote about Katharine's own views on footnoting. One graduate student recalled that in criticism he had received on term papers and master's thesis, he had been advised to avoid footnotes. Katharine told him, "If an item of information is important enough to mention, work it into the text itself, or else leave it out altogether." He took her advice to heart and when he later did his doctoral dissertation at another university, he realized that his new habit of omitting footnotes had influenced his writing in other ways. His style had become much simpler, and was consequently clearer and easier for the reader to understand what was being communicated.

Her efforts as a teacher in lecturing, editing, and counseling are paralleled by her constant urging of students to undertake original collecting of folklore within their own communities or segments of society. She makes the point that anyone can be an amateur collector of folklore upon learning a few basic requirements of the art (see 1949b). Her encouragement along this line has on several occasions motivated students to refine and polish up term papers for possible publication. A number of these writings have been accepted in journals devoted to folklore. As Katharine has approached retirement the thought has been with her, she says, to bring together for publication as a book a selection of papers on folklore written by former students. It should come as no surprise, therefore, when watching Katharine practice her craft as a teacher, to see the relationship between student and professor gradually change to a relationship between colleagues—once she is assured that the other person takes scholarship seriously. She displays very little patience with students who lack this quality.

RESEARCHER

Despite her readiness to work closely with serious students revising research reports for publication, Katharine Luomala is an individualist in conducting her own research. The record of her writings reveals but few exceptions. While a graduate student, as mentioned earlier, she co-authored an article based on collaborative field work among the Diegueño. During the war years her name appeared in joint authorship of several government reports.

She has recorded her awareness of this dilemma of individual versus cooperative research, and does recognize the advantage sometimes of the latter practice. From the vantage point of a quarter century following World War II, she recalls how American anthropologists critically evaluated themselves and their work in wartime service:

"One of the things that most [anthropologists] had been forced to learn ... was to work together on projects, and unfortunately they had had to learn it under the stress of war. The prima donna habit of work has always been, and still is, strong in anthropology. Perhaps it has grown out of necessity, born of a formerly limited number of personnel in the science, shortage of funds, and difficulties of travel, to work alone in the field and later to write up alone the results of the solitary work. ... It took World War II for the American anthropologists to demonstrate the benefits of their disciplinary training and of their solo orientation in the way of independence, endurance, [and] resourcefulness. ... However, it also revealed their difficulties in learning to work in teams, to write up the results of their solo or team research in such a way that an administrator could and would read their reports ..." (1970c, pp. 9-10).

However, upon returning to the academic scene in 1945, she resumed the more traditional posture of independent researcher, adhering to a mode which in the long run would better suit her personal style.

In the interest of developing a strong postwar emphasis in Pacific Islands research, the University of Hawaii administration had arranged for several faculty members in the social and natural sciences to divide their time between teaching and research. Katharine was one of those to benefit by this arrangement. The partial relief from teaching enabled her in 1946 to complete the manuscript for her definitive work on the demigod Maui (1949a, p. i), and before long to become involved in several new projects. Though serving full time on the University faculty, she continued to be formally affiliated with Bishop Museum as an Honorary Associate in Anthropology. This title, originally conferred on her in 1941, was more than honorary in that for many years it provided certain study facilities in support of her Polynesian researches. All of Katharine's major works have been published by Bishop Museum.

Katharine has been deservedly fortunate in obtaining supplemental support from sources outside Hawaii for her research activities during summers and sabbatical leaves. The Wenner-Gren Foundation for Anthropological Research, then known as The Viking Fund, provided financial assistance in 1948-1949 for field work in the Gilbert Islands. Twice, in 1956 and again in 1960, she secured fellowship aid from the John Simon Guggenheim Foundation to study collections of Gilbertese materials in European and American museums and archives. With Federal research funds she spent the year 1966-1967 at the Smithsonian Institution as Visiting Senior Research Fellow to work up her Gilbertese notes for publication. At various times over the years funding for travel to professional meetings at home and abroad has been available from the American Council of Learned Societies and other sources.

When it comes to memberships and attendance at annual meetings of professional organizations, Katharine is neither strongly motivated socially nor is she a joiner for the sake of belonging. She discriminates, and that discrimination seems to be based on both the scholarly responsibility she feels and the scholarly stimulation to be derived. Invariably she contributes a research paper, perhaps ostensibly to insure travel support to the meeting, but inevitably the paper turns up later in revised or expanded form in a professional journal or an editor's collection of essays. The Anthropological Society of Washington for a time provided her with opportunities to exchange views with other anthropologists in wartime service in that city. Her brief experience as a government analyst led to membership in the Society for Applied Anthropology, but her enthusiasm for that kind of anthropology had waned by the early 1950's. Already noted is her continuing support for the honorary scholastic societies Phi Beta Kappa and Sigma Xi. Her life membership in The Polynesian Society is an obvious commitment, considering her primary research interests. A Fellow of both the American Anthropological Association and the American Folklore Society, she has evidenced a greater identification with the latter through service for varying periods as Editor and Council Member. In postwar Hawaii she served at different times until the early 1960's as President, Editor, and Councillor of the Anthropological Society of Hawaii, discharging a professional responsibility she felt toward strengthening the local community group. In more recent years she has extended her regional participation by attending meetings of a number of international associations. On that aspect of her scholarly activity I will comment further in reviewing her role as Traveler.

In thirty-five years of consistent productivity following completion of her doctoral dissertation, Katharine has published about 120 items as listed in the appended bibliography—an impressive record by any standard. In anthropology one can identify certain researchers who concentrate their output in a few major works which appear as books or monographs, while others seek broader exposure by achieving a continuous outflow of journal articles and book reviews. Katharine has done both, maintaining a nice balance between the two extremes. From the year of her doctorate until now she has been a perennial reviewer of books for professional journals, most of them books about folklore in all regions of the world and about ethnography in Polynesia and related parts of the Pacific. In a somewhat similar pattern she has published one article after another, averaging one or two a year. Expectedly, she has published mainly in the field of oral art, a term she sometimes prefers instead of folklore. But readers may be surprised at her periodic forays into the fields of ethnohistory and ethnoscience, not to mention her ethnographic concern with material culture, religion, and social relationships.

Her first major publication, on the Navaho (1938a), was followed shortly afterward by her comparative monograph on sun-snaring myths (1940a). Then, after the war, in quick succession, appeared her definitive treatments of Maui (1949a) and the Menehune (1951a), an ethnobotanical study of the Gilbert Islands (1953a), and her immensely popular work, *Voices on the Wind* (1955a). Since that time, she has worked steadily on the preparation of a comprehensive ethnography of the Gilbert Islanders. This promises to be as extensive as her persistent search of the world's museums and archives on Gilbertese materials plus her own considerable field notes will permit.

One measure of the fascination which binds Katharine Luomala the researcher to the wide world of Polynesian oral art as a field of inquiry is revealed here in her own words: "Without question, the literary specialization of Polynesia ranks the area with ancient Greece, India, and Scandinavia in the earliest era of bards before the introduction of writing. In Polynesian mythology, as in the oral literatures of these classic areas, there is much that is strange and tedious until one knows the cultural background of the narrators and tries to define their literary standards to see how nearly the individual narrators have attained them" (1950c, p. 879). In communicating the results of this inquiry to her reading audiences, she demonstrates her remarkable capacity to move freely from literary description and insightful synthesis to painstaking analysis and methodological criticism.

One anthropologist, who regards *Maui-of-a-Thousand-Tricks* as Katharine Luomala's best work, characterizes it as displaying imagination, literary talent, insight, and tremendous scholarship. He admitted to me that he uses it as a model in his own folkloristic research. A prominent American folklorist writes that specialists in his field have come to rely upon Katharine's comparative studies in Polynesian oral literature and such collections as her *Voices on the Wind,* and like to claim her as "one of our own." One professor of English literature has praised *Voices* as "the best modern literary treatment of Polynesian poetry" (Day, 1971, p. 7). A reviewer in *Western Folklore* has cited the same book as a "graceful synthesis ... presented in brilliant prose, without sacrificing scholarship" (Dorson, 1959, p. 67). An anthropologist, referring to her monograph on the Menehune as a "mock-serious" ethnographic account of Hawaii's mythical leprechauns (Lessa, 1952, p. 195), wrote me that students in his religion class are very often convinced that Katharine is writing about *real* people so thoroughly does she describe the Menehune.

In writing *Voices on the Wind,* Katharine quite arbitrarily chose "certain of those Polynesian mythological characters ... whom both their Polynesian creators and I like best, and whose familiar biographies we never weary of hearing or telling once more ..." (1955a, p. 18). Elsewhere, in a more encyclopedic manner, she has produced syntheses of Polynesian literature (1946b) and Polynesian poetry (1965a) for those who desire a comprehensive overview as introduction to the subject. Of special note for their Pacific-wide coverage are the descriptive summaries she compiled for *Funk & Wagnalls Standard Dictionary of Folklore, Mythology, and Legend* which deal separately with the mythologies of Australian Aboriginal, Indonesian, Melanesian, Micronesian, and Polynesian peoples (1949c, 1949d, 1950a, 1950b, 1950c).

The principal focus of Katharine's researches in oral literature as first enunciated in her doctoral dissertation (1936a, p. 10) continues to guide her investigations and analyses in this area. Her primary concern to understand the processes of re-interpretation resulting in diversity of structure and function between local variants of the same tale or myth has relevance for studies of change in the present as well as in the traditional past. Thus, in reviewing Dorothy Barrère's report on late 19th-century Hawaiian creation "legends," Katharine advocates going beyond the specific history of the re-interpretations, "to investigate them from the standpoint of the creativity of the native artist-scholars who had shifted from a purely oral to a partly oral and partly written medium of communication and had produced something new through the inspiration of the large world opened up to them by the foreign culture. . . . There is, too, the question of the social and psychological functions that these revised accounts served the artist-scholars and their contemporaries, native and foreign alike, in a period of rapid cultural change" (1971b, p. 472).

Strongly rejecting both diffusionist and evolutionary types of theory that depend upon the uncritical interpretation of mythological evidence to explain historical connections between the New and Old Worlds, she argues instead for "more definitive conclusions derived from intensive analyses, such as those of the Finnish School, of all variants based on each clearcut [mythological] theme shared by the two hemispheres" (1950h, p. 271). In an earlier review, criticizing Lord Raglan's methodology in *The Hero,* she stated the same conviction more colorfully: "One turns with relief to examine the pedestrian plodding of American anthropologists in the field of mythology [under the leadership of Boas], their preoccupation with myth elements, and their cautious and modest generalizations. . . . Like the Finnish geographical-historical school of folklore, they present the evidence for their conclusions in great and wearying detail" (1938d, p. 518).

She aims her critical barbs also at those who utilize oral traditions and genealogies in reconstruction of biased and speculative ethnohistory. She recalls her student training under Robert H. Lowie, "I may have acquired his skepticism (or common sense) and extreme caution about accepting as historically true statements about past events in oral traditions" (1965e, p. 374). She viewed Alphonse Riesenfeld's reconstruction in *The Megalithic Cultures of Melanesia* as both "unorganized" and "depressing" in spite of the impressive accumulation of mythological data he presented in support of his historical hypothesis. In reviewing his book she concluded, "[Edward B.] Tylor's remark that far from elucidating history the myths need history to elucidate them fits my feeling" (1952b, p. 98). She deplored Thor Heyerdahl's resurrection of the "two-strata" theory of Polynesian origins and berated those Polynesianists who "still use this chronology for lack of anything better." Her review of his *American Indians in the Pacific* ended with a judgment that "traditions and genealogies have been as much a curse as a crutch for progress in reconstructing Polynesian history. What a curse they can be may be judged from Heyerdahl's statement" (1953b, p. 231).

Yet in all honesty Katharine stops short of rejecting completely the evidence from mythology in attempts to clarify culture history. Against her background of research on Pacific folk narratives, she poses this qualification, "the nagging question of what history [the myths] might contain and how to evaluate it persisted especially when I found myself in the Gilbert Islands sometimes acting as if certain oral traditions told to me actually had some valid historical content" (1965e, p. 374).

Among folklorists the "motif-index" and the "tale-type index" have an importance as classificatory aids perhaps comparable to that of the "cross-cultural method" linked with the Human Relations Area Files (HRAF) in anthropology. Practitioners in both fields tend to segregate as either advocates or critics of the aids in question depending on how essential to work in the discipline they judge the aids to be. As folklorist Katharine is not an indexer. (Neither, as anthropologist, is she committed to the cross-cultural method.) With regard to the two indexes, she views them as "helpful guides to source material as I try first one path then another, in hopefully travelling toward some comprehension of the nature and meaning of oral narrative art and the culture of which it is a part. . . . The indexes like any reference works are tools of the trade" (1963c, p. 748). Nevertheless, she pays tribute to folklorist Stith Thompson whose name is intimately associated with development of both indexes: "even as we wholeheartedly admire the devotion and cohesion of the folklorists who have aided Thompson in the two monumental indexes of motifs and tale types we must salute him as a leader whose unselfish and singlehearted dedication and industry to the Herculean labor have put amateur and professional folklorists the world over into his everlasting debt" (p. 750).

To insure the scientific value of reports of folklore research, Katharine insists upon a number of essentials. One, as she has advised amateur collectors in the Pacific Islands, is to "keep your theories and facts separate" (1949b, p. 317). Another is suggested in her criticism of J.F. Stimson's work on Tuamotuan legends, which lacked "even a brief summary of information" regarding narrators, recording method, whether with an audience or not, and so forth (1939a, p. 326). A third essential is detailed in her review of Carl Etter's work on Ainu folklore, where she finds it unfortunate "that in his book he merely tells *about* the myths, without giving the myths as told. [It is] hoped that the author will eventually publish literal translations of the myths he obtained" (1950i, p. 271). And, lastly, she is particularly insistent about the need to report variants from the characteristic form of a myth in a certain area. Any deviations collected in the field may represent genuine native adaptations. Myths published by European scholars as characteristic may contain misunderstandings and misquotations from the native source, and must be evaluated in comparison with known variants (1940c, p. 176). With such reporting criteria in mind, Katharine is understandably annoyed by the too casual manner of fellow ethnographers who "get 'buck fever' when it comes to collecting myths and presenting them as an integral part of their study of the total culture. Either they feel impelled on the basis of a few myths to psychoanalyze the culture as a whole to the extent that the myths themselves have to be left out to save space, or they slap a title 'Myths and Folk Tales' at the heading of the last chapter, and write *Finis*" (1950f, p. 123).

By no means all of Katharine's research has been about oral literature. A secondary interest relates to plants and animals associated with human living. Her ventures into ethnoscience or cultural ecology may well be rooted in her earlier years on the family farm in Minnesota and exposure to the animal-oriented folklore of her Finnish heritage. Certainly biological subjects attracted her both in high school and in college, and she credits teachers in those classes with having opened the doors of science to her (1953a, p. 2). To date she has written on two principal topics arising from her research in Polynesian mythology and Gilbertese ethnography. The first of these is the native dog of Polynesia and the second is the plant biota of the Gilbert Islands. A third preoccupation might well be added here, although I am not aware that Katharine has published on the subject. For years she bred and reared Siamese fighting fish *(Betta)* in aquariums in her apartment, scientifically recording their habits and enjoying their beauty and companionship. She once gave a talk on her experiences with bettas at a meeting of the Honolulu Aquarium Society.

Her research on the Polynesian native dog includes a review of myths about Maui and the dog (1958a), a zoological survey based on literary references going back to the early 17th century (1960a), and a discussion of the dog in the Polynesian system of values as modified by the succession of European influences (1960b). A glimpse of Katharine's personal philosophy about animal pets appears in this last item: "The dog, or any creature, on whom man projects his way of life, recreates him in turn. Both must adjust to each other if their partnership is to continue. Emotionality about the creature arises. 'Love me love my dog,' which implies preferences and values, reveals the dependence, whether sentimental, economic, or both, and the extension of self and personal and cultural values into a non-human part of society" (p. 214).

In the late 1940's Katharine collected plants of more than one hundred species on Tabiteuea Atoll in the Gilberts and on Canton Island in the nearby Phoenix group. The specimens, identified by Bishop Museum botanists, are available at the Museum for study by others. In two ethnobotanical reports (1951b, 1953a) she presented all available information on the use and care of these plants from her Gilbertese informants, from published accounts of the mid-19th century to the present, and from unpublished letters written by missionaries of the so-called Boston Mission. She modestly disclaims completeness and professional qualification in the plant collecting, which was incidental to her principal field work. A preliminary paper on the arum known as *Cyrtosperma* (*babai*, in Gilbertese), a prestige food figuring prominently in social exchanges, has appeared (1970b) as part of a more detailed study to be included in her projected monograph on Gilbertese ethnography.

Much of Katharine's research falls within the developing field of ethnohistory, which calls for the concurrent use of literary documents, field observations, and native accounts of past events in reconstructing particular culture history. Her paper on documentary research in Polynesian mythology (1940c) validated her status as an anthropologist who not only utilized documentary sources but also showed skill in their evaluation. Her article on missionary contributions to Pacific anthropology (1947b) testified to her conviction, born of experience, that untrained, nonnative observers with "A discerning ear, curiosity, patient application, talent for keen and accurate observation, insight born of sympathy for all human beings however different, and mother wit" can render an important service in recording descriptions of aboriginal life and natural history (p. 13). H.E. Maude, a former Administrator of the Gilbert and Ellice Islands Colony, wrote to me about his feeling of obligation to Katharine: "Actually I owe more to Katharine Luomala than she suspects herself, for it was her article ... that first inspired me to pursue a line of ethnohistorical research which I have followed ever since." After his retirement from the British colonial service, Maude joined the faculty of Australian National University to become one of the principal exponents of Pacific ethnohistory.

True to her tradition of encouraging native islanders to narrate their own history, Katharine in 1948 obtained a complete account in Gilbertese, translated into English, from a Gilbertese leader and resident of the site in Tabiteuea Atoll where sixty-eight years earlier a massacre of pagans by Christian converts had taken place. "I expect to write more fully later about this particular historical event," she promised in a preliminary report on the massacre (1954a, p. 19).

At times Katharine seems to be completely absorbed with the past, whether it be traditional or ethnohistorical, yet she manifests a sense of urgency about the need to record changes in island custom that may be observed in process today. Thus, while praising H.E. Maude's ethnohistorical interpretation of the evolution of the Gilbertese *boti,* a major institution in that society, she appends a caveat: "what continues to operate in the present should, it seems to me, be regarded as more than a decayed survival of a past form; it should also be investigated as an adjustment to change that has meaning and validity in the present and represents native efforts to adapt older traditional beliefs and customs to bring them into harmony with the changes that have occurred since European contact and missionization. *Otherwise, scholars of the future will be looking for manucripts and memoirs about the present era to reconstruct the history of these adjustments"* (1965d, p. 134; italics added).

FIELD WORKER

For anthropologists, field work is usually more than just a means of gathering information about another people and their customs. It has been aptly termed a kind of vision quest. "By immersing himself in another way of life, [the anthropologist] comes to view himself, his own way of life, and man, in a new perspective. It is a profound experience, uncomfortable and sometimes shattering, but richly rewarding as well" (Keesing and Keesing, 1971, p. 12). Katharine's own experience would appear to fit this pattern, especially her last and most extended sojourn in the field, five months living among the little known Gilbertese of Tabiteuea Atoll in the central Pacific.

Her introduction to field work in the declining Diegueño Indian culture of southern California was reported as a feature of her graduate student training in the mid-1930's. Brief encounter that it was, barely two months long and confined to interviewing a single Diegueño informant, it could hardly be called "immersion." Her second venture, during World War II, was more ambitious. As noted in regard to her association with the War Relocation Authority, she worked intensively for ten weeks with a subcultural segment of her own society. That research aimed at sampling opinion among the townspeople of several communities in California's central valley. In her own words, it was "a time of strain and anxiety." Under trying conditions she collected information relative to the return of Japanese-Americans and analyzed it for use by head-office administrators. Here, more certainly, she experienced immersion. But when one recalls that she chose to return to academic life only a year or two later, it would seem that employment involving that type of field research suited neither her personal nor her professional needs. Her third and latest field undertaking, in a culture and environment markedly different from any she had ever before encountered, reflects the kind of immersion cited in the lead paragraph of this section. It was to have a more lasting influence on her, both as a person and as an anthropologist.

For ten months in 1948 and 1949 Katharine took leave from her post at the University of Hawaii to conduct an ethnographic survey of the Gilbert Islands which straddle the equator in easternmost Micronesia. It is indicative of then existing travel conditions that she required fully half of that time to get to and return from the site of her field research. She traveled by scheduled airline and nonscheduled freighter, schooner, motor launch, and outrigger canoe and, of necessity, covered a major portion of the South Pacific en route. "Old hands" in the islands had recommended Tabiteuea of all the atoll groups in the Gilberts as the most culturally conservative and the most likely to welcome an anthropologist. She has described with mixed emotions the island environment where she worked those five months: "To me, the scenery of sand, sky, sun, coconuts, and water is beautiful, most of all on the lonely weather side; but monotony soon dulls lyric inclination" (1953a, p. 27). In truth, there is not much variety in the six square miles of Tabiteuea's land area divided into sixty islets resting on a coral reef around the large lagoon and supporting seventeen villages populated by some four thousand Gilbertese.

Those are the bare statistics, but they do not portray the island scene as colorfully as Katharine did in a public lecture about her field experiences following her return to Honolulu. She entitled her talk "Logbook of a Voyage to the Middle of the Earth," taking her cue from the image the Tabiteueans have of themselves as living "at the center of the world." Later a version of her presentation was published in *Pacific Discovery* (1951d). Katharine, and others before her, have called the Gilbertese the Irishmen of the Pacific, an apt characterization illustrated by this excerpt from her account: "Many a time I returned from a *maneaba* [traditional assembly house] on the verge of shell shock from the noise and fury of the arguments over . . . privileges and duties. Men shout . . . dogs bark, children cry, and the women cackle with shrill laughter or make ringing, impromptu remarks, stinging enough at times to make the speaker gulp and sit down" (p. 10).

When she began her investigations, she explained to the villagers her desire to record their myths and chants, as well as other ethnographic features. She soon learned that many of these oral traditions served to validate privileges and obligations of various family lines as the latter constantly maneuvered for relative social position within the community. The *unimane* (old men) of Eita Village, one of several in which she lived during her field work, envisioned her work as a means of possibly reducing disputes between families by reference to her "book," and asked to adopt her as their favorite daughter with appropriate ceremonies in the *maneaba*. They named her Nei Marewen-Eita, "literally, Lady Top-of-the-coconut-tree-of-Eita, or poetically, Lady Top-of-the-hopes-of-Eita" (meaning, hopes for settling future arguments). "The adoption proved," she hoped, "mutually satisfying. . . . Eita loyalty and strong sense of duty toward me became one of my most cherished psychological supports" (p. 11).

Discussion of the traditional intervillage rivalries aggravated by intra-village differences in religious conviction has prompted Katharine to identify some of those islanders who in one way or another were closely associated with her in the field. "My cook and his wife, the laundress, were staunch [London Missionary Society]; my interpreter was the chief lay Catholic of the island; and the native magistrate was leader of the pagans and reputedly the most outstanding magician" (1951d, p. 10). Her comments further suggest some of the conflicts in Gilbertese culture today resulting from the introduction of European practices. Of Bakoa, her interpreter and the only Gilbertese she mentions by name in her writings, she says: "His education outside the Gilberts to be a medical practitioner, his later wide practice throughout the archipelago, his contact with foreigners and their culture, and the negative attitude of his Christian religious sect toward the traditional assembly house had increased his doubts [of the value of the old customs associated with the assembly-house social structure] but not enough to make him reject the system completely" (1965b, p. 39). Bakoa, reviewing his own village's many status-giving "firsts" to his employer, betrayed his still active commitment to Gilbertese values when he boasted, "And now our village is the first again because I'm the first interpreter for the first anthropologist to come to Tabiteuea!" (p. 34).

One of the paradoxes of field work in another society is that the researcher is almost never physically alone, and yet there persists a sense of exclusion by virtue of the differences in language and culture between him and his study community. Katharine remarks on this feeling of loneliness. At times it "proved so deep and insidiously penetrating that I didn't even know what was the matter with me" (1951d, p. 5). "Sometimes," she recalls, "after a day spent struggling with a foreign language and hearing English only in the limited, cultural context of island life, I would sit on the furthermost extension of the wooden pier ... and look at the heavy, dark blue, evening clouds massed after sunset low on the horizon in a semicircle about me." Those precious few moments by herself would bring her "a measure of perspective to a field life in which there is no real relaxation except in sleep" (p. 12).

Near the end of her stay on Tabiteuea, her work was unexpectedly handicapped by the onset of the stormy, westerly season. A change in the weather "reached a climax [one day in early December] when at midnight in a violent storm the posts supporting my roof on the west side gave way and the roof moved several feet toward the east before it slid toward the floor, stopping miraculously a half palm's height from my head" (1951d, p. 14). She moved into a little native hut nearby, and in three weeks was celebrating Christmas with her "relatives" of Eita Village. Part of her plant collection for Bishop Museum had been destroyed but, in spite of the poor weather, the villagers aided her in gathering replacements during the short time left to her (1953a, p. 2). At the end of the month, during a break in the weather, she departed Tabiteuea on the Colony schooner *Kiakia* to begin the long road back to Hawaii from "the middle of the earth."

Katharine has talked about returning to Tabiteuea to continue her ethnographic researches. Beyond that, and perhaps more important, she has noted the desirability of undertaking specialized studies relative to Tabiteuean acculturation, whether she will do this herself or leave it for someone else to tackle. For example, in 1949, she suggested that a tantalizing problem exists in the contrast between the conservative traditionalism persisting in Tabiteuea itself and the fact that Tabiteuean workers were leaders the year before in a labor strike at the phosphate mines operated by Europeans on Ocean Island.

A very nice thing happened to Katharine the summer following her field work in the Gilberts. A silver tray arrived in the mail one day, inscribed with her name as "Woman of the Day, Anna and Eleanor Roosevelt Radio Program." In their nightly talk fest on the ABC network, the "Roosevelt Ladies" had accorded Katharine nationwide acclaim for her accomplishments in ethnographic research on faraway Tabiteuea Atoll.

WRITER

Katharine's penchant for combining literary expression with critical scholarship must be admitted as a relatively rare quality among writers of anthropological treatises. Her assessment of the problem is captured in a comment in her review of a collection of essays written for a general audience: "Brevity is often associated with a careful selection and organization of material to interest and inform the amateur, and a willingness to abandon for this purpose the mental baggage that a scholar hauls around when he writes for a fellow specialist. It requires both skill and enthusiasm to be able to look freshly at one's specialty—to figure out how to captivate the nonspecialist—with honest knowledge. It can also be a mentally revivifying experience for the scholar" (1962d, p. 140).

Her reviews of others' works frequently mention the author's facility (or lack of it) to make his book not only informative but enjoyable as well. By such comment she implies a criterion important to successful writing. Her own attraction to fun and humor in research she explains in an account of Gilbertese numskull tales: "Humorous narratives, especially those which burlesque solemn and staid social custom and behavior, are usually my favorites for reading and research. ... I find that rereading them and once more enjoying their humor soon dissipates any weariness from my endless dissection and attempts at synthesizing information about them and about the cultures in which they are popular" (1966a, p. 157). And, she confesses, "Perhaps it is unscientific to admit that the funny stories I study strike me as funny. Most of the stories I write about I still enjoy rereading; I cannot say the same for what I have written about them, but at the time it was fun" (p. 158).

Although Katharine urges scholars to adopt a more pleasurable and less pedantic approach to their material, she insists that they maintain a scholarly integrity in presenting their observations. In reviewing J.F. Stimson's *Songs and Tales of the Sea Kings*, she resorts to innuendo to make this point: "Stimson's interpretations [thus she terms his 'translations'] I find, as always, a delight to read, and recommend them to lovers of poetry. ... However, love of mystery and the undiscoverable (preferably in capital letters) belong to the Romantic Tradition, and that, not the Scientific Tradition, binds all four parts of this book into unity as escape literature in the nineteenth century tradition of von Arnim and Brentano, who were friends but not followers of Jakob and Wilhelm Grimm" (1959c, pp 80-81).

Unquestionably her best work as a writer is her *Voices on the Wind: Polynesian Myths and Chants* (1955a). When she wrote this book she had in mind a more general audience. Favorite mythological characters are portrayed against her rich experience of two decades of painstaking comparative research and publication. Production of those prior studies represented countless hours tinged with "the weariness from my endless dissection." By comparison, *Voices* is an adventurous fun fest inspired with her great affection for the heroic players. Here I have the feeling that Katharine really let herself go, enjoying to the fullest the composing of each chapter as a gift of love, and saddened at the end when the final chapter had been completed. Even her selection of a title suggests this relaxed attitude toward her material. After quoting a bit of Polynesian poetry, "Wild scud the clouds,/Hurled by the tempest,/A tale-bearing wind/That gossips afar," she explains with a delight that all gossips must exhibit, "This book is another tale-bearing wind to carry beyond the islands the news about the favorite heroes and heroines of Polynesian tradition" (pp. 3-4).

Those who reviewed *Voices on the Wind* in professional journals give testimony to her ability to both charm and educate her readers. Lowell Holmes, anthropologist, finds the material "presented in a pleasing marriage of prose and traditional poetry" (1957, p. 288). Edwin G. Burrows, noting that the book was written to entertain as well as to inform a more general audience, recommends it also to the serious student, "for no such sampling and illustration of the character of the verbal arts in Polynesia has been previously available. . . . Few if any other collections of folklore bring out the cultural setting as richly as is done here" (1957, p. 386). Folklorist Richard M. Dorson praises it as "a wise and beautiful book . . . a work of art, consummately contrived . . . all presented without the taint of jargon and with no interruption to the threads of the discussion. Literary and anthropological approaches to folklore are here admirably joined" (1959, p. 66). He continues, "Luomala's own artistry in describing Polynesian landscapes and settings itself illuminates the Polynesian oral style. . . . In spite of the sustained poetic quality of the work, the true rawness of oral narrative emerges" (p. 68).

This same flair for poetic expression and witty humor pervades the many public lectures Katharine is asked to give at home in Hawaii and during her frequent travels abroad. Audiences relish her depiction of the gods, heroes, and mortals she has researched. She seems to find equal enjoyment in sharing her professional experiences with lay listeners. As noted earlier, many of these oral popularizations show up at a later date in written form, after she has polished, elaborated, and documented them for a more academic audience. However, even as professional pieces, they retain the clarity of prose and illustration that many anthropologists would do well to adopt as a model for communicating their own observations and conclusions.

Administrator

Some anthropologists find principal satisfaction in becoming good teachers. Probably more devote their primary attention to conducting research, whether by personal inclination or because of the "publish-or-perish" principle. A few seek status and personal gratification by following the route of professional administrator. Katharine's success as teacher and researcher is well established, as we have seen, and she likes both of those activities for what they are and not for what they promise in academic acclaim. The role of administrator, however, is simply not her cup of tea, although she has accepted her share of that responsibility whenever occasion demanded. I suppose Katharine regards good administration (by others, of course) to be that which guarantees her the time and facilities to do well what she most prefers, namely, to teach and to do research. To become personally involved in almost any aspect of administration, she is convinced, just detracts in time and effort from getting on with the job as university professor. Actually, Katharine is not very much different from most professors in her attitudes about university administration.

Despite her antipathy for administrative duties, Katharine did serve a full three-year term in the mid-1950's as Department Chairman at Hawaii. For shorter periods, both before and after, she agreed to fill in while the incumbent Chairman was away. As department head, she always met her responsibilities conscientiously, though sometimes with considerable frustration and mental anguish in dealing with deans and vice-presidents. Within the Department she has borne her part of the burden of committee work in supervising degree candidates, reviewing departmental curricula, and selecting applicants for graduate study and teaching assistantships. Regular departmental meetings, usually taking up more time than desirable, she regards as occasionally necessary (but not often). She resents the time taken away from "more important" activities. Within the University she has served terms on the Research, Publications, and Pacific Islands Library Committees, the functions of which, understandably, she views as sufficiently significant to merit the time she contributes to them.

For the major part of two decades Katharine took an active interest in administering the affairs of the Anthropological Society of Hawaii. This modest local organization functioned as a forum on matters concerning anthropology and the Pacific Islands, periodically bringing together interested persons from Bishop Museum, the University of Hawaii, and other segments of the Hawaii community. At different times Katharine was elected to almost every office in the Society. As president she was successful in obtaining for the Society national recognition by the American Anthropological Association. In the 1960's she helped organize several annual spring conferences sponsored by the Society to provide opportunities for local amateurs, anthropology students, and professionals to present papers and hold discussions on current researches.

The American Folklore Society has also benefited from Katharine's occasional role as an elected officer, especially in regard to the Society's publication policy. She has at times served terms in elective posts within professional organizations of larger, international scope.

EDITOR

In wartime Washington, Katharine had learned to write reports for administrators who required clear and concise prose in what they would read. This experience worked to her advantage in subsequent years of objective, anthropological reporting. Her work with students on term papers and graduate theses, discussed earlier, was an attempt on her part to instill in the younger generation the same standards she had come to demand of herself. And part of these standards was a quality of literary expression Katharine had labored to achieve since her own graduate student days at Berkeley.

Her comparative study of sun-snaring myths and her competent reviews of books on oral literature for the *Journal of American Folklore* had brought her to the attention of folklorists in the United States even before the war. In 1947 she accepted an Associate Editorship with the *Journal*, which she retained until 1952. In 1950-1951 she also edited a quarterly news bulletin about anthropological activities in the Pacific for the Anthropological Society of Hawaii. This bulletin, named *News from the Pacific*, had been inaugurated just the year before when the Society decided to sponsor something more ambitious than the casual newsletter which had served the membership for several years.

During the Christmas season in 1949, Katharine visited Berkeley to help celebrate the fiftieth anniversary of the founding of the Department of Anthropology where she had earned her university degrees. At the same time several professional organizations to which Katharine belonged were meeting there. It was at the meeting of the American Folklore Society that she was named Editor-elect of the Society's journal for which she was already Associate Editor. In her new position she would replace Editor Wayland Hand in 1952. Many years later she wrote about her immediate reaction to this honor in a statement memorializing the late MacEdward Leach who had been Secretary-Treasurer of the Society at the time of her appointment: "In his warm, friendly, and completely disarming manner, MacEdward Leach took me aside at our first meeting in Berkeley when I had just been appointed ... and felt like a stranger and even trespasser among so many nonanthropologists who had long known each other and could run circles around me in their knowledge of editing, for I knew nothing. Maybe [he] realized my self-doubt or was concerned for the future of the *Journal,* for he offered me his cooperation and assistance in every way in my new appointment. His quiet sincerity charged me with confidence at a time when I most needed it. ... Although I knew Mac only through that memorable Berkeley meeting and our voluminous correspondence during my editorship, the example of his great kindness and thoughtfulness to a novice is one which I wish I could remember to emulate every day of my life" (1968a, pp. 115-116).

Katharine edited Volumes 65 and 66 of the *Journal* during the two years of her term. Lack of finances proved to be a serious problem in meeting expenses of postage and typing, even though Bishop Museum and the University of Hawaii assisted her editorship in minor ways. Much of the final typing of manuscripts she was compelled to do herself. Her lengthy correspondence with Secretary-Treasurer Leach dealt with this problem much of the time. "Both of us," she wrote, "were anxious about Society finances. Every penny saved helped, and I can still see the blue sheets with their columns of figures on *Journal* costs" (1968a, p. 116). In her Editor's Report in 1953, after enumerating the financial handicaps she had to contend with, she regretfully submitted her resignation as Editor to take effect at the end of 1953 "in order to spend more time on [my] paid duties of research and teaching" (1953c, p. 250).

I know, from her frequent comments while editing the *Journal,* that she was greatly disappointed in the condition of manuscripts submitted to her. Many were not only poorly written by her standards but were also inadequately prepared for publication. In the first year, Katharine dedicated many hours going over those manuscripts with the same critical attention that she was accustomed to give in reviewing student research papers. Then, finally, she decided that her time was too precious to continue editing the work of hopeful authors who had failed to do their homework as professional writers. And so, she resigned the editorship.

TRAVELER

To view this last of seven aspects of Katharine Luomala's fullness of life is to follow the beautiful flowering of an individual from the geographic and cultural narrowness of her childhood in Minnesota—step by step, hesitantly at first and then with growing confidence—to awareness and participation in ever widening circles until the whole world becomes a stage for her expression. Until Katharine boarded ship for Hawaii in 1934, she had never left the continent. She felt really at home only in the vicinity of Cloquet or of Berkeley, the first and second of the three cities in this tale that is being told. The summer's sojourn in Honolulu seems to have parted the bonds of her mainland existence, because she returned again to Hawaii in 1938 to 1941, and yet a third time, finally to stay, in 1946 following her retirement from wartime service.

The next major step in this flowering was Katharine's decision to undertake ethnographic field work in the far-off Gilbert Islands. Those ten long months away from Hawaii took her not only to the Gilberts. As we have seen, she became acquainted en route with Fiji, Nauru and Ocean Islands, the Ellices, New Caledonia, and New Zealand. Her enforced detour to New Zealand served a second purpose, for she was in time to attend the Pacific Science Congress, in Christchurch. Earlier, in 1939, she had presented a research paper at the Pacific Science Congress, in Berkeley; she would participate in still other Congress meetings in subsequent years.

Assisted by a Guggenheim grant Katharine spent most of the spring and summer of 1956 searching for Gilbertese materials in museums and libraries on the mainland. She found time to attend the International Congress of Anthropological and Ethnological Sciences, in Philadelphia. When delegates to assemblages of this scope come together from so many different countries, the world appears to shrink, for the time being, to a size more comprehensible to those present as they take advantage of the unique occasion for international scholarly exchanges in person. To have once or twice experienced this unusual opportunity could only have infected Katharine with a desire to travel more frequently and more widely in order to savor to the fullest the gratifying enrichment to be derived from such meetings. In any case, the next year saw her off again, this time briefly to the Pacific Science Congress in Bangkok as delegate from the University of Hawaii. Field trips to Chieng-Mai in northern Thailand and to Angkor Wat in Cambodia, and brief stopovers in the Philippines and such islands as Iwo Jima, Guam, and Kwajalein which had figured in World War II actions, widened Katharine's acquaintance with the Pacific to include the other, western half.

During a sabbatical leave from the University in 1960, she took the spring and summer months to circumnavigate the globe. Armed with another Guggenheim grant to study research collections in Europe, she traveled through east and south Asia to her destination and returned via the United States mainland—the distance from Honolulu is about the same either way. Her itinerary read like a Cook's Tour, and included such stopovers as Japan, Hong Kong, Singapore, Java, Thailand, India, Egypt, Israel, Turkey, and Greece (to name but a few), until she arrived in Finland, the homeland of her ancestors. While in Europe she read papers about her research at the International Congress of Americanists, meeting in Vienna, and at the International Congress of Anthropological and Ethnological Sciences, in Paris. She explored ethnographic and folk museums, libraries, archives, and many places of anthropological repute, such as the Paleolithic cave sites in the Dordogne. Her research aims were mainly to locate and to identify Gilbertese materials, photographing the artifacts and microfilming historical documents as she worked over one collection after another. She reaped a particularly abundant harvest at institutions located in Stockholm, Stuttgart, Frankfurt, and London, and also at the Universities of Helsinki and Turku.

Since 1960 and her sampling of the smorgasbord available to the researcher-*cum*-world traveler, Katharine has held to a schedule, whether intended or fortuitous, of returning to Europe about every two or three years, except that in 1966-1967 she chose to spend her sabbatical leave as Visiting Senior Research Fellow at the Smithsonian Institution. She has been a fairly frequent participant in meetings of the International Society for Folk-Narrative Research, having attended sessions in Antwerp, Athens, and Bucharest during the past decade. Where circumstances allow, economical person that Katharine is, she manages to work in one or two other folklore or ethnographic conferences that are convened within a reasonable distance of her primary objective. For example, on her way to Belgium in 1962 she stopped over in Mexico City for a meeting of the International Congress of Americanists, and in 1964 she paused long enough in Moscow to read a paper at the International Congress of Anthropological and Ethnological Sciences while en route to a folklore conclave in Athens.

In applying for travel funds, which she has been remarkably successful in obtaining, Katharine points out the principal advantages of travel for herself as being the enrichment and improvement of her own capabilities as teacher and researcher in the fields of folklore and ethnography. Follow-up reports on what she has accomplished during her travels further document the nature of these advantages. For instance, when reporting to the University administration on her sabbatical leave in 1960, she wrote of her interest in museums: "Museums are important ... to get clues or hunches for further study in one's specialty, to acquire first hand familiarity with other cultures—even fleetingly, to refresh one's enthusiasm for teaching or any other communication with people, by seeing for oneself the specimens mentioned in one's courses ... to learn systems of arrangement and classification ... to meet the people concerned with collecting, classifying, and describing museum materials."

In the same report she describes the character and consequences of travel *per se* as they appear to her: "The word [travel] should be used in quotation marks. Perhaps fieldwork would be a more applicable term, for my feeling was much the same as in fieldwork. The working schedule is twenty-four hours a day, because everything is different, and there is sometimes literally no rest from new impressions. . . . [As] in fieldwork, a person undergoes a fission, with one part participating in the life at hand, the other thinking, noting, and relating what is seen and heard and felt, to what is already known. . . . The anthropologist gets jolted from his pigeonholing of customs or of tracing their interrelations or of describing the material manifestations when he sees the whole cultural panorama spread before him in all its infinite complexity. It reminds him that his science still gets at only a small sector of even the simplest cultures."

RETIREMENT—WHAT LIES AHEAD?

Certain themes of interest and activity in Katharine Luomala's career to this time are identified in this tale that I have related. As she takes formal leave of her University obligations, a whole new way of life opens up for her to mold and shape as she will. For many of us old-timers, to reach retirement has scarcely been an ending but rather a beginning. I am confident this will be the case as Katharine leaves the campus.

I think Katharine will miss her students, at least the more serious ones, if she gives up teaching entirely. I think she will continue her researches in those fields she has already distinguished by her many contributions. Certainly we all look forward to further publication of her Gilbertese material on which she has labored so diligently. I think she will find travel abroad to international meetings increasingly of benefit and satisfaction as she shares her experiences with those of scholars from other regions of the world. Certainly the latter are anticipating her continued participation. I will not be surprised if Katharine shows a greater interest in contemporary change, possibly even indulging herself a bit in the application of anthropology toward meeting some of the critical concerns of today's world.

I hope that she will devote a larger portion of her time in future to that which she does so much better than most of her colleagues, and that is to write more in the manner of her *Voices on the Wind*, translating her treasury of anthropological knowledge and experience into literary fare for a more general readership. A wider audience awaits her popular offerings, should she decide to cast her lot in that direction.

LITERATURE CITED IN THE TEXT*

BUCK, PETER H. (TE RANGI HIROA)
  1945. *An Introduction to Polynesian Anthropology.* Bishop Mus. Bull. 187. Honolulu.
BURROWS, EDWIN G.
  1957. Review of *Voices on the Wind,* by Katharine Luomala. *American Anthropologist*
    59(2): 386.
DAY, A. GROVE
  1971. *Pacific Island Literature: One Hundred Basic Books.* Honolulu: Univ. Press
    Hawaii.
DORSON, RICHARD M.
  1959. Review of *Voices on the Wind,* by Katharine Luomala. *Western Folklore*
    18(1): 65-67.
FEDERAL WRITERS PROJECT, WORKS PROGRESS ADMINISTRATION
  1938. *Minnesota: A State Guide.* American Guide Ser. New York: Viking.
GRINNELL, HILDA W.
  1958. *Annie Montague Alexander* [1867-1950]. Grinnell Naturalists Soc.
HOLMES, LOWELL D.
  1957. Review of *Voices on the Wind,* by Katharine Luomala. *J. American Folklore*
    70(277): 288-289.
KEESING, ROGER M., and FELIX M. KEESING
  1971. *New Perspectives in Cultural Anthropology.* New York: Holt, Rinehart and Win-
    ston.
KING, PAULINE
  1958. "She Likes Fairy Tales and Folklore." *Honolulu Advertiser,* June 5, B3:1.
KLUCKHOHN, CLYDE
  1939. Review of *Navaho Life Yesterday and Today,* by Katharine Luomala. *American
    Anthropologist* **41**(2): 310-313.
KROEBER, A.L.
  1957. *Ronald Leroy Olson, Retired, 1956.* Kroeber Anthropological Soc. Pap. 16, pp.
    1-4.
LESSA, WILLIAM A.
  1952. Review of *The Menehune of Polynesia and Other Mythical Little People of*
    Oceania, by Katharine Luomala. *J. American Folklore* **65**(256): 195-196.
McCOWN, THEODORE D.
  1969. *Teaching Anthropology at Berkeley.* Kroeber Anthropological Soc. Pap. 40, pp.
    82-92.
SANDERS, IRWIN T., and RICHARD B. WOODBURY (Editors)
  1953. *Societies Around the World.* 2 vols. New York: Dryden.
SPICER, E. H., and OTHERS
  1946. *Impounded People: Japanese-Americans in the Relocation Centers.* Washington,
    D.C.: War Relocation Authority, U.S. Dept. Interior.
STEWART, LOIS
  1952. "Dr. Luomala Expert in Isle History, Mythology." *Honolulu Advertiser,* June
    22, 12:7.
THOMPSON, STITH
  1946. *The Folktale.* New York: Dryden.

---

*For references from Luomala's works, see "Bibliography of Katharine Luomala"
herein.

BIBLIOGRAPHY OF KATHARINE LUOMALA
Compiled by Leonard Mason

1933 "Turtle's War Party: A Study in Comparative Mythology." M. A. thesis, University of California at Berkeley.

1936a "Maui the Demigod: Factors in the Development of a Polynesian Hero Cycle." Ph.D. dissertation, University of California at Berkeley.

1936b " . . . Prize Winning Article on Famous 1918 Fire." *The Pine Knot* (Cloquet, Minnesota), No. 50 (May 15), pp. 1, 8.

1936c (with Gertrude Toffelmier) "Dreams and Dream Interpretation of the Diegueño Indians of Southern California." *Psychoanalytic Quart.* **5**:195-225.

1936d Review of *The Legends of Maui and Tahaki,* by J. F. Stimson (trans.). *J. American Folklore* **49**:272-273.

1937 Review of *Tales from a Finnish Tupa,* by James Cloyd Bowman,Margery Bianco, and Aili Kohelmainen. *J. American Folklore* **50**:105.

1938a *Navaho Life of Yesterday and Today.* Berkeley: National Park Service (Western Museums Laboratories), U.S. Dept. Interior. (Portions reprinted, in 1953, in *Societies Around the World,* Irwin T. Sanders and Richard B. Woodbury (eds.). New York: Dryden Press, Vol. 1, pp. 205-206, "The Navaho Country;" pp. 264-265, "Clan Origins.")

1938b "Hoopaapaa." *California Monthly* (November), pp. 16-17, 41-44.

1938c Review of *Twenty-fifth Anniversary Studies,* D. S. Davidson (ed.). *J. American Folklore* **51**:351-352.

1938d Review of *The Hero: A Study in Tradition, Myth, and Drama,* by Lord Raglan. *American Anthropologist* **40**:517-519.

1938e. Application for Bishop Museum Fellowship for Research, Yale University Graduate School. In Bishop Museum, Honolulu.

1939a Review of *Tuamotuan Legends (Island of Anaa), Part I: The Demigods,* by J. F. Stimson (trans.). *American Anthropologist* **41**:326.

1939b Review of *Mangareva: l'Histoire Ancienne d'un Peuple Polynésien,* by Père Honoré Laval. *American Anthropologist* **41**:495-496.

1940a *Oceanic, American Indian, and African Myths of Snaring the Sun.* B. P. Bishop Mus. Bull. 168. Honolulu.

1940b "A Hero Among Gods." *International House Quart.* (Summer), pp. 25-27.

1940c "Documentary Research in Polynesian Mythology." *J. Polynesian Soc.* **49**:175-195. (Reprinted, in 1941, in *Polynesian Anthropological Studies,* issued by The Polynesian Society as Memoir 17. New Plymouth: Thomas Avery and Sons.)

1940d "More Notes on Ra'a." *J. Polynesian Soc.* **49**:303-304. (Reprinted, in 1941, in *Polynesian Anthropological Studies,* issued by The Polynesian Society as Memoir 17, New Plymouth: Thomas Avery and Sons.)

1940e "Notes on the Development of Polynesian Hero-Cycles." *J. Polynesian Soc.* **49**:367-374. (Reprinted, in 1941, in *Polynesian Anthropological Studies,* issued by The Polynesian Society as Memoir 17. New Plymouth: Thomas Avery and Sons.)

1942a Review of *Myths and Tales of the Matako Indians,* by Alfred Métraux. *J. American Folklore* **55**: 188-190.

1942b Review of *An Analogy Between a South American and Oceanic Myth Motif and Negro Influence in Darien,* by Henry Wassén. *J. American Folklore* **55**:190-191.

1942-1943 Restricted reports, mimeographed, on attitudinal surveys on various subjects for the Program Surveys Division, Bureau of Agricultural Economics, U.S. Dept. Agriculture.

1944a (with Anne O. Freed) *Buddhism in the United States.* Community Analysis Report 9. Washington: War Relocation Authority (Community Analysis Section), U.S. Dept. Interior.

1944b (with Charles Wisdom) *Relocatjon at Rohwer Center. Part I: The Relocated Population.* Project Analysis Series 17. Washington: War Relocation Authority (Community Analysis Section), U. S. Dept. Interior.

1944c (with Charles Wisdom) *Relocation at Rohwer Center. Part II: Issei Relocation Problems.* Project Analysis Series 18. Washington: War Relocation Authority (Community Analysis Section), U. S. Dept. Interior.

1945a *Exploratory Survey of California Attitudes Toward the Return of the Japanese.* Community Analysis Report 11. Washington: War Relocation Authority (Community Analysis Section), U. S. Dept. Interior.

1945b *Effect of the Housing Shortage on Central Valley, California: Attitudes Toward the Return of the Evacuees.* Community Analysis Report 12. Washington: War Relocation Authority (Community Analysis Section), U.S. Dept. Interior.

1945-1946 (with Joan Ishiyama, Edward H. Spicer, and Rachel R. Sady) *Annotated Bibliography of the Community Analysis Section.* Community Analysis Reports 14-19, (14, Nov. 1945; 15, Feb. 1946; 16, Feb. 1946; 17, Apr. 1946; 18, (n. d.); 19, Jun. 1946). Washington: War Relocation Authority (Community Analysis Section), U.S. Dept. Interior.

1946a (with E. H. Spicer, A. T. Hansen, and M. K. Opler) *Impounded People: Japanese-Americans in the Relocation Centers.* Washington: War Relocation Authority (Community Analysis Section), U. S. Dept. Interior. (Re-issued, in 1969. Tucson: University of Arizona Press.)

1946b "Polynesian Literature." In *Encyclopedia of Literature,* Joseph T. Shipley (ed.), Vol. 2, pp. 772-789. New York: Philosophical Library.

1946c "Fellow Californians . . . Fellow Americans." *J. American Assoc. University Women* **39**:208-211.

1946d "California Takes Back Its Japanese Evacuees: The Readjustment of California to the Return of the Japanese Evacuees." *Applied Anthropology (Human Organization)* **5**:25-39. (Reprinted, in 1947, in *Pacific Citizen* (Salt Lake City, Utah) **24**:4, 5.)

1947a "Community Analysis by the War Relocation Authority Outside the Relocation Centers." *Applied Anthropology (Human Organization)* **6**:25-31.

1947b "Missionary Contributions to Polynesian Anthropology." In *Specialized Studies in Polynesian Anthropology,* by Katharine Luomala and Others, pp. 5-31. B. P. Bishop Mus. Bull. 193. Honolulu.

1948 "Research and the Records of the War Relocation Authority." *Applied Anthropology (Human Organization)* **7**:23-32.

1949a *Maui-of-a-Thousand-Tricks: His Oceanic and European Biographers.* B. P. Bishop Mus. Bull. 198. Honolulu.

1949b "The Amateur Collector in Pacific Islands." *J. American Folklore* **62**:317.

1949c "Australian Aboriginal Mythology." In *Funk & Wagnalls Standard Dictionary of Folklore, Mythology, and Legend,* Maria Leach (ed.), Vol. 1, pp. 92-94. New York: Funk & Wagnalls.

1949d "Indonesian (Malaysian) Mythology." In *Funk & Wagnalls Standard Dictionary of Folklore, Mythology, and Legend,* Maria Leach (ed.), Vol. 1, pp. 518-521. New York: Funk & Wagnalls.

1949e Review of *Anatomy of Paradise: Hawaii and the Islands of the South Seas,* by J. C. Furnas. *Pacific Discovery* **2**(6):28-29.

1950a "Melanesian Mythology." In *Funk & Wagnalls Standard Dictionary of Folklore, Mythology, and Legend,* Maria Leach (ed.), Vol. 2, pp. 701-705. New York: Funk & Wagnalls.

1950b "Micronesian Mythology." In *Funk & Wagnalls Standard Dictionary of Folklore, Mythology, and Legend,* Maria Leach (ed.), Vol. 2, pp. 717-722. New York: Funk & Wagnalls.

1950c "Polynesian Mythology." In *Funk & Wagnalls Standard Dictionary of Folklore, Mythology, and Legend,* Maria Leach (ed.), Vol. 2, pp. 876-879. New York: Funk & Wagnalls.

1950d "South Sea Superman." *International House Quart.* **14**:210-215.

1950e Review of *The Hero With a Thousand Faces,* by Joseph Campbell. *J. American Folklore* **63**:121.

1950f Review of *Seven Mohave Myths,* by A. L. Kroeber. *J. American Folklore* **63**:122-123.

1950g Review of *A Harvest of World Folk Tales,* by Milton Rugoff (ed.) *J. American Folklore* **63**:380.

1950h Review of *Asiatic Influences in American Folklore,* by Gudmund Hatt. *American Anthropologist* **52**:270-271.

1950i Review of *Ainu Folklore,* by Carl Etter. *American Anthropologist* **52**:271.

1951a *The Menehune of Polynesia and Other Mythical Little People of Oceania.* B. P. Bishop Mus. Bull. 203. Honolulu.

1951b "Plants of Canton Island, Phoenix Islands." *B. P. Bishop Mus. Occ. Pap.* **20**:157-174.

1951c "Micronesian Informants as Collectors." *J. American Folklore* **64**:221.

1951d "Logbook of a Voyage to the Middle of the Earth." *Pacific Discovery* **4**(2):4-14.

1951e Review of *The Kumulipo: A Hawaiian Creation Chant,* by Martha Warren Beckwith. *J. American Folklore* **64**:429-432.

1951f Review of *Art in Arnhem Land,* by A. P. Elkin and R. and C. Berndt. *J. American Folklore* **64**:445.

1952a *Peter Henry Buck (Te Rangi Hiroa) [1880-1951].* B. P. Bishop Mus. Bull. 208, pp 36-44. Honolulu

1952b Review of *The Megalithic Cultures of Melanesia,* by Alphonse Riesenfeld. *J. American Folklore* **65**:95-98.

1953a *Ethnobotany of the Gilbert Islands.* B. P. Bishop Mus. Bull. 213. Honolulu.

1953b Review of *American Indians in the Pacific: The Theory Behind the Kon-Tiki Expedition,* by Thor Heyerdahl. *Norveg* **3**:228-233.

1953c "Editor's Report." *J. American Folklore* **66**:248-250.

1954a "A Gilbertese Tradition of a Religious Massacre." *62nd Annual Report (for the Year 1953).* Hawaiian Historical Society (Honolulu), pp. 19-25.

1954b Review of *Missionary Influence as a Political Factor in the Pacific Islands,* by Aarne A. Koskinen. *Far Eastern Quart.* **13**:373-374.

1954c "Editor's Report." *J. American Folklore,* Suppl. (January), pp. 9-10.

1955a *Voices on the Wind: Polynesian Myths and Chants.* Honolulu: Bishop Mus. Press.

1955b "Western Polynesian Classification of Prose Forms." *J. Oriental Literature* **6**(2):16-23.

1957 "Lono: Essence of Wisdom." In *The University of Hawaii, 1907-1957: Higher Education in the Pacific: A Foundation for Freedom.* Honolulu: Univ. Hawaii, 2 pp.

1958a "Polynesian Myths About Maui and the Dog." *Fabula* **2**:139-162.

1958b Review of *Easter Island: A Stone Age Civilization of the Pacific,* by Alfred Métraux (trans. from the French by Michael Bullock). *Western Folklore* **17**:144-146.

1958c Review of *Tribal Myths of Orissa,* by Verrier Elwin. *Western Folklore* **17**:146-147.

1958d Review of *Taboo,* by Franz Steiner. *Western Folklore* 17:289-292.

1958e Review of *Easter Island: A Stone Age Civilization of the Pacific,* by Alfred Métraux (trans. from the French by Michael Bullock). *American Anthropologist* 60:405.

1958f Review of *The Mythology of the Ifugaos,* by Roy Franklin Barton. *American Anthropologist* 60:419-420.

1958g Review of *Ancient Voyagers in the Pacific,* by Andrew Sharp. *American Anthropologist* 60:776-778.

1958h Review of *Die Wiener Cook-Sammlung: Südsee-Teil,* by Irmgard Moschner. *American Anthropologist* 60:778-779.

1958i Review of *Among the Savages of the South Seas: Memoirs of Micronesia, 1862-1868,* by Alfred Tetens (trans. from the German by Florence Mann Spoehr). *American Anthropologist* 60: 1232-1233.

1959a " 'Don't Call Me,' the Menehune Said. . . ." In "The Professor's Notebook," *Honolulu Star-Bulletin* (Nov. 15).

1959b Review of *Arts and Crafts of Hawaii,* by Te Rangi Hiroa (Peter H. Buck). *Anthropos* 54:309-311.

1959c Review of *Songs and Tales of the Sea Kings,* by J. Frank Stimson (Donald Marshall, ed.). *J. American Folklore* 72:80-81.

1960a "A History of the Binomial Classification of the Polynesian Native Dog." *Pacific Science* 14:193-223.

1960b "The Native Dog in the Polynesian System of Values." In *Culture in History: Essays in Honor of Paul Radin,* Stanley Diamond (ed.) pp. 190-240. New York: Columbia Univ. Press.

1961a "Survey of Research on Polynesian Prose and Poetry." *J. American Folklore* 74:421-439. (Reprinted, in 1961, in *Folklore Research Around the World: A North American Point of View,* Richard M. Dorson (ed.). Bloomington: Indiana Univ. Press.)

1961b "A Dynamic in Oceanic Maui Myths: Visual Illustration with Reference to Hawaiian Localization." *Fabula* 4:137-162.

1961c Review of *Ariki the First-Born: An Analysis of a Polynesian Chieftain Title,* by Aarne A. Koskinen. *J. Polynesian Soc.* 70:386-388.

1961d Review of *The Games of New Zealand Children,* by Brian Sutton-Smith. *American Anthropologist* 63:608-610.

1961e (Abstract) "The Fantasy of Distinguished Parentage in Polynesian Narratives." In *Abstracts of Symposium Papers, 10th Pacific Science Congress* (Honolulu), p. 93.

1962a "Additional Eighteenth-Century Sketches of the Polynesian Native Dog, Including the Maori." *Pacific Science* 16: 170-180.

1962b "Martha Warren Beckwith: A Commemorative Essay." *J. American Folklore* 75:341-353.

1962c Review of *History and Traditions of Tikopia,* by Raymond Firth. *Ethnohistory* 9:285-287.

1962d Review of *Mythologies of the Ancient World,* Samuel N. Kramer (ed.). *Western Folklore* 21:139-140.

1963a "Flexibility in Sib Affiliation Among the Diegueño." *Ethnology* 2:282-301. (Based on a paper, Individual Changes in Sib Membership, Diegueño Indians, read at 35th International Congress of Americanists (Mexico, 1962)). Summary in *Actas y Memorias,* 35th I. C. A., Vol. 2, p. 99. Mexico: 1964.

1963b Review of *Flower in My Ear: Arts and Ethos of Ifaluk Atoll,* by Edwin Grant Burrows. *Pacific Historical Rev.* 32:419-420.

1963c Review of *The Types of the Folktale: A Classification and Bibliography,* by Antti Aarne (2nd ed., trans. and enlarged by Stith Thompson). *American Anthropologist* **65**:747-750.

1963d (Abstract) "The Tragedy of the Demigod Maui." *VIe Congrès International des Sciences Anthropologiques et Ethnologiques* (Paris, 1960). Tome II, *Ethnologie* (premier volume), pp. 183-184. Paris:Musée de l'Homme.

1963e The Ropes of the Sun (unpublished trans. from the French of "Les Liens du Soleil," by Alexandre Haggerty Krappe, in *Rev. Archeologique* **13**:248-252. 1939). Original manuscript in Hamilton Library, University of Hawaii, 7 pp.

1964a "Motif A 728: Sun Caught in Snare and Certain Related Motifs." *Fabula* **6**:213-252.

1964b Review of *Alpha: The Myths of Creation,* by Charles H. Long; *The Two Hands of God: The Myths of Polarity,* by Alan W. Watts; and *The Wisdom of the Serpent: The Myths of Death, Rebirth, and Resurrection,* by Joseph L. Henderson and Maud Oakes. *American Anthropologist* **66**:960-962.

1964c "Report to the Executive Board by the Publications Policy Committee," submitted by Katharine Luomala, chairman. *J. American Folklore,* Suppl. (April), pp. 12-13.

1965a "Polynesian Poetry." In *Encyclopedia of Poetry and Poetics,* by Alex Preminger (ed.), pp. 654-655. Princeton: Princeton Univ. Press.

1965b "Humorous Narratives About Individual Resistance to Food-Distribution Customs in Tabiteuea, Gilbert Islands." *J. American Folklore* **78**:28-45.

1965c "Creative Processes in Hawaiian Use of Place Names in Chants." In "Lectures and Reports," Georgios A. Megas (ed.), 4th International Congress for Folk-Narrative Research (Athens, 1964). *Laographia* **22**:734-741.

1965d Review of *The Evolution of the Gilbertese Boti: An Ethnohistorical Interpretation,* by H. E. Maude. *Man* **65**:134.

1965e Review of *The Oral Tradition: A Study in Historical Methodology,* by Jan Vansina (H. M. Wright, trans.). *Ethnohistory* **12**:373-375.

1965f "Nareau's Tricks in the Assembly House." In *The Primitive Reader,* John Greenway (ed.), pp. 59-62. Hatboro, Pennsylvania: Folklore Assoc. (Reprinted from Luomala, 1965b, pp. 36-37.)

1965g "Snaring the Sun." In *The Primitive Reader,* John Greenway (ed.), pp. 102-104. Hatboro, Pennsylvania: Folklore Assoc. (Reprinted from Luomala, 1949a, pp. 44-45.)

1966a "Numskull Clans and Tales: Their Structure and Function in Oceanic Asymmetrical Joking Relationships." *J. American Folklore* **79**:157-194. (Reprinted, in 1966, in *The Anthropologist Looks at Myth* (Melville Jacobs, comp., John Greenway, ed.) Bibliographical and Spec. Ser. 17, Pub. American Folklore Soc. Austin: Univ. Texas Press.)

1966b Review of *Ka Po'e Kahiko: The People of Old,* by Samuel Manaiakalani Kamakau (Mary Kawena Pukui, trans., Dorothy B. Barrère, ed.). *J. American Folklore* **79**:501-502.

1967 Review of *Temenos: Studies in Comparative Religion Presented by Scholars in Denmark, Finland, Norway and Sweden* (Vol. 1, 1965). *Western Folklore* **26**:281-282.

1968a "MacEdward Leach, 1892-1967." *J. American Folklore* **81**:115-116.

1968b Review of *Kapingamarangi: Social and Religious Life of a Polynesian Atoll,* by Kenneth P. Emory. *J. American Folklore* **81**:86-87.

1968c Review of *A Bibliography of South Asian Folklore,* by Edwin Capers Kirkland. *Western Folklore* **27**:282-283.

1968d Review of *American Indian Mythology*, by Alice Marriott and Carol K. Rachlin. *Science* **162**:785-786.

1970a "Four Aspects of Twelve Korean Proverbs Used in Hawaii." *Proverbium* **15**:75-78.

1970b "Babai *(Cyrtosperma chamissonis)* a Prestige Food in the Gilbert Islands Culture." In *VIIe Congrès International des Sciences Anthropologiques et Ethnologiques* (Moscow, 1964), Vol. 5, pp. 488-499.

1970c "Imponderabilia for a History of Anthropology at University of Hawaii, 1922-1946." *News From the Pacific* (Anthropological Soc. Hawaii) **19**:1-32.

1970d "Introduction." In a re-issue of *Hawaiian Mythology*, by Martha Beckwith, pp. vii-xxix. Honolulu: Univ. Hawaii Press.

1971a "Proverbs from Korean Visiting-Students in Hawaii." *Proverbium* **16**:602-606.

1971b Review of *The Kumuhonua Legends: A Study of Late 19th Century Hawaiian Stories of Creation and Origins*, by Dorothy B. Barrère. *J. American Folklore* **83**:471-472.

1971c Review of *Legends of the South Seas: The World of the Polynesians Seen Through Their Myths and Legends, Poetry and Art*, by Antony Alpers. *American Anthropologist* **73**:1368.

1971d " 'Drowning the Otter': Comment on a Danish Wellerism." *Proverbium* **17**:630.

1972a "Foreword." In *The Kumulipo: A Hawaiian Creation Chant*, by Martha Warren Beckwith, pp. ix-xix. Honolulu: Univ. Press Hawaii. (Reprint ed., first printed 1951.)

1972b "Degeneration and Regeneration: The Hawaiian Phantom Hitchhiker Legend." *Fabula* **13**:20-59.

1973a "The Narrative Source of a Hawaiian Proverb and Related Problems." *Proverbium* **21**:783-787.

1973b "Moving and Movable Images in Easter Island Custom and Myth." *J. Polynesian Soc.* **82**:28-46.

1974a "The *Cyrtosperma* Systemic Pattern: Aspects of Production in the Gilbert Islands." *J. Polynesian Soc.* **83**:14-34.

1974b "The Ear-Flyers and Related Motifs in the Gilbert Islands and Its Neighbors." *J. American Folklore* **86**:260-271.

1975a "Cultural Associations of Land Mammals in the Gilbert Islands," *B. P. Bishop Mus. Occasional Pap.* **24**(13): 227-274.

MICRONESIA

THE APOTHEOSIS OF MARESPA

WILLIAM A. LESSA

University of California, Los Angeles

V ERIDICAL ACCOUNTS of apotheosis are of importance in bringing reason into the sporadically emergent myth-ritual controversy, as well as establishing the potentialities of oral tradition for history But such accounts are lamentably few and are vastly outnumbered by others that are either inadequately documented or not documented at all. At the heart of the problem is the verbal nature of the transmitting process, for the cultural milieu in which apotheosis takes place is ordinarily a preliterate or nonliterate one. Even where written accounts of deification are known and enjoy the aura of age, they are usually based ultimately on spoken tradition and give the semblance of historicity only by virtue of their having been finally committed to writing. The recording may come many years or even centuries later.

My central purpose is to provide an instance from Micronesia of the deification of a mortal by his kinsmen. It is supported by a considerable amount of evidence, some of it written, most of it oral, and all of it having a high degree of internal consistency that should give no offense to credibility. I shall also endeavor to show that both myth and ritual arose out of this event. In doing so I, of course, do not deny that other myths and other rituals may have arisen out of fantasy or dreams, or that one may inspire the other in sequence.

But in tracing the simultaneous development of myth and ritual from a real event, I hope to bury still further those uncompromising aspects of the ritualistic theory, made popular by the Cambridge school and Lord Raglan, which allege that all myths originate in ritual and that no myths have an historical basis. I shall oppose, too, an opposite theory—just as repugnant but less polemically championed—that all rituals have their antecedents in myths. Of course, I do not purport to be the first or even among the first to document the fallacy of such extreme hypotheses. For example, more than three decades ago Clyde Kluckhohn wrote a masterful refutation of such monistic schemes (Kluckhohn, 1942). He demonstrated beyond cavil that some rituals have their genesis in myths, and vice versa, and that some myths and rituals even occur without reference to one another. His contribution was to insist that the almost universal tendency for myth and ritual to be associated results from a common functional basis for the two: ritual is a symbolic representation or dramatization of fundamental societal needs; mythology is a rationalization of these same needs. If myth and ritual are very frequently concomitant and interrelated, the answer can be found without recourse to any putative causal sequence that would have ritual leading to myth, or the other way around.

Ulithi Atoll, the locale of the apotheosis under consideration, has been the object of my field research on four separate occasions totaling a year. The bulk of the data pertinent to the present article was gathered in 1948; other probings took place during the summer of 1960, when I made an effort to amplify certain points that were not clear from the previous inquiries.

The atoll is situated in the western Carolines, not far from Yap. The natives are simple agriculturalists, dependent for subsistence chiefly on the coconut and various arums, supplementing their predominantly starchy diet with fish, pork, and chicken.[1] There were only 421 inhabitants in the island group in 1949, but in the middle of the last century there were probably about 700. Social structure is dominated by matrilineages, with a modified form of patrilocal residence and a modified type of Crow kinship terminology. The lineages are important because the pagan religion centers essentially around a system of ancestor worship in which the ghosts of lineage mates are the object of an everyday cult. To be sure, there is also a belief in celestial gods, paralleled by some less lofty terrestrial spirits; in practice, however, the ghosts of departed relatives are most significant to the natives. Since 1937 there has been a steady and now almost complete conversion to Roman Catholicism, but at the time when the earlier field study was made, many of the older and more influential people were still pagans and most others had a keen remembrance of the old cult. There is virtually no social stratification; wealth is evenly distributed. Land is held by the lineages and portioned

---

[1]This article deals with Ulithi essentially as I found it in 1948. The time is a modified "ethnological present." When I switch to 1960 I have endeavored to make this clear. By now the atoll has undergone such drastic acculturation that little of what I say would apply.

out to individual families for their own needs. There are various kinds of chiefs, including those with territorial jurisdiction and others with lineage authority. Political problems are the concern of the village council of elders, with chiefs functioning primarily either as lineage leaders or as liaison agents with outside islands. It should be mentioned that divorce is easy and remarriage common (prior to conversion to Christianity).

TYPES OF LINEAGE GHOSTS

Ghosts, as distinguished from nonhuman spirits, are known collectively on Ulithi as *tuthup.*

Ghosts associated with particular lineages, of which there are forty-five on the atoll (many of them now extinct or moribund), are called *tuthup bwelbwohat.* Of the great pool of such lineage ghosts, most are undistinguished and soon pass into oblivion, but some achieve remembrance for a while because of a temporary display of necromantic aptitudes. During their lifetime, that is before becoming ancestral ghosts, these individuals never gained great importance, nor did they hold high positions. After they had died and gone to the sky world, Lang, they would return to earth and possess relatives who served as their mouthpieces during a trance, but in so doing they failed to make noteworthy or even accurate disclosures, or otherwise render significant aid to the living. Despite their failures, such ghosts are not innominate, as are the rest of the ordinary ghosts, who never possessed anyone at all. These special name-bearing ghosts are credited with having attempted to act as benefactors for their kinsmen by possessing at least one of their relatives. In the course of time they are forgotten.

The next class of lineage ghosts are those who stand at the head of all the ghosts of a given lineage by virtue of their consistent ability to render greater service to their living relatives than any other ghost. They are known as "little ghosts," *tuthup wachich,* but little only in contrast to two great ghosts of whom we shall speak shortly. Every lineage, except very minor ones, possesses "little ghosts," and, for the most part, the names of these ghosts, who may be either male or female, are still remembered even by persons who have renounced paganism. Each of these successful ghosts has, or once had, a shrine of his own called a *fangelialus,* or spirit shrine, to which his lineage descendants bring offerings. It is only in recent years that these shrines have disappeared.

These successful "little ghosts" must continue to aid their kinsmen, lest they lose their status as the leading ghosts of their lineages and be supplanted by other ghosts of greater power and reliability. This replacement takes place by elevating a ghost within the lineage. It is not clear what happens to *tuthup wachich* who are deposed, they seem to revert to the status of a minor lineage ghost or simply be forgotten. It is of historical interest that these "little ghosts" were mentioned in a letter written in 1722 by Father Cantova after he had interviewed some west Carolinians cast away on Guam. He writes:

> There are among them some priests and priestesses who claim to have dealings with the souls of the dead. These priests tell authoritatively who has gone to Heaven and who to Hell. The former are honored as benevolent spirits and are given the name of *tahutup*, which means "patron saint." Each family has its *tahutup* to which it appeals when in need. If they are sick, undertake a voyage, go fishing, work at the cultivation of their lands, they invoke their *tahutup*. It is to him that they address their requests for the restoration of their health, the success of their voyages, the abundance of fish, and the fertility of their lands. They present gifts to him, which they suspend in the house of their *tamoles* [chiefs], either to obtain favors they have asked of him, or to thank him for assistance already received from his liberal hand (Cantova, 1728, pp. 230-231).

There is on Ulithi still a third class of lineage ghosts called *tuthup paling*, or "great ghosts," and these are the subject of our concern. Only two such ghosts are known to exist. The *tuthup paling* are lineage ghosts who have achieved such superior eminence that they have a special status setting them apart from all other lineage ghosts. So successful are these two "great ghosts" that they are opportunistically embraced by many local lineages as their own major ghost. In fact, their power is respected to the extent that they are known and adopted over a wide portion of the Carolines.

IONGOLAP

The first of these "great ghosts" is Iongolap. Some Ulithians say that Iongolap was born on nearby Yap, where he certainly is well known and holds a major place in the religious system, but most informants maintain that he really came from Ulithi, where he was born "a long time ago" to a Yapese woman. There are many Carolinian myths surrounding him and his origins, and he fits well into the whole pattern of the religion of Yap and many of the islands that are tributary to it, including Ulithi. The literature on this apotheosized ghost and his cult is substantial (see especially Müller 1917-1918, Vol. 1, pp. 324-337; Damm and Others, 1938, pp. 198, 352-354, 359-360), yet for all his prominence he has been almost abandoned on Ulithi. Ulithians recognize his great importance, but they do not any longer implement this recognition very much except in deference to their overlords on Yap, who require them to bring tribute to him there. It would appear that Iongolap was once truly important—possibly the most important of all local ghosts—but that he has fallen into discard because of the great success of another "great ghost," Marespa.

Although Iongolap is alleged by Ulithians to have been an actual person, there is no available evidence to confirm this, yet some ethnologists tend to accept his historicity. Thus, Yanaihara writes (1939, p. 22):

Yonolav [Iongolap] may have been the chieftain of a powerful gens in the Gagil district [of Yap] and the hero of the expedition which subdued the three islands [Ulithi, Fais, Sorol] of the Central Carolines. Perhaps he was deified by the people of Gagil on account of his heroic exploits.

MARESPA

The other "great ghost" honored in Ulithi is Marespa, who is the principal object of our attention.

Since so much of my argument involves historicity and accuracy, I am confronted with the need to go into detailed particulars, and I hope that the reader will bear with me. Oral information comes in the form of anecdotes, genealogies, songs, tales, and rites. Written sources are derived from various German anthropologists who made mention of the personage in question many years ago and are able to provide some control not only over the matter of historicity but the time factor as well.

About Marespa there is little of the obfuscation that surrounds the origins of the older Iongolap. He was a child born in the middle of the last century on the islet of Lam in the northwestern part of the Ulithi group. His parents were Remal and Fahoi. When he was a few months old, much too young to either walk or talk, he died.

His grave, according to various natives to whom I spoke, still stands on the island of Lam. I infinitely regret that I never visited the place, the island having been uninhabited for some time and off the beaten track; but I have no reason to doubt that a grave did exist and that the people were sincere in their conviction that it belonged to Marespa. The presence of such a grave would of course provide further evidence of Marespa's reality.

When Marespa died his soul is said to have gone to Lang. After a short stay there, he returned to earth in the form of a ghostly spirit and possessed one of his relatives, a man named Mare, who lived on the island of Lam. Mare's lineage is not known to us but I suspect that he may have been the same man as Maremar, Remal's brother and therefore a member of the Muruch lineage. Ulithians often condense personal names to one or two syllables. At any rate, on this occasion Maresepa is said to have revealed his identity and ordered that the people build a shrine for him on the island of Mogmog, and to prepare coconut oil for hanging in the shrine as an offering. Later, he asked for two more shrines, and these were built for him on the islands of Mangejang and Pigelelel (Pokhalei). Mare, then, was the first person selected by Marespa to be his *wasoama,* or medium. I am told that sometimes when possessed he would swim from Lam to Mangejang, then to Pigelelel, and back to Lam, aided, I presume, by a log.

Later, Marespa began to possess other relatives, announcing his name and causing them to predict typhoons, reveal the fate of voyagers at sea, warn of impending epidemics, forecast an abundance of fish, describe events in distant places, and so on. So renowned did he become that people hastened to gain his favor when they were in need.

Until the recent past there were many persons who had been possessed by Marespa. Those who served habitually as his mouthpiece had the status of true *wasoama.* Others, being possessed only once or twice, could not lay claim to being his mediums, for they were merely male and female relatives whose connection with the ghost could not be sustained. In 1948 there were several old men who remembered the true mediums, who included not only the boy's own father, Remal, but four other men of his father's Muruch lineage. The mediums, always men, were never possessed contemporaneously; one would be utilized only after the other had been terminated as a medium. The effect of an experience with Marespa was to cause the medium to shake all over while being possessed, after which he would become limp and sick, with headaches, nausea, and lack of appetite. This malaise, say my informants, would last about a day.

Marespa's three shrines no longer existed as such in 1948, but they were well remembered. These houses, called *fangelmarespa,* were devoted entirely to him, thus contrasting with the ordinary spirit shrines, or *fangelialus,* which never existed as separate structures but were incorporated with ordinary dwelling huts. The former shrines located on Mangejang and Pigelelel were on the lands known respectively as Muruch and Wilimathol, the first belonging to the lineage of Marespa's father and the latter to that of his mother. The houses were abandoned when the Japanese, early in their administration, reserved these two islands for the production of copra and forced the inhabitants to leave. In time, the houses deteriorated and eventually vanished. The only other *fangelmarespa* was the one on the island of Mogmog, on the land called Iarau, and it was the last to survive, having been destroyed by the Americans during World War II.

In 1948 a makeshift shrine was being maintained for Marespa on the island of Fassarai by the chief of Mangejang, who had had to move to Fassarai when the Japanese commandeered his island. This chief, Chuoior by name, was the head of the Muruch lineage and the son of one of Marespa's paternal cross cousins. I had occasion to interview this man and to see his makeshift shrine. He was not a medium but a custodian who received, on behalf of supplicants, the sacred oil used as an offering to the great ghost. He hung the oil (in ancient whiskey bottles!) in the forepart of the house where he lived. The oil, called *loi,* has special merit in winning the favor of ancestral ghosts.[2]

In addition to oil, the offerings taken to the three great shrines were: wreaths, turmeric, loincloths, women's shell belts, shell necklaces, and turtle shells. If the custodian was eager to keep an offering for himself he could exchange it for something else. Along with these sacrifices went the supplications of the donor, who had to use a custodian as an intermediary because he alone could intercede directly with the ghost.

Obviously, Marespa was destined to burst out of the confines of his own lineage. This indeed was what happened. He became the "little ghost" not only of his own Fasilus lineage but eighteen others as well.[3] It is possible that Marespa owed some of his prominence to the fact that his lineage was that of the hereditary paramount chiefs, although my informants were emphatic in denying this. Certainly it is unusual that a child who had never exerted influence as a living individual should become deified.

Soon after Marespa had demonstrated his talents to the people of Ulithi he moved beyond the confines of his atoll and came to be sought after in Fais, the islands to the southeast known collectively as The Woleai, and such islands in the southwest as Yap, Ngulu, Palau, and others. But this is a story whose telling I wish to hold in abeyance because it represents a major step in the process of deification.

EARLY ETHNOGRAPHIC NOTICES

The earliest written mention of Marespa was made by Jan S. Kubary, and we cherish it less for its accuracy than its priority. Discussing the influence of Yap on Palau, he asserts that one of the ways in which

---

[2]Apparently, oil for Marespa was originally manufactured only by members of the boy's lineage. When he came to transcend strictly lineage lines, this custom was abrogated. The reason for Muruch lineage's importance is that Marespa's father belonged to it. Apparently, however, there was no technical obstacle to the assumption of custodianship of a *fangelmarespa* by lineages other than Fasilus and Muruch. Incidentally, I learned that the custodianship of a shrine could be shared by a woman but that she would be an unequal partner; her main function was to make leis to place in the shrine, but they could only be put there by a man.

[3]Some of these were sublineages and some were actually extinct, with their estates being managed by other unilinear groups. One was a macroclan.

this can be documented is in personal names, as for example "Maresseba," a personal name on Palau which in Yap is the name of the local god of Guror (Kubary, 1889-1895, Vol. 1, p. 26).[4] I am indebted to Inez de Beauclair not only for her ferreting out this obscure reference to Marespa but also her comment that Kubary was wrong about his being the local god of Guror (de Beauclair, pers. comm., Sept. 8, 1967). The important thing, however, is that Kubary, sometime between 1871 and 1885, discovered that Marespa had already made his presence felt in Yap.

The next ethnographic report, by Wilhelm Müller, stems from interviews in 1909-1910 with a chief from Ngulu while Müller was working on Yap. Although we shall have occasion to wrangle over some of the facts, it is obvious that this is an important piece of documentation whose broad outlines have been depicted with a good grasp of the essential events of the Marespa phenomenon.

. . . in other cases real spirits (kan) assume the foretelling of future events. An example of this, already mentioned fleetingly by Kubary, is Merasepa, who is not a god but a human soul which had strayed from its customary paths. Tatse,[5] the chief of Nulu, calls him a "moonian."[6] He lived about the time of Tatse's grandfather. His father, Ramal, was a man from Mogemog who lived temporarily on Nulu; his mother was Lte. The child was born in Mogemog, and died after a week. His soul remained there and from then on spoke through the mouth of his father, who sat and walked as if in a sleep. It could be clearly distinguished when Ramal spoke and when Merasepa. If the latter was speaking, Ramal spoke in a falsetto voice like a baby, but always in distinct words. Usually the child could be induced to speak only by artificial means. Ramal had to drink coconut oil and eat mint leaves in order to fall into a trance. In this condition he was an oracle to be questioned in matters of disease, approaching typhoons, and so on. He went into the houses of the sick and announced the remedy that he was inspired to tell. Once when Ramal went to Palau and passed through Nulu, the people of Nulu asked him to leave Merasepa with them. They offered him turmeric, turtle shell, and fiega belts. A man named Waethog took oil and mint leaves, whereupon Merasepa possessed him. This man had not previously distinguished himself from his fellowmen or shown any special traits that could have made him suitable as a medium for the spirit.

---

[4]Kubary was a remarkable young Polish-born Hungarian-German who worked in the South Seas for the Museum Godeffroy of Hamburg. Self-taught, he began work in the Carolines at the age of twenty-four and became the first of the Carolinian ethnographers.

[5]My chief informant, Melchethal, knew Tatse on Ngulu and gave me the name of his father as Marekhul and his mother as Malie. He said that Tatse was an old man when he himself was about thirty-five (ca. 1926). He believes Tatse was in error about Lte. My informant knew Waethog, mentioned by Müller, only by reputation, saying he was a Nguluan who was either the real or adoptive father of Sorekh, who serves as a time marker in reconstructing Marespa's time of birth.

[6]The meaning of the Yapese word *moonian* is not entirely clear and in any event does not seem to fit Marespa, even though it was applied to him by Chief Tatse of Ngulu as referring to a class of *kan* or demons who "haunt the villages" (Müller, 1917-1918, Vol. 1, p. 367). Some explanations by Walleser (1913, pp. 615 and 615, n. 4) are not helpful.

It is said that recently Merasepa has been visiting Mogemog on his own, which probably means that this artificial transfer does not always function. After the death of the first medium he possessed another, Vier; but he has not possessed any new mediums since the death of this last. No one knows what became of him (Müller, 1917-1918, Vol. 1, pp. 376-377).

The wide swath cut by Marespa through the islands of the east is documented by Augustin Krämer's observation that his name was alluded to in a verse used on the atoll of Lamotrek in connection with a medicine that has proved to be successful (Krämer, 1937, p 139). Krämer recorded the verse in 1909. Incidentally, William Alkire found that there was a *fangelmarespa* and a Marespa medium on Lamotrek when he was doing field work there in 1962-1963 (Alkire, 1965, pp. 121-123).

Paul Hambruch, a member of the Thilenius expedition who spent two weeks on Ulithi itself in 1909, gathered a fair amount of miscellaneous ethnographic information but not much about the religious system of the atoll. He devotes some space to Yonelap (Iongolap), and describes the preparations made by the people of Ulithi for the occasional visits by that god when he joins the crews of the canoes returning home after having brought tribute to Yap. The passage relevant for our purposes is as follows:

The natives pick coconuts, catch fish, and lay them together with mats, oil, tobacco and garlands in the Fathuulus house, which has been elaborately decorated. . . . Yonelap stays here when he is on Mogemog, and his grandson Liogefalu . . . and the spirit of the deceased Mogemog inhabitant Marethupar live here too (Damm and Others, 1938, p. 354).

In that publication we are most fortunate in having two photographs of the *fangelialus* on Mogmog taken in 1909 by F. E. Hellwig (Plate 28), two sets of sketches by Elisabeth Krämer and Hambruch himself (p. 333), and a full page water color by Frau Krämer (Plate 33). I have reproduced Frau Krämer's sketch of this important shrine, whose site I often visited, even though the little house was gone (see Fig. 1).

MARESPA'S GENEALOGY

The genealogical facts about Marespa bear examination not only because they help to verify his very existence and his place in the scheme of things but also because they serve to pinpoint the time of his birth.

His father was Remal of the Muruch lineage, his mother Fahoi of the ranking Fasilus lineage. His father's name is corroborated in the account given by Müller (1917-1918, Vol. 1, p. 376). Although Müller's informant, who came from a different atoll, gave his mother's name as Lte, my own informants insist this is incorrect.

Marespa had a brother named Harong, about whom nothing is

FIGURE 1—The *fangelialus* on Mogmog in 1909 (after a sketch by Elisabeth Krämer).

known beyond the fact that he seems to have died before reaching the age of marriage. (I note, however, that one of Marespa's *wasoama* was a Harong.) He had two sisters, whom we must assume were older than he; they were Soilim and Lifohoi.

Soilim had a husband named Rolmei, who was head of the Lamrui lineage and thereby the second most important chieftain of the atoll. They had a daughter named Lifohothul, who married but apparently bore no children. She is important to us because living informants heard her relate how she held Marespa in her arms when she was a girl. Although she was the baby's niece, obviously she must have been born before he. Lifohothul had the following siblings, apparently in this order of birth: a sister named Ifelakh; three brothers named Iurul, Lathisemel, and the third unidentified; and a sister named Ilemokh who married and had grandchildren who were alive in 1948, particularly a woman by the name of Lemang, whom I knew.

Marespa's other sister, Lifohoi, had a son named Sorekh, who seems to be the same Sorekh whom Ulithians told me had been a *wasoama* for Marespa. Sorekh's father, Waethog, from Ngulu Atoll, was said by Müller's informant, Tatse, to have been possessed by Marespa, it will be recalled. Figure 2 is an abridged genealogy that I have drawn up to show the chief kinsmen in Marespa's genealogy.

THE TIME OF MARESPA'S BIRTH

Knowing these names and these genealogical facts we can make certain inferences regarding the years when various persons lived and when Marespa must have been born.

We may begin with Marespa's elder sister, Soilim. My chief informant says that he remembered her when he was a lad of eleven or twelve, and that she was so weak from old age that she had to be carried about when she had to eliminate or be moved anywhere. This was about the year 1902, and if she was approximately ninety years old then, she would have been born about 1812.

This approximate age for Soilim would not do offense to what is known about her husband, Rolmei, who is mentioned in the literature by Captain Tetens, who said that two ruling chiefs, Giurr and Ronneme, were on Ulithi when he visited there in 1870 (Tetens and Kubary, 1873, p. 56). Giurr was probably Huior, whom an informant says was already dead when he himself was born in 1891; but in any event he does not enter into the picture. The other chief, Ronneme, was really the aforementioned Rolmei, Marespa's sister's husband. If he was alive in 1870 and was, let us say, sixty years old, he would have been born in 1810,

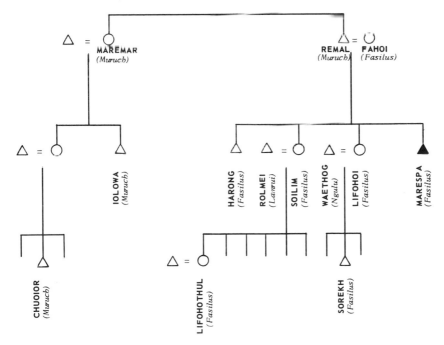

FIGURE 2—Marespa's genealogy, abbreviated. Lineages are indicated in parentheses.

two years prior to his wife. This date could vary one way or the other, but even so it would not be too inconsistent with our estimate for Soilim.

Now we immediately take up Lifohothal, child of the above Rolmei and Soilim. She used to describe vividly how she held Marespa in her arms when she was a young girl. Lifohothal is said to have died a decrepit old woman in about 1932, and if an age of 100 is subtracted from that year, she would have been born in 1832. I know that such an age may seem excessive, but Ulithians often live very long. I am motivated by the fact that Lifohothal was a first child and her mother might have been about twenty when giving birth to her. Twenty added to 1812, of course, again gives us 1832.

Next we turn our attention to Marespa's other sister, Lifohoi. Her husband was the Waethog possessed by Marespa on Ngulu; but we have no particular means of estimating his birth. Nor can we date the birth of Lifohoi herself, except that it must have been later than 1812 if she was younger than her sister Soilim. We can make further inferences through her son, Sorekh, about whom we have more facts.

We have indisputable evidence that Sorekh died between 1907 and 1909. He survived the dreadful typhoon of 1907 and, together with many other Ulithians, was evacuated to Yap aboard the schooner *Germania* after he had unsuccessfully appealed to Iongolap to stop the storm (Damm and Others, 1938, p. 348). When Hambruch arrived in Ulithi in 1909 to do field work, Sorekh had already died on Yap and been replaced by Rawe (Damm and Others, 1938, p. 348). If we assume that he was seventy when he died, and that his mother Lifohoi bore him when she was twenty, she would have been born about 1818, a few years after Soilim, her sister.

Now we come to Marespa himself. If Lifohothal was a girl of seven (my assumption) when she held Marespa in her arms, this would have had to be in the year 1839, approximately. The time is not an unreasonable one in terms of Kubary's report and the events reported about Marespa's ghostly career. But it has one drawback: the interval between Marespa's year of birth and that of his elder sister would be twenty-seven years. If we strain things a bit and say his mother started having children at the age of sixteen and had her last child, Marespa, twenty-seven year later, she would have been forty-three years old at the time. This would not make medical history, of course, but asks a good deal of us .

The dilemma could be partially resolved by making adjustments here and there in our estimates, but they could not alter the fact that Soilim would have had to have a child, and that this child would have had to be old enough to hold a baby. The time span between niece and uncle would perforce remain great.

There are certain possibilities to consider in trying to understand the genealogy given me—a genealogy which, by the way, cross-checks with several independent genealogies involving Marespa but supplied by different informants using different points of reference. Remal may have had more than one wife. Perhaps Müller's informant was right, after all, and a woman named Lte enters into the picture. But why should Ulithians withhold this information, assuming they knew about it? Polygamy was permitted on Ulithi, and of course so was remarriage after divorce or the death of a spouse. Another source of confusion may lie in adoptions. Ideally, they should not affect genealogies but in practice they do, especially since they are so common (45.0 percent of the population in 1949).

To sum up, Marespa probably was born and died in 1839. This date fits in well with almost all genealogical and historical facts, except that it imposes a great time interval between his birth and that of his elder sister. There is no certain way of explaining or reducing that interval.

TRANSCENDING ULITHI

Intimations have already been given of Marespa's recognition beyond the confines of his atoll. To the east and south he came to be embraced by the island of Fais and the many islands known collectively to Ulith ians as the Woleai. All these islands have a kinship and political relationship to Ulithi, which is their superior in the complex hierarchial structure of the Yap (Gagil) empire (see Lessa, 1950); but it is likely that Marespa's acceptance owed as much to the enthusiasm inspired by his great accomplishments as to the superordinate position of his native land. The people of Fais and the Woleai, I am told, offered *mepel* to Marespa on each of their own islands. On the occasion of the great annual tribute voyages to Yap, when a fleet of canoes from all over would assemble on Ulithi, the people of these islands were received in the great assembly house known as Rolang, whose site is still sacred today. In accepting them the paramount chief of Ulithi, who was by heredity a Fasilus, would say a prayer and then take the *mepel* to the nearby *fangelmarespa*, west of the building. However, some of the offerings were transmitted to Yap, together with Ulithi's own offerings.

To the southeast, Marespa gained a foothold in Ngulu, a small atoll with close ties to Ulithi. It will be recalled that Müller gave us an account of this episode, so we need not repeat it.

More astounding was Marespa's acceptance on Yap, where in Gagil district he became second in importance only to Iongolap among the grade one and grade two classes of the proud *pilung* or upper caste of those islands. What is remarkable about this is that the people of Ulithi are considered by the Yapese to belong to the same inferior caste as the *pemilngai* of Yap. The offerings taken to Yap consisted of coconut oil, sleeping mats, and loincloths of the *machi* type,[7] but not turmeric, which comes from Yap. They were sent approximately in May as part of the intricate complex of political tribute, "rent," and religious offerings in which Ulithi and its own satellite islands were locked with Yap. I have detailed data on these great expeditions but will withhold discussing them until the section on "The Process of Apotheosis." Suffice it to say for now that the apparent reason why offerings were taken to Yap was that the Yapese, as "parents" of their "children" on Ulithi and the other islands, took a chauvinistic attitude in these matters and felt that they could intervene more successfully with Marespa than could such inferiors.

Even Palau, which has a disdain for everyone, including the Yapese, saw fit to accept Marespa. While he did not usurp the position of their already entrenched high ghosts, he was hailed for his remarkable abilities. It will be recalled that Müller's informant maintained that Marespa was brought to Palau by Remal. I have been told that at least one lineage there asked for and received permission from Ulithi to erect a *fangelmarespa* in his honor. According to one informant, people on Palau were still manufacturing the coconut oil in 1948 and placing it inside Marespa's shrine when making their supplications.

Far to the west, near Indonesia, are the four islands of Sonsorol, Pulo Anna, Merir, and Tobi, and I am told that they too found a place for Marespa, even though they are said to have reckoned a certain ghost by the name of Matefoi as the most powerful of all. The natives of these islands built their own local shrines to Marespa and did not take offerings to him on Ulithi, which is at least 700 miles away.

THE PROCESS OF APOTHEOSIS

Apotheosis, defined as the act of raising a person who has died to the rank of a god, may be of two kinds. It is logically possible for a god to have developed from a mortal whose kinship status is not a factor. But where kinship does enter in, the situation is different and we are confronted with the problem as to where ancestor worship leaves

---

[7]These are woven on a loom out of very fine banana fiber threads and are characterized by an intricate red and black design. *Machi* are highly prized and are used only by chiefs. As for the oil, its importance is attested to by a Yapese remark about "the god in the Spanish oil bottle," meaning Marespa (de Beauclair, pers. comm., Aug. 28, 1971).

off and apotheosis begins. It is necessary to make at least some effort
to define the difference.

Where a ghost comes to be venerated beyond the confines of a kin
group, where he is not one of the ancestors of the people who have
come to embrace him, then he has attained the qualities of a god. Furthermore, when he has become the object of a myth-making process
whereby experiences and attributes are given him beyond those of merely powerful, superior men, then again he may be said to have acquired
the status of a deity. Ancestor worship already presupposes his historicity.
It also entails the transference to him of specifically religious acts and
attitudes, including worship and sacrifice. What it does not include is
the "public" character of his cult and the leveling of supernatural sanctions against wrongdoers beyond his kinsmen. An additional but purely
incidental distinction, perhaps, is that a god enjoys some measure of
perdurability, whereas a worshiped ancestor suffers the fate of evanes-
cence.

Regarding Marespa, the question of historicity has already been dealt
with. So has his emergence as a supralineage spirit. What remains is
to demonstrate that he had transcended the shamanistic sphere and had
achieved functions beyond prognostication and familial admonishments
—or at least was in the process of doing so before his posthumous career
was terminated by the encroachments of Christianity and the skeptical
world of alien powers.

We may begin with traditional narrative. I did not in the course
of my research on Ulithi attempt to uncover the presence of Marespa
tales, but in my notes I have found a simple story that partially lifts
the boy out of the ancestral sphere and into the realm of the gods.
The tale is short and was narrated to me by an elderly man who first
heard it as a boy from some people who were making leis for a *fangelmarespa*. Rather than present it verbatim, I have thought it wise to para-
phrase it and incorporate various explanatory notes that will make it
more intelligible and meaningful. It goes as follows:

Marespa died. His ghost went to live inside a taro leaf. There was a spirit named
Mitou whose function was to catch the souls of living people and take them up to Ialulep,
the foremost god of Lang, the sky world. Mitou went to Marespa and made him his
"child," and Marespa did everything that he told him. They had a net and with it they
would start out in the east and make their way west as far as the Philippines, trying
to catch the souls of people and make them die. They worked only at the full moon.
Once when the moon was full they started out to do their work. There was a spirit named
Sathawolemethau, who lived on a long log in the sea, and when they tried to catch him
they could not because he broke the net and escaped. Marespa said to Sathawolemethau,
"Be ready! I will come the next full moon and catch you." He replied, "You are a very
wicked man. You are catching all your 'children' on these islands. You were born on

earth." Marespa had not known that he was born on earth until he found this out from
the spirit. He felt remorse. One full moon he and his friend came back to catch souls,
but Marespa set free all those caught in the net. His friend was unaware of this. Every
time Marespa and his friend went to catch souls, he would do that. One time when Marespa
was in Lang, another spirit named Ilurang said to him, "You were born on this island
(Ulithi)." Then Marespa entered into mediums. They made a *fangelmarespa* for him and
the people of the island prayed to him. After that, other islands too made *fangelmarespa.*
That is why Marespa became our ghost.[8]

I am indebted to Inez de Beauclair for a brief reference to a Marespa
story that she obtained from a middle-aged man from Ngulu whom
she interviewed on Yap. She writes: "He told a strange story, in which
Marespa figured as guiding a man dropped to the bottom of the sea,
reaching the *falu* (men's house) of the dead, who were all sitting silently
twisting coconut fibre ropes (sennit)" (de Beauclair, pers. comm., Apr.
23, 1965).

Obviously, for Marespa the myth-making process had never reached
the stage achieved by that other "great ghost," Iongolap. I am convinced,
however, that had Marespa enjoyed the more or less pristine cultural
milieu in which Iongolap's genesis as a god had proceeded, things might
have been otherwise.

Songs from various islands still preserving some paganism have
served to perpetuate memories of Marespa, and of this there is no better
example than that of Ifaluk.

In 1947 during the course of field work on this little atoll, Burrows
and Spiro came to know him under the name of Mwarisepa or Morisepa,
listing him as one of the ten "foreign supernaturals" known on the atoll.
They reported that he was said to be the ghost of a boy who died at
sea, and they presumed that he was from Ulithi because he was invoked
in a series of songs attributed to that island group but still being sung
on Ifaluk. "This spirit," they wrote, "helps mariners lost at sea" (Burrows
and Spiro, 1953, p. 349).

Burrows had occasion to revisit Ifaluk in 1953 while it was still pagan
and collected among others a number of religious dance songs that were
published posthumously in his book, *Flower in My Ear* (1963). Of these
songs, known as *ur,* three are concerned almost entirely with Mwarisepa
(pp. 389-394, 394-400, 400-403), while three others make passing reference to him (pp. 141, 363-370, 379-389). Although *ur* in general are

---

[8]Sathawolemethau is a spirit to whom people present an offering after successfully
completing a voyage. The offering consists of coconut husks carried by voyagers as a
reserve to be eaten (?) if necessary. When they arrived they would throw them into the
water and say, "I give you garbage for your water channel, Sathawolemethau!" The attitude
of the people seems to have been that they were not giving him anything good. I cannot
explain this attitude.

"not intended to express adoration directly, but rather to please the gods with entertainment" (Burrows, 1963, p. 63), those in question reveal an unmistakably supplicative attitude toward the young godling. He is ardently courted, and with good reason. In his home in the sky he takes pity on those on earth; he talks to them with kindly words. He guides mariners safely to shore and saves the people from sickness. One song tells us that the former chiefs used to be bad men, but now because of him the chiefs agree to pray for the people's welfare. The god teaches the women their *bwarux* or serenade dance songs, and he dances with them, each woman giving him a garland of flowers. The songs are like paeans—praising, thanking, exulting. The women are anxious always for him to descend from his abode in the sky and they try to coax him with blossoms, songs, and dances. He is not averse to their blandishments, although something further also draws him earthward (Burrows, 1963, p. 393).

> *The boy in the sky remembers, down on*
> *earth below*
> *His mother still among the living,*
> *Remembers when he was a babe in her arms.*
> *He comes down to earth,*
> *Wanting to stay there with her*
> *Or take her to the sky with him . . . .*

Deprecation of Mwarisepa is hinted at by Burrows and Spiro when they say that "people on Ifaluk seem to have no active faith in him" (Burrows and Spiro, 1953, p. 349), but it should be remembered that they were recording an impression of him formed late in time by the Ifaluk. Regardless of this, one of the songs itself, undoubtedly composed much earlier in time, contains the following passage (Burrows, 1963, p. 385):

> *Sometimes he speaks the truth,*
> *Sometimes he lies, they say . . . .*

But the song hastens to defend him against such calumny (Burrows, 1963, p. 385).

> *His talk does not swerve from the truth*
> *Whatever backbiters may say.*
> *He gives the people the truth!*

It will be recalled, however, that all six of the *ur* having anything to do with Marespa originated on Ulithi; even so, he must have been held in some esteem on Ifaluk for the pagan natives to have preserved his memory for so long in the dances they danced and the songs they sang.

De Beauclair tells me that on Yap she heard of and collected parts of a women's dance song that had been inspired by Marespa. It deals with the catastrophe that met a fleet from Ulithi sailing to Fais. The canoes were punished by the chief, Sorek (Marespa's nephew, Sorekh?) by means of the most powerful Yapese magic, the red earth *eria,* put on the masts. This happened during German times (de Beauclair, pers. comm., Apr. 23, 1965). I regret that I do not know from her account how Marespa himself participated in this episode, but it is interesting to see him associated with the kind of magic power which Yap is said to use to close and open the seaways.

In turning now to the rituals that came to be built up around Marespa we shall, of course, ignore those associated purely with lineage ancestor worship and proceed to those that treated the boy as a godling. First is an annual ritual of major importance performed on Ulithi over a period of two lunar months and designed to bring an abundance of fish to the atoll. This rite would open up on Mogmog with the fish magician, commissioned to act by the paramount chief, taking a loincloth to the *fangelmarespa* on that island and leaving it with the custodian. The whole ritual was an elaborate and dangerous one, taking place for the most part during sea trips about the atoll, and in the course of events there would be prayers to many great sky and ocean deities, so that to a certain extent Marespa may be said to have been associated with the gods.

Marespa was linked with an even greater annual event, comparable in magnitude with the expeditions made by members of the intricate *kula* ring off eastern New Guinea made famous by Malinowski's writings. This annual event was the so-called tribute voyage to Yap. I have already alluded to the trips made to Yap by its satellite islands, and much has been written about them by German ethnographers, as well as myself. I shall confine myself to excerpts from an eyewitness account from the point of view of Ulithi and try to make simple what is in fact a complex matter.

The purpose of the expeditions was to bring "rent," political tribute, and religious offerings to Gagil district in Yap. I shall discuss only the offerings, called *mepel.* They were for both Iongolap and Marespa.

Of the great fleet of canoes assembled on Ulithi from all over the eastern islands, about five or more were from the atoll. Coconut oil for Marespa was put in the windward and leeward cabins of the canoe belonging to the paramount chief of Ulithi, who, of course, was a member of the Fasilus lineage. The other canoes, too, carried oil, but in this instance for their own lineage ghosts, not Marespa. The paramount chief would pray to Marespa for a safe voyage, while the navigators of each of the other canoes prayed to the great navigation god, Ialuluwe. Strict precedent determined that the lead canoe and its pilot be always from the island of Falalop.

On reaching Yap a sort of quarantine was placed on all the canoes to guard against any harm from spirits that might have followed the canoes to Yap. The passengers remained in their canoes, with the sails down but the masts up, until a certain magician for travel, who lived in Gagil district, had taken steps to lift the quarantine. He would walk up to each canoe, and as he did so, men and women would shout "Hai! Hai!" as they pounded the ground with coconuts and blew on shell trumpets to drive away the spirits. The magician would work purificatory magic over each canoe, and when he was finished the paramount chief from Ulithi would disembark with his men. They carried *mepel* for Iongolap and Marespa and these were hung in a house on a spot called Lamrui. In front of the house on the west side were about ten stone slabs used as back rests by chiefs and other important people as the prayers were being said with the offerings. These stones were not exclusively used for this one occasion, however, but also for any important meetings throughout the year concerning Iongolap and Marespa. The reason the offerings were brought to Yap was that the Yapese of Gatschapar village recognized the great power of both of the two great ghosts, Iongolap and Marespa. (We know from other accounts that the islands east and south of Ulithi were likewise required to take *mepel* to Yap.)

The return voyage from Yap to Ulithi was surrounded with further ritual and prayer. Marespa was again called upon to safeguard the travelers and their canoes.

I have not endeavored to ascertain other ways in which the Marespa cult involved ritual but am sure that Marespa was often invoked ritualistically not only in prayer but other ways as well, if the example of his companion ghost, Iongolap, is of any value. The career of the one closely follows the other and it is most likely that it followed a well-established pattern in the Carolines. Indeed, although I have not referred to them, there are ample examples in the literature of the apotheosis of local Carolinian ghosts, although I have found none that approximated the high status of the two "great ghosts."

CONCLUSION

I have, then, described an instance of the deification of a small boy on Ulithi. He died, became a lineage ghost, transcended the bounds of his lineage, and finally was well on his way to becoming a full divinity when his metamorphosis was interrupted by Westernization. This instance deals with the question as to whether or not humans are ever at all deified, and more particularly whether real persons give rise to religious rituals and myths.

This article has not purported to be a comprehensive discussion of the myth-ritual theory, but it is possible that examples such as that of Marespa will help refute the more dogmatic kind of ritual theory, which, maintaining as it does that all myth has a ritual origin, is obviously untenable. Much of what the ritualists have to say is perfectly true, but by their own criteria their position becomes invalid if even one instance can successfully be opposed to their notion that myths never have historicity but emerge only out of ritual.[9]

LITERATURE CITED

ALKIRE, WILLIAM H.
    1965. *Lamotrek Atoll and Inter-island Socioeconomic Ties.* Illinois Studies in Anthropology. Urbana: Univ. Illinois Press.
BURROWS, EDWIN G.
    1963. *Flower in My Ear.* Univ. Washington Publ. Anthropology. Seattle: Univ. Washington Press.
BURROWS, EDWIN G., and MELFORD E. SPIRO
    1953. *An Atoll Culture: Ethnography of Ifaluk in the Central Carolines.* Behavior Science Monogr. New Haven: Human Relations Area Files.
CANTOVA, JUAN ANTONIO
    1728. "Lettre du P. Jean Cantova, Missionair de C. de J. au R. P. Guillaume Daubenton. Mar. 20, 1722." *Lettres Edifiantes et Curieuses, Escrits des Missions Etrangères, par Quelques Missionaires de la Compagnie de Jésus.* 34 vols. N. LeClerc and Others, 1707-1775. Vol. 18 (1728), pp. 188-247.
DAMM, HANS, and OTHERS
    1938. "Zentralkarolinen, 2 Halbband: Ifaluk, Aurepik, Faraulip, Sorol, Mogemog." In G. Thilenius (ed.), *Ergebnisse der Südsee-Expedition, 1908-1910.* II Ethnographie; B Mikronesien. Band 10, 2. Hamburg: Friederichsen, De Gruyter.
KLUCKHOHN, CLYDE
    1942. "Myths and Rituals: A General Theory." *Harvard Theological Rev.* **35:** 45-79.

---

[9] I wish to make special mention of the assistance given me in my library research by Charlotte E. Spence, Indo-Pacific Bibliographer of the UCLA Research Library.

Krämer, Augustin

1937. "Zentralkarolinen, 1 Halbband: Lamotrek-Gruppe, Oleai, Feis," In G. Thilenius (ed.), *Ergebnisse der Südsee-Expedition, 1908-1910*. II Ethnographie: B Mikronesien. Band 10, 1. Hamburg: Friederichsen, De Gruyter.

Kubary, Jan S.

1889-1895. *Ethnographische Beiträge zur Kenntnis der Karolinen Archipels*. 3 vols. Leiden: P.W.M. Trap.

Lessa, William A.

1950. "Ulithi and the Outer Native World." *American Anthropologist* **52**:27-52.

Müller, Wilhelm

1917-1918. "Yap." In G. Thilenius (ed.), *Ergebnisse der Südsee-Expedition, 1908-1910*. II Ethnographie; B Mikronesien. Band 2, 2. Hamburg: L. Friederichsen.

Tetens, Alfred, and Johann Kubary

1873. "Die Carolineninsel Yap oder Guap nebst den Matelotas-, Makenzie-, Fais- und Woléa-Inseln [Bearbeitet von Dr. E. Gräffe]." *J. Mus. Godeffroy* **1**:84-130.

Walleser, Sixtus

1913. "Religiöse Anschauungen und Gebräuche der Bewohner von Yap." *Anthropos* **8**:607-629, 1044-1068.

Yanaihara, Tadao

1939. *Pacific Islands under Japanese Mandate*. Shanghai: Kelley and Walsh.

THE ORIGIN OF CLANS ON NAMU, MARSHALL ISLANDS

NANCY J. POLLOCK*
Victoria University, Wellington

T WO IMPORTANT MODES of establishing social identity exist for a Marshallese; namely, the atoll he considers his home island and his clan. The need to identify with others, and the means by which that identification is brought about, make social identity an important part of Marshallese social structure.

In general, identity units are the means by which persons locate themselves within their society's framework.[1] Moreover, these units are given time depth by links to ancestors. Kinship often figures prominently in these units which may or may not be corporate entities; sometimes the unit has a specific name, and it may be built into the oral tradition. By providing the categories from which face-to-face groups are drawn, such a unit is an important means by which an individual establishes himself within his society's traditions. This paper will examine these features as they occur in one Marshallese society, Namu.

Part of the identification process rests in establishing connections with a founding ancestor; thus we must examine what the people know about these ancestors and their clan origins. Traditional accounts tell how the clans came into being and the places with which they were associated. Katharine Luomala, in her discussion of Micronesian mythol-

*Field work on Namu was carried out from February, 1968, to January, 1969, supported by a Research Grant from the National Institute of Mental Health #1 F1 - MH - 39. 045 - 01 (Cuan) and MH - 11,300 - 01.

[1]The term "identity unit" is used to convey the Marshallese individual conceptualization of himself in his social context by means of certain culturally prescribed factors which give him a discreteness at the same time as he holds a sense of belonging (compare Goodenough, 1970; Keesing, 1971; Rigby, 1969; Strathern, 1971.)

ogy, states that "Traditions about the origin of clans constitute a major part of Micronesian mythology" (1950, p. 719).

Data on how clans of chiefs were formed can be found in documents of the German Thilenius expedition (Erdland, 1914; Krämer and Nevermann, 1938), as well as in tales of some of the major ancestral figures and totems. This information, unpublished material collected by Commander Buckingham of the U.S. Navy and given to Dr. Leonard Mason, and my own field data on Namu atoll will be used. The views of Marshallese ideology discussed in this paper are based on the expressions of Namu persons in 1968-1969, together with my interpretation of these. Thus where the term "Marshallese" is used, it must be borne in mind that this is my Namu informants' views of Marshallese.[2] This factor highlights the many levels of relativity at which any social group establishes its identity.

A Marshallese clan *(jowi)* is a widespread social entity with two major features—the common name of a putative ancestor inherited matrilineally, and the feeling that an individual is in some way related to the other members of that named clan, even though he may not be able to trace the exact genealogical relationship. Clan affiliation restricts the range of potential marriage partners; clan exogamy is a structural principle which has not been violated, as far as we can tell, over the past generations. Clan affiliation is also evoked to obtain hospitality when a Namu person is away from his home atoll; for instance, there was a household in Majuro which some Namu people joined because they were of the Jemeliwut clan. Namu people also indicated that each clan had major attributes that were useful to other members of the society; that is, Raij clan members were known to have unique healing powers. No activities bring clan members together as such, although a person's presence at a particular event may be justified by his clan identity.

The right of an individual to use a particular clan name as his own may be the only form of recognition he gives to clan membership. A particular clan name is spread over many atolls of the Marshalls and may also be found in the social groups of neighboring islands.[3] Thus the name of the clan is an important symbol of unity for this very dispersed group of people. Within a clan are found several unnamed

[2]After reading a draft of this paper, Bob Kiste asserted that the Bikini and Eniwetok peoples each have their own version of its origins, which differs from this Namu version. Mike Rynkiewich commented similarly for his interpretation of Arno people's origins.

[3]Complete lists of clan names for social groups continuous to the Marshalls do not appear in the literature. Riesenberg's list (1968) is the sole exception. Possible homonyms between clans of Mokil, Pingelap, and Ponape has been suggested by Morton (n.d.) but further investigation of this question for other neighboring populations is needed.

lineages *(bwij)*. A lineage is more localized to a particular atoll and is the important group for day-by-day activities.

The significance of a name lies in its use as a label through which membership in a particular category is established. The name then stands as a symbol for the category. The name of a clan indicates the discreteness of one clan from another. It is interesting to note that Marshallese clans, for which there are very few group activities, have names, whereas Marshallese lineages, whose members are in constant interaction, have no names.

This paper will indicate how accounts of clan origins are a means by which a Marshallese connects living members of his social group to members of past groups and categories. Second, it will discuss the process of clan segmentation and the consequent dispersal of clans throughout several atolls, and suggest how this development may have brought about the present form of the clan. Finally, it will briefly examine clan names to see if they can help in the reconstruction of clan origins.

Namu atoll is traditionally known as the seat of origin of the Marshallese.[4] "Legend relates that originally the Ralik Chain had seven clans, all of which had originated on Namu atoll" (Bryan, 1965, No. 13). Examining the current (1968) representation of clans on Namu (see Table 1) gives some indication of how clans dispersed throughout the Marshall Islands. Admittedly, the postulation of the origins of clans is only "conjectural history"; nevertheless, it is instructive to try to reconstruct this aspect of development in Marshallese social structure. Emphasis in the published accounts is on the development of the chiefly clans. This may be attributed to the way in which the information was sought, or perhaps it is inherent in the thinking of the Marshallese. At any rate, it gives the analysis a royal or noble bias.

One of the most complete accounts of clan origins can be found in Buckingham (n.d.):

> This is the story of the Iroij, a now vanished race of kings, whose descendants are till the feudal lords of the Marshall Islands. It is the story of the Iroij of Ralik, the western or "Sunset" chain of the Marshalls. The facts related here were told to the writer from memory by Lokrap of Ebon atoll, himself a descendant of the line. It is written here for the first time, and is a story new to Western ears. Indeed it is known to only a very few of the Marshallese themselves, such knowledge having been reserved only for the ears of the chiefs.
>
> In Namo the story begins, and its beginning is as misty as the windward beaches of

---

[4]We must assume for this paper that the Marshalls population is a discrete social unit. However, implicit in the discussion and the mythology is the idea that the first residents arrived from the west and/or south and were probably of diverse origins. Their navigational skills enabled them to survive, but this does not indicate homogeneity of origins. Thus the question of who the Marshallese were before they became discrete as a group is beyond the scope of this paper. Identity as Marshallese starts with Liwatoinmour and Lijjeleijet.

that island. Lijjeleijet and Liwatoinmour were sisters, but they and their children were to contend in a most unsisterly fashion for the rule of the islands. Of that struggle a full account will be given. But let it be pointed out in the beginning that a position of importance in this story is given to women. For in the Marshall Islands, the line of succession is through the mother only, and to be of the Iroij one must come of a royal mother.

Little is known of these two sisters of Namo atoll, except that until recent years both were still there. One is visible even yet, on certain days when the wind blows, and the breakers pile foaming on the reef. Lijjeleijet, whose name means "woman of the sea," was driven by her sister to live in the sea. But she did not die. Nowhere does the surf smoke as on the reefs of Namo. Like the white smoke of a great fire it drifts over the island. The people call this smoke "Lijjeleijet," but few of them realize that this is the spirit of that ancient woman of the sea returning to her beloved home.

And as for Liwatoinmour, although she founded a line of royal kings, her ultimate fate was rather shameful. Her name has a sound like Radak words meaning "Come from the east to live." But no matter from whence she came, Liwatoinmour stayed on Namo for a long, long time. In fact, she was still there a few years ago, in the form of a certain rock, receiving the worship and gifts of the people, until a missionary named Dr. Rife picked her up and cast her into the sea. He said she was only a stone, and perhaps the good man was right. For Liwatoinmour remained where he cast her.

Now the daughter of Liwatoinmour was named Iroij. She it was who gave her name to the royal descendants of her line. Iroij, too, was of the misty past, and may, or perhaps may not have been a person. The word "Iroij" means a group of people. It may signify the large retinue of a royal personage, or the large number of his subjects. Once the title was won by wisdom and courage in battle, the title became hereditary. And now the Iroij are gone, and in the descendants the blood of commoners is mixed. But still they are called princes and princesses, and still they are the chiefs in their islands and the owners of all land.

Only one descendant of Lijjeleijet is remembered, and he because he dared to challenge the rule of the Iroij. When he, Jemaliut, was defeated, his family passed into the obscurity which history reserved for defeated aspirants to royal crowns.

Lokrap's account highlights many important features of the ethnohistory of the Marshallese people, even though it deals primarily with the development of the Iroij line. Buckingham's manuscript contains only the English version of Lokrap's tale, and one would expect that at least some of the narrative is couched in Western rather than Marshallese terms; however, some of the points can be verified from the German material which includes the Marshallese original, as well as German and English translations.

This account will be used as a basis for discussing four major aspects of the origins issue. First, we will examine how the descent line has been traced through women, and how this ideology may have led to the dispersal of clans over several atolls. Second, we will examine how clans came to have a hierarchical structure vis-a-vis one another. Third, we will suggest what some of the symbolic representations of the clan structure might be. And fourth, we will discuss the clans and their traditional places of association.

TABLE 1
REPRESENTATION OF CLANS ON NAMU, 1968

	Persons	Percent
Riaur	79	13
Ribikarij	83	12
Ejowa	98	16
Raij	55	8.8
Jemeliwut	140	24
Rilujen Namu	24	3.2
Mckauliej	114	19
Lo Baren	4	
RiMeijor	4	
RiKwajalein	1	
Kuaro	1	4
Ijirik	4	
Erebra	2	
Jol	5	
TOTAL		100

DESCENT LINE TRACED THROUGH WOMEN

Lokrap's account indicates that the most important personages in Marshallese ancestry were two sisters. From these two female founding ancestors an emphasis on descent in the female line has developed. Although Lokrap emphasizes the development of the chiefly class, namely the Iroij line, it seems clear from both his and the Namu people's thinking and the literature that Ralik Chain Marshallese consider themselves as descendants of Liwatoinmour. Her name, and the rock which symbolized her existence, were venerated because they represented the chiefly line, and were the source of their existence. It is not known if this applies to people of the Ratak Chain, or if they trace their origin from another rock which was said to exist on Aur. Pre-eminence in the literature has been given to Namu rock, and my own data collected on Namu itself further indicate that Namu rock and its associated ideology is the source of all Marshallese origin beliefs.

The German reports throw some light on clan origins and indicate where Iroij and Jemeliwut stood in relation to other clans:

At first seven sibs *(djoui)* commonly called *djirik* existed from which all others stem:

1. Irodj ⎱ the two strongest
2. djirik ⎰
3. the woman from Namo
4. reludjen Namo
5. riGuadjlen
6. djemeliwut   s. gesch.S.246 (Regenbogen)
                (Rainbow) v. Gesang s.281
7. rikebinailingin (s.Lae)

These are the seven mother clans of Ralik Chain. When a woman comes from another island, her children must found a new sib; marriage within the sib was naturally forbidden (Krämer and Nevermann, 1938, p. 42).

Neither the reason for the numerical ordering nor background information on any of these *jowi* is given. This listing does bear out Lokrap's account of the Iroij clan as separate and opposed to Jemeliwut clan. The German listing also indicates a geographical spread covering Namu, Kwajalein, and Lae atolls, but it does not establish how these first seven clans came to be on these three atolls lying in close proximity to one another.

However, it is established that Liwatoinmour and Lijjeleijet are considered the founders of Iroij clan and Jemeliwut clan, respectively. From this beginning, the names of these clans and other derived clans have become symbols of specific groups to which each Marshallese belongs. An individual inherits the right to belong to his mother's clan by virtue of being her child, a concept known as matrifiliation (Fortes, 1959). An individual considers himself as belonging to a larger category of people, that is, all those who share the same clan name as he does—who are descendants of a common eponymous ancestor. It is this latter, wider concept of descent which makes the clan an identity unit.

For the purposes of membership in Marshallese society, the clan name gives a Marshallese an identification by which other Marshallese can place him in the total set of social relationships. It means that, through the possibility of genealogical links (traced to past or present members of the same clan), the individual can be included in a network wider than that of his immediate nuclear family and lineage. The individual may interact very little with the larger group of persons sharing a clan name, but he uses the name as an identity marker; thus we may call this a descent category, rather than a descent group (compare Silverman, 1971, p. 54; Keesing, 1971, p. 161). Even though the entity of persons belonging to the same clan may be said to be corporate because they share the same name and have certain rights and obligations to one another, nevertheless the clan is not the unit in Namu society that draws people together for common action. The group that acts together is the lineage (for a discussion of lineage activities, see Pollock, 1974). In Namu society, then, the term descent group is best applied to the lineage, to distinguish this from the wider more ideological entity, the clan. Inheritance of a common name in the matriline is the major, perhaps the only, warrant for membership in the clan category. In the sense that the clan name performs some of the same functions as the surname in Western society, it indicates to another person where that individual belongs in his society, but gives little information beyond this.

HIERARCHY OF CLANS

From various accounts we are led to believe that individual status was derived from being a member of a particular clan. This was especially true of the Iroij group, which may have been conceived as a high status clan because of its close associations with Liwatoinmour, or it may have achieved its definition and pre-eminence through warfare. Lokrap's account indicates that Liwatoinmour was the most powerful sister in the sibling set and was thus able to bring about the physical removal of Lijeleijet, and perhaps other sisters who are not mentioned in this account. Clan fission based on whom an individual chooses to associate himself with at the time of the split, and power, may be further bases for clan hierarchies. Thus a clan with known links to a founding ancestor, and which also had numerical strength in terms of the numbers of persons on one atoll who shared the clan identity, may have been ranked higher than one not possessing these attributes. The Marshallese conceptualization of clans as hierarchically arranged was reported by German ethnographers and by Mason (1947), but was not found on Namu by this writer in 1968.

Erdland gives a more complete account of the ranking of what the translator calls "kin groups" in his chapter entitled "Origin of the Kin Groups and Totemism" (1914, p. 343). Ranking is based on two factors, status derived from the *akejab* (spirits), and status derived from residence location.

The history of the various kin groups of the natives is closely connected with the gods *akejab* ... which also explains, partially at least, the difference in rank of the individual kin groups.

First it should be mentioned that the rank of the individual kin groups, as well as of the different lineages within the same kin group, is indicated by where they live on the island, whether on the lagoon side, farther in the interior of the island, or not far from the outer shore. The soil on the lagoon side of an island is the most fertile. Besides, canoe traffic on the lagoon starts from the lagoon shore, and all the traffic can be observed from there. Because of all these advantages, settling closest to the lagoon is a birthright of the families of high chiefs. The lower the rank the farther interior is the place of residence. The lowest families live closest to the outer shore, there where the ground is covered with stony debris, where shrubs that require the least to grow, like the salt-water bush, are neighbors of equal status, where the surf'breaking on the outer reef pounds loudly, and where, finally, the outer reef, as the place where everybody, rich and poor alike, relieves himself, does not exactly smell like narcissuses and roses, particularly at ebb tide. The low families are therefore likened to wild pandanus trees, which likewise thrive on the outer shore. When the word *lik* (outer shore) occurs in the name of a kin group, it is evident that this group is an inferior one, usually the lowest lineage of a kin group or set of kin groups.

The kin groups of the Ralik chain and the most important ones of the Ratak chain are listed here, along with their totems *(wune ak* or *morair)* insofar as they could be determined. The kin groups *(jowi* or *buij,* reckoned through the mother) are:

1. Iroja	2. Irrebra	3. Jowin Jemaliwut
Rimae	Magawuliej	Tilan
Ribugienjekjeken	Rimej	Ijjirik
Rijirika	Jibuilul	Rukuajlen
Rilikinbulujo	Rabrib	Rikibinailinin
		Rilujiennamo
		Rilikijine

Standing alone are: Ribikarej, Jol, Rimeijor, R'arno, R'aur, Ribogo (Erdland, 1914, pp. 263-264; HRAF Trans., pp. 342-343).

Erdland gives the major characteristics of each clan:

The Iroja are from Ebon and are higher than the Larrebra and Ijjirik. Their totem is the thunder (Lakota). . . . The Iroja have a characteristic trait of constantly urging and entreating. . . .

The high Larrebra are from Namorik; their totem is the bird *kalo* (red goose . . .). They excel in decisiveness and firmness. . . .

The Ijjirik of Namu were originally of third rank *(laadokdok)* and for this reason in ancient times a chief dared to offer them rat excrement as food. Their totem is a hibiscus bush from Bikini, and their district is the northern islands of the Ralik group. They are said to be fickle and changeable in character. . . . The Magawuliej are from Bikini and venerate Wurijabado as their *akejab,* since they originated from the incestuous intercourse of Wurijabado with his sister Luajet.

The Rimae or Rilobaren come from Bajjur, a reef north of Pingelab (Jaluit).

The Rukuajlen are from Kwajalein; they have as totem a *kamin* bush and a shark that stays in the lagoon opposite the island of Kwajalein.

The Rilujiennamo stem from the sister of an unnamed Lajjirik chief. When the latter tried to have intercourse with his sister, she refused, and therefore, her brother gave her the order: "Now then, move to the middle of the island!" Her doing so reduced her rank, but it was honorable.

The Rikibinailinin are from Ebaden (Kwajalein); their totem is a salt-water bush.

The Rilikijine are from Likijine on Kwajalein.

The Jibuilul or Rimeik descend from "the roots of a breadfruit tree, spreading over the ground." A woman once relieved herself thinking it to be one of the roots of the tree. To make these people feel ashamed, one need only say: "O . . . Jibuilul rej koorlok air konono. The Jibuilul (buttock grabbers) are beginning to talk presumptuously!"

The Rilikinbulujo come from Bulujo on Namu.

The Ribugienjekjeken live mainly on Woja (Ailinglablab).

The Ribikarej are to be found everywhere. . . .

The Jol descend from the "foot end of the chief's bed." When during a famine a woman cried out, "Jol o!" the chief gave her some of his food; the Jol, therefore, may eat food that has lain in the sacred place of the chief's hut, something that other common kin groups are not permitted to do.

In the Ratak group the chiefs Ujilan and Lailan belong to the kin group Rimeijor, Kaibuki and Labareo to the kin group R'arno, and the chiefs of Mejit to the kin group R'aur. On Eniwetok there are some Ejoa, and on Bikini a few Jelablab; the Menokenani are extinct. The kin group Ribogo lives on Mili and traces its origin back to Linomeme (Erdland, 1914, pp. 343-345).

Erdland gives no reasons for arranging the clans into three groups, nor for the order in which he treats their characteristics and atolls of affiliation. It appears that he is suggesting a development of the clans to indicate their status vis-a-vis one another—higher status clans heading each of his three lists. If this is correct, he seems to be suggesting that the oldest clan is at the head of each group and those listed below each head are subclans of that particular group. This status, however, was not permanent since it was achieved, and not wholly ascribed by birth. An individual could advance his status by being successful in battle, and by so doing his whole kin group achieved higher status. Therefore, we must conclude that the relative status of the clans was constantly changing with the fortunes of war. For example, Erdland reports that:

The Jowin Jemaliwut of Namu was the highest kin group of chiefs. It has been warred upon by other kin groups, however, so that its present members are only of lower rank (jiboge) (Erdland, 1914, p. 343).

Thus any ranking of clans represents only one point in time. As Mason (1947, p. 22) states, "Today, civil war is a thing of the past, and the relative ranking of clan groups has been frozen as of the last aggressive action during the German administration."

Lokrap's account indicates that highest status was denoted to those who inherited membership in the Iroja or Irodj clan of their mothers. We must note that the name given to the line is now synonymous with (or has become attenuated to refer to) the most important status in Marshallese social structure, namely the Iroij (paramount chief). Accounts of the founding of this line include how it became distinguished from other clans because of it direct link to Liwatoinmour, the most powerful woman in Marshallese tradition. Gulick suggests that a chief married into a clan in which it would be appropriate for his children to become members (1862, p. 302). Lokrap's reference to the demise of the Iroij group indicates that the overall superiority of the Iroij had become weakened by the lack of women to pass on the group name. Present-day Iroij (chiefs) are members of several different clans, and their relative status, by no means clear, is a matter of some contention. Namu informants stated that members of Iroja clan today have the same status as members of all the other clans. It is essential to clarify the status of Iroij in relation to other ranked positions, as well as the status of Iroja clan in relation to the other clans.

We have the conflicting statements of Erdland, who claims that the Jowin Jemaliwut was once the highest kin group, and Lokrap's account which claims that Iroij clan status was supreme, being derived from success in war. Whatever the case, it appears that early in Marshallese history, Liwatoinmour and her descendants of the Iroja line were on a par with the opposing group of Lijjeleijet and her descendants of the Jemaliwut line. These groups must have met in frequent wars to decide dominance over a particular area, and when one clan became overly powerful it could dictate the residence areas assigned to subgroups, as Erdland describes. If the relations between the dominant clan and one or more subclans became excessively strained, then the weaker clan probably moved out to become more independent of the dominant clan. It would appear that Jemeliwut clan became dominant on Namu while the Iroij clan became dominant on Ebon. Superiority probably fluctuated with the changing fortunes of war. Since these two clans were closely connected through founding ancestors, they probably had many members who, together with their spouses, had to choose on which side to fight and from which group they obtained land. The dominant group was determined by who won the last battle as well as by demographic factors such as the size and age structure of that clan. Gulick (1862, pp. 304-305) gives a vivid account of the welcoming performance on Ebon in 1860 for Kaibuki and his retinue returning from a long voyage to the north. In 1857 a group of 800 had left Ebon in forty *proas* (canoes) for the northern islands where they had been engaged in wars. This must have been a major power struggle.

Mason (1947, pp. 23-25), in his survey of social organization throughout the Marshalls, regards some clans as subgroups of more inclusive clans, such as Iroja clan, Magaoliej clan, and RiBikarej clan; however, these groupings of subclans under an inclusive clan are not found on Namu. Although the rule of clan exogamy appears to have been generally practiced, occasionally members of the Iroja clan could marry in order to consolidate their status position (Erdland, 1914; Krämer and Nevermann, 1938). If this report is reliable, the practice is similar to other Pacific island societies where endogamy was accepted between members of the highest ranking clans (compare Goldman, 1970, p. 188, for the Society Islands; 1970, p. 228, for the Hawaiian Islands).

Problems of maintaining status and clan viability when no women were born to a clan, or when no clan women bore children, is pointed out in Lokrap's account. When this occurred, the status of the clan was sure to drop and the clan itself might eventually die out.

In regard to present-day strength of clans, Jemeliwut was the largest clan on Namu in 1968, and included many lineages that cannot trace exact links to one another. Despite its numerical dominance, its members were not accorded status higher than that of members of any other clans. We need to know whether the Iroja clan has a similarly large number of members on Ebon today in order to make observations about the continuity and strength of these two founding clans. Erdland claims that Ijjirik clan originated on Namorik, but Mason (1947, p. 22) says that the people of Lajirik clan came from the stone on Aur. They may not be considering the same level of the clan, which would account for the variation. Some of these problems may be solved by examining the present-day dispersal of clans throughout all the atolls of the Marshalls.

In summary, being a member of a clan closely connected to Liwatoin-mour, that is, one of the original seven, appears to have given higher social status than membership in clans derived from fissioned units or from an immigrating woman. This link to the founding ancestor is an important feature of Marshallese identity and is symbolized by the clan name. Achievements in war helped to maintain this status, but could not create it without the all-important link to the founding ancestor. Eligibility to clan membership has been strongly maintained in the matriline; however, eligibility to Iroij status is based on demographic variables, such as numbers of women in a sibling set who bear children. Thus if Iroij clan membership and high status were interdependent at one stage in Marshallese history, they are now two separate aspects of Marshallese social structure, each with its own identity criteria.

SYMBOLIC REPRESENTATIONS OF CLANS

The association between Liwatoinmour, the female ancestress of the Marshallese, and a rock is common to all versions of Marshallese clan origin myths. Erdland's account of this association runs:

The memory of the totem of all the high kin groups was refreshed when two ships were stranded on Namu atoll. A basalt rock, *Luwatonmour* (the one who gives long life), was found there, located near the hut Manjenninean in the village of Bojar. Chiefs and subjects gathered annually around this "mother of all kin groups," sacrificing and practicing magic. A magic formula, for the most part incomprehensible to me, which refers to Chief Kabua (formerly Lebon), asks for an increase of the family, names *Lijman* and *Liolir*, and then points to Eonwuj (Majuro as the island of the handsomest race of people) and Aur, where Luwatonmour's sister, Lirebrebju, also a basalt rock, lived. The striking thing about the gathering of the natives celebrating at the place of Luwatonmour was that, contrary to the usual custom, the subjects remained erect in the presence of the sitting chief and did not have to go bent over. This walking with the body erect was called: *Ededal in Bojar*, the walking of Bojar. Is this supposed to indicate the common origin of all the kin groups and their original equality of rank? In any case this idea is suggested (Erdland, 1914, p. 345).

The Namu rock is important in the association between myth and clan origins and seems to be the tangible representation of the Marshallese as a people. This is particularly important on an atoll where artifacts and remains of earlier times are very rare. This rock is geologically alien to the coralline Marshalls and possibly was transported purposefully as a reminder of an earlier homeland.[5] Or its significance may lie in the very fact of its distinctiveness. Finsch states his feelings about the associations with the rock thus:

On the atoll Namo is the large stone Luadonmul, according to Kabua a true story, and not a coral rock, only for Irodsche, but it remained unclear whether it was the site of the Anitsche (gods) of the chiefs, or merely accessible only to the latter; for it is difficult to obtain clear information from the natives in matters of this kind (Finsch, 1893, p. 44).

This rock is also associated with ancestral spirits *(akejab* or *ekjab)*. Rocks are sometimes considered the visible links between the supernatural and the earthly. Erdland discusses two kinds of spirits as if they were ranked, the higher being the time-honored spirits and the lower being transformed spirits. The lower *ekjab*, one type of spirit, live on or near individual atolls and humans are constrained by their presence. Namu informants did not refer to these two ranks but claimed that *ekjab* were spirits of human beings who upon death were transformed into fish, birds, trees, or rocks. Natural objects therefore are thought to embody some of the spirits of deceased persons. An example of this belief most frequently cited by Namu people is a rock situated on the southeastern reef islets whose spirits have enabled previously childless women to have children.

Representation of the supernatural and the past in tangible form runs throughout much of the creation mythology of the Marshallese people. For example, one version of creation refers to the first living beings as two serpents; the female was Lejman and the male Ullip.

---

[5]Sachet's discussion of the occurrence of noncorraline rocks on atolls in the Pacific does not mention this particular rock (Sachet, 1955).

Lejman was considered the mother of Edao, the notorious trickster (Erdland, 1914, p. 311), who is linked in myth as the brother of Jemaliwut. Together they form the core of Marshallese mythology. Accounts of myth and history incorporate the natural and supernatural into one reality, and are valuable in providing an important identity symbol for successive generations of Marshallese.

A few examples of totems are also seen as tangible representations of the links between human social groups, particularly kin groups, and important natural phenomena in their environment. Perhaps reflecting the anthropological thinking of the time, Erdland, and Krämer and Nevermann were predisposed to make a direct association between certain totems (wunenok) with various kin groups. Yet Erdland (1914, p. 345) recognizes that "the traces of totemism are almost obliterated today, and the present generation has hardly any notion of its former existence." This was even more true in 1968. In seeking such information, I was told that only the shark remains as a totem for some lineages, and thus they must not eat shark. Otherwise totems were unknown.

The significance of the rock appears to have been extensive throughout Marshallese legendary history. The missionary, Dr. Rife, was presumably struck by the idolatrous nature of the rock and felt that the continued presence of such a hallowed object would be detrimental to the Marshallese acceptance of Christianity, and had it thrown into the sea. He thus recognized the power of this rock in Marshallese thinking, but did not realize that the power would persist even if its representation was cast into the sea.

The rock has not been cast out of Marshallese traditions, and is still remembered as a symbol of clan origins. Its presence was pointed out to this writer with some pride. It lay on the reef on the ocean side of Namu Namu islet and was only visible at mid-tide, some three hundred yards from land.

The rock reputedly stood at Bojar, which is still a very hallowed spot. Bojar is a plot measuring 200 by 600 yards and lies adjacent to and on the lagoon side of the plot of land named Mwojeninean. This place is still tabu today; one may not move across it and children may not play there. No coconut palm trees grow there, and the grass is cut regularly by one person with special authority from the Iroij to do so. It is also reputed to be the site of a major battle, and remains and weapons are buried there. It is close to the house of the present Iroij and is a conspicuous piece of ground, partly because it lacks the palm trees which grow on every uninhabited piece of the lagoon shore, and partly because of its elevated nature.

As a symbol of Marshallese identity, then, the rock has fixed associations, first with the ancestral spirits, and second as the site of original birth. Given this beginning, it is clear that the derived clans also had to have their fixed places of association. An individual is associated with a particular atoll. This is the place to which he belongs, that is, from which he draws his identity because of its association with the spirits of his ancestors, but is not necessarily the atoll on which he was born.

CLANS AND PLACES OF ASSOCIATION

Besides the important association with the spirits of his "home" atoll, the Marshallese is tied to his atoll through the important concept of *lamoren* land which is inherited in the matriline within the lineage and is the main source of rights to land (Pollock, 1974). These rights are lifelong and associate an individual with a specific atoll. To the question "Where are you from?" a Marshallese is likely to give the name of the atoll where his ancestral spirits are embodied in his *lamoren* land rights, even though he may never have set foot on that atoll.

This sense of belonging is carried further by the etymological form that most clan names take. Of the sixty clan names listed by Bender (see Table 2), thirty-five are marked by the prefix *ri* - or a contraction thereof, meaning "a person of." For example, *ri-Majol* is a "person of the Marshalls," and *ri-Namu* is a "person of Namu atoll" (Bender, 1963, p. 153). Thus, from the clan name we can discern the clan's possible affiliation with a specific place. Some refer to atolls within the Marshalls, for example, riNamu, r'Arno, riKuajlen; others such as riMejiko and ripit refer to persons from Mexico and the Gilberts, respectively; others such as riMae, rikin ailin in, and riBojar refer to places on atolls. Whether or not the place reference in a clan name indicates the place from which a founding ancestress came is difficult to assess. A new settlement may have been necessary because of the greater strength of a sister in resources of people or land. This was suggested by Lokrap as the reason for the original split between Liwatoinmour and Lijjeleijet. A move may also have been triggered by demographic necessity. If a clan had several large sibling sets in two or three consecutive generations, it may have been advisable for one branch, probably the more junior, to move out and start a new line elsewhere. This internal segmentation may have led to the widespread geographic dispersal of clans as found today.

If the move were prompted by demographic necessity, or if there was no bad feeling between the branches, the new branch may have regarded itself as still part of the old clan, thus giving rise to the idea of subclans as discussed by Mason (1947, pp. 23-25). For example, riMae is a subclan of Iroja. Possibly the Iroja clan became too large to meet

TABLE 2
NAMES OF MARSHALLESE CLANS (JOWI-JOU)*
(From Bender, 1963, p. 153)

1. depdip	31. rilo-bar-en
2. ijjidik (RAL)	32. rilo-tobu
jidikdik (RAT)	33. riluujien-namu
3. ijjidik in kapinmeto	34. riluut
4. irooj	35. mekijko
5. irribra	36. rimatol-en
6. irruja	37 rimeik
7. irruja kijeek	38. rimaae
8. irruja pako-likae-lal	39. rimalel
9. irruja ribikien-jikjik-en	40. rime-joor
10. irruja rilikin-bilujo	41. rinamu
11. jejed	42. ripako
12. jemeluut	43. ripikaar-ij
13. jibilu jibilul	44. rikipin-ailin-in
(14.) see 2 above	45. rikipin-bilujo
15. jikublik	46. ripit
16. jinkabo	47. ripit in namdik
17. jilaplap	48. ripit in mejru
18. jol	49. ruoojje
19. jowa (RAT) ejowa (RAL)	50. rilo-kelanc
20. ka-lo	51. ribojaar
21. kotra	52. riebaten
22. luuk	53. riikjit
23. meka-uliij	54. rikin-ailin-in
24. raarno	55. rilikijjini
25. raij	56. rilikin-jepakina
26. rail	57. rilo-kileni
27. raur	58. rilo-malo
28. rijiluuj rijaluuj	59. ritebaal
29. riikjit	60. tilan
30. rikuajleen	

*Straight letter symbols have been substituted for the linguistic orthography in the original.

its needs on Ebon (Erdland, 1914, p. 343) and a branch was established on the islet of Mae in Namu atoll. Descendants of the woman who first went to Mae would regard themselves as riMae, while at the same time consider themselves as Iroja. With time the Iroja connection might be forgotten and the subclan association lost in importance. Thus, internal segmentation may be seen to have produced subclans and an individual might view himself as a member of both a subclan and the larger whole clan unit (especially if the subclan was small and new, or if he wanted to establish his common identity with a person in another subclan of the same major clan).

When a woman came from another atoll she brought her clan name with her, but if she came from a place which had no clans, she was given the name of the place from which she came, hence riMejiko, a clan whose founder(s) came from Mexico, and ripit, a clan whose founders came from the Gilberts.

Other clan names are not as easily identified as those associated with places. Some of these may be linked to each other, perhaps by segmentation, as suggested by the practice of adding suffixes to a major clan name. In his analysis of place names in the Marshall Islands, Bender (1963, p. 35) examines "whether we can say that some repeated names seem to have been the favorites of certain clans and thus probably transferred by their members, and . . . whether these land units with names identical with or containing the names of clans are in fact [still] owned by members of those clans." He was unable to obtain this information and thus was forced to conclude that:

> More needs to be known of the history of the clans . . . for example did the clan that now owns Mae descend from the riMae? We think such questions and whether or not some lineages (families, clans) had favorite names which they took with them from atoll to atoll are worthy of further investigation (Bender, 1963, p. 257).

An examination of accounts of origins of clans in the Marshalls has shown that social identity is derived from descent from a founding ancestor and from a connection to a specific place. Marshallese often move about on their own atolls and others close by. In identifying themselves, the place of birth or atoll of affiliation would be used. One might give his clan name if he thought his questioner would recognize it and identify him with a person the questioner already knew. Places and clan names as links to persons were both likely to be important identification factors, depending on the context. Forde has noted a similar conceptualization in African societies:

> Frequent displacement of homesteads and the wider intercommunication involved has both favoured and given value to the maintenance and transmission within households of the traditions of origin and of links to other households that are expressed in common clanship (Forde, 1970, p. 24).

And again:

> non-corporate dispersed clans . . . [have] an orientation function for the individual within the tribe or district (Forde, 1970, p. 28).

Thus where clan identity is the only unifying principle for a highly dispersed group, origin myths and tales of the putative founding ancestors may be the basis for the corporateness of the group.

Atoll affiliation is the second major part of Marshallese identity. This link with people complements the link to places. Often a tangible object represents a geographical place. Rocks, trees, lagoon side, center of the island, are symbols with special group meaning and form the basis for commonly held beliefs. Lokrap suggests that the links to ancestors and the fission of groups is specialized knowledge that was formerly reserved only for chiefs. If such knowledge was restricted to the highest ranks, the identifying factor might have been the belief that the chief possessed some secret knowledge belonging to the group and his position would be reinforced by this specialized knowledge. Apparently only he knew the links between his clan and those of others and their symbols. Knowing that their chiefs possessed such specialized knowledge was sufficient to enable the whole unit to identify itself as part of wider Marshallese society.

Today many Marshallese know stories of their origins, and it would seem that the chiefs spread this knowledge among them. Powerful foreigners encouraged telling of the tales and caused a widespread dissemination among Marshallese themselves at the same time that the local people were confronted with the values of a very different cultural tradition from their own. Thus, on the one hand, cultural traditions may have been weakened by European contact, while, on the other hand, these traditions were strengthened as they reinforced Marshallese distinctiveness.

We have not considered the problem of Marshallese identity as a total unit in pre-European times, since that is beyond the scope of this paper. The connection between myths of clan origins and the identification of the Marshallese as a group who consider themselves as descendants of Liwatoinmour and Lijjeleijet raises the interesting questions of how and when ethnic boundaries are drawn and the concept of a discrete identity emerges. These are questions which perhaps can never be answered, or at any rate await future research.

LITERATURE CITED

BENDER, BYRON
1963. A Linguistic Analysis of the Place-Names of the Marshall Islands. Ph.D. Dissertation, Indiana Univ.
BRYAN, E.H., JR.
1965-1966. *The Marshalls and the Pacific.* Hourglass Special, Kwajalein, Marshall Islands.
BUCKINGHAM, H.A.
[n.d.] Collection of Folk-tales of the Marshall Islands. Manuscript, 1949.

ERDLAND, AUGUST

1914. *Die Marshall Insulaner: Leben und Sitte, Sinn und Religion eines Südsee-volkes.* Munster: Aschendorff. JJH (Trans. for HRAF, Yale Univ.).

FINSCH, O.

1893. *Ethnologische Erfahrungen und Belegstücke aus der Südsee.* Vienna: Holder.

FORDE, C. DARYL

1970. "Ecology and Social Structure." *Proc. Royal Anthropological Inst.,* London, pp. 15-29.

FORTES, M.

1959. "Descent, Filiation, and Affinity." *Man* **59** (309, 331): 193-197, 206-212.

GOLDMAN, IRVING

1970. *Ancient Polynesian Society.* Chicago: Univ. Chicago Press.

GOODENOUGH, WARD H.

1970. *Description and Comparison in Cultural Anthropology.* Chicago: Aldine.

GULICK, L.H.

1862. "Micronesia." *Nautical Magazine and Naval Chronicle* **6**:302-305; **8**:408-417.

KEESING, ROGER

1971. *New Perspectives in Cultural Anthropology.* New York: Holt, Rinehart, Winston.

KRÄMER, A., and H. NEVERMANN

1938. "Ralik-Ratak (Marshall Inseln)." In G. THILENIUS (ed.), *Ergebnisse der Südsee Expedition 1908-1910.* II Ethnographie, B Mikronesien. Band 11. Hamburg: Friederischen, De Gruyter

LUOMALA, KATHARINE

1950. "Micronesian Mythology." In MARIE LEACH (ed.), *Standard Dictionary of Folklore, Mythology and Legend.* New York: Funk and Wagnalls.

MASON, LEONARD E.

1947. "The Economic Organization of the Marshall Islands." *Economic Survey of Micronesia.* U.S. Commercial Co., Vol. 9.

MORTON, N.E.

[n.d.] Population Structure of Micronesia. Manuscript.

POLLOCK, NANCY J.

1974. "Landholding on Namu Atoll, Marshall Islands." In H. LUNDSGAARDE (ed.) *Land Tenure in the Pacific,* Vol. 2. Honolulu: Univ. Press Hawaii.

RIESENBERG, SAUL H.

1968. *The Native Polity of Ponape.* Washington, D.C.: Smithsonian Inst. Press.

RIGBY, PETER

1969. *Cattle and Kinship among the Gogo.* Ithaca: Cornell Univ. Press.

SACHET, MARIE-HÉLÈNE

1955. "Pumice and other Extraneous Volcanic Materials on Coral Atolls." *Atoll Research Bull* **37**:1-27.

SILVERMAN, MARTIN

1971. *Disconcerting Issue.* Chicago: Univ. Chicago Press.

STRATHERN, ANDREW

1971. *The Rope of Moka.* Cambridge: Cambridge Univ. Press.

POLYNESIA

ASPECTS OF THE WORD LEI

MARY KAWENA PUKUI*

B.P. Bishop Museum, Honolulu

T O A HAWAIIAN the word *lei* means many things. A lei is a baby, dearly loved. A lei lovingly remembered by those who reared the baby to adulthood—parents, grandparents, uncles, aunts, other senior relatives, and those closest to the child.

A lei is a sweetheart, and hence another reason for having so many songs about loving and cherishing a lei. It is a wife and a husband also, for that is what sweethearts often become, do they not?

A lei is a chanted poem or song accompanying a flower lei that is given to a person esteemed, especially an *ali'i* (chief, chiefess, king, queen, noble). When the lei of flowers withered and was discarded, the lei of poetry remained always as a reminder of a happy occasion. Two of these lei chants are still being sung today, *"Lei Loke O Kawika,"* for Prince David Kawananakoa, and *"He Lei No Ka'iulani,"* for Princess Victoria Ka'iulani Cleghorn. In this latter chant the word lei is used with yet another meaning—the "royal lei" of line 15 refers to the Hawaiian monarchy.

HE LEI NO KA'IULANI (1893)

He lei keia no Ka'iulani	This is a lei chant for Ka'iulani
Pāpahi kalaunu a o Hawai'i,	The Crown Princess of Hawai'i
Ola o Kalaninuiahilapalapa	Long may Kalaninuiahilapalapa live
O ka wohi kukahi o ka lahui,	The most esteemed one from Hawai'i

---

*This paper was transcribed from a tape in Bishop Museum made on February 24, 1964, in answer to the question "What is a lei?"

Ua hui hoʻokahi a o Europa,
Kaōhi i ka ea a o Hawaiʻi
Walohia e ka leo o Kaʻiulani
Ua hewa anei au e Maleka,
I hoʻole ia ai koʻu kuleana,
I ka noho kalaunu o Hawaiʻi nei
Aia i ka nuʻa o Hale-Keʻokeʻo,
Ka healiʻi o Wasinetona,
E noi ana hoʻi me ka hopo ʻole,
I ka ea aloha o Hawaiʻi nei.
Hoʻihoʻi ia mai ka lei aliʻi
O ka ʻihi kapu hoʻi a o Hawaiʻi,
Kukā ana hoʻi me ka ʻoluʻolu,
Ma ka ʻaha Senete o Amerika,

Aia o Kaʻiulani i ke alo,
Imi ana i ke ola a o Hawaiʻi,
O ka leo aliʻi i paʻē mai,
Ua noi aʻe nei au i kuʻu lahui,
I manaʻo ʻia ai a e kāʻili

I ka noho kalaunu a o Hawaiʻi,
Koʻu kuleana hoʻi mai ka po mai
I ʻimi ʻia e Kalani-Kaulilua
Papa Laʻamea Koʻu makua
ʻIkea ʻia au a he wohi kapu,
He kama kahi au na ka lāhui,
Na ka ēwe aloha o na kūpuna
Māpu ke aloha i ka puʻuwai
Hana mau ana hoʻi i ka iwihilo,

O Vitoria ia o Kaʻiulani
Hoʻoilina kalaunu a o Hawaiʻi,
Haʻina ko lei e Kaʻiulani
E ola o Kalaninuiahilapalapa.

Mixed with the stream of Europe.
To control the life of Hawaiʻi
Is Kaʻiulani's plea,
Is America being unjust
In denying me my right
To occupy the throne of Hawaiʻi?
There at the great White House
The royal house of Washington
Pleading courageously
For the beloved life of Hawaiʻi.
Restore the royal lei
The sacredness of our Hawaiʻi.
Discussing pleasantly
With the members of the Senate of
America
Kaʻiulani is in their presence
Pleading for the life of Hawaiʻi.
The royal voice had reached us from afar
I have spoken in behalf of my people
That which was planned to be snatched
from us
The royal throne of Hawaiʻi
My rightful inheritance from the gods
That was founded by Kalani-Kaulilua
My uncle, Laʻamea
I am recognized of the sacred rank
An only child of the nation
The beloved strain of our ancestors
Love wells up within the heart
Remaining always within the very core of
one's being
O Victoria Kaʻiulani
Crown Princess of Hawaiʻi
This is your lei chant, Kaʻiulani
Long may Kalaninuiahilapalapa live.

After Kalākaua and his Queen, Kapiʻolani, ascended the throne, people came from various islands of the Hawaiian chain with tributes of chants and leis to honor Queen Kapiʻolani. From Hawaiʻi, the *lehua (Metrosideros macropus)*[1] of Mokaulele; from Maui the *lehua* of Līhau; from Oʻahu the *ʻahihi (Metrosideros tremuloides)* of Nuʻuanu; and from Kauaʻi the *ʻōhai (Sesbania tomentosa)* of Papiohuli.

A lei is an expression of affection and loyalty voiced in a chant and not necessarily accompanied with a flower lei. Two such chants are still in existence, but very rarely heard. One of these chants originated in Puna. This chant for Queen Emma Kaleleonalani compared the love

---

[1]Scientific names in this paper are taken from Pukui and Elbert (1971) and Neal (1965).

of the Hilo and Puna native for his queen to the string, needle, flowers, container, and the tying of the cord ends, thus completing a lei of respect, love, and esteem. The second chant is called "Lei O Ke Kipi," composed by the adherents of Queen Emma in 1874 following the riot which broke out when Kalākaua won the kingdom of Hawai'i through election. The lei in this case is the loyalty with which Queen Emma was adorned by her supporters. But in addition it is a chant of resentment. Queen Emma, who had been pro-British, was criticized by some of the American supporters of Kalākaua, and this expression of resentment was written in retaliation.

LEI O KE KIPI

He lei keia no Ema	This is a "lei" chant for Emma
Ko lei kaulana i ke kipi.	A lei known as the wreath of rebellion.
Ua kau ko lei i ka waha,	Your lei is much talked about
I ka lehelehe o ka loko 'ino.	By the lips of heartless people.
Kueka'a pau 'ia mai	Out in a heap they come rolling,
Na kui, na 'oi o loko	The nails and other sharp objects within.
O ke kolea kau ahua,	They come from the "mound-perching plovers,"
Noinoi 'oihana aupuni.	Who beg for government jobs,
O ka hana loko maika'i 'ia	Those who were kindly treated
E ka na'au lani ha'aha'a,	By a gracious and royal heart.
Ua pono 'oe ke lino a'e	Your pride is well justified
Ua lohe na kupa o Kahiki.	For you are known in foreign lands.
Elua 'oi o ke ao nei	There are two great women in the world,
O Wikolia ko Lakana	(Queen) Victoria of London
O Kuini Ema ko Hawai'i	And Queen Emma of Hawai'i.
Kohukohu i ka lei kalaunu.	Both are worthy of their crowns.
Ha'ina 'ia mai ka puana	This ends my chant
Ka-lele-o-na-lani he inoa.	In praise of Ka-lele-o-na-lani.

So you see that there are many loving strands in the word *lei*, which means not only a string of flowers to be worn and later cast aside.

We also have our island leis today as the *lehua (Metrosideros collina)* for Hawai'i; *lokelani (Rosa)* for Maui; *kukui* blossoms *(Aleurites moluccana)* for Moloka'i; *hinahina (Tillandsia)* for Kaho'olawe; *kaunao'a (Cuscuta-sandwichiana)* for Lana'i; *'ilima (Sida fallax)* for O'ahu; *mokihana (Pelea anista)* for Kaua'i; and the sea-shell beads for Ni'ihau.

It is interesting to note that the *lokelani* is really a small red rose, but the color chosen for Maui is the pink of the *loke Hawai'i*, a Hawaiian rose. This rose is fragrant and quite thorny, a garden favorite in my childhood. It probably was the first rose introduced here to have the name of *loke Hawai'i*. Miss Marie Neal, the late Botanist of Bishop Museum, was interested in tracing this rose before it became known locally as *loke Hawai'i* and discovered its older name, the Castillian rose.

There were other leis mentioned in songs and story, and one of these is the *mānewanewa* of Lana'i, the name given for a beach grass. It was said, "If you have seen Lana'i, but have not worn a *lei* of *mānewanewa* while on the island, you have not seen the whole of Lana'i." *I 'ike 'oe ia Lana'i, a i lei 'ole i ka mānewanewa, 'a'ole no 'oe i 'ike ia Lana'i.*

The *mānewanewa* grows, or grew, at Polihua, where the turtles went to lay their eggs. An informant recalled a stone turtle in the sea that someone or something carried away, for no longer is the stone turtle seen. Where turtles once were numerous, they now are rarely seen.

At Ka'au, in Palolo, a rare grass grew whose blossoms were made into leis by visitors to show that they had been there to see the place where Ka'au-hele-moa, a supernatural cock, lived. At one time, this cock roused the wrath of Kamapua'a, the hog god who went there to fight Ka'au-hele-moa. Kamaunuaniho, grandmother of Kamapua'a, had told him that if and when he overcame his foe, Ka'au-hele-moa, the hog god must eat the cock. The fight was furious and the rooster feathers flew everywhere. Battered and weak, Ka'au-hele-moa fell into a pool, reddening the water with his blood. Kamapua'a went home thinking the cock was dead. However, upon awakening the following morning, Kamapua'a heard the loud crowing of the cock, Ka'au-hele-moa. His feathers that fell to the ground sprouted into grass which was made into wreaths. Only once have I seen this lei, when one of my aunts came home after a visit to Ka'au wearing a lei of this grass. I was a little girl then, and whether the grass still grows or not, I do not know.

The *pahapaha* of Polihale was often mentioned in chants of Kaua'i. Nowhere else was the *pahapaha*, or sea lettuce, worn as a lei, but that of Polihale had a quality that other *pahapaha* did not. When dried, the lei was revived by soaking in sea water. What better proof of a visit to this locality than to wear a lei of this odd seaweed to show the folks at home?

Another seaweed, the *limu kala (Sargassum* spp.), was worn as leis in the *hula hoe* or canoe paddling hula, a dance used not for fun and entertainment in olden days, but in respect to the gods of the sea. Sometimes the *limu kala* was worn in religious ceremonies to *kala,* or free, one from an evil influence which ended when the lei was set adrift in the sea.

When the goddess Pele migrated here to Hawai'i, many members of her family came with her. Upon arriving at a small island just beyond Ni'ihau, one of Pele's brothers, Kane-'apua, chose that islet as his dwelling place. As a token of her affection for Kane-'apua, the youngest sister,

Hiʻiaka, left one of her *lehua* leis on a rock, thus naming the island Lehua.

This flower, the *lehua*, was associated with Pele. In going to the mountains as children, we were reminded never to pick any *lehua* on the way up to the mountains lest we be surrounded by the mists and rain. It was permissible to pick *lehua* on the way back to the lowland.

Hiʻiaka was said to have owned a grove of *lehua* trees that bore many blossoms of many colors. In a fit of jealous rage, Pele destroyed all but four, the dark red *lehua* *ʻapane*, the lighter red *lehua* *ʻula*, the orange hued *lehua* *mamo*, and the very pale yellow *lehua* *kea*. The last two are rare, but the reds are commonly seen on the ride between Kaʻū and Kona. Those who ride by do not always notice the difference in the redness of the *lehua* blossoms unless someone points them out. The bronze red leaf buds, *liko lehua*, were also used in leis.

Another name for the *lehua* trees on Hawaiʻi was the *ʻōhiʻa kumakua*. This tree was a *kino lau*, or one of the many forms assumed by the god Ku-ōhiʻa-laka. By the name of the god, I see the connection between the *lehua* of Hawaiʻi and the *rata* of New Zealand, they are one and the same. This flower, the *lehua*, was one of the five plants essential to the building of the hula altar.

An ancient hula school was at Moʻohelaia on Molokaʻi, a spot that no one on the island living today can point out. The famous *lehua* trees of Kaʻana grew nearby. We were told by a native on Molokaʻi that he remembered seeing the *lehua* as a boy, but that they had been completely destroyed by introduced animals.

Another tree that furnished beautiful leis is the *hala (Pandanus odoratissimus)*. When Hawaiians speak of *pua hala*, they do not mean the blossom, but the soft yellow part of the key which is cut off and strung. The blossom is called *hinano* and is not used in lei making. The bracts of the blossoms were used to make the very fine mats employed by medical *kahuna* to teach with pebbles the location of internal organs of the body and their diseases.

The *hala* of Kekele was said to be the most fragrant on Oʻahu. Kekele was located at the foot of the pali on the Koʻolau side and extended to about as far as where the Kaneohe Memorial Park is today. As my informants, William Kaioe and Ka-aoao-loa Kukahiko, told me more than thirty years ago, it was "from where the house stands at the turn of the road at the foot of the Pali to the big cow pasture." And as I remember, that cow pasture is where the Kaneohe Memorial Park is now. The *hala* grove of Kekele is gone completely, but I recall the natives of that side of the island telling me that the sweetness of the *hala* still lingered in the air even after the grove was destroyed. They would smell the *hala* when passing by at night. Love sometimes retains the sweetness in one's memory long after all is gone. The *hala pia,* a small pale yellow variety, was found among the others here at Kekele. The *hala* was much worn by Hawaiians at times of festivity, but never on business. It was, and still is, a favorite lei at New Year. The word *hala* has other meanings besides the name for pandanus. It also means "gone, past, dead, departed," and for this reason the *hala* was not worn when on the quest of something. Politicians dreaded the *hala* when campaigning. What better lei for the New Year than the *hala* when the old year with its joys and sorrows has passed.

This thought of the *hala* being significant for a departure originated with the goddess Hi'iaka. While walking along with her companion, Wahine-'oma'o, they came upon some girls stringing leis. The girls gave each of the travelers a lei to wear. Glancing down at the lei she was wearing, Hi'iaka remarked to her companion, "This is very significant, but we will see what lies before us." They had walked some distance when someone, recognizing Hi'iaka, ran to ask her help for a sick relative. Hi'iaka replied, "He is beyond help now, he is gone, *ua hala.*" Since that time, *hala* leis were worn on some occasions and never on others, lest trouble be encountered. Fishermen preparing to launch a canoe would change their minds at once if someone went by wearing a lei of *hala.* It was a warning not to go to sea, lest there be no returning.

The *kauna'oa* was brought hither by Pele and left on the beaches. It was also worn as a lei, especially by those who go to the seashore. *Kauna'oa* was not regarded as lucky or unlucky, but there was an old expression, *Hihi kauna'oa, hihi i Māna, aloha wale ia la'au kumu 'ole.* "The *kauna'oa* creeps along at Māna, how sad for that trunkless plant." The *kauna'oa* is a parasite clinging to other plants for support, hence compared to a destitute or helpless person who depends on others for help.

As a child I heard a chant by my grandmother, telling of Kane'apua returning to the ancient homeland to visit. Then, coming back to Hawai'i, Kane'apua came adorned with strands of *'ilima.* Whether he was said to have introduced the *'ilima* here, I do not remember.

There were many kinds of *'ilima,* and all were medicinal, but since we are on the subject of the lei, I would rather go on with that. I know of three varieties used for lei making, the pale yellow *'ilima okea,* the bronze red *'ilima koli-kukui,* and the yellow *'ilima* whose descriptive name I have never heard. The pale yellow and the bronze red were rare, even when *'ilima* leis were sold by the lei vendors on Maunakea and Kekaulike Streets in Honolulu.

The petals of the domesticated *'ilima* are rounded, while those of the wild *'ilima* are irregular in shape. Those used for leis were called *'āpiki*, "tricky," because they were believed to attract mischievous spirits who were very fond of *'ilima*. When the abodes of these mischievous ones were known, wearers of *'ilima* leis avoided passing those places.

We have been hearing recently that *'ilima* leis were reserved exclusively for royalty, but I doubt that very much. I used to grow *'ilima*, and at one time I had so many seedlings that I shared these with Jonah Kumalae, Sr. Later, he had a larger and better *'ilima* garden than I did. Today this flower is very scarce and to have a lei of *'ilima* would be an honor indeed. Probably the story of the *'ilima* being reserved for royalty stemmed from the fondness that Princess Abigail Kawananakoa had for these blossoms. She was a beautiful Scottish-Hawaiian woman, and to see her in a black or white *holokū* wearing strands of the yellow *'ilima* is a sight to remember always. Princess Kawananakoa was particular that the flowers were of uniform size and every *'ilima* lei was strung to perfection.

Maile (Alyxia olivaeformis), once very common, is not as plentiful today. To wear a two-strand *maile* lei today is a joy, but in my youth such a lei would have been regarded as very skimpy. *Maile* leis were much thicker then and some were entwined with *pala (Marattia douglasii)* fern to enhance the fragrance. There are four kinds of *maile*: the *maile-lau-li'i*, small-leaved; *maile-kaluhea*, sweet-smelling; *maile-ha'iwale*, brittle; and *maile-pākaha*.

The large-leaved, very fragrant *maile* found in Hilo is the *maile-kaluhea*. A *maile* often mentioned in poetry is that of Ko'iahi in Wai'anae, O'ahu, but according to an informant who is a native of that district, wild goats have destroyed this *maile-lau-li'i* of Ko'iahi.

The *maile* was used in some religious ceremonies and no hula altar was complete without it. With introduced animals and the clearing away of forest lands, unfortunately in time the *maile* perhaps will vanish.

Everybody and anybody wore leis, the fisherman, cowboy, driver of ox carts, farmer—anyone who wanted to. Plantation laborers wore leis on their hats to go to work, just for the sheer love of them. Where there were no flowers, leis were fashioned of leaves, blossoms of grasses, ferns, the eyes of pineapple strung together, chili peppers, or shredded *ti (Cordyline terminalis)* leaves—any plant that could be braided, strung, or wound fast together with a cord. They were worn on hats, on the head, around the neck, or over one shoulder and tied at the opposite hip. When visitors went to see relatives, they never departed without a lei or two from that locality.

At Waikapuna, in Ka'ū, the *leihua* or globe amaranth *(Gomphrena globosa),* a garden escape sowed on the hillside by the wind, presented a beautiful sight after the winter showers were past. The whole hillside was purple with *leihua*. When the beach dwellers came to the plantation villages, leis of this flower adorned their hats, and when we went to the beach, we came home bedecked. Anybody seeing the leis knew instantly where one had been. A few years ago, I went to Waikapuna and the sight that met my eyes filled me with unhappiness. Cane trash piled up along the shore from one to ten feet deep, sea pools once teeming with small fish were shallow with a muddy deposit, and the hillside was covered with *ēkoa* or *koa haole (Leucaena glauca)* for the cattle to munch on. A large fig tree was the only thing growing there among the *ēkoa*. The *leihua* that once glorified the landscape was all gone.

I remember when the *waikahuli (Coreopsis nuecensis)*, or gaillardia, was found everywhere at La'ie, O'ahu—along the roadside, bordering the cane field, and in the pastures—red ones and yellow ones everywhere! But I have not seen any in recent times. Perhaps it is gone also.

Pregnant women were discouraged from wearing leis lest the umbilical cord wind around and strangle the unborn baby. But after delivery if there was not milk enough to nurse the baby, the mother wore a lei of sweet potato vines to induce a better flow of milk.

Leis, when worn, were never given away except to the nearest kin. Should a worn lei fall into the hands of a sorcerer, a scrofulous sore could develop on the neck of the wearer. It was considered rude to ask for a lei worn by another.

A lei worn in the hula was never given, not even to the nearest of kin. After a prayer for inspiration had been uttered, that particular lei worn by the dancer belonged also to the goddess of the dance.

When a descendant of our hereditary chiefs visited our home in Ka'ū, etiquette was observed. Nobody walked up to put the lei on the royal visitor, lest the hand or hands passed above the head of the *ali'i*. The lei was handed to the personal attendant for the *ali'i*, if one was present. Otherwise the lei was given to the royal person with a bow and then the giver backed away until the door was reached where one could turn around. At no time was the back ever turned to the *ali'i*, that was *kapu*, prohibited.

When Mrs. Lahilahi Webb was guide to exhibits at Bishop Museum, I asked her how leis were presented to an *ali'i* and the description furnished by Mrs. Webb was exactly as I remembered similar occasions. Leis were always presented with the utmost respect. Mrs. Webb was nurse and companion for Queen Lili'uokalani until Her Majesty passed away.

If the lei had to be put on an *ali'i*, the ends of the lei were untied first. With the greatest of care, one side of the lei was held, while the other hand guided the other end of the lei around without ever passing the hand of the lei giver over the head of the *ali'i*. With a little practice, this may be done with ease, as one stood to one side of the *ali'i*.

The passing years have brought us new ways and customs. In my youth a lei reached just about to the waistline or higher. Today, dancers wear leis which fall between the ankles and the knees. I consider that much too long.

Before World War II, I never saw leis presented to all and sundry accompanied by a kiss. True, our greeting was the *honi,* kiss, almost like the *hongi* of the Maoris of New Zealand, but we did not greet everybody that way with a lei—and so I wondered how a kiss with lei giving began.

One day, I wondered out loud at the Waikiki Camouflage Unit where I worked shortly after the beginning of World War II. A worker who was a cutter in the Camouflage Unit by day and a U.S.O. entertainer at night, heard me and laughed. She then told me that while entertaining one evening, her fellow musicians dared her to kiss a homely officer sitting nearby. She could not just barge up to kiss him, so she sat thinking a while until an idea came. When there was a little recess, she walked up to him, removed her lei, placed it on his shoulder, and said loud enough for those about to hear, "This is a Hawaiian custom," and implanted a kiss upon the man's cheek. Thus a neo-Hawaiian custom was born.

Another of those so-called Hawaiian customs is the cutting of a lei at the dedication of a building or a road. I am sure that there is a connection between this and the cutting of the ribbon by the *haoles.* Probably someone had an idea that it would impart something Hawaiian if a lei was cut instead. Had this been an old custom among the Hawaiians, surely a voyager, missionary, visitor, or a Hawaiian historian would have mentioned it. We have instead accounts of the ceremonial cutting of the thatch above the door of a thatched house, called the cutting of the umbilical cord. A house, so it was believed, acquired a personality of its own. Some had the warmth of welcome that one felt immediately, while other houses did not, in spite of the graciousness of the host.

To string something across the doorway or any entrance as with a cord or a ribbon was called a block, or *ālaina.* A tree whose branches reached across the entrance of a house was an *ālaina* which should be removed. This was thought to block prosperity, but when houses were without windows the blockage of sunlight was indeed a detriment to the welfare of the occupants. We were taught from infancy never to sit or stand directly in the doorway, lest we make an *ālaina* of ourselves.

When a *kahuna* was sent for, the door was kept open lest it become an *ālaina* against the progress of healing. As an open unobstructed entrance was desirable, surely no old-timer would stretch a ribbon, cord, or a lei across the doorway. Besides, a lei, among other things, signified the encompassing love of family. The thought of snipping the lei with scissors and allowing the severed ends to fall and be trampled by feet or crushed by wheels is just unthinkable.

At the 1954 dedication of the Kamehameha Schools Preparatory Department, on the Charles Reed Bishop campus, the following ceremony was performed. William Bishop Taylor and I untied the long *maile* lei, at its center. Then, the separated *maile* leis were tied at each end, to form two shorter *maile* leis.

One of the interesting sights in the Honolulu of my youthful years was the lei venders sitting along the sidewalks of Maunakea Street with their baskets of flowers and leis—some stringing leis, some just talking about the events of the day. Those were the days when twenty-five cents bought a pink carnation or a gardenia lei; and *'ilima,* still numerous in home gardens or the Pauoa School, sold for fifty cents.

There were plumerias *(Plumeria acuminata),* but these were rarely ever sold by the lei vendors because the plumeria was regarded then as a "graveyard" flower. Every cemetery in Honolulu had growing plumeria then, but only in white or yellow. I was a grown woman when the various shades of pink and reds came in. Today, I think more plumeria leis are sold than all of the others put together.

Fewer rose, pansy, or violet leis are seen today. The *melekule (Calendula officinalis)* were also fairly common and were reminders of the feather lei in shades of yellow. The yellow-orange *mamo (Carthamus tinctorius* L.) was strung into leis that also resembled feathers.

At Waimea, O'ahu, and Lumaha'i, Kaua'i, the shells of the small bivalve were gathered and sewed into hat bands. The shells of Waimea were predominately white, while those of Lumaha'i were brown. Mixed among the shells were some yellows and grays. These were sorted for size and color then sewn into bands, either plain or with designs. Every curio store in town sold these, but now that the sand has been removed from this area for construction projects, the Waimea shells are rarely seen today.

Other seashells worn were the *leho,* cowry; the *kūpe'e (Nerita polita);* the *pūpū 'alā, (Conus auratus),* a cone called *pōniuniu* in the locality I hailed from in the Ka'ū area on the island of Hawai'i, because of the dizziness that resulted when one was stung by the animal within the shell. There is another small shell, dark brown in color and similar to the famed lei shell of Ni'ihau, that is worn in leis but its native name I do not know. The *pūpū* Ni'ihau *(Columbella),* called *momi* by the natives of that island, is the most admired and best known of our island lei shells.

As I previously mentioned, leis made of the feathers of our native birds were reserved for royalty only. It was not until foreign birds, such as the dove, parrot, peacock, pheasant, and others, were introduced, and our women acquired skill in hat making, that the flat hatbands, also called leis, came into vogue. When the art of dyeing was learned, white chicken or duck feathers were colored and made into imitations of the royal leis, as well as hat bands.

I shall tell you now of the story that produced the belief that peacock leis produced bad luck.

When Queen Kapi'olani and Princess Lili'uokalani were preparing to attend Queen Victoria's Jubilee in England, a dress and *holokū* trimmed with peacock feathers were made for Queen Kapi'olani. The dress was completed, but the *holokū* ran short of the blue feathers to finish it as there were no more blue peacock feathers to be found. An idea came to a young man in the royal court, James Lono McGuire. He went among the people, and whenever he saw a lei with the desired feathers he would mention casually of hearing that peacock feathers were unlucky to own and wear. When the owner expressed a wish to dispose of these feathers lest ill luck befall him, Mr. McGuire offered to dispose of the feathers, misfortune and all. Before long the Queen's *holokū* was completed.

The *holokū* was inherited by Kahanu-Pau-o-kaulele-a-iwi Kalani-ana'ole, niece of Queen Kapi'olani. After the death of Kahanu, the *holokū* was sold at public auction to Miss Vivienne Mader of New York for fifty dollars. Under one sleeve was a small rip which I mended for Miss Mader. The *holokū* was of blue velvet, of the exact shade of the peacock feathers which trimmed the cuffs, yoke, and wide hem.

The story of the completing of the Queen's *holokū* was told me by James McGuire himself, and the belief still persists among some people that a hat band of peacock feathers brings bad luck to the wearer. McGuire accompanied the Queen and Princess to England and wrote a diary of their visit in England—all in Hawaiian. Those who were interested bought copies of it, and I deem myself fortunate in owning a copy.

Some years ago there were two stones at Wahiawa that were taken to Kūkaniloko. As they were said to be healing stones named Lae-nihi, female, and Ke-aniani'ula-o-ka-lani, male, and had nothing to do with royal births, the two stones were again moved beside some pineapple land. Lahilahi Webb told me that she assisted Mrs. Julia Swanzy in directing the removal of the stones to the site of the second relocation.

Someone claimed to have been healed by the stones, and so the newspapers published the story with pictures of the two stones—the tall male stone and the low boot-shaped female stone. That started visitors going there. Some went to satisfy curiosity and others to seek relief from pain. After two weeks, Keahi Luahine and I decided to go and we saw the crowds coming and going.

A lei stand there made a thriving business selling leis to Hawaiians and a hot dog stand appeased the hunger of visitors who desired food.

I found it most interesting to observe those who came, for people brought gifts that they thought were appropriate to these healing, spirit-possessed stones. Filipinos brought candles. Chinese brought punk sticks and cakes. Japanese brought artificial flowers and food. Portuguese brought money, and Hawaiians brought leis. In front of the two stones was an elongated sand-filled box to hold the gifts brought by the Orientals. At the entrance of the enclosure, a box with a coin slot was nailed to a post to hold the monetary gifts. The stones were adorned with flower and *maile* leis from the Hawaiians. To Hawaiians, leis of flowers or even of leaves were always appropriate gifts for supernatural beings who lived in stones and imparted *mana*.

Some years later, I revisited the stones, practically forgotten by now, and was shocked to see initials cut into them. The stones themselves are far more interesting, and who really cares whether Kilroy or anyone else had been there?

Later I met a native Hawaiian of Wahiawa who told me that he remembered the tall stone in his boyhood. At that time, the stone was believed to bring or to clear away the rain, to heal the earth rather than human ailments. I asked whether the people then adorned the stone with leis. "Certainly," he replied. Immortals as well as mortals were fond of flower or leafy leis.

Lae-nihi, the name given to the boot-shaped stone, was also the name of Halemano's supernatural sister. Lae-nihi always went to assist Halemano in trouble. The setting of the legend of Halemano was in that portion of the island of O'ahu. This legend may be found in Fornander (1919, pp. 228-262).

When early voyagers brought jet beads here, the supply could not fill the demand, so someone thought of making beads of *kukui* nuts. cut in grooves, in facets, or just smoothed. I wish I knew the name of the originator and where he lived—for he deserves praise for the happiness he gave us. Women wore *kukui* nuts as leis until the fad wore out, then like many old things some became neglected and lost, and others vanished into trunks. Then the fashion of wearing *kukui* nut leis was revived and those who kept their *kukui* leis found that they had heirlooms. Those who did not, had *kukui* leis made. *Kukui* leis are early post-European and not ancient. Dr. Kenneth P. Emory of Bishop Museum told me that he had not ever found a *kukui* lei or bead in any of his archaeological digs.

I remember leis made of worsted, manila rope dyed red in imitation of *lehua,* of satin ribbon, and of crepe paper. Some remain and some are gone entirely.

For a while all kinds of seeds became the vogue in leis and now we have rick-rack and plastic flowers. All of these are beautiful, but I hope we will never be without flower leis.

Hawai'i would not be Hawai'i at all without the flower leis.

LITERATURE CITED

FORNANDER, ABRAHAM
    1919. "Hawaiian Antiquities and Folk-lore." *Mem. B. P. Bishop Mus.* 5(2):228-263.
NEAL, MARIE C.
    1965. *In Gardens of Hawaii.* B. P. Bishop Mus. Spec. Pub. 50. Honolulu.
PUKUI, MARY KAWENA, and SAMUEL H. ELBERT
    1971. *Hawaiian Dictionary.* Honolulu: Univ. Hawaii Press.

CONNOTATIVE VALUES
OF HAWAIIAN PLACE NAMES

SAMUEL H. ELBERT*

University of Hawaii, Honolulu

I N A REVIEW of George P. Stewart's *Names on the Land,* George L. Trager (1946) outlined his idea of an optimum place-name study, and one of the stipulations was that the connotations of the names be stated. He criticized Stewart for several reasons, one being that his work read like a novel rather than like a scientific work.

A pioneering study of Hawai'i's place names was published in 1965 by Katharine Luomala in a source not apt to be seen by Polynesianists. It is a scientific article and it reads like a novel, as do other Luomala writings, thus belying Trager's divorcing of the two media.

Luomala's study has been called "pioneering" because it seems to have been the first to concentrate on poetic uses of place names in Polynesia. Beckwith mentions such usage in connection with the fondness for names (1919, p 313). The Biblical genealogies immediately found favor with the Hawaiians, she says, an aristocratic people who memorized their genealogies (even padded some) and who filled their chants with all manner of categories, as of types of gods, clouds, winds, rains, and especially places. Gifford in his study of Tongan place names (1923)

*Portions of this article, somewhat altered, are a part of the introduction to the second edition of *Place Names of Hawai'i,* which includes an introduction by Samuel H. Elbert and a glossary of 3,906 place names by Mary Kawena Pukui, Samuel H. Elbert, and Esther T. Mookini (1974). Mrs. Pukui has, as is her custom of many years, been most helpful in interpreting the sayings and texts included in the present article. Koana Wilcox supplied the song *Honua = 'ula* and its composer's name and homeland. Elizabeth K. Bushnell and Albert J. Schütz critically read an early version of the manuscript. To all of these, *mahalo,* and *mahalo,* too, to the University of Hawaii for a teaching reduction that gave me time to work on this undertaking.

includes songs filled with place names. Other Oceanic place-name studies, such as those by Reed (1961) on New Zealand, Bender (1963) on the Marshalls, Goodenough (1966) on Truk, and Barthel (1962) on Easter Island, satisfactory as they may be in many respects, say nothing about this important cultural use of place names that gives the names connotative values quite apart from that of mere nomenclature.

The purpose of this contribution is to expand Luomala's study of Hawaiian place names to include those found in proverbial sayings, narratives, chants, and songs.

Like most Polynesians, Hawaiians are fond of proverbial sayings that are memorized verbatim, and are used less for didactic purposes than as displays of wit, and as praise of the land. They differ from Euro-American proverbial sayings in that they rely heavily on place names. Rather rare in the West are such phrases as "castles in Spain," "crossing the Rubicon," and "sent to Siberia." These traditional expressions say a great deal in a few words and are slightly elliptic, but they are not encountered frequently and are not particularly admired; some may consider them too trite for respectability. In the traditional Hawaiian culture, however, such expressions were greatly admired, and a few people still use them today. Not many years ago Mary Kawena Pukui found a colleague. Ke = oho = kapu, hard at work. Instead of the banal comment that a *haole* would make, she asked cryptically: "Are /you/ limping along the Beach of Weariness?" *(E kū'o'i a'e ana i ke One o Luhi?).*[1] Ke = oho = kapu, quick as a flash, said resignedly: "/I'm/ just climbing up Drudgery Hill." *(He pi'i-na kē-ia i mauna Pa'u-pa'u):* Both Mrs. Pukui and Ke = oho = kapu were pleased, and the latter's work may have, as a result of his repartee, seemed less like drudgery. The core of these sayings is the double meaning in the place names *Luhi* 'weariness' and *Pa'u-pa'u* 'drudgery.'

The English sayings cited above do not rely on word play, nor do the places mentioned in *The Pilgrim's Progress.* The places in that masterpiece are fictitious and didactic—Slough of Despond, Delectable Mountains, Celestial Country, Carnal Policy, and others.

Hawaiian sayings also may be didactic. The two in the preceding paragraph seem to express resignation and patience. Others, not didactic describe emotional states or important events, but the largest proportior show *aloha 'āi-na,* 'love for the land and the people of the land,' an

---

[1]Hawaiian words herein are written as they are in the Elbert and Pukui *Hawaiian Grammar,* now in press, except that words in names here are separated by equal signs, and that affixes and compound members in the names are set off by hyphens. The glottal stop is shown by the reverse apostrophe; the macron indicates long vowels and stress not conforming to the usual patterns.

this function, so important in Hawai'i, seems completely lacking in Euro-American proverbial sayings. (It is not noted, for instance, in Archer Taylor's *The Proverb and An Index to the Proverb*, 1962.)

A few sayings containing place names and descriptive of human emotions follow.

Anger: *Nā-pele-pele nā pali o Ka=lalau i ka wili 'ia e ka makani.* 'Crumbling are the cliffs of Astray, twisted by the wind.'
Naue Ka=lalau, pōniu ka Lawakua. 'Astray trembles, the Lawakua wind whirls.'
Ke lau-ahi mai-la 'o Pele iā Puna. 'Pele is pouring lava out on Puna.'

Grief: *Lu'u-lu'u Hana-lei i ka ua nui, kaumaha i ka noe o Alaka'i.* 'Hana-lei is downcast with great rains, heavy with the mists of Alaka'i.'

Love: *'O ka ua o Hilo e mao ana, 'o ke alohu i ka ipo, meu pau 'ole.* 'The rain of Hilo clears, love of a sweetheart—endless.'
A aloha wale 'ia kā ho'i 'o Ka=unu=o=Hua, he wahi pu'u wale iho nō ia. 'Even Ka=unu=o=Hua is loved, it's just a mountain.'

Trouble. *Alu i Kē'ē* 'There at Kē'ē' (a remote cliff difficult or impossible to climb on the Nā=pali coast, Kaua'i).

Hospitality: *Ke ala-nui hele ma-uka o Pu'u=kā-hea.* 'The pathway going inland of Calling-hill.'

Coals to Newcastle: *Ho'i hou ka pa'a-kai i Wai=mea.* 'The salt goes back again to Wai=mea.' (Lots of salt is already available at Wai=mea, leeward Kaua'i.)

Intelligence: *No Ka=lae nō ka wahine.* 'The lady is from The=forehead.'

Stupidity: *He po'e una-unahi he'e 'o Kula: 'o Kula hoe hewa.* 'The people of Kula scale squids; the people of Kula paddle badly.' (Kula is high on Hale=a=ka=lā, Maui; where the people don't know how to paddle, and don't know that squids have no scales.)
Mai Ke='ā-'ā mai paha. 'Maybe from Dumbness.'

Drinking: *Aia aku i Ka=nenelu.* '/He's/ over there at The=Bog.'
I Hala =pē akū nei paha. 'Maybe at Missing=drenched.'

Not returning home. *Ua kō'ia paha e ke au o Hala'ea.* 'Perhaps /he/ is dragged away by the current of Hala'ea.' (The currents at Hala'ea, on the Ka'ū side of South Point, Hawai'i, are very strong. A Midas-like story here is of a chief who claimed too many fish. The people piled fish high in his canoe and it was carried away by the current.)

Being poorly dressed: *Aia i Ka'ū i Ka = 'alu-'alu.* 'There in Ka'ū at Sagging.' (Of baggy, poorly-fitting clothes.)

Recovery from sickness: *'Ane-'ane e pae aku i Moku = ola.* 'Almost landed at Isle /of/ Life.'

Success: *Ka pi'i nō ia ā Kōkī = o = Wai-lau.* 'He has climbed Summit of Wai-lau.' (A Moloka'i peak that is difficult to climb.)

Failure: *Ua pae ka wa'a i Nānā = wale.* 'The canoe landed at Profitless = looking.'
Aia aku-la paha i Waī = kī-kī i Hamo-hamo i ka 'imi 'ahu-'awa. 'Maybe just at Wai = kī-kī Groping-about *(Hamo-hamo)* looking for bitter grass *('ahu-'awa).*'
'A'ole i ke'ehi kapua'i i ke one o Hau = iki. 'Soles of /their/ feet have never trod on the sands of Strike = a = little.' Strike = a = little may be something like 'strike it rich,' and exemplifies Hawaiian fondness for understatement. Something in the worst possible taste is described as *'a'ohe kohu iki* 'not a little suitable' and of a beautiful girl one says that she is without pimples, crooks, or blemishes *('a'ohe pu'u, 'a'ohe ke'e, kīnā 'ole).*

Or one may point out, usually in jest, some unpleasant physical characteristic, past happening, or unpleasant meaning associated with a rival island or place. And place names by extension include the people of the place.

O'ahu: *O'ahu maka 'ewa-'ewa.* 'Unjust-eyed O'ahu.' (The goddess Hi'iaka of Hawai'i said this when her O'ahu relatives refused to help her mend her canoes. 'Ewa, a district on O'ahu, has the meaning 'crooked'; the saying applies to people who do not welcome and help visitors.)

Puna, Hawai'i: *Lohi'au Puna i ke akua wahine.* 'Puna is backward because of the goddess.' *Weli-weli 'ino Puna i ke akua wahine.* 'Puna is terrified by the goddess.' (These are references to Pele, the volcano goddess, who still ravages in Puna.)

Kaʻū, Hawaiʻi: *E hoʻi Kaʻū i Pala=hemo.* 'Go back /to/ Excreta = dab in Kaʻū.'

Ka = laoa, Hawaiʻi: *Ka = laoa ʻai pō ʻele-ʻele.* 'Ka = laoa eats /in the/ dark night.' (The people are stingy and don't want to share their food.)

Hawaiʻi palu lāʻī. 'Hawaiians lick ti leaves.' (Ka = meha-meha was invited to a party on Oʻahu. He brought an army with him, and when the food ran out the Hawaiian folk had to lick the ti leaves in which food had been baked.)

Maui: *Maui poʻo hakahaka.* 'Empty-headed Mauians.'

Sayings that praise the land are called *aloha ʻāi-na* sayings, a phrase taken from the famous song *Kau-lana nā Pua* 'Famous /are/ the Children' that describes the support of Hawaiians for the last queen, Liliʻu = o = ka = lani, and their sorrow that she was forced to sign "the paper of the enemy" *(ka pepa o ka ʻenemi)* brought by the evil-hearted messenger *(ka ʻelele o ka loko ʻino)* with its sin of annexation *(hoʻo-hui ʻāi-na kūʻai hewa)* to America. The song (Elbert and Mahoe, 1970, pp. 62-63) ends with a salutation to the people who love the land *(ka poʻe i aloha i ka ʻāi-na).*

There are probably thousands of *aloha ʻāi-na* sayings. They name illustrious chiefs and places, important rains, seas, winds, and distinctive features. Speakers of Hawaiian never tire of hearing them over and over, and on hearing them one recalls his own grandmother or older relative who used to say them, and one has heard some of them in songs. They thus reinforce ties to family as well as to places, and are a link with a past that in many ways seems still a glorious never-never land. To the outsider some of them may sound foolish, and this may be why Kepelino (Beckwith, 1932, pp. 142-143) said, more than a hundred years ago, that when the foreigners ask and ask they get only a heap of foolishness *(ʻahu nā kupaianaha).* Did he mean that Hawaiian lore seems foolish to the foreigners, or that the Hawaiians refuse to tell the truth and told only foolish things? But the outsiders are outsiders, and so they remain today. Even Pele, the volcano goddess, is called a *malihini* (foreigner) because, aeons ago, she came from Kahiki.

Even more cogent than the association of *aloha ʻāi-na* sayings with friends and relatives were the ties with the land and the seas, the source of life. Today, young people look to the excitement of a city and the opportunities believed to lie there for an independent existence and for acquiring what are now considered the good things of life. Not so before.

Opportunity was on the land and in the sea. The present and the future lay in the gardens, fishing grounds, and surfing sites. This attachment to the land and the sea was reflected in the poetic *aloha 'ai-na* sayings that one heard in conversation and in songs. Poetic? Yes, in the sense that the sayings brought to mind mental pictures of familiar places and cast a golden aura of affection over them.

Only a few of the many thousand *aloha 'ai-na* sayings can be mentioned here, some of the phrases naming chiefs, rains, winds, seas, and famous features associated with the various islands. Each island, for example, is coupled with a chief's name; thus *Hawai'i o Keawe, Kaua'i o Mano = ka = lani = pō* ('multitudes/of/chiefs/from the /gods'). *Lāna'i o Ka = ulu = lā'au* ('the forest'). *Maui o Kama, Moloka'i o Ka = meha-meha = nui, Ni'ihau o Mano = 'ōpū = pa'i-pa'i* ('many belly slappings /as in childbirth/'), and *O'ahu o Kākuhihewa.*

Rains, seas, winds, and features were associated with places on the various islands.

Rains: Hawai'i: *Ka ua kani lehua o Hilo.* 'The lehua sounding rain of Hilo.'

Kaua'i: *Ka ua loku o Hana-lei.* 'The pouring rain of Hana-lei.'

Maui: *Ka ua lani ha'a-ha'a o Hāna.* 'The rain of Hāna's low-lying sky.'

O'ahu: *Ka ua Kuahine o Mānoa.* 'The Sister rain of Mānoa.' (For songs with a rain name, see Elbert and Mahoe, 1970, pp. 43, 50.)

Seas: Hawai'i: *Kona kai 'ōpua i ka la'i* 'Kona seas with cloud billows that tell of peace to come.'

Kaua'i: *Ke kai malino mai Ke = kaha a Milo = li'i.* 'The quiet seas from Ke = kaha to Milo = li'i.'

O'ahu: *ka 'ehu kai o Pua = 'ena.* 'The sea spray of Pua = 'ena.'

Winds: Hawai'i: *'Apa'apa'a* (Kohala). *Kuehu = lepo.* 'Dust scattering' (Ka'ū).

Kaua'i: *Ala = 'oli.* 'Joyful pathway.'

Maui: *Ka = ua = 'ula.* 'The red rain.'

Moloka'i: *Ala = hou.* 'New pathway.'

O'ahu: *Ala = eli* 'eroded pathway' (Mānoa, Hono-lulu).

For songs with wind names, see Elbert and Mahoe, 1970, pp. 50, 56. For long lists of winds, see Fornander, 1918, pp. 92-103), in which 12 winds are named in the single valley of Hālawa, Moloka'i.

Famous features: Hawai'i: *I kala = pana i ka niu moe.* 'At

Kala=pana, the coconut palms lie flat.' (A traditional way to honor a very high chief was to ask the chief to hold on to the tip of the fronds of a young coconut tree, while the people bent the tree over and subsequently trained it to grow flat on the ground. Queen Emma was probably the last *ali'i* to be honored thus, at Kala-pana, when she visited there on horseback shortly before the death of Princess Ruth in 1883. Emma died in 1885.)

Kaua'i: *Ka limu kā kanaka o Manu'a=kepa.* 'The man-striking moss of Manu'a=kepa' (a slippery moss on which people slip and fall).

Maui: *Kau=pō 'ai loli,* 'Kau-pō people eat sea slugs.' (A local chief long ago was so fond of this food that he had a special oven in which to bake all the *loli* that the people brought him.)

Moloka'i: *Ulu kukui o Lani=kāula.* '*Kukui* groves of Lani=kāula.' (Here in this grove the famous prophet, Lani=kāula, was buried by his sons. The grave was believed to have mana.)

Ni'ihau: *Kō 'eli lima a'o Halāli'i.* 'Sugar cane hand-dug at Halāli'i.' (A peculiar sugar cane concealed by wind-blown sand. People saw protruding green leaves and dug out the cane stalks.)

O'ahu: *Ka i'a hāmau leo o 'Ewa.* 'Sea bivalves of 'Ewa that silence voices.' (A taboo of silence was enforced on persons looking for pearl oysters at Pearl Harbor.)

When Kamehameha dreamed of conquest of Kaua'i, he mentioned these places which he wished to enjoy: *E holo a inu i ka wai o Wai=lua, a hume i ka wai o Nā=molo=kama, a 'ai i ka 'anae 'au o Ka=wai=ma-kua i Hā-'ena, a lei ho'i i ka pahapaha o Poli=hale, a laila, ho'i mai a O'ahu, ia ka 'āi-na e noho ai. (Ka Nupepa Kuokou,* Iulai 20, 1867, rewritten in present orthography; the translation that appeared in Kamakau, 1961, p. 187, has been slightly altered.)

'Let /us/ go and drink the water of Wai lua, wear a loincloth in the water of Nā=molo=kama, eat the mullet that swim in Ka=wai=makua at Hā-'ena, wreathe /ourselves/ with the seaweed of Poli=hale, then return to O'ahu, the land to dwell upon.'

The preceding gives merely a sampling of place names that appear in sayings. Some are remembered because of double meanings, and some are merely tag lines attached to places great and small throughout the islands. Some are derogatory, but most of them express affection for the land.

PLACE NAMES IN NARRATIVES

Hawaiian narratives are replete with place names. Many such tales were collected by Abraham Fornander's helpers in the 1860's and have been translated and published in Hawaiian and English. Others have appeared in Hawaiian only in Hawaiian newspapers. Some of these have been translated. The Fornander stories are called in Hawaiian *mo'olelo* and *ka'ao*. The former were considered true, and the latter not always true (Beckwith, 1970, p. 1), a distinction not maintained by Fornander's later editor, Thomas G. Thrum. Many place names are found too in Kamakau's *Ruling Chiefs of Hawaii* (1961) and still more in Emerson's *Pele and Hiiaka* (1915). This is an epic describing the journey of Hi'iaka, Pele's younger sister, from Kī=lau=ea Volcano on Hawai'i to Kaua'i in order to find Lohi'au, whom Pele had met in her dreams and fallen in love with. On her long journey Hi'iaka encountered a succession of *mo'o* 'water supernaturals,' whom she fought with and vanquished, usually turning them into stones that still stand. *Mo'o* is also the name for 'lizard,' but the *mo'o* of the legends are fearful and gigantic, and usually lived in water. The islet Moko=li'i 'little lizard' (or Chinaman's Hat) in Kāne='ohe Bay, O'ahu, was the tail of a *mo'o* defeated by Hi'iaka, and its body is the long flat section near the shore (Emerson, 1915, p. 91). A nearby rock called today Crouching Lion, formerly named Ka=uhi='imaka=o=ka=lani 'the observant cover of the heavens,' was a *kupua* 'demigod' already turned to stone who rose to a crouching position and vainly begged Hi'iaka to restore him to life. A cave, Ke=awa='ula, at Yokohama Beach, Wai='anae, O'ahu, is said to have been opened by Hi'iaka to get water.

Many gulches and ridges were formed by the rooting of the pig-god, Kama=pua'a, a symbol of erosion and lechery. Some of the stories concerning him are racy. In one account he chased Pele to Pua'a=kanu ('pig planted') in Puna, Hawai'i. He was about to molest her when Pele's sister, Kapo=kohe=lele ('flying vagina Kapo') sent her special part flying to lure away the erotic pig-god. He forgot Pele and followed the part to Koko Crater, O'ahu, where it left an imprint. Kama got there too late, however, as the part had already flown off to Ka=lihi.

Places in stories such as these are termed *pana*, and in their imaginations people ally the place with amusement and affection to the wondrous events of the past.

A second use of place names in narrative is nonpoetic, and the teller becomes a reporter of detail rather than a reteller of adventure. To the outsider, such detailed lists of places are boring, but not so to the narrator or his Hawaiian audience. Listed in travel-guide order, the places are a witness both to the story's veracity and the teller's memory, and again, are ties of *aloha 'āi-na*.

The following passage described a swim from Wai='anae, O'ahu, to Puna, Hawai'i, by a female *laenihi* ('labroid') fish. The fish was on a noble mission—to find her brother a wife. Before leaving she told her brother that he would know where she was by natural phenomena (she could create lightning, thunder, and earthquakes when she wished to). In a brief paragraph 19 places are named (if we count Maui twice). They appear here in bold-face type, and in the English version are translated when possible. Of the 18 different names, 4 (25 percent) are not listed in Coulter's *Gazetteer* (1935) or Pukui and Elbert (1966): *Hana-ka-'ie'ie, Pōloli = ka = manu, Mahiki,* and *Kukulu.* This may give some idea of the number of places mentioned in the tales that are not recorded on maps.

Holo mai = la 'o Laenihi i ke ahiahi, a hiki i **Hale = o = Lono** *ma* **Pā = lā'au** *i* **Moloka'i,** *ua ka ua. Kāhāhā 'o hope no ka hiki = wawe loa. Ma = laila aku a* **Hana-ka-'ie'ie,** *ma* **Kahiki = nui** *i* **Honua-'ula** *ma* **Maui,** *'ōlapa ka uwila. Kāhāhā hou 'o hope no ka 'emo 'ole loa. Mai* **Maui** *aku a* **'Umi = wai,** *ma* **Kohala** *i* **Hawai'i,** *ku'i ka hekili; ma = laila aku a* **Pōloli = ka = manu,** *ma = waho o* **Mahiki** *i* **Hāmā-kua,** *nei ke ōla'i. Ma = laila aku a hala 'o* **Hilo,** *a komo i loko o* **Pana = 'ewa,** *a hiki i* **Kukulu** *ma = waho o* **Puna,** *kahe ka wai 'ula. A laila, no'o-no'o 'o hope nei, ua lou'a 'o* **Kama = lālā = walu.** (Elbert, ed., 1959, p. 255.)

'Laenihi came in the evening, going to **House = of = Lono** at **Wooden = fence** on **Moloka'i**—the rain rained. The people behind were astonished at the great speed. From there on to **The-'ie'ie vine = bay** at **Great = Tahiti** at **Red = earth** on **Maui**—the lightning flashed. The people behind were astonished, quick-as-a-flash. From **Maui** to **'Umi's = water,** at **Kohala** on **Hawai'i**—the thunder roared; from there to **The = bird = is = hungry,** beyond **Mahiki** at **Hāmākua**—the earth quaked. From there past **Hilo,** entering within **Pana = 'ewa** and on to **Kukulu** outside **Puna**—the red rain water ran. Then the people behind thought that **Kama = lālā = walu** had been found.'

The following passage by the noted writer, Kamakau, is from *Ke Au Okoa* of June 10, 1869. It describes the beauties of Hāna, Maui, in the late 18th century. A translation appears in Kamakau's *Ruling Chiefs of Hawaii* (1961, p. 385), and recently in Wenkam (1970, p. 34). The text has been rewritten in the present orthography, and the translation slightly altered. An unclear portion is marked with a question mark. Of the 12 places named, only 5 are in a glossary of Hawaiian place names by Pukui, Elbert, and Mookini (1974), or are in Coulter (1935)—another example of the high percentage of names not listed on maps and probably destined to be soon forgotten, if not already so.

A he 'āi-na kaulana 'o Hāna i ka wā kahiko. 'O ka pā kaua ka mea i kaulana ai 'o Hāna, 'o ka nalu o Pūhele ma ka wai 'au'au o Kū = maka, o ka he'e pu'e wai o Wai = 'ōhinu, o ka lele ma'opu mai a ka wai o Kama, 'o ke kāhuli a ka lau o ka 'ama'u, 'o ka 'awa lau lena o Lanakila. 'O ka momona o ka o (?) Pu'e = kahi, 'o ka poi ono o Kua = kahi, 'o nā 'opihi momona o Ka = wai = papa, 'o ka uhu palu-palu momona o Hane = o'o, 'o nā pua'a kū-palu me nā 'īlio nahu maka; aloha nō nā li'i i kē-lā 'āi-na 'olu-'olu, i ho'o-pulu 'ia e ka ua 'Āpua = kea, ka ua wāwahi i luna o ka hala, ka hala mai Wā-kiu a Hono-ka = lani (Kamakau, 1961, p. 385).

'Hāna was in olden days a noted place. Hāna was famous for the fortified hill, the surf at Pūhele, the fresh-water bathing pool of Kū = maka, the surfing to the stream mouth at Wai = 'ōhinu, the leaping to dive in the waters of Kama, the changing color of the fronds of the *'ama'u* fern, the yellow-leafed kava of Lanakila. The fat [?] of Pu'e = kahi, the delicious poi of Kua = kahi, the fat limpets of Ka = wai = papa, the fat soft parrotfish of Hane = o'o, and the fattened pigs and eye-biting dogs dear to the memory of chiefs of that pleasant land moistened by the 'Āpua = kea rain, the rain that rattles on the *hala* trees passing from Wā = kiu to Hono-ka = lani.'

Such an insistence on place must have seemed dull to Moses Nākuina (1867-1911), the gifted author of the story of Paka'a and the gourd that controlled the winds (n. d.), a retelling of legends for the amusement and moral improvement of the youth in his Christian Endeavor Society, of which he was president for the last eight years of his life. His literary style contrasts notably with that of the legends in the Fornander volumes, collected about a half century earlier. Nākuina's phrases are longer, he piled up sequences of homonyms, and he mentioned only important places. On a journey of Pāka'a from Kaua'i to Hawai'i he mentions only Ka = pa'a on Kaua'i; Waī = kī-kī on O'ahu; Kaunakakai and Pū = ko'o on Moloka'i; Lele, Lahaina, 'Uo, and Hāna on Maui; and Wai = pi'o and Hilo on Hawai'i. The reader is not presented a time table that tells everywhere the hero slept and took a bath. Nākuina's slighting of place names is similar to that in the literature of the west, and must have pleased his younger readers but left his older ones with the feeling that the story was too meagerly documented to be believed! And if such readers knew small places between Kaua'i and Hawai'i they were disappointed at not hearing them in the narrative.

PLACE NAMES IN SONGS AND CHANTS

The most complete discussion of the role of place names in Hawaiian poetry is by Katharine Luomala. She has described with sensitivity and delicacy the emotional effect that place names may have, even when the "specific associations with specific places have blurred ... a halo of happiness or sorrow clings to the poet's recollection ... " (1965, p. 243).

The discussion here will begin with examples of the love chants of the legendary antihero, Hale = mano (*antihero*, a currently fashionable term, seems appropriate because Hale = mano is unable to hold his lover and because he himself proves inconstant, a sophistication perhaps rare in the usual folktale). As he sings the chant to follow, Hale = mano has been looking at the summit of the volcanic dome of Hale = a = ka = lā on Maui with clouds flying over, now concealing and now revealing, and he sings of places where he has been with his lover (again the original is rewritten in the present orthography):

Kau = pō 'ai-na pali huki i luna,	Kau = pō land of cliffs rising high,
Huki a'e-la e like me Kahiki = nui,	Rising upwards like Great-Tahiti,
He nui nō wau nāu, e ke aloha.	Great was I, you /thought/, O love.
	(Elbert, ed., 1959, p. 275)

A Hawaiian poetic device sometimes known as linked assonance, as an echo of the last word of a line in the next line, is found in lines 2 and 3. Kau = pō and Kahiki — nui are places on Maui where Hale = mano shared joy and sorrow with his wife.

Hale = mano then goes on to the next island, Hawai'i, where he and his wife enjoyed the surfing of Kai — mū, but where she deserted him for the chiefs of Hilo and Puna, and he administers the saddest and most gentle of rebukes:

Ke kua 'ia mai = la i ke kai ka hala o Puna	Chopped to bits by the sea are the hala trees
E hala'o'a ana mehe kanaka lā	Standing up like human beings
Lulumi iho= la i ke kai o Hilo—ē	Drowned in the Hilo sea
Hā-nu'u ke kai i luna o Moku = ola	Rises up the sea of the Isle = of = Life
Ua ola a'e nei loko i kō aloha ē (Elbert, ed., 1959, p. 277).	This heart lives upon your love

Later in the love-matching game of *kilu* (Malo, 1951, pp. 216-218) another woman makes a sure bet with Hale = mano (if I win you are mine and if you win I am yours), and this unsubtle arrangement arouses the heroine's jealousy and she now sings back a love song to Hale = mano (Elbert, ed., 1959, p. 285).

Auwē ku'u hoa pili, 'o ke kāne ē,	Alas my dear companion, /my/ man,
Ku'u hoa o ka hale wai anu o Hilo.	My companion of the cool waters of the house of Hilo.

No Hilo ho'i au no ka ipu a Kulukulu'ā   From Hilo I and the calabash of
                                                  Kulukulu'ā
No ke one holu i Wai=o=lama,   Where sands ripple at Wai=o=lama,
No ka ua hehi lau 'ulu o Pi'i=honua.   Where rain treads upon breadfruit leaves at
                                                  Pi'i=honua.
I noho kā-ua i nā ulu o Mālama ē,   We stayed in the groves of Keep.
Mālama ke aloha i ka wai-maka   Keep love in tears

Three places are recalled here with joy and sorrow: the rippling sands of *Wai=o=lama* (a stream and beach near the town of Hilo), *Pi'i=honua* (at least five places on the island of Hawai'i have this name), and *Mālama*, a famous place in the Puna District.

The juxtaposition of *Malama* and *mālama* is a favorite of poets, and in the well-known song about the ship *Pueo Kahi* a similar *Māmala* (Honolulu harbor) contrasts with *mālama:*

Ma ka 'ili-kai a'o Māmala   On the surface of the sea at Māmala
Mālama 'ia iho ke aloha.   Keep your love.

This sort of echoism is extremely popular. One more example will be given, also from Elbert and Mahoe (1970, p. 29):

He aloha nō 'o 'Ahulili—   Love for 'Ahulili—
A he lili paha ko ia-la.   Perhaps she's jealous.

'Ahulili is a prominent East Maui peak, but the theme of the song is a woman's jealousy *(lili).*

The following song, given in its entirety, differs from the previously cited extracts in that punning is lacking. Its appeal is in its subtlety and in the repetition of the names of places, rains, and winds of the poet's birthplace, together with sayings, mostly of the *aloha 'āi-na* kind. It jumps about from East Maui to West Maui in a seemingly helter-skelter way. This is an example of a song that might seem a heap of foolishness to the outsider but that delights the child of the land. Koana Wilcox, who contributed the song, said that the song's composer, David K. Ka=pōhā=kimo=hewa, lived at Kula, high on Hale=a=ka=lā mountain on East Maui, in the first decades of this century. In keeping with the penchant for understatement and veiled meanings, Kula is not mentioned by name, but is identified by the mists and by the derisive reference in the chorus to scaling squids (quoted earlier in its entirety).

Place names on East Maui include *Honua='ula, 'Auwahi,* and *Ka='uiki.* Hāna is identified by the *aloha 'āi-na* saying about the low skies (previously mentioned). Tributes to West Maui include mention of *La'i='e-lua* and the *Hono-* bays (Hono-kahua, Hono-ke=ana, Hono-kō=hau, Hono-kō=wai, Hono-lua, Hono-nana) and Koa'e. The skin-stinging rain is at Wai = 'ehu and the Kili'o'opu wind at Wai = he'e ('o'opu fish were caught here). The school at Lahaina Luna is praised as the light of knowledge not blown out by the Red = rain gales. The taboo fish and the famous stones have not been explained.

HONUA = 'ULA
By David K. Ka = pōhā = kimo = ñewa

Honua – 'ulu kua la'o-la'o,	Honua = 'ula, pitted back,
Nā pu'u o La'i = 'e-lua.	Hills of Doubly = peaceful.

Chorus

He aloha wale a'e ana	A greeting
I ku'u 'āi-na kaulana,	For my famous land,
I ka unahi-nahi i ka pika he'e,	For scaling squid suction cups,
I ka uahi kokololio.	And gusty mists.

Ka ua Pe'e = pā = pōhaku,	The rain hiding /behind/ stone walls,
Hanohano i ka i'a kapu,	Distinguished by taboo fish,
Nā pōhaku kaulana,	Famous stones,
'O'Auwahi wela i ka la'i.	'Auwahi hot in the sun.

E nā-hono = a = Pi'i-lani	O bays of Pi'ilani
I ka malu hēkuawa.	In the valley shade.
E ka ua hō'eha 'ili	O rain that stings the skin
A me ka ua Kili'o'opu.	And the rain and Kili'o'opu wind.

Alai 'oe, e Ka = 'uiki,	You block, Ka = 'uiki,
I ka wai 'āwili me ke kai	Streams mingling with seas
I ka ua Lani = ha'a-ha'a	In the Low = lying rain
Ma nā pali o Ko'olau.	And windward cliffs

Moloka'i nui a Hina,	Great Moloka'i, /child/ of Hina,
E ka pu'u o Koa'e,	O hill, Koa'e,
I ka ipu kukui pio 'ole	Light never extinguished
I ka makani Ka = ua = 'ula.	By the Red = rain gales.

The many sayings in this song raise the question: which comes first, the saying or the song? According to Mrs. Pukui, either may be first. She told of a famous chant that later became a saying. A colleague at Bishop Museum many years ago became suddenly angry. Seeing this, Mrs. Pukui chanted thus:

Ua pau k-o-'u lihi hoi-hoi i ka nani o Poka 'Ailana. 'My pleasure in the beauty of Ford Island is no more.'

This is all, but the angry person's wrath vanished and she burst into laughter. She well knew the story of the person for whose anger the chant was composed, a resident of 'Ewa. The chant was a mild rebuke for a lost temper, and has long been admired for several reasons, two of them not touched upon in this article:

(1) It's indirect; one never calls an adz by its own name. And the incident is thinly disguised by change of locale from 'Ewa to nearby Ford Island.

(2) It's understated. This is a favorite rhetorical device not unrelated to the fondness for indirection. Strong condemnatory phrases are 'not a little suitable' *(a'ohe kohu iki)* meaning 'ridiculous' and 'not a little good' *('a'ole maika'i iki)* meaning 'god-awful.' A beautiful person is one without pimples and flaws *('a'ohe pu'u, kīnā 'ole).*

(3) It recalls the past, past stories, past jokes, and suggests one's own childhood and a generation older than one's own; to hear it might bring tears as well as laughter.

HAWAIIAN GRAMMAR AND LITERARY USE OF PLACE NAMES

It has been often suggested that traditional sayings, narratives, and songs indicate the values of a culture, and in this article I have mentioned that the many references to place in these media indicate fondness for punning, love of land, and tendencies for indirection and understatement. I have mentioned elsewhere (Elbert, 1960) that the phonemic poverty of Hawaiian makes for a plethora of homonyms, and near homonyms, and this gives the literary artist who plays with words very malleable materials. We can say that the phonemic structure bears some relationship to the poetic devices. Can we say also that the interest of place in the literary media is matched by an interest in place in the grammar?

Words indicating spatiotemporal relationships, in John Lyons' terminology (1969, p. 275), are called deictic categories, a technical term taken from the Greek word 'to point.' In these categories are usually included personal pronouns, demonstratives, tenses, and sometimes honorifics. In Hawaiian tenses are meagerly developed and we do not have honorifics other than polite ways to address a chief, but we do have an elaborate use of directional particles, and these pre-eminently express spatial relations.

The three (pronouns, demonstratives, and directionals) are briefly discussed below. Possessives must be included with pronouns because they contain many of the same morphemes. Both pronouns and possessives are far richer than their English equivalents and include dual as well as singular and plural forms, and in the first person dual and plural, both inclusive and exclusive forms. The possessives, furthermore indicate the nature of the relationship of possessor to possessed object and the number of the possessed objects. The English pronoun 'our' has sixteen translations in Hawaiian:

Dual, *a*-form, inclusive, singular possessed object: *kā kā-ua;* *o*-form, inclusive, singular possessed object: *kō kā-ua.*
The above with plural possessed objects: *ā kā-ua; ō kā-ua.*
The same, exclusive; *kā mā-ua; kō mā-ua; ā mā-ua; ō mā-ua.*
The same, plural: *kā kā-kou; kō kā-kou; ā kā-kou; ō kā-kou; kā mā-kou; kō mā-kou; ā mā-kou; ō mā-kou.*

These pronouns and possessives may be considered deictic because they refer to spatial relationships of people. More obviously deictic are the demonstratives and directional particles, many of which have a four-fold sectioning. (In Table 1 words beginning *pē-* 'like unto' are called *similitude demonstratives.* Only the singular pronouns are listed in the table, but of course the threefold categorizations of the singular pronouns would apply also to the dual and plural pronouns.)

TABLE 1

	NEAR SPEAKER	NEAR ADDRESSEE	FAR FROM SPEAKER AND ADDRESSEE	NEUTRAL DISTANCE
Singular pronouns	*(w)au, a'u*	*'oe*	*ia*	
Demonstratives	*ke-la, nei*	*kē-nā, nā*	*kē-lā, lā*	*ia*
Similitude demonstratives	*pē-nei*	*pē-nā*	*pē-lā*	*pē-ia*
Directional particles	*mai* 'hither' *iho* 'down'	*a'e* 'up'	*aku* 'away'	

This is not the place to discuss the differences in meaning and distribution of the demonstratives beginning with *kē-* and *pē-*, and those that begin with neither *kē-* nor *pē-*, nor the differences of the three proximal directional particles, far more complicated than as indicated by the above glosses.

It seems certain, however, that it is almost impossible to say much of anything in Hawaiian without frequent use of the four directionals. Most verbs of motion (such as *hele,* 'to go,' *'au,* 'to swim,' or *nānā,* 'to look' are usually followed by one or the other of these particles. This forces the Hawaiian speaker and literary artist to show *relative space* in nearly every utterance, sentence, or verse. This may have some relationship, however remote, with his interest in place, in his use of traditional sayings, and in his stories and songs, especially when this is coupled with love of nature and of the land and sea. It would be interesting to compare use of place names elsewhere in the Pacific in sayings, narrative, and poetry. The grammatical structure in many related languages is similar to that of Hawaiian. Can it be said that the use of place names is equally compelling?

Pīpī holo ka'ao
Sprinkled, runs on the tale.

LITERATURE CITED

BARTHEL, THOMAS S.
    1962. "Easter Island Place-Names." *J. Soc. Océanistes* **18**:100-107.
BECKWITH, MARTHA WARREN
    1919. "The Hawaiian Romance of Laieikawai: With Introduction and Translation."
    *Bur. American Ethnology Annual Rep.*33 (for 1911-1912), pp. 285-677.
    1932. *Kepelino's Traditions of Hawaii.* B. P. Bishop Mus. Bull. 95. Honolulu.
    1970. *Hawaiian Mythology.* Honolulu: Univ. Hawaii Press. (First published in 1940.)
BENDER, BYRON WILBUR
    1963. A Linguistic Analysis of the Place-Names of the Marshall Islands. Ph.D. dissertation, Indiana University.
COULTER, JOHN WESLEY
    1935. *A Gazetteer of the Territory of Hawaii.* Univ. Hawaii Research Publ. 11. Honolulu.
ELBERT, SAMUEL H.
    1960. "The Structure of Hawaiian as a Factor in Symbolic Proliferation." *Actes VIe Congrès International Sciences Anthropologiques et Ethnologiques,* Vol. 2, pp. 65-70. Paris.
ELBERT, SAMUEL H. (Editor)
    1959. *Selections from Fornander's Hawaiian Antiquities and Folk-Lore.* Honolulu: Univ. Hawaii Press.
ELBERT, SAMUEL H., and NOELANI MAHOE
    1970. *Nā Mele o Hawai'i Nei; 101 Hawaiian Songs.* Honolulu: Univ. Hawaii Press.
ELBERT, SAMUEL H., and MARY KAWENA PUKUI
    In press. *Hawaiian Grammar.* Honolulu: Univ. Press Hawaii.
EMERSON, NATHANIEL B.
    1915. *Pele and Hiiaka: A Myth from Hawaii.* Honolulu.
FORNANDER, ABRAHAM
    1918-1919. "Fornander Collection of Hawaiian Antiquities and Folk-Lore." *Mem. B. P. Bishop Mus,* Vol. 5. Honolulu.
GIFFORD, EDWARD WINSLOW
    1923. *Tongan Place Names.* B. P. Bishop Mus. Bull. 6. Honolulu.
GOODENOUGH, WARD H.
    1966. "Notes on Truk's Place Names." *Micronesica* **2**(2):95-129.

KAMAKAU, SAMUEL M.
1961. *Ruling Chiefs of Hawaii.* Honolulu: Kamehameha Schools Press.
LUOMALA, KATHARINE
1965. "Creative Processes in Hawaiian Use of Place Names in Chants." In GEORGIOS A. MEGAS (ed.), "Lectures and Reports." 4th International Congress for Folk-Narrative Research (Athens, 1964). *Laographia* **22**:234-247.
LYONS, JOHN
1969. *Introduction to Theoretical Linguistics.* Cambridge: Cambridge Univ. Press.
MALO, DAVID
1951. *Hawaiian Antiquities (Moolelo Hawaii).* Nathaniel B. Emerson (Trans.). B. P. Bishop Mus. Spec. Pub. 2(2nd ed.). Honolulu: Bishop Mus. Press.
NAKUINA, MOSES
[n.d.] Moolelo Hawaii o Pakaa a me Ku-a- Pakaa, na Kahu Iwikuamoo o Keawenuiaumi, ke Alii o Hawaii, a o na Moopuna Hoi a Laamaomao. (Hawaiian Story of Pakaa and Ku-a-Pakaa, High Stewards of Keawenuiaumi, the Chief of Hawaii, and the Grandchildren of Laamaomao.) In Univ. Hawaii Library.
PUKUI, MARY KAWENA, and SAMUEL H. ELBERT
1966. *Place Names of Hawaii.* Honolulu: Univ. Hawaii Press.
PUKUI, MARY KAWENA, SAMUEL H. ELBERT, and ESTHER T. MOOKINI
1974. *Place Names of Hawaii.* (Revised and enlarged ed.) Honolulu: Univ. Press Hawaii.
REED, A. W.
1961. *A Dictionary of Maori Place Names.* Wellington: Reed.
STEWART, GEORGE R.
1945. *Names on the Land.* New York: Random House.
TAYLOR, ARCHER
1962. *The Proverb and an Index to the Proverb.* Hatboro, Pennsylvania: Folklore Assoc. (First printed in 1931 and 1934.)
TRAGER, GEORGE L.
1946. Review of *Names on the Land,* by George R. Stewart. *International J. American Linguistics* **12**:108-110.
WENKAM, ROBERT G.
1970. *Maui: The Last Hawaiian Place.* San Francisco: Friends of the Earth.

NEWSPAPERS

Ka Nupepa Kuokoa (The Independent Newspaper). Honolulu, 1861-1920.
Ke Au Okoa (The Independent Era). Honolulu, 1865-1873.

HAWAIIAN CHANTS AND SONGS USED IN POLITICAL CAMPAIGNS

ELEANOR WILLIAMSON

B.P. Bishop Museum, Honolulu

E ola o ka Lani
E Pauahi Lani nui
Na kau a kau.

The Chiefess lives
O Royal Pauahi
From season to season.

ALWAYS AND FOREVER ALIVE is the memory of the Princess Pauahi."
The brief introductory phrase figuratively expresses this, in a Pauahi
Lani *mele inoa*—a name song.

Charles Reed Bishop, five years after his wife's death, established
Bernice Pauahi Bishop Museum as a memorial to her. The Museum,
founded in 1889, was to be located "within the grounds of the Kamehameha School for Boys at Palama, near Honolulu." The Museum Deed
of Trust, dating to 1896, states that monies are to be spent for the
"development of . . . Bernice P. Bishop Museum as a scientific institution
for collecting, preserving, storing and exhibiting specimens of Polynesian
and Kindred Antiquities, Ethnology and Natural History and books
treating of, and pictures illustrating the same, and for the examination,
investigation, treatment and study of said specimens, and the publication
of pictures thereof, and of the results of such investigation and study."

Testimony of Mr. Bishop's foresight and continued concern is revealed
in this letter (now in Bishop Museum) to one of the seven Museum
Trustees:

San Francisco June 14, 1898

Rev.d C.M. Hyde D. D.
Honolulu

Dear Sir -

A number of years ago I attended a feast given by Liliuokalani, then Princess, at which two old natives, male and female, recited with excellent effect some old meles, one of which was said to have belonged to A. Paki. It occurred to me that those chants and others could and should be preserved by aid of the phonograph. Mr. Brigham was present and approved of the idea. Later when it was said that a phonograph was to be taken to Honolulu I sent some cylinders to Mr. Brigham, and I think that he did use some of them with what effect I do not know. At that time and most of the time since the instruments were rented on close terms and were not for sale. Now they can be bought, and I understand that a fairly good one can be bought for about $30. exclusive of cylinders. It seems to me worth while for the Museum to own a good phonograph and to secure a considerable number of native meles (ancient and modern) songs, speeches, etc. for preservation.
What do you say to it?

Yours very truly
Chas R Bishop

"Native meles (ancient and modern) songs, speeches, etc." preserved on cylinders recorded in the early 1920's are among the first Bishop Museum sound artifacts collected. These were accumulated, as funds became available, by means of recording techniques that remained in step with advances in recording technology. This evolutionary development included record discs, wire recordings, and today's sound media of vinyl discs, magnetic tapes, and cassettes.

Concentrated and systematic collection of oral narratives in the Hawaiian Islands was made possible through the cooperation of the University of Hawaii Committee for the Preservation and Study of Hawaiian Language, Art and Culture.[1] One of the aims of this Committee has been to secure proper equipment to assist Mrs. Mary Kawena Pukui, Bishop Museum Associate in Hawaiian Culture Emeritus, and myself, Assistant in Anthropology, in our recording of willing informants with

[1]The 1959 Hawaii Territorial Legislature appropriated $25,000 to the University of Hawaii. President Laurence H. Snyder appointed, in June, 1959, Father John H. McDonald of St. Catherine's Catholic Church, Kauai, as chairman of the University of Hawaii Committee for the Preservation and Study of Hawaiian Language, Art and Culture. Serving as Committee members were: Dr. Samuel H. Elbert, Professor of Pacific Languages and Linguistics, University of Hawaii, and Associate in Linguistics at the B. P. Bishop Museum; Dr. Kenneth P. Emory, Chairman Anthropology Department, Bishop Museum, and Professor of Anthropology, University of Hawaii; Mr. William C. Kea, General Commercial Manager, Hawaiian Telephone Company; Mr. Thomas Nickerson, Director Office of Publication and Information, University of Hawaii; Miss Barbara B. Smith, Associate Professor of Music, University of Hawaii; and Mr. James H. Shoemaker, Vice-President and Economist, Bank of Hawaii.

knowledge about the past throughout the Hawaiian Islands.

Such an informant was Mr. William Kaho ʻowaiwai Kāmaʻu ("Uncle Bill") of Hilo, where he died in February, 1974. The voices of his father and sister, both deceased, were already preserved on magnetic tape in the Museum's collection. Mr. Kāmaʻu's father, the Reverend W. Kāmaʻu, served as pastor of the Kawaiahaʻo Church, Honolulu, from 1934 until his death on February 4, 1944, and Mr. Charles Kenn had recorded the Reverend Kāmaʻu chanting in the early 1930's. A copy of this recording was presented to the Museum in 1951 (Bishop Mus. Tape Rec., 1951). Mrs. Anna Kāmaʻu Hoʻopiʻi was recorded in Hilo, chanting and telling a shortened version of the legend Lau-kia-manu-i-Kahiki, Bird-trapping-leaf-of-Kahiki. This recording (Bishop Mus. Tape Rec., 1952) was done by Mrs. Dorothy B. Barrère, then a Museum volunteer.

It was on June 16, 1962, during one of the visits of Mr. Kāmaʻu to Honolulu, that Uncle Bill invited Mrs. Pukui and me to visit him in Hilo, in order to record him and other Hawaii residents. August 21 and 22 of that year were spent at his home recording (Bishop Mus. Tape Rec., 1962a). These recording sessions were friendly and congenial, for Uncle Bill knew and often stayed with my father and his family in Hilo during youth and early manhood.

Uncle Bill was born July 5, 1892, at Kamaʻili, Puna District—one of ten children. His schooling was obtained at Hilo Boarding School and through correspondence courses. He retired from the Hilo County Engineering Office.

The year 1962, being an election year, provided Uncle Bill with conversational topics of deep personal interest, for in 1925 he had been elected to the Territorial Legislature as a member of the House of Representatives. In 1928, he campaigned for and won a seat in the Senate. He credits his victories to his father, who taught him the art of chanting with this advice: "Your voice is like that of the ocean. Let the voice ride along as the sea, sometimes going up and down, and then crash it against the shore."

"You'd be surprised to know that's one of the things that helped put me into politics. I quote some of them," said Uncle Bill. He then commenced chanting in the Kepakepa style of Hawaiian rhythmic recitation, which requires distinct pronunciation.

He makamaka no ka ua ia Hilo one
I ka hele no a kipa i Hanakahi.
Kipa aku, ua hala i Makakalo
Ua hele no ā nā ʻale kakali mai.
Ke kakali aʻe nei no paha ʻoukou ia Kāmaʻu
Eia au he moho e alualu nei i ka moho senetoa.

The rain is a friend of the sands of Hilo,
And goes a-calling at Hanakahi.
Now that you have called, one is gone to Makakalo,
Has gone where the billows are and there awaits.
Perhaps you are waiting for Kāmaʻu,
Here am I,
A candidate seeking to become Senator.

After Uncle Bill had chanted, Mrs. Pukui said that she recognized the poetry as part of an old *mele* belonging to Kamāmalu, and offered the older version for comparison:[2]

> He makamaka ka ua no Hilo one
> I ka hele no a kipa i Hanakahi.
> Kipa aku la ʻoe
> Ua hala aku la i Makakalo.
> Ua hele no ā nā ʻale kakali mai
> E nānā ana i ka huikau a nā lehua,
> I ka luʻuluʻu o na pua i ka nahele.
> He wahine ʻako pua ia no ka Puʻulena.
> Aia la i kai o Punahoa,
> He hoa ia la,
> No ka nahunahu ka hewa,
> He hākānele wahi a ka ʻōlelo.
> He lola ia la,
> He hepa na ke aliʻi
> O . . . e . . . anei. . . e

> The rain is a friend of the sands of Hilo,
> And goes a-calling at Hanakahi.
> Now that you have called,
> She has gone to Makakalo.
> She goes where the billows are and there awaits you.
> She looks at the lehua blossoms blooming in profusion
> At the flower-laden boughs in the forest.
> She is a flower picking woman for the Puʻulena breeze.
> There she is, down at Punahoa.
> A companion indeed!
> Except for her back-biting,
> Uttering only worthless words.
> A lazy one!
> A stupid one in the presence of the chief.
> That . . . is what she is!

The origin of this older chant can be traced to Kamāmalu, wife and half-sister of Liholiho, who became King Kamehameha II. Kamā-

---

[2]Translations are by Mrs. Pukui unless otherwise noted.

malu was jealous of the king's interest in a certain young woman, and composed this derisive chant, thus exposing the wrath of an envious female. According to Mrs. Pukui, it was certainly permissible to use small sections of another person's *mele;* however, this example was particularly interesting because of the very different intentions of the two versions.

From this recording session with Uncle Bill began an interest in the origins and use of Hawaiian chants and songs in political campaigns, for Uncle Bill was a storehouse of Hawaiian oral traditions. He said that the older people who attended his political rallies often chanted along with him and were delighted to hear the old chants once again. When he spoke to the audience of another district, he would chant a selection that would have meaning for them. For example, he said: "When we got to Kona this is what I chanted."

> Ua lupea 'ope a Kona i ka lā
> Ua hinua ke kai la'i a 'Ehu.
> Ua kā ia i ka waimaka
> Hanini a e la ma uka o 'Alana-po.
> Pō mai nei o uka i na 'ulu o Weli.
> E ho'oweliweli na ka moe ia'u,
> E like me ka hanini a ka ua pakapaka
> O ma uka a 'Alana po.
> Pela no,
> Hanini mai ana mana koho pāloka
> No William Kāma'u.

Listening to Uncle Bill, it was pleasurable to hear the clever usage of linked assonance, indicative of high poetic attainment. Unfortunately, this characteristic of Hawaiian chants becomes difficult to transmit in translation.

> Pleasingly bundled is Kona in the sun
> Sparkling on the peaceful sea of 'Ehu.
> Kona is smitten by pouring tears of the rain
> That spills yonder at 'Alana-po.
> Dark with mist is the upland breadfruit grove of Weli.
> And my dreams cause misgivings
> Like the pouring of heavy raindrops
> In the land of 'Alana-po.
> So too,
> Let your votes pour down
> On William Kāma'u.

"Then, Kohala, not much you know," said Uncle Bill as he chanted the following:

Aloha Waikā ia'u me he ipo ala
Me he ipo ala
Ka maka lena o ke ko'olau,
Ke puapua mai 'ia i luna.
A 'eha e, a 'eha e, a 'eha ho'i
'Eha i ku'iku'i a ka Ulumano
Ku i ka pahu, ku a ka 'awa'awa
Hanane'e ke kīkala i kō Hilo Kini
Hō 'īa mai a nui ka paloka
I hanane'e ai
Ke kīkala o William Kāma'u,
Ho'i hau'oli kākou a pau.

Waikā loves me as a sweetheart,
As a sweetheart
Is the yellow eye of the ko'olau blossom,
A blossoming on high.
Hurt, hurt, aye hurt,
Hurt by the pounding of the Ulumano wind
Pierced by the strong, hurling harsh wind
With laden backs, those of Hilo
Give freely of your votes
To William Kāma'u,
Let his back be laden with them,
And together we will return rejoicing.

If several lines of this chant seem familiar, it is probably because they are heard today on popular recordings under the titles "Hole Waimea" or "Waika." The latter is on Gabe Kila's *Paniolo Country* record album (1974). "Hole Waimea" may be heard on The Kamehameha Schools' recording (n.d.), *Kamehameha Sings Again;* the Hilo Hawaiians album (n.d.), *Honeymoon in Hawaii;* or Tom Kaulaheaonamoku Hiona's Folkways record (1962), *Hawaiian Chants, Hula and Music.* On this latter disc, Hiona chants "Hole Waimea" using the dance gourd, *ipu hula,* as an accompanying instrument.

Other lines from Uncle Bill's Kohala chant can be traced to "Hoe Puna i ka wa'a" (see Emerson, 1909, p. 70), skillfully blended to make a meaningful experience for his audience.

The use of Hawaiian *mele* did not end with soliciting votes, however, for a letter dated October 26, 1923, from the Reverend W. Kāma'u to the Hawaiian language newspaper *Kuokoa* (Nov. 1, 1923a), shows yet another use of traditional Hawaiian chant—a transmission of thanks to the voters who "on election day cast their 648 votes for W. K. Kāma'u, Jr., showing their faith (in him). For them my gratitude—from the waterless cliff of Panau (district of Puna) to the cliffs of spraying waterfalls at Waipi'o."

O maikaʻi Waipiʻo	Beautiful Waipiʻo
He alolua na pali	Where cliffs face each other
Pīhoihoi ka piʻina o Koaʻekea	Anxiously one ascends Koaʻekea
Hoʻo āʻiaʻi ka wai o Hiʻilawe i luna	Clear is the water of Hiʻilawe
Ua hele wale no a hoʻohuelo i na pali	Streaming tail-like down the cliffs
E ō e Hawaiʻi Hikina i ko inoa - e	Answer O East Hawaiʻi to your name,
Me ke aloha.	With affection

The Reverend Kāmaʻu's adeptness with traditional *mele* is indicated by his perceptive usage of "Maikaʻi Waipiʻo." Charles E. King set three lines of this chant to a piano arrangement in four-four time, with ukulele and guitar accompaniment. King's *Hawaiian Melodies* (1923a, p. 123) lists Princess Likelike as the composer. She is also recognized as the composer in Smith's paper, "Hawaii's Royal Composers" (1956, p. 98), and on the sound recording *Meet Palani Vaughn and the Sunday Manoa* (n.d.).

On a copy of "Maikai Waipio—Lovely Waipio," illustrated here (Fig. 1) from the Queen Liliʻuokalani music manuscripts in the Bishop Museum Library, the Queen wrote "Tune by Liliuokalani." Her music and the Hawaiian text with English translation afford the opportunity for comparisons with those of Kāmaʻu, King, Smith, and Vaughn.

The versions by the Queen and the Reverend Kamaʻu bear resemblances to "Mele Oli No Ema," discovered in a handwritten manuscript (Museum manuscript library). The *oli* is entitled "Maikai Waipio" and was described "as a famous *mele* for Queen Ema. The *mele* was very lengthy, but only a few stanzas were written. It was a *mele* liked by Kaleleonalani." The manuscript reveals several important points. The *mele oli* "was not danced to," and was delivered "with prolonged phrases chanted in one breath, often with a trill *(ʻiʻi)* at the end of each phrase (Pukui and Elbert, 1971, p. 262). Other than spelling the Queen's English name, Emma, in the Hawaiian form of Ema, the inclusion of one of the Queen's Hawaiian names, Kaleleonalani, uncovers a date, 1863, and the death of King Kamehameha IV. The husband of Queen Emma died only fifteen months after the tragic loss of their only child, the Prince of Hawaii. Ka-lele-o-na-lani, "The-flight-of-the-chiefs," became the Queen's name to commemorate her sorrowful loss.

"Maikaʻi Waipiʻo" is but one of numerous chants that chronicled Kaleleonalani's travels after the deaths of her young son and her husband. "Mele Oli No Ema" detailed her visit in Waipiʻo valley, Hawaii.

The Reverend Kāmaʻu expressed gratitude to those voters who supported his son in "Maikaʻi Waipiʻo," the poetry of which became lastingly enhanced with the "Tune by Liliuokalani."

Queen Emma's travelogue *oli* described her travels on Maui. There

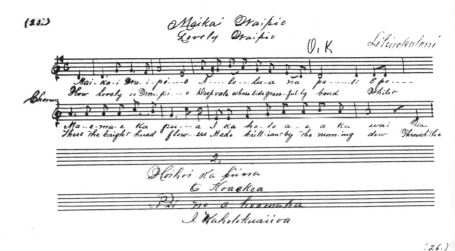

FIGURE 1

in the Makāwao district, Kaleleonalani saw the vegetation and beauties of Piʻiholo Kokomo and Haʻiku, geographic place names still used today.

MELE OLI NO EMA

Maikaʻi Waipiʻo he alolua na pali
E pōʻai a puni a hapa makai
Pīhoihoi i ka piʻina o Koaʻekea

Pi'i no a ho'omau i Ka-holo-kuaiwa
Ho'ā'ia'i ka wai o Hi'ilawe i luna
Ua hele a ho'ohuelo i na pali,
O ke ki'o wai kapu ia o Ha'iwahine
He 'oiā'i'o, 'oia paha e?
E pā wai au, a kepa kaua.

Lapa ka 'ohu o Malu-o-pokahi
Mākaukau ka 'upena lawai'a a ke kupa
E ho'āla lū ana a puni hei a manu.
Hei ma ka 'ākau, ulu mai me ka hema,
'Ohi hāpuku ka makapehu o ka uka
E ho'olale ana i ahi no ka i'a
Me he i'a ho'omalu alo o Kaukini
He 'oiā'i'o, 'oia paha e?
E pā wai au, a kepa kaua.

Maika'i Lili hemolele i ka lā
Lenalena ke oho o ke kukui nono i ka lā
Ma'ū ka 'awapuhi nolu i ka palai,
Maopopo ka 'ike i na nani o Pi'iholo
Ohi ka 'i'o o ka la'au o Makāwao.
He nani ia la he mōhala ka pali o Kokomo
E huia mai a pau na Ha'iku,
He 'oiā'i'o, 'oia paha e?
E pā wai au, a kepa kaua.

OLI CHANT FOR EMA

Beautiful is Waipi'o with cliffs facing each other.
Enclosed by cliffs except on the seaward side.
Difficult is the climb to Koa'ekea
And the continuation up to Ka-holo-kuaiwa.
Sparkling white appears the falls of Hi'ilawe
Streaming tail-like down the cliffs
Into the sacred pool of the woman, Ha'iwahine
This is true, is it not?
Let me sip some water, and let us go on our way.

The mists play about at Malu-o-pokahi
Where the native sons make ready with their nets
To stretch and shake among the aroused birds to ensnare them
Birds are caught on the right, captured on the left;
The people of the upland gather birds greedily
And urge that a fire be lit to cook their meat
To bring under the protection of Kaukini.
This is true, is it not?
Let me sip some water, and let us go on our way.

Beautiful is Lili, peaceful in the sunlight.
Yellowed are the leaves of the kukui warmed by the sun.
Moist are the ginger stalks that shelter the ferns
One can clearly see the beauties of Pi'iholo.
The bark of the trees of Makāwao, grow in thickness
Beautiful and expansive is the cliff of Kokomo,
Combined with the charms of Ha'iku.
This is true, is it not?
Let me sip some water and let us go on our way.

The Hawaiian language newspaper *Kuokoa* published numerous
songs composed for political candidates. Selected as representative of
the County of Maui is the following song for Mr. Samuel E. Kalama,
who served twenty successive years as Maui County Chairman *(Maui
News,* 1933, p. 1). His widow, Mrs. Minerva L. Kalama of Makāwao,
Maui, is now 91 years old. When asked if she remembered any of Uncle
Sam's political campaign songs, she could not recall any in its entirety.
Discovering the following song in the *Kuokoa* brought much joy to Auntie Minerva, as it did to me. I suspect that a hula tempo was sung,
as informants indicated that "lively tunes" were used at political rallies.

HE WEHI A HE LEI NO KALAMA

Ha'aheo no 'oe la e Maui,
Ua puka e ka moho a ka lāhui
Ua koho pono 'ia me ka lōkahi
I Lunamaka'ainana no ke Kalana,
Pū'iwa nā manu noho kuahiwi,
I ka 'aeko nui ho'i o ka lewa,
A he lono hau'oli kai lohe 'ia mai
Ua kau o Kalama i ka helu ki'ekie.
Ua pi'i nā hae me ka lanakila,
Ma nā moku huia o Maui nei.
Lilo i mea 'ole nā ēnēmi,
'Opu loko'ino he aloha 'ole
Kanikani pila me ka waiolina
'A'ohe hua-pa; a e loa'a mai
Ui aku ui mai nā ēnēmi
A heaha neia pilikia nui,
Ua hūhewa ia paha ke kahuna,
Ua nele i ka 'ike kilokilo lani,
Ua pa'a i ka mana o ke kūpuna,
I ka mana Kāhikolu ho'i o luna.
Welo kīhei a ke A'eloa,
I ka moho lanakila a ka Repubalika
Ku mai o Kalama me ka hiehie,
Ua 'ohu i ka lei o ka roselani,
A 'o Maui no la e ka 'oi.

Ha'ina ia mai ka puana,
A he wehi kēia nou e Kalama
Ha'ina hou ia mai ana ka puana,
Hipa, hipa, hipa, huro!

Haku ia e Alani Hikina (Kuokoa, 1923b)

A LEI OF ADORNMENT FOR KALAMA

You are proud indeed, O Maui
The people's candidate has won,
You are chosen in unity
A representative of the County,
The mountain-dwelling birds are startled
By the great eagle soaring aloft,
Joyous news has been heard
That Kalama reached the highest point
And made the banners of victory float on high
Over all the districts of Maui,
His enemies were as naught
Those with evil and unkind hearts,
That sound like fiddles
Without charms to attract sweethearts.
The enemies turn to each other
To ask what caused their failure.
Perhaps, the kahuna went off his course
In his observations of omens in the sky.
They were held down by the mana of (his) ancestors
And the Trinity from above.
The cloak of the runner waves in the A'eloa breeze.
The victorious candidate of the Republicans
Kalama stands forth in triumph
Adorned with roselani wreaths,
Which denotes Maui's excellence.
This ends our praise
A song to adorn you, O Kalama.
Again, another ending, we sing,
Hip, hip, hip, hurrah!

Composed by Alani Hikina

In a discussion of Uncle Sam's song with Mrs. Pukui, she indicated the line, "Welo kihei a ke A'eloa," is an old saying applicable to a swift person resembling the *A'eloa* wind of Ka'ū, Hawai'i. The *A'eloa* wind blew steadily, thereby causing the cloak of a swift runner to billow out from his shoulders.

Reference to *Kāhikolu,* Trinity, is found here in the line preceding that of the *A'eloa* breeze, and also in the Samuel King campaign song. Without a doubt, the composers believed that the power, *mana,* of the Trinity would assist the candidates in their political bids.

William Haʻehaʻe Heen was in his eighties when I showed him two songs from the *Kuokoa*. Although it was almost forty years since Bill Heen had seen the two songs, which were used to attract voters in his political campaigns, he remembered that "He ʻOhu Lei No W. H. Heen" was sung to the tune of "Na Lii" (King, 1948, p. 86). The music of "Na Moku Eha" (King, 1923b, p. 80), was the melody for "He Inoa Keia No Haʻehaʻe."

The practice of setting poetry to another person's melody reveals a characteristic feature of Hawaiian music, for the poetry is of primary importance in conveying the message, whether in chanted or melodic form.

When Mr. Heen campaigned for his second term as City and County Attorney of Honolulu, these two songs were performed while political supporters presented colorful leis to adorn the candidate. The flower leis have withered, but the poetic descriptions of the event in the "lei" songs have remained fresh for more than forty years.

HE ʻOHU LEI NO W. H. HEEN

He wehi kēia no Haʻehaʻe,
Ka moho lanakila a ka lehulehu.
Ka wehi ʻohuʻohu no ke kanaka,
A nau ia e lei mau aku,
Ua piha ʻoliʻoli Oʻahu nui,
Nā kini o ka ua Kūkalahale,
Ua hōʻike mai nā mana koho,
Ka manaʻo hiaʻai o ka lōkāhi,
Aia me ʻoe ka ipo nohea,
A ka puʻuwai a e haulani nei
Ua lono e ka iʻa hāmau leo
I ka leo o ke kai o Waialua,
Haʻehaʻe ke kilo kānāwai,
Kuhikuhi puʻuone o Hawaiʻi.
This is your lei of honor,
O William Haʻehaʻe Heen,
Haʻina ko wehi lei hanohano,
Wiliama Haʻehaʻe Heen.
E ... ō ....

Haku ia e S. K. K. (*Kuokoa*, 1923c, p. 4)

The Kūkalahale is a famous rain in Honolulu (Pukui and Elbert 1971, p. 334). The poetic name of the area surrounding Pearl Harbor is "ka iʻa hāmau leo," the land of the silent fish, literally, "sea creature that silences the voice, so called for a taboo of silence maintained by fishermen there" (Pukui and Elbert, 1971, p. 88).

LEI TO ADORN W. H. HEEN

This is an adornment for Ha'eha'e
The victorious candidate of the people
To decorate and adorn a man.
It is for you to wear always,
Much joy fills great O'ahu,
The dwellers in the Kūkalahele rain.
The voters have expressed their thoughts
Of delight and of unity.
With you, their love like that of a lover
A joy that dwells in the heart.
The land of the "silent fish" hears of him,
And the voice of the sea of Waialua,
Ha'eha'e shall be the guardian of the law.
As advisor for the benefit of the land.
This is your lei of honor,
O William Ha'eha'e Heen,
Answer us.

Composed by S. K. K.

When a chant or song concluded with "E . . . ō," Hawaiian etiquette
required that the person being honored reply with, "Yes, I am here."
ȝ . . . ō.

HE INOA KEIA NO HA'EHA'E

He inoa kēia no Ha'eha'e,
Ka moho a ka lāhui ua lanakila,
Ko lei kēia o ka hanohano,
Eia me 'oe e lei mau ai.
He wehi me kilakila i nohea 'ia,
Ho'okāhi pu'uwai a ka lehulehu.
Ka hea mai nei a o Ha'eha'e,
O'oe ka mākou a e li'a mau ai.
E ō ka inoa a o Ha'eha'e,
Ka moho lanakila me ka hanohano.
Ha'ina mai ka puana he lei aloha,
Ua kau i ka hanohano ka luna wēkiu.
Ha'ina ka puana he lei i aloha ia,
Ha'eha'e e ka moho ua lanakila.

Hakua ia e Helen K. Davis (*Kuokoa*, 1923d)

THIS IS A NAME SONG FOR HA'EHA'E

This is a name song for Ha'eha'e
The victorious candidate of the people.
A "lei" this is, to honor him,

FIGURE 2

Adornment of victory to bedeck him.
All of the people are in harmony
As they call upon Ha'eha'e,
You are the one we delight in
Answer to your name, O Ha'eha'e,
A victorious and honored candidate.
This ends our affectionate praise,
(For one) who has reached the pinnacle.
Again, a repetition of our "lei" of affection,
Ha'eha'e, the candidate who is victorious.

Composed by Helen K. Davis

The "lei aloha," strung by the composer, comprises the words in her lei of affection.

A political song for Mr. Curtis Piehu Iaukea was recorded on a commercial disc (Columbia Y-20, n.d.) by Ernest Ka'ai and Glee Club. Mr. Ka'ai published the song "Lanakila Iaukea," in *Souvenir Collection of Hawaiian Songs and Views*, a copy of which was a gift to the Museum from Mike Fern of Kauai. No indication of date is noted in the book, which was "Published with the approval of the Hawaii Promotion Committee." The Hilo Hawaiians and the *Kamehameha Sings Again* recordings of "Hole Waimea," mentioned earlier in this paper, follow the melodic line of the music of Mr. Ka'ai, illustrated here as Figure 2, for "Lanakila Iaukea." The song was remembered by Mrs. Minerva Ka-ama from her Hawaiian 78-rpm record collection. The Hawaii State Archives documents 1906-1908 as the period in which Mr. Iaukea served as Oahu County Sheriff. Was the song composed for that election period? The dating of music, in published or on audio recordings, as done on the Kila *Paniolo* disc (1974) assists toward accurate research into Hawaiian music.

LANAKILA IAUKEA

He aloha 'aina   An (expression of) love for the land
'U'uwai o ka 'onipa'a   Held firmly in the heart
Kukilakila no ka lāhui   Majestically standing for the people,
Nā ēwe o Hawai'i.   Descendants of Hawaii.
A kau i ka lanakila   Go on to victory,
I ka moho Iaukea.   O, candidate Iaukea.

Hui   Chorus
Kui ia e ka leihiwahiwa   String the choice lei
Wili ia ke aloha me ka lōkāhi.   Entwine it with love and peace.
hōkū alaka'i Iaukea.   Let Iaukea be the guiding star.

Na ka 'I me ka mahi   To the 'I and Mahi Chiefs,
Nei lei mamo liko.   This choice mamo wreath belongs.
'Ōiwi pono'i no ka iwikuamo'o   A true native, of royal descent
Imua e ke alo e na poki'i   Go forward for your younger brethren
A welo e ka hae Iaukea.   Let the flag be unfurled for Iaukea.

Colonel Iaukea and the Honorable Robert William Kalanihiapo Wilcox played important roles during the reigns of King David Kalākaua and his sister, Queen Lili'uokalani. From the *Kuokoa* (1900) comes this report and song for Wilcox.

Because of the selections of most of the eligible voters, that the honors at this election time were given to R. W. Wilcox, to be delegate to Congress in Washington. Having received this victory, the members of the Home Rule party were filled with joy, and when the cock crowed at dawn, several nights ago, the "ko-ko" (cluck-cluck) of the mother hens could be heard below.

MELE NO WILIKOKI

Kaulana e ka moho o ka lāhui   Famed is the people's choice
Ka 'Elele a nā maka'ainana   The Delegate for plain people
Noho mai Hawai'i puni o Keawe   Hawai'i land of Keawe abides
Ua lawe i ka hae o ka lanakila.   To bear the banner of victory.

Mikioi na hana a Maui o Hina   Maui of Hina works with neatness
No'ono'o kaulike me ka noe'au   Thinks fairly and with wisdom
Eia Moloka'i nui o Kama   Here is Moloka'i, great isle of Kama
Hi'ipoi mai ana i ke aloha.   Who embraces her gift of love.

A Wilikoki a mau loa   May Wilcox abide forever more
Me na keiki a o ke kaona.   With the lads of the town.
Kako'o mai Kaua'i o Mano   Kaua'i of Mano lends support
I ka pua kaulana a Kamehameha.   To a famous son of Kamehameha.

Ku'i mai e ka lono lohe ke kaona   News went forth to be heard in town
Ua puka Wilikoki me ka hanohano.   That Wilcox had won with honors,
Hanohano ke aloha ua kuni ia   Wonderful is love, firmly affixed,
Ma na welelau a o ka makani.   Borne along by the tips of the breeze.

Ia 'oe e O'ahu Kakuhihewa   O O'ahu, Kakuhihewa's island,
Mālama ia iho ko milimili   Take good care of your cherished one.
O ka mea kaunui a ka lāhui   He, on whom the people depend
Ma na 'Ailana a'o Hawai'i.   Throughout the islands of Hawai'i.

Me 'oe ke aloha ua poni ia   Love for him has been established
Me na pu'uwai o ka lehulehu   From the hearts of the people.
E ola ka 'Elele a ka lāhui   Long live the People's Delegate
A kau i ka heke o ka lanakila.   To be at the very top of victory.

Ia'ina ia mai ana ka puana	Here ends our song for
Wilikoki ka 'Elele i aloha ia.	Wilcox, the beloved Delegate.

Haku ia e David Umi, Honolulu	Composed by David Umi, Honolulu

Mrs. Helen W. Salazar, a granddaughter of R. W. Wilcox, has set "Mele No Wilikoki" to a hula melody, so that "this song for Hawai'i's first delegate will live." Mrs. Salazar has altered the first and third lines of the second stanza to: "Mikioi na hana a Maui o Kama/Eia Moloka'i nui o Hina." Kama, shortened from Kamalalawalu, was the chief of Maui and Hina's island is Moloka'i. The next *mele,* for Prince Jonah Kuhio Kalaniana'ole, followed the traditional position of Kama for Maui, and Hina to Moloka'i.

Prince Kuhio was the second Delegate to the United States Congress, and represented the Territory of Hawaii in 1902, serving ten consecutive terms (Sixty-seventh Congress, 1924, p. 7). As a political aspirant for the Delegate's position, he found it expedient to convince voters from each island as evidenced in the following twenty-eight poetic lines, from Mrs. Pukui's collection.

KALANIANA'OLE	KALANIANA'OLE
anakila ka 'elele ho'opono	Victory for the rightful delegate
Kalaniana'ole kau i ka wēkiu.	Kalaniana'ole appears at the summit.
ō'ike o Makoa ka'u kukini	Makoa, my swift messenger revealed
ohe Wakinekona puni ka honua.	Washington and the world heard.
iloka lōkahi me ka 'i'ini.	Votes united with desire
uni 'ia a pa'a i ka pu'uwai.	Firmly kindled in the heart.
O'ahu-a-aKākuhihewa	O O'ahu, island of Kakuhihewa,
a ko lei, ko milimili.	Here is your darling, your pet.
'oe e ka pua o ke kalaunu	He was a child, close to the crowned (heads)
e ke kapa 'ahu'ula o ke kūpuna.	His ancestors wore the sacred feathered capes.
Hawai'i nui o Keawe,	O great Hawai'i, island of Keawe,
a ko mamo ua lanakila.	Here is your offspring, he has won the victory.
ō'ike mai e ka pae 'ōpua	The horizon clouds reveal this
a pūnohu 'ula i ka malie.	The red rainbow in the clouds, also.
Maui-nui-o-Kama.	O great Maui, island of Kama,
'ipoi mai ia Kūhiō.	Cherish Prince Kuhio.

FIGURE 3

A ka hiwahiwa 'oe a ka mākua
A he lei 'ā'ī na ke kūpuna.

A beloved child of his parents,
A choice one to his grandparents.

Kaua'i-nui-o-Mano e
Kia'i 'ia mai ko pulapula.

O great Kauá'i, island of Mano,
Watch over your hereditary chief.

E Hiku, e Lono o ke kuahiwi
Mālama i ka wohi a ka lāhui.

O Hiku and Lono of the mountains
Take care of the people's pride.

E Moloka'i-nui-a-Hina
Na Mana Nui e aloha mai.

O great Moloka'i, island of Hina,
May the Great Powers show their love.

Kaupaona 'ia mai na 'ōlelo,
Kōkua na lani ua poni 'ia.

By weighing the spoken words carefully
May they give support to the anointed one.

E ola 'oe me kou lāhui,
O Kalaniana'ole ua lanakila.

Long may you and your people live,
O Kalaniana'ole, the victory is yours.

The late Miss Johanna Niau Wilcox, one of Dr. Samuel Elbert's students in Hawaiian language, began to do volunteer work at the Museum in May, 1962. Miss Wilcox, a retired Hawaii State employee of the Transportation Division and a Hawaiian musician of note, died in June of 1974. She began assisting with tape transcriptions in the record ing lab of the Museum's Department of Anthropology and soon realized the value of taped oral preservation. As opportunity arose, she recorded old songs that she recalled, and songs of her own composition. One of these is a song for former Governor Samuel Wilder King, with words and music by Miss Wilcox (Fig. 3).

She wrote this in 1936 when Mr. King ran for re-election to the office of Delegate to Congress from the Territory of Hawaii. Her translation is included with these comments.

For campaign purposes, a song must be short. After the candidate launches into his speech, and his plea for votes to elect him to the office he seeks, his musicians would sing campaign songs, as the candidate received leis from his supporters. My song was favored by Sam King.

KAMUELA KING	SAMUEL KING
Kaulana Kamuela King i kou inoa	Distinguished is Samuel King
Ka 'Elele Lāhui i Wakinekona.	Hawai'i's Delegate in Washington.
E pua nani 'oe nō Hawai'i	You are a choice flower of Hawai'i
A ka lehulehu a'e hi'ipoi nei.	Cherished by its people
Eala e Hawai'i nui ākea,	Arise — All you of Hawai'i
E kāhi ka mana'o me ke aloha.	Stand together in unity and love.

Ka Makua Mau Loa kou kōkua.   May our Heavenly Father help you.
Ka Mana Kāhikolu kou Alaka'i.   And the Holy Trinity guide you.

E ō 'e Kamuela King i kou inoa   Respond to your name song, Samuel King
Ka 'Elele Lāhui i Wakinekona.   Delegate of the people in Washington
                                          (Bishop Mus. Tape Rec. 1962b)

The music transcription was done by Stephen La'anui Salazar, great grandson of Robert W. Wilcox and a grand nephew of Johanna N Wilcox.

Another composer and collector of Hawaiian political campaign songs is Mrs. Alice Namakelua. From the age of sixteen, she attended political rallies with pencil and paper to collect songs which were present-ed for various candidates on the island of Hawai'i. She recorded the following: "Sometimes, one would hear the same tune four times, bu with different words for each candidate. That never bothered anyone because the words were what people listened to" (Bishop Mus. Tape Rec., 1961).

Although the composition of Hawaiian political campaign songs fo various candidates has dwindled, the 1962 Hawai'i State elections re vealed the creativeness of Mrs. Namakelua. She composed a campaign song for Mr. Theodore Nobriga, who was a candidate for the office of Lieutenant Governor. Although an unsuccessful candidate, Mr. Nobri ga stands out as the only candidate on this island for whom a politica campaign song was specially composed with words and music by a devot ed employee, for Mrs. Namakelua is retired from the City Parks an Recreation Department, where Mr. Nobriga was Director. She also com posed campaign songs for Mayor Neal Blaisdell, and for Governor John A. Burns when he was a candidate in 1956 for Delegate to Washingto (Namakelua, 1973, unnumbered pages).

Much more on political campaigns remains to be translated from the Hawaiian language newspapers and transcribed from the magneti tapes in Bishop Museum. The rewarding task of transcribing and trans lating continues with Mrs. Pukui for, although she was officially retire in 1961 from the Museum, she still offers her untiring service to he life interest—that of preserving Hawaiian culture and presenting it from the Hawaiian viewpoint. Although these accounts are considered b some to be "old fashioned and superstitious," it is apparent from th information presented here that, in "collecting, preserving, storing an exhibiting" Hawaiian oral and written traditions, Mr. Bishop's question "What do you say to it?" is being answered.

E ola o ka Lani
E Pauahi Lani nui
Na kau a kau.

The Chiefess lives
O Royal Pauahi
From season to season.

"Always and forever alive is the memory of the Princess Pauahi."

LITERATURE CITED

COMMITTEE FOR THE PRESERVATION AND STUDY OF HAWAIIAN LANGUAGE, ART AND CULTURE
    1970. *Preserving Hawaiian Culture: Progress Report.* Honolulu: Univ. Hawaii.
EMERSON, NATHANIEL B.
    1909. *Unwritten Literature of Hawaii: The Sacred Songs of the Hula.* Bur. American Ethnology Bull. 38. Washington, D.C.
FORNANDER, ABRAHAM
    1916-1917. "Hawaiian Antiquities and Folk-lore." *Mem. B.P. Bishop Mus.* 4:596-609.
HODGES, WM. C., JR., and ERNEST KAAI
    (n.d.) "Lanakila Iaukea." *Souvenir Collection of Hawaiian Songs and Views*, pp. 37-38. Honolulu.
KUOKOA, KA NUPEPA [The Independent Newspaper]
    1900. "Mele No Wilikoki." Nov. 16, p. 2. Honolulu.
    1923a. "Letter from William Kamau." Nov. 11, p. 8. Honolulu.
    1923b. "He Wehi A He Lei No Kalama." Nov. 15, p. 4. Honolulu.
    1923c. "He Ohu Lei No W.H. Heen." Nov. 15, p. 4. Honolulu.
    1923d. "He Inoa Keia No Haehae." Nov. 15, p. 4. Honolulu.
KING, CHARLES E.
    1923a. "Maikai Waipio." *Hawaiian Melodies*, p. 123. Honolulu.
    1923b. "Na Moku Eha." *Hawaiian Melodies*, p. 80. Honolulu.
    1948. "Na Lii." *Hawaiian Melodies*, p. 86. Honolulu.
MAUI NEWS
    1933. "Samuel E. Kalama, Maui County Chairman." Feb. 28, p. 1. Wailuku.
NAMAKELUA, ALICE
    1973. *"Aunty Alice" Namakelua's Lifetime Hawaiian Compositions.* Honolulu: Heinz-Guenther Pink.
PUKUI, MARY KAWENA, and S. H. ELBERT
    1971. *Hawaiian Dictionary.* Honolulu: Univ. Hawaii Press.
SIXTY-SEVENTH CONGRESS OF THE UNITED STATES.
    1924. "Memorial Address. Jonah Kuhio Kalanianaole." Jan. 7, 1923, p. 7. Washington, D.C.
SMITH, EMERSON
    1956. "Hawaii's Royal Composers." *Paradise of the Pacific Holiday Annual.* Honolulu.

RECORDINGS CITED
MUSEUM RECORDINGS

BERNICE P. BISHOP MUSEUM TAPE RECORDINGS
1951. H-15 Reverend William K. Kamau. Honolulu.
1952. H-25.1 Mrs. Anna K. Hoopii. Hilo.
1961. H-86 E Mrs. Alice Namakelua. Honolulu.
1962a. H-110 A Mr. William K. Kamau. Hilo.
1962b. H-104 A Miss Johanna N. Wilcox. Honolulu.

COMMERCIAL RECORDINGS

HILO HAWAIIANS
[n.d.] "Hole Waimea." *Honeymoon in Hawaii*. Concert Disc M-1046.
HIONA, TOM
1962. "Hole Waimea." *Hawaiian Chant, Hula and Music*. Folkways Records FW 8750
New York.
KAAI, ERNEST, AND GLEE CLUB
[n.d.] "Lanakila Iaukea." Columbia Y-20.
KAMEHAMEHA SCHOOLS, THE
[n.d.] "Hole Waimea." *Kamehameha Sings Again*. Kamehameha Schools KA 10
Honolulu.
KILA, GABE, AND THE NANAKULI SONS
1974. "Waika," and "Waimea Waltz." *Panilo Country*. J-San Records JSR 1974-
Kailua, Hawaii.
VAUGHN, PALANI, AND THE SUNDAY MANOA
[n.d.] "Maikai Waipio." *Meet Palani Vaughn and the Sunday Manoa*. Hula Record
HS 524. Honolulu.

THE FIREBALL IN HAWAIIAN FOLKLORE

WILLIAM K. KIKUCHI*

University of Arizona, Tucson

A LMOST EVERY CHILD raised in the Hawaiian Islands has participated in circles of storytelling. The most requested and awe-inspiring stories are those dealing with the supernatural, commonly called *kahuna* in Hawaiian, *obake* in Japanese, and "chicken-skin," or ghost stories, in English. The popularity of these tales cuts across ethnic groups and includes persons of all ages. Various ethnic groups in Hawaii have contributed their own motifs, resulting in creolized tales that are the legends of 20th-century Hawaii.

Supernatural tales and legends of pre-European Hawaii and multi-ethnic Hawaii all have a common role, that is, to instruct the listener in what can be termed appropriate behavior patterns. Fitting rewards and punishments are learned from each tale. By entertaining the listener, by attracting and holding his attention, these tales educate in a subtle manner and instill a respect for right and wrong in selected areas of behavior.

One of the motifs of Hawaiian supernatural tales is *akualele,* the "flying god" or fireball. *Akualele* seems to be a supernatural phenomenon and not a physical manifestation. It cannot or has not been associated with natural phenomena, such as flaming balls of gas or firebrands. This paper will examine the role and function of *akualele* tales in pre- and post-European Hawaii.

Pre-European Hawaiian society was a highly stratified, integrated, and cohesive organization. The physical universe was the result of the

*I would like to acknowledge the late Professor James E. McDonald of the University of Arizona for his encouragement and kind assistance in the preparation of this paper. Also, I extend my appreciation to Mrs. Mary Kawena Pukui, without whose help this paper would not have been completed.

mating of the gods. Every object in it was named and had its own role and function. Men and women were but a portion of this network, and in order to regulate or perpetuate the order and nature of things, it was necessary to practice life within the rules and regulations set down by supernatural beings as well as by human beings. Gods, demons, and spirits permeated the realm of man, rewarding him who lived according to the supernatural dictates and punishing him who lived in violation of such dictates. Appropriate behavior was the key to a successful life in ancient Hawaii. Man's universe worked smoothly until he disrupted it by inappropriate actions.

Chiefs and priests commanded the power needed to enforce organized and ritual sanctions in order to maintain, insure, and integrate the worldly society. Priests had wide sacred powers, but narrow political powers, whereas the converse was true for the chiefs. The concept of chiefly sanctity was brought to its peak development in Hawaii, in contrast to its Polynesian neighbors (Goldman, 1970, p. 521).

In 1819, with the overthrow of the *kapu* system, Liholiho and his faction of chiefs sought to abolish the physical manifestations of the ancient religion by ordering the destruction of temples and images. This political maneuver sought to destroy the religious and supernatural foundations of the society (Levin, 1968, pp. 402, 427), which then caused the believers of the old faith to "go underground." The myths, traditions and legends of Hawaii were slowly to atrophy. From 1820 the islands were to undergo considerable acculturation in the life styles of the people and an increasing intermarriage of both the genetic and the cultural aspects of the society.

The influx of a great number of Asiatic immigrants in the late 1800's and early 1900's brought a strong source of cultural and genetic influence into Hawaii. These were, in the majority, peasants in the working class who were under contract to the dominating minority of the Western Caucasian group who had settled earlier and sought financial gains in the islands.

Hawaiian values, ethics, morals, and traditions are still perpetuated today in spite of 150 years of Western acculturation and nearly 100 years of strong Asiatic influence. The identity of the Hawaiians, as studied by Beaglehole (1937), Handy and Pukui (1958), Forster (1960), and Gallimore and Howard (1968) in widely separated areas around th islands, is maintained in many ways. One of these is supernatural tales

THE FIREBALL MOTIF IN OCEANIA

Many fireball motifs have been recorded and indexed by Kirtle

(1971) and Thompson (1936), as shown in the accompanying table. In these motifs, common items are the luminous nature of each, the relationship of light to astral bodies, and fire. Many of the fireball motifs center on vengeance and sorcery, and in essence relate light and fire to demons and vengeful gods.

The motifs are found principally in Polynesia, the Polynesian Outliers, and in Japan. (The presence of fireball motifs does not here imply a common origin, but rather that the development of similar themes occurred independently both temporally and spatially.) In Polynesia the motif has been recorded in the Hawaiian Islands, Society Islands, Mangareva, Ellice Islands, Rangiroa Atoll in the Tuamotu Archipelago, Samoa, Rarotonga in the Cook Islands, Rurutu in the Austral Group, Chatham Island, and New Zealand.

In Tahiti, Tane, one of the major gods in the pantheon of gods, was represented as a meteor which was cone-shaped and had a large head with the body terminating in a point and a long tail (Beckwith, 1970, p. 113). Ave-aitu and nameless spirits were sent as fetchers on errands of sorcery. Ave-aitu, a guide for Tane's host in time of war, flew about shaped as a comet (Henry, 1928, p 379). Ave-aitu and deified warriors were embedded in a sacred wood *(pua)* and sent as agents of sorcery (Beckwith, 1970, p. 114).

On Rangiroa the fireball was called *kaha,* an object supposedly half man and half animal, and was buried in a specific temple. This *kaha* would leave its home and rise to the tops of the coconut trees while changing its color from blue to green to red and then would fly to another temple. Its flight was an omen of a forthcoming event.

In Rurutu the fireball, *walua-ino,* is greatly feared. This fireball represents the souls of men who were sacrificed at the temples in ancient times. It is oval, has a yellowish glow, and its flight leaves a trail much like a neon light. Its mission is to cause sickness and death. There was no way to stop or divert such fireballs, and one reason for the acceptance of Christianity was to counter these evil spirits.

Among the Maoris of New Zealand, Rongo-mai, another of the major Polynesian gods, came to earth "like a shooting star or comet or flame of fire" (White, 1887, p. 109). On one occasion Rongo-mai's mission was to lead the attack of the Nga-ti-hau against the Nga-ti-awa.

In the Polynesian Outliers fireball motifs are known from Rennell, Bellona, Tikopia, and Kapingamarangi. On Rennell "shooting stars" were not considered stars or any other astronomical phenomena, but rather gods in flight. There were three types, *ta'e hetu'u, bulighoba,* and *tangagoa,* each larger than the preceding one. *Tangagoa* is described as a huge fireball, red at night, but whitish during the day (Elbert and

Monberg, 1965, pp. 91-92). As in the case of *Tangagoa,* who, as a fireball, kills a girl for speaking his name at night, the fireball, or *ugaimami,* is related to the meting out of a punishment.

It is only in Japan that documentation of each story can pinpoint the dates at which the fireball motifs began. Japanese mythology contains at least twelve types of fire or lights of supernatural origin (Davis, 1920, p. 357), and the numerous tales of these supernatural occurrences make entertaining listening. Usually the fireball motif is connected with humans who have been wronged. They were either killed or died, and then returned to the living as a reminder of a misdeed (Davis, 1920, pp. 344, 357-358; Ferguson and Anesaki, 1928, pp. 237, 239).

The words for the phenomenon in Japan are *tama-shii,* ball-wind, and *hinotama,* fireball. The Japanese motif equates the fireball with a human soul, which burns and glows with the torment of hatred, jealousy, revenge, or love. The appearance of a fireball can be related to an offense in the mortal world which must be revenged or cleared before the soul of the offended can rest. Hence the fireball has a sanction-fulfilling role, either to revenge itself, or, less drastically, to warn close ones of a break in the harmonious relationship between the mortal and supernatural worlds.

Only one example of the fireball motif was found in Melanesia, on Dobu in the Solomon Islands. Beckwith (1970, p. 113) reports that on

TABLE 1

FIREBALL MOTIFS RECORDED AND INDEXED BY
KIRTLEY AND THOMPSON

	KIRTLEY	THOMPSON
(1) Luminous (blazing) ghosts	E 421.3	F 574
(2) God in form of comet	A 124.5	
(3) God descends in form of shooting star	A 171.0.3.2	
(4) God represented as meteor	A 137.16	
(5) Comet's appearance as omen of death	D 1812.5.1.6.2	
(6) Shooting stars magically caused to kill	D 2061.2.10	
(7) Ghost as firebrand	E 421.3.2	E 421.3.2
(8) Luminous spirits	F 401.2	E 421.3
(9) Spirit resembles meteor	F 401.19	
(10) Will-o'-the-Wisp	F 491	K 1888
(11) Comet as evil spirit	F 499.4	
(12) Soul as light		E 742
(13) Soul as Will-o'-the-Wisp		E 742.2

Dobu the idea of the fireball as fetchers may be a primitive theme. The Dobuans believed that the fireball was the flaming pubes of witches as they flew at night. A similar theme is found in the Hawaiian Islands where Kapo-'ula-kina'u flew as a fireball and had the power to detach her vagina and send it flying away. This idea may be related to the tremendous powers which the sight of women's vaginas and buttocks had in influencing spirits and as the ultimate gesture of defiance.

Further search into the literature of Micronesia and Southeast Asia might reveal other examples of the fireball motif. However, enough has been stated for comparative purposes.

NATIVE HAWAIIAN BELIEFS

The *akualele* seems to be related to sorcery, a pervasive force in Hawaiian life. Indeed, Beckwith (1970, p.105) felt that it "had become one of the strongest forces in shaping the life and character of the Hawaiian people and in determining the careers of their leaders."

The antiquity and evolution of sorcery in the Hawaiian Islands is unknown. In the author's opinion, the development and refinement of sorcery can be related to the second migration of peoples into the islands from the Society Islands. During this period, the sophistication of the arts and crafts and the development of classes of professionals with their guardian gods seem to be the seeding bed for the development of sorcery, which had its origin in the gods and demigods to be discussed. The fireball was one of the body forms of these supernatural beings.

One of the families of lesser gods who came from Tahiti to dwell in Hawaii was the family of Pele, goddess of the volcano. Pele's family consisted of seven brothers and six sisters, all expert in some form of sorcery and in the *hula*. As was typical of Hawaiian demigods, Pele could assume many body and object forms, or *kino lau*. She was able to change her form to become a blazing flame, a beautiful young girl, or an old hag (Pukui and Elbert, 1957, p.141). One of her forms of travel was as a ball of fire traversing the mountains (Handy, 1968, p.52).

Born from the same mother as Pele, the sorceress Haumea, was Laka, patron of the *hula*, the goddess of love, the fertile, the impregnated one from whom future generations issued (Beckwith, 1970, p.186). She was conceptualized as two individuals residing in one body. As Laka, she was the mild, loving patron of the *hula*, but as Kapo-'ula-Kina'u she became the angry sanctioneer, the keeper and guardian of *hula* tabus.

Kapo-'ula-Kina'u, Kapo-of-the-red-streak or Kapo-red-spotted, preceded the Pele family migration to the islands. Wherever Kapo and her sisters stopped in their migration through the islands, she established a school for the *hula* (Handy and Pukui, 1958, p.124). She was represented by the color red, the plant *hala-pepe (Dracaena aurea)*, and the *'ohe* tree *(Reynoldsia sandwicensis)*. The *kahuna'anā'anā*, or sorcerers, who served Kapo, wore dress items of red, such as red loincloths, and displayed red banners (Emerson, 1965, p.42). Kapo's principal function was to guard the rituals of the *hula* and to punish those who violated its rules. In her missions of punishment Kapo assumed the form of a fireball.

Kāne-i-kaulana'ula, Kāne-in-the-floating-red-cloud or Kāne-in-the-red-flush-of-victory, a god who was also associated with Kapo-'ula-Kina'u and who punished those violating the *hula* rituals, was seen as an avenging fireball (Emerson, 1965, p.33). Red was also the color identified with him.

In the prehistory of the islands, three gods, Kapo-'ula-Kina'u, Kāne-i-kaulana-'ula, and Ka-huila-o-ka-lani, entered a grove of trees on Molokai with a tremendous flash of lightning. They entered the *'ohe* tree, *nīoi* tree *(Eugenia)*, and *a'e* tree *(Sapindus saponaria* f. *inaequalis)*, respectively, and transmitted their powers into the wood (Beckwith, 1970, p.111; Westervelt, 1963, p.114). Pukui and Elbert (1957, p.112), refer to the *kauila, Alphitonia ponderosa*, rather than the *a'e* tree. The *nīoi* tree with the body of Kāne-i-kaulana-'ula was hewn into an image which was called Kālai-pāhoa, cut with a *pāhoa* adz. This *nīoi* tree was so filled with power that its chips killed the carvers on contact. Any portion of this image of the poison god, whether touched or consumed, would kill. Even physical contact of the image with the same type of wood transmitted its power to that wood. Consequently, *nīoi* wood was sought and brought into contact with Kālai-pāhoa so that the wood could be used for sorcery. When the caretaker wished to send the spirit within the wood on a mission, he scratched the wood and the spirit would fly at night in the form of a fireball, large at the head and tapering off to a tail (Beckwith, 1970, p.113).

The war god of Liloa, king of part of the island of Hawaii, was named Kā'ili (the snatcher) and was passed on to Liloa's son 'Umi (Beckwith, 1970, p.113). Ellis, in his tour of the island of Hawaii in 1823, noted that the location where the image of Tairi (Kā'ili) once stood was the area from which *akualele* were seen to come, flying in the evening in the form of a luminous substance like a flame, much like a comet with a tail (Ellis, 1917, p.90). His informants mentioned that since the abolition of idolatry, in 1819, Tairi had not been seen, because his image had been destroyed and his worship discontinued.

There were two principal types of spirits that associated themselves with individuals—the *'aumakua* and the *'unihipili*. The *'aumakua* ranked below the gods and demigods and existed in many forms, from animals to astral bodies. These were ancestral gods or gods worshiped by craft guilds and did not manifest themselves as *akualele*.

The *'unihipili*, on the other hand, were spirits of dead people and could be acquired by invoking them, feeding and caring for them. The keeper gave the spirit *mana*, or power, by feeding it. The spirit would rest on its keeper and whisper information to him. At times the spirit was seen as a blazing light on the shoulder of the keeper (Westervelt, 1963, p.251).

Both *'aumakua* and *'unihipili* could be beneficial as well as harmful. They punished their human caretakers if they violated laws of the spirits. It was the caretaker who decided the role of his spirit, that is, whether it would be beneficial or harmful. Thus, it was the caretaker who decided his own fate. On errands of sorcery the *'unihipili* were sent as *akualele*, and the death of the victim soon followed.

In the legend of Pūma'ia, Fornander describes Pūma'ia's soul as a blazing spirit that flew about seeking its human body and finally finding it in the temple of Kūali'i. He flew about and raided the Kūali'i neighborhood of food and valuables seeking vengeance for a misdeed (Fornander, 1916, pp.472, 474).

According to Kamakau, after Kamehameha returned to the island of Hawaii in 1812, sorcery became widespread (Kamakau, 1964, p.134). Much of the sorcery at this time was concerned with wooden bundles containing Kālai-pāhoa *mana* and was called *akua-kumu-haka* sorcery. *Akualele* were described as resembling "fire rockets," flying great distances. When it was within the wood, the god-spirit was content. However, when scratched by its keeper, it would fly out, pulsating as though throbbing in anger at being hurt. After Kamehameha's death, the original Kālai-pāhoa image was cut into sections and distributed among selected chiefs.

Akualele, or *akua-kumu-haka*, was said to have been a common occurrence from the time of the abolition of the *kapu* in 1819 until 1830 (Kamakau, 1964, p.135). This may be related to the increasing frequency of deaths of native Hawaiians from foreign diseases. In the Puna district of Hawaii Kālai-pāhoa sorcery was still very much feared as late as the 1920's. Deaths by tuberculosis were attributed to the fetchers which flew about without any keepers to care for them (Beckwith, 1970, p.113 and Notes).

HISTORIC PERIOD

Well into the historic period, as late as the turn of the 20th century, *akualele* were only occasionally seen. The diminishing indigenous Hawaiian population and the increasing pressures of Western acculturation probably account for the smaller number of *akualele* sightings. The changing composition of the population tended to dilute the "Hawaiianness" of the total culture and folklore. However, the influx of a large Japanese immigrant labor force tended to reinforce the local beliefs in *akualele*. It is only among the Hawaiian and Japanese ethnic groups in Hawaii that one finds a similarity of folklore concerning fireballs and luminous flying objects. In the late 1800's and the early 1900's a revival of sorts was seen concerning these fireball phenomena. The stories from that period can be divided into those with either Hawaiian or Japanese affiliations.

An account of Queen Emma's visit to Puna, Hawaii, as told by Joseph Ilalaole (1937), traced an *akualele* sighting.

Then one night she [Queen Emma] heard the people outside exclaim at a strange sight. The Queen came to see what the excitement was about and when she saw it she cried out, "Please don't go until I get home." Then to her people she said, "Hurry and get everything ready for my departure; I must go without delay in the morning." The Queen went to Hilo and caught the boat there for Honolulu. She was sad and anxious to be gone and soon after her arrival in Honolulu her sister-in-law, Princess Ruth Ke'elikolani died. The sign the Queen saw in Puna was an omen of her death. [Princess Ruth died May 24, 1883.]

An article published in the newspaper *Hōkū o Hawaii* (Kalioahaialii, 1917) described another *akualele* sighting, which is remarkably similar to present-day UFO (Unidentified Flying Objects) reports.

On Friday morning, May 25, at 8 A.M., while I was working in my patch, I turned to look seaward. There I saw each detail of an object flying northeast on the Kohala side of the land, moving toward Kona over the hills of Anahulu, this was the appearance of this strange flying object that I saw; it had a large rounded head in front and a long tail behind like that of a kite. In front it was white and lengthened out like a beak of a sword-fish, the middle part was green, the tail glowed like fire and it sent out sparks that flew about in space. I noticed that it fell where the hills of Anahulu joined, where Anahulu stands to fall on Waawaa .... Is it telling me that days of peace will come and that human life will no more be sacrificed on the altar of the god of war?

The last question was in reference to World War I, which was then in progress, and indicated an interpretation of this sighting as an omen, unlike the aboriginal sign of sorcery and death.

In the newspaper *Ku'oko'a*, J.K. Mokumaia (1922) wrote about strange fireball sightings occurring in the Moanalua area on the island of Oahu.

It was customary that when a company of people passed time away on the Ewa side of Moanalua, facing the edge of that hill, at eventide, a fire would be seen crawling on the edge of the cliff and drop down on that hill. It was like a rocket. Your writer had seen it himself, and being too young to know better, we children shouted aloud, "O, see the fire with a head in front of it and a long tail." We children liked it, we older ones, and were always eager to see this flying object. We questioned each other about this flying fire. We used to form a group to watch it. For two or three nights there was no sign of it and on the fifth night everyone of the boys that came, including the writer, saw its head and eyes. It was as red as fire and frightful. We screamed aloud in fear and later learned the truth. It was fed and was tame. It took the form of a man and went up there to look for food.

This account, dated April 22, 1922, is significant because the *akualele* had the fireball configuration, yet it also had a distinguishable head and eyes. Likewise, this phenomenon was similar to the ancient belief that the *akualele* had a form, once human, and that it became tame because it was fed.

A caretaker at Moanalua told a Hawaiian-English female, Informant A, that in one of the caves along the cliffs an *akualele* lived and every so often it would come out and fly about the area. Years later the daughter of this informant and her friends visited the same area. The daughter was coaxed into chanting, and, while she was doing so, a bright ball of fire arose and approached the car in which she and her friends were seated. Frightened, they drove away with the fireball accompanying them for a distance, whereupon it returned to its cave, leaving the frightened occupants of the car speeding away.

A series of stories cluster around the motif that fireballs seen at one's residence indicate disharmony, jealousy, or hatred. The appearance of fireballs nearly always occurs at night and is striking as well as frightening. *Akualele* can be stopped and destroyed by swearing. Some informants attest to the fact that *akualele* in themselves are not like flying mines which harm one by explosion, but that they explode and break up into many individual flames which move about giving the appearance that the bits of light are individual animate things.

When Informant A married, one of her husband's cousins strenuously objected to the marriage on racial as well as religious grounds. The cousin brought in a *kahuna-pule-'umi* who recited a prayer, sending an *akualele* to the informant's house. The fireball was seen by neighbors to fall on the informant's house. The priest, who was an old man, could not properly execute the prayer, because it required long breath control and, thus, he fell exhausted, dying later in a hospital. The fireball, further, had no effect, because the informant was a descendant of the Ma'iola god and had no need to swear in order to avoid the evil of the fireball.

Informant B, an 88-year-old female Hawaiian living at Maunalani

Heights on Oahu, was startled sometime in the 1940's by a bright white light at her front door. It was a huge fireball. The informant asked an older woman about this apparition and was told that someone in the family was against her. She prayed, asking for divine guidance, and in a dream that night, she discovered that a particular member of the family was jealous of her.

Informant C, a male Hawaiian aged 50+, lived in the Kailua area on the Kona Coast of Hawaii. He related that when he was a young man, a fireball of bright yellow came crashing through the air and flew over and under the trees there. Before anyone could swear, the *akualele* crashed into a tree and exploded into many small fireballs.

Informant D, a Hawaiian-Chinese female aged 50+ of Wailua, Kauai, and Informant E, a Hawaiian male aged 60+ of Kalaheo, Kauai, related that whenever an *akualele* was seen, it was a sign for the observer to turn back from wherever he was going and to desist from any activity he was engaged in at the time. The *akualele* was an omen of impending danger.

Informant F, a male Caucasian aged 31, noted that while he was driving down the Old Pali Road on Oahu an *akualele* passed slowly in front of his car. Immediately the engine was killed by it. As soon as the fireball passed the car, the engine started again. Another informant, Informant G, a male Hawaiian-Chinese-Filipino aged 29, stated that along the same Pali Road, a fireball stopped a car in which he was riding. The driver, an older man, got out and began swearing, whereupon the fireball burst into smaller fragments. The driver claimed that these fragments became little mythical men called *'e'epa*.

Many isolated sightings of individual *akualele* are just that, only sightings. However, they all seem to contain bits of data which, when pieced together, provide for a better synthesis of this phenomenon.

Informant H, a 17-year-old part-Hawaiian female, observed a fireball of bright red-orange color hovering about 50 feet in the air. It was curved while spinning in flight and then it fell to the ground.

A male Hawaiian-Caucasian aged about 40, Informant I, was leaving his job late one night when a large luminous blue fireball fell almost at his feet. He and his wife stood before it quite shocked. The wife was about to touch it when it flew upward and disappeared.

Informant J, a Hawaiian-Chinese-Caucasian female aged 24, said that her relatives claim that when a fireball explodes, the fragments become individual objects which move and scamper about.

Informant A recalled that when she was sitting with several other girls in the court of Kawaiaha'o Church, a fireball came from above, bounced about the place, and burst in a glimmer of light. All of the girls were shocked and quite upset at this surprising appearance. This same fireball left a trail of sparks as it flew about.

The *akualele* motif, then, among the informants who were part-Hawaiian and who identified themselves as ethnically Hawaiian, closely follows some of the indigenous beliefs: (1) fireballs are sent by someone human; (2) fireballs can be stopped by swearing; (3) fireballs fly leaving sparks; (4) fireballs vary in color from red, orange, and white to blue; and (5) fireballs are omens.

After examining the remaining stories concerning fireballs and noting their ethnic composition, a high correlation between the motifs in the stories and the ethnicity of the informants becomes apparent. The remaining stories, fragments of tales, were all told to the author by Japanese or part-Japanese informants.

On the island of Kauai, in the Koloa district, fireballs were commonly seen in the vicinity of the horse stables and near graveyards. Among the Japanese immigrant plantation workers these apparitions were feared.

During the anniversary of my grandfather's death, a special memorial service was held with relatives and friends in attendance. A fireball was observed by three individuals, each noting that it was the spirit or soul of my grandfather on its return to man's domain for the last time.

A 50-year-old Japanese male who resided at Hanalei on Kauai also observed a fireball at the door of the house where a funeral service was being held. Again, the informant stated that it was the spirit of the deceased. He also claimed that fireballs were most commonly seen along the beach area of Hanalei.

Gwladys Hughes, in her study of the folk beliefs and customs of school children at Waialua on the island of Oahu, noted this statement made by a Japanese girl, aged 14: "A fireball is said to be a spirit going through the sky. It has tails. I think it is shooting star." Five of the children in the same class said they were afraid of fireballs (Hughes, 1949, p.295).

A most complex and interesting story was told to me by a young Japanese insurance salesman who resided at Hakipuu on the island of Oahu.

The head of the Japanese household went to use the outdoor toilet one night and was astonished when the area lit up as if a bright meteor had just flashed by. When he returned to his house, his wife and his father said they saw a fireball fly by and disappear into a thicket of *hau* trees. It seems that the fireball was frequently seen at night flying into the same location. The family decided to investigate the next day and, after a considerable tedious search, they found a decapitated skeleton. The family then consulted a local priest of Hawaiian ancestry and were told that the skeleton belonged to a murdered man whose body had never been found. The priest's advice was for the family to seek the direction from which the fireball originated and that its source would be the location of the head. The family then followed the priest's advice and soon after found the skull. The skull and body were brought together and buried. After this the fireball was no longer seen flying in the area. The spirit had not been able to rest as long as its body and the misdeed had not been discovered, and so in its nightly flights, the spirit had been trying to attract the attention of someone who might help.

The tale combines both Hawaiian and Japanese motifs in that the soul could not rest as long as the murder was not known by others and, like the story of Pūmaiʻa, the spirit blazed in anger as it sought its whole body.

Several fragments of tales told by Japanese informants point to the motif that an entire universe exists which must remain in balance and in a state of smooth functioning. Similarly, the Hawaiian universe of appropriate behavior was based on this fine balance. Dysfunction, friction, discord, hate, or lack of care in Japanese life styles was, in some cases, resolved only through supernatural intervention. Several informants noted that after the death of an individual, memorial services must be held at set dates and in certain traditions and that the graves of the dead must be properly cared for.

In three cases neglecting to perform these mortal services for the deceased resulted in *hinotama* appearing before the relatives and friends, warning them that some dysfunction existed in their lives. A Japanese Buddhist priest was consulted and, as did the Hawaiian priest, he interpreted the manifestation as a simple warning that the graves of the deceased were overgrown and that their memory was being lost by the relatives.

Among the Japanese informants the *hinotama* were always blazing lights of no particular color, but nearly always of small-fist to baseball size. Their flight was not high in the air, but normally at about the height of a man. These never seem to have left any trail of sparks or to have had a definite shape as recorded for Hawaiian *akualele*.

Recently a man of Chinese ancestry observed a "hippie-type" man approaching him from out of the bushes. The individual wore a loincloth and his hair was quite disheveled. The Lahaina, Maui, area where this occurred is a haven for many such transients, so the informant was not too concerned about the man's weird dress. Reportedly the informant carried a camera, and two pictures which he took of the "hippie" shocked him. The first showed only a bright sphere like a sun halo reflection off the lens and the second picture showed a blazing fireball. The informant was quite astonished and, although he was unaware of fireball stories and local superstitions, he was afraid that he may have experienced a supernatural happening. This man was a land developer whose future development was being surveyed at the time. As in many stories before, this event influenced the developer to stop construction in the area. Whether the story and its events are actually true or not, the tale exists with its *akualele*, fortifying the belief that the supernatural does exist and, at times, intervenes as a sanctioning force into man's life.

Professor James E. McDonald of the University of Arizona's Institute of Atmospheric Physics, kindly made available a copy of a UFO sighting which happened soon after the beginning of World War II in the Mana area of the island of Kauai. Each of the observers, one a Caucasian and the other a Hawaiian, confirmed the other's sighting, although the Hawaiian informant did not wish to go into details. Her cultural background evidently conditioned her to what she had seen, leading her to interpret the bright white and green object as an *akualele*.

SUMMARY AND CONCLUSIONS

The fireball motif in the Hawaiian Islands derives its origins principally from two ethnic groups: the indigenous Hawaiian and the immigrant Japanese. The Hawaiian fireball is called an *akualele* or "flying god." It is generally described as an elongated ball which in flight resembles a tadpole with a long tail leaving sparks as it flies. This is called the *pū'ali* shape. Its flight seems to be directional at above tree level, but at times haphazard at lower levels. Because of their color range, these *akualele* can be identified as to the sex of the captured spirit. Red was said to signify male, whereas all lighter shades, from yellow to blue, signified the female, according to Informant A. The spirit manifests itself as a blazing, pulsating fireball, and, as it pulsates, it reaches some optimum size in its flight. The fireball can be stopped in flight and destroyed simply by swearing at it. Its destruction always starts with a brilliant explosion which does not harm people standing nearby; neither does it cause secondary fires. Upon explosion, each piece moves about on the ground; and these, according to one informant, are the *'e'epa* people, who scamper about to do their missions of mischief. The motif in which the fireballs stop car engines is localized to the Pali Road area of Oahu. It is likely that this motif is related to and, perhaps, has become confused with other legends of the same area, some of which have to do with the stopping of car engines because the occupants carried pork with them. This motif stems from the presence of a stone guardian which once stood near the Pali Lookout Point. Offerings were made there to insure safe passage along the cliff journey. A simple offering, such as a leaf, or more elaborate ones, such as foods, were quite commonly placed before the guardian. Obviously no such tributes are offered today by the many cars and buses passing over the Pali.

In ancient Hawaii the *akualele* were once the *kino lau*—multiple bodies—of gods and demigods, and their mission was mainly to punish those people who broke the laws of the land. The later development of *akualele* as captured spirits who were not of the same class as the gods and demigods shows an evolution toward sorcery for many purposes, used mainly by humans against their fellow men. Sanctions and their execution became less the domain of the gods and more under the control of man.

In contrast, the Japanese *hinotama,* which in Japan can be more accurately described and dated to show its development as a motif, seems to be a vague phenomenon in Hawaii. There was very little recorded information describing its color, relative size, or even shape. It seems to be of small size in contrast to the *akualele,* and appears as a constantly moving flame from a candle with no focal point. It may be yellow or reddish-yellow, although no sex is represented by its hues. Its flight is swift, directional, sometimes hovering, and always close to the ground.

Hinotama were most commonly seen at or near manure piles, around marshy areas, in graveyards, and along sandy corraline coastal spots. Such locations strongly hint that *hinotama* have physical rather than supernatural origins, for example, marsh gas-methane, phosphorus, and the like.

In Japanese folk tradition, the *Obon,* or festival-of-the-dead memorial services which are held during the summer months, are for the souls of the departed who return to the mortal world for a short time. Their return is manifested sometimes as *hinotama;* other times the souls return in invisible forms.

Acculturation in the Hawaiian Islands has been increasingly toward the Westernization of a predominantly non-Western population. The perpetuation of motifs such as the fireball is a fair index of how nonindigenous traditions and folklore are retained and how, in a subtle and entertaining manner, ethnic identification is maintained. Storytelling is one of the many ways in which education of the listener takes place. In an increasingly multi-ethnic Hawaiian population the once indigenous Hawaiian folklore motifs are being transmitted to the listener, and the result is truly a new multicultural identification. Importantly, *akualele* and *hinotama* tales capture the listener's attention by infusing him with awe and wonder of things supernatural. The *akualele* and *hinotama* tales are not merely stories. They all have a moral, and attempt to instruct the listener in behavior appropriate in given situations.

LITERATURE CITED

BEAGLEHOLE, ERNEST
  1937. *Some Modern Hawaiians.* Univ. Hawaii Pub. 19. Honolulu.
BECKWITH, MARTHA W.
  1970. *Hawaiian Mythology.* Honolulu: Univ. Hawaii Press.
DAVIS, HADLAND F.
  1920. *Myths and Legends of Japan.* London: Harrap.
ELBERT, SAMUEL H., and TORBEN MONBERG
  1965. *From the Two Canoes: Oral Traditions of Rennell and Bellona Islands.* Honolulu
    and Copenhagen: Univ. Hawaii Press and Danish Nat. Mus.
ELLIS, WILLIAM
  1917. *A Narrative of a Tour through Hawaii* . . . . Honolulu: Hawaiian Gazette.
EMERSON, NATHANIEL B.
  1915. *Pele and Hiiaka.* Honolulu: Star-Bulletin.
  1965. *Unwritten Literature of Hawaii: The Sacred Songs of the Hula.* Rutland: Tuttle.
FERGUSON, JOHN C., and MASAHARU ANESAKI
  1928. *The Mythology of All Races.* Boston: Archaeological Inst. America.
FORNANDER, ABRAHAM
  1916. "Collection of Hawaiian Antiquities and Folk-lore." *Mem. B.P. Bishop Mus.,*
    Vol. 4, Pt. 3.
FORSTER, JOHN
  1960. "The Hawaiian Family System of Hana, Maui, 1957." *J. Polynesian Soc.* **69**:92-
    103
GALLIMORE, RONALD, and ALAN HOWARD, editors
  1968. *Studies in a Hawaiian Community: Na Makamaka o Nanakuli.* Pacific Anthro-
    pological Rec. 1. Honolulu: Dept. Anthropology Bishop Mus.
GOLDMAN, IRVING
  1970. *Ancient Polynesian Society.* Chicago: Univ. Chicago Press.
HANDY, E. S. CRAIGHILL
  1968. "Traces of Totemism in Polynesia." *J. Polynesian Soc.* **77**:43-56.
HANDY, E.S. CRAIGHILL, and MARY KAWENA PUKUI
  1958. *The Polynesian Family System in Ka-'u, Hawai'i.* Wellington: Polynesian Soc.
HENRY, TEUIRA
  1928. *Ancient Tahiti.* B.P. Bishop Mus. Bull. 48. Honolulu.
HUGHES, GWLADYS F.
  1949. "Folk Beliefs and Customs in an Hawaiian Community." *J. American Folklore*
    62(245):294-311.
ILALAOLE, JOSEPH
  1937. An Account of Queen Emma's Visit to Puna. MARY K. PUKUI (trans.) B.P.
    Bishop Mus. Hawaiian Ethnological Notes. Honolulu.
KALIOAHAIALII, GEORGE
  1917. "A Strange Flying Object." *Hoku o Hawaii.* June 12.
KAMAKAU, SAMUEL M.
  1964. *Ka Po'e Kahiko: The People of Old.* MARY KAWENA PUKUI (trans.); DOROTHY
    B. BARRÈRE (ed.). B.P. Bishop Mus. Spec. Pub. 51. Honolulu.
KIRTLEY, BACIL F.
  1971. *A Motif-Index of Traditional Polynesian Narratives.* Honolulu: Univ. Hawaii
    Press.

LEVIN, STEPHENIE SETO
     1968. "The Overthrow of the *Kapu* System in Hawaii." *J. Polynesian Soc.* **77**:402-430.
MOKUMAIA, J. K.
     1922. "Moanalua Past and Present." *Nupepa Kuokoa,* April 22. Trans. by MARY K. PUKUI in Bishop Museum Library.
PUKUI, MARY KAWENA, and SAMUEL H. ELBERT
     1957. *Hawaiian-English Dictionary.* Honolulu: Univ. Hawaii Press.
THOMPSON, STITH
     1936. *Motif-Index of Folk Literature,* Vol. 6. Bloomington: Indiana Univ. Studies Vol. XXIII.
WESTERVELT, WILLIAM D.
     1963. *Hawaiian Legends of Ghosts and Ghost-Gods.* Tokyo: Tuttle.
WHITE, JOHN
     1887. *The Ancient History of the Maori: His Mythology and Traditions.* Vols 1-3. Wellington: Government Printer.

TUAMOTUAN CHANTS AND SONGS
FROM NAPUKA

KENNETH P. EMORY

B. P. Bishop Museum, Honolulu

I N THE COURSE of Bernice P. Bishop Museum's field work in the Tuamotu
Archipelago, April, 1929, to December, 1930, and May to December,
1934 (Emory, 1932; 1935; Stimson, 1935), I became very much aware
that the surviving pre-European chants and songs offered a great
opportunity to reach the traditional thinking, feelings, beliefs, and
practices of the Tuamotuans. When modified or composed since then,
the chants and songs reflect most tellingly the impact of foreign influences.

The collection of chants and songs, therefore, became a major
occupation of the expeditions. They were copied from existing manuscript
books, written down by our informants, or taken directly by dictation.
In addition, as many as possible were recorded on dictaphone wax-cylin-
ders. The larger part of this work fell to J. Frank Stimson, who was
engaged to record and study the language. However, our first stay at
Napuka, September 21 to October 4, 1930 (Emory, 1932, pp. 46, 50)
was too short for Stimson to record more than three chants. On our
second visit to the Tuamotus, Stimson elected to visit and concentrate
on islands to the southeast so that further collection of chants and songs
from Napuka during the stay from May 15 to July 29, 1934 (Emory,
1935, pp. 61-62) was left entirely to me.

In all, 120 chants and songs were collected; 49 with text and sound
recording, 61 with text only, and 10 with sound recording only. So far,
only three of the chants have been published, all three connected with
religious ceremonies on the *marae* temples (Emory, 1947, pp. 69, 71-72).

The Napukans gave terms to their categories of songs and chants. The general term for the slow, solemn songs was *fagu,* of which there were several kinds and which often expressed grief. In a lighter vein were the *koivi,* usually rendered in a fast, gay manner, but sometimes sung in chorus in a slower tempo. *Koivi* were the equivalent of the Tahitian *ute,* and elsewhere in the Tuamotus were called *teki. Pehepehe* were rhythmic recitations which served various functions, such as glorification of the land (more specifically called *fakataratara)* or the exaltation of individuals (called more specifically *fakateniteni).* Another major category was dance songs, called *papa ruta.*

In this paper I shall present examples of the various types of songs and chants in order to indicate their range and content. The translations should be taken as provisional.[1] None of the texts used here were transcribed from the dictaphone cylinders.[2] They were written down by me from dictation or by a Tuamotuan helper, except for the one modern composition which was copied from the manuscript book of Chief Maono.

FAGU

During our stay, there was reluctance to sing *fagu* during the day or before the children had gone to sleep, but there was no hesitation about singing them at night. This was probably because a quiet atmosphere was the appropriate setting. But at many other atolls in the Tuamotus, among people of the first or second generation of Christian converts, some felt it incumbent upon them to refuse to speak to us about prayers, chants, and songs associated with their "heathen past" *(tau eteni),* lest they be judged as not having turned away from that period of "darkness." But at the gathering of relatives and friends at a death, emotion was so strong that the mourners would break into an ancient *fagu,* in which they had all participated in the past, and thus many of these have survived.[3]

---

[1]Of great help in the translating, has been the Tuamotuan dictionary of Stimson and Marshall (1964) in which most of the words and meanings I collected at Napuka have been incorporated.

[2]It would have been of great assistance to follow the chants as recorded on the cylinders, but repeated playing would have meant their virtual destruction. These cylinders are being copied onto magnetic tape at the Edison re-recording laboratory at the University of Syracuse, New York. After this work is completed it is hoped to make them available on recorded discs.

[3]Father Paul Maze, later to become Monsignor Hermel, told us that he had no objection to their singing their ancient songs if this brought unity of spirit and assuaging of grief. It was not, however, until after our visits that he turned his attention to their content and became aware of their harmlessness and beauty. He then devoted considerable time to collecting additional texts for Bishop Museum and forming a collection at the Catholic Mission, headquarters in Tahiti, which is now openly encouraging the preservation of the ancient songs and dances of the eastern Tuamotus.

Another favorite time for singing *fagu* was on the capture of a *manihini* turtle; that is, one supposed to have been sent by an ancestral spirit. As it lay on its back on the former site of an ancient *marae,* people gathered around it to sing *fagu* to please the spirit of the one that sent it. Should they fail to do so it was believed the spirit *(varua)* would come, turn over the turtle in the night, and so allow it to escape, and, furthermore, would not deliver another turtle into their hands.

Traditionally when *fagu* were sung by a group of people, a leader sang the first line, called the *pepenu* (head). A second person answered with the next line, called the *maro,* a word ordinarily meaning "to oppose." Then all joined in what is termed the *rena,* a stanza of the song. The *pepenu* and *maro* were usually repeated before each of the succeeding *rena.* When one person became out of breath, another who had been saving his might join in to carry on the song. He was said to *haru* (grab away) that voice. After European contact *fagu* were converted into the Tahitian form of singing known as *himene.*

Some Napukans gave additional descriptive terms for *fagu* — those expressing grief for an absent or dead person were called *fagu heva* or *fagu tutagi,* and *fagu kiri* was a special term for songs sung at superincision ceremonies.

Grieving songs were favorites of the old people and were often sung by a parent while thinking of his child who had departed. The day that Hiti, age 50, left for Tepoto atoll, I was at his house just after dark, and heard his aged mother singing *fagu* to herself as she thought of him. Two of the *fagu* she sang were *E uhu ra i roto e* (wax cylinders 404 (T4A) and 405 (T4B)) and *E rigorigo ki toga ra.*

E UHU RA I ROTO E

Pepenu	First Voice
E uhu ra i roto e, te arofa e, te arofa.	That which wells up within is love, is love.

Maro	Second Voice
E muna iti roto e, te arofa e, te arofa.	That which is whispering softly within is love, is love.

Rena	Verse 1 (all voices)
E muni iti roto e, e uhu ra i roto e,	That which is whispering secretly within, welling up within,
Jhu atu ki tai e,	Is stirring seaward,
Te henua e tuki, a ro i a.	Is the land bearing its burden (of love), *a ro i a.*
E muna iti roto e, te arofa e, te arofa.	That which is whispering softly within is love, is love.

Rena	Verse 2
E muna iti roto e, te i taku vaka,	The gentle whispering within, is
tei taku vaka garo e,	because of my canoe, my canoe lost,
Garo atu ki motu e,	Lost over the horizon,
Te henua e tuki a ro i a.	The land bears its burden (of love) *a ro i a.*
E muna iti roto e, te arofa e,	That which is whispering softly
te arofa.	within is love, is love.

E RIGORIGO KI TOGA RA[4]
SONG OF THE DISEMBODIED SPIRIT

Pepenu	First Voice
E rigorigo!	A disembodied spirit!
Ki toga ra te rigorigo,	In the south is the spirit.

Maro	Second Voice
E rigorigo mate.	A spirit informing of death
E rigorigo ora hoki!	(Or) a spirit messenger telling that all is well indeed!
Ko mai a ro i a e.[5]	*Ko mai a ro i a e.*

Rena	Verse 1 (All Voices)
E rigorigo mate e!	A spirit of one dead!
Koa ka haere mai;	Come, gladness;
Koa ka haere mai toga	Joy, come from the south,
Kua puna te atu motu henua	The remotest lands are covered
i te kimi haga i taku nei tama	in the searching for my child,
ho i i te rigorigo.	by the *rigorigo.*

Rena	Verse 2
E rigorigo mate, e naki,	A spirit of one dead, hurrying
Nakinaki ra o a tagata.	Hurrying of a person.
Kai heko e	Eating of a crab
ki te atua ra koga hoki.	at the place of the god, indeed.
Te rigorigo!	The spirit!

During our 1934 visit to Napuka, Chief Maono and his wife had to leave for Tahiti. Hei and Tuata composed this *himene* for their departure (wax cylinder 412). Although it is a modern composition, it takes the place of a *fagu* which expresses grief for an absent person.

---

[4]Wax cylinders 408, 409, as sung by Te Urupo. I was told that when a *rigorigo* came from the south *(toga),* it was a portent of death; when, however, it came from the north *(tokerau),* it was a sign that all was well.

[5]The ending *ko mai a ro i a e* can start with *ho* as well as *ko.*

E MAONO TAVANA E

1.

E Maono tavana e, te reva ana koe,
Hopere mai koe to haga tamariki
Kaore makui e, ki runga i te henua.

Maono, our chief, you are leaving
You are casting off your children
To be left on the land without parents.

2.

Egere koe hopere ai no tetahi
    tumu ke atu e
Kia tae koe ti Tahiti
Kia hava hia e, korua e.

Do not abandon your children for
    any reason whatever
When you reach Tahiti
Where you two have to appear in court.

3.

Kia tae koe ki te ara, mihi mai
    koe kia matou,
ko nei matou e, heva tika atu ae
E) kore ravea e, kua ta tatou e.

When you are on the road, miss us,

Here we will be, deeply grieving
It can not be helped, we are separated.

4.

Ko hoki mai koe, ki ruga i te
    henua nei,
Kia kitc atu matou, koa iho nci matou.
ei koa hoki, kua tae mai koe.

When you return upon the land here,

When we see you, we will rejoice.
There will be happiness, you will have
    returned.

Dirges, sometimes called *fagu tutagi,* were sung at funerals and inherited within families. The following *fagu tutagi* was composed for Te
Kopeka, a Napuka chief of long ago, and was also used for his descendants (wax cylinder 407).

UHU ATU PATIU

Pepenu

Uhu atu patiu ko tona mate
    ko Te Kopeka

First Voice

The storm announces the death of
    Kopeka.

Maro

Kopeka ariki, a re i re
o huna ki te pea au
Guihaguiha aku patiu.
Kua tau tagata roto fare
Ko tona mate ko Te Kopeka.

Second Voice

Chief Kopeka, *a re i re,*
Lost in the waves
Rages my storm.
People sit down at the house
At the death of Kopeka.

Rena

Kopeka ariki, a re i re,
Uhu atu patiu ki vaho i Te-roroma.

ue mahiti e konohi.

Verse (All Voices)

Kopeka the chief, *a re i re,*
The storm announces the death outside
    Te-roroma.
Alas, an eye has been plucked out.

Kua tupu te karero i vaho i Te-roroma.	Words spring up outside of Te-roroma.
Ko tona mate ko Te Kopeka e.	At the death of beloved Kopeka.
Kopeka ariki, a re i re,	Kopeka the chief, *a re i re,*
Ua ina te riri te matangi	The anger of the wind rages.
E fano te maomao piri kuru	The thrush clinging to the breadfruit tree flies away
A tukamoa te tapairu	The loveliness of the young people, shine,
O tona mate ko Te Kopeka	At the death of Kopeka.

Fagu kiri (kiri = skin) were songs accompanying the rite of superincision *(tehe)*. At Napuka, upon reaching the age of 12 or 13, every male undergoes the operation of superincision, akin to circumcision. The operation has been described by Harry L. Shapiro (1930, p. 140). Traditionally the act was performed at the *marae*. No person was allowed to participate in the ceremonies on the *marae* and to partake of turtle feasts unless he had been so incised. The chants and the feast accompanying it were his initiation into manhood, and the duties of adulthood. During our field work the principal motive was the knowledge that girls would not readily accept a lover who was not superincised. After the operation the initiate is no longer a *tamaroa* (boy), but a *tamatika* (adult). The boy was not informed of the coming operation until the morning when everything was made ready for it and the father had completed all arrangements with the *tahuga,* the priest and doctor. The afternoon of the ceremony *(paku),* a feast was held. Only males were allowed and only those who could be classed as siblings or cousins and who were *tamatika.* Pig, baked flour dough, and drinking nuts made a typical feast. All the food not eaten the first afternoon was put away and on the next day the men assembled to eat again. No food other than the feast food, called *kai o te kiri* (food of the skin), could be eaten until all was consumed, which might take three days.

At the time of our visit two *tahuga* took part in the superincision Chief Maono and his younger brother Tokoriu who served as an assistant. In addition there was a male nurse called a *kiri kopaki* who took the boy to the lagoon and washed and bandaged the wound. After the operation the boy sat on a stool in the house and his male and female relatives came to console him and to sing *fagu kiri.* After the incision came a feast for friends and relatives called a *fakanoa haga,* a lifting of tabu.

KA MAU HOKI TO KIRI

Pepenu	First Voice
Ka mau hoki to kiri,	Hold firmly the skin,
Ka motumotu te tamarua hoki.	Cut the boy.

Maro	Second Voice
E teie hoki koe ru e,	And this will bring contentment,
E ru e te metua.	The father is pleased.

Rena	Verse 1 (All Voices)
Ka hau hoki to tokotoko, ko	Your support, god Tane-who-leveled-
Tane-tuki-henua	the-earth, bring untroubled life
Kia tu na, ka higa, ka mate, ka veri	That he be established, fall, faint, spear
Ka to i oro ki tana hare	?Crawl to his house.
E fana to, e poro.	Fly forth, speak.

Rena	Verse 2
Ko tama e, i kiritia mai e	The child is released
He tau titi e, e rakei e	A turnstone, a white tern,
No ka hau hoki to tokotoko, ko	That your support Tane, may bring
Tane-tuki-henua.	untroubled life.

Rena	Verse 3
No tae ake, no tae ake	Arrive, arrive (ancestral spirits)
No Te Uru-fano-ariki, no Te Aia,	Te-uru, Te Aia, Te Ahi,
no Te Ahi-purapura,	
No Te Nini-tapu ki Taharoa	Te Nini, at Taharoa,
Kia tu na.	That he be established.

PUREA RA KI MUA KI TE MARAE HOKI

Pepenu	First Voice
Purea ra ki mua ki te marae hoki	A prayer before the *marae* indeed

Maro	Second Voice
E koti horo puna	That the cutting be straight,
Ka karo tau e.	. . . .
Tagitagi te tama ki te fakaroha e.	The child cries for sympathy.

Rena	Verse 1 (All Voices)
Purea ki mua ki te marae,	Praying before the *marae*
Kia tae to koro e takoto raua	That swelling comes when they two lie down
Ko vai hoki te tagata	Who will appear
E ranga ma to tahua?	On your meeting place?

Rena	Verse 2
E koti oro puna	A straight cutting
Metaki te tuahine, metaki koa.	The sister is glad, very glad.
Ka nefa ki atu, nau mai	Stemming out, coming back,
Ko vai hoki te tagata	Who will be the one
E raga mai to tahua e.	Appearing at your meeting ground?

Songs and chants from the legend of Tahaki were rendered in the form of *fagu*. The culture hero Tahaki, who avenges the treatment of his father Hema, is known throughout East Polynesia. Full versions of the Tahaki legend from Fagatau and from Anaa have been published (Stimson, 1934, pp. 50-100; 1937, pp 60-96), as well as my own bibliography of Polynesian Tahaki legends published in Stimson (1934, pp. 89-90). In this latter volume, E. G. Burrows has included music notation to the songs, derived from listening to the dictaphone cylinders of the solo singing of the woman Reva from Fagatau. I did not attempt to learn the entire Napuka version, but I recorded from old Te Mae six parts which belong to the legend and disclose knowledge of some of the episodes as related in the Fagatau and Anaa versions. The most important of these is the *fagu tutagi,* lament of Hema's wife Huarei and son Tahaki, over Tahaki's departure to rescue Hema (wax cylinders 413, 414, sung by Te Mae, Kararo, and the latter's wife Tagie).

LAMENT OF HUAREI AND TAHAKI

Pepenu

First Voice

Purutia te tama riro i tere, e ragai

The son is a wanderer setting out on a voyage, a far searching

Maro

Second Voice

E korua i toro, e tagi.

And you two are overcome with grief.

Rena

Verse 1 (All Voices)

Korua i toro,
Purutia te tama riro i te tere
Poroporo faki karoharoha
Ma te kitea te mata o te metua.

You two are consumed with grief,
As the son sets out on a voyage
Professing deep love
For the face of the parent may not be seen again.

E ragai, e korua i toro, e tagi.

A voyage of danger, and you two are aflame with grief,

E tagi te tama ki te metua.

As the son weeps before the parent.

Rena

Verse 2

E korua i toro,
Ko Te-muri, ko Te-muri-aroha mai Havaiki.
Puapua karoharoha
Ma te kitea te mata o te metua.

You two are aflame with grief,
It is the Wind-bearing-love from (homeland) Havaiki.
Tender love blossoms
Because the eyes of the parent will not be seen.

E ragai, e korua i toro, purutia.

A venture, and you two grieve, a wandering.

Rena

Verse 3

Korua i toro,
Henua, henua tagi hoki koe,
    na Ru, ko Vaerota

You two are consumed with grief,
A land, a land weeping deeply, you are under god Ru, the land Vaerota.

E tagi ki te hitihaga te	Weeping from the rising of the sun
mata te metua.	the eyes of the parent.
E ragai, e korua i toro	A voyaging, and you two are overcome
E tagi te tama ki te metua.	As the son weeps with the parent.
E purutia.	(The son) a far wanderer.

In the manuscript book of Te Atua-hagai-rua of Hao atoll, Stimson found, and copied in 1930, a Hao version of this episode (Emory and Stimson, n.d., Vol. ZZ-VH-17) and in 1934 he recorded at Vahitahi another Hao version (Vol. ZZ-VH-4). At Tatakoto in 1934 Stimson transcribed the text of still another Hao version from Te Uira a Maio (Vol. ZZ-VH-4-17). All three are essentially alike. To demonstrate the remarkable degree of similarity between versions of the same *fagu* from such isolated Tuamotuan communities as Napuka, Fagatau, and Hao-Vahitahi, the version sung (except for verses 2 and 3) at Vahitahi by Huarei, her younger sister Ruea a Raka, Tahakura, and Te Hina is presented for comparison (wax cylinder 521-A).

HAO-VAHITAHI VERSION OF THE LAMENT
OF HUAREI AND TAHAKI

First Voice

Purutia te tama riro i te toro,	The son is a wanderer setting out on
he ragai e	a voyage, a far searching
E korua i toro i tagi	And there are two overcome with grief.
E tagi te tama ki te metua, purutia	The son weeps before the parent, a wanderer
E korua i toro. A ra.	And there are two who grieve. *A ra.*
E ko tu e te ipo kino	And the beloved one is established (in our hearts).
Mai a rau ui i i c.	*Mai a rau ui i i e.*

All Voices I

Purutia te tama riro i te tere	The son sets out on a voyage
Poroporo kia Ruaroa	Professing his love before Ruaroa (Long-grave)
Ki te kitea te mata o te metua.	Because will not be seen the face of the parent.
E ragai e, kua heke ragai ai.	A voyage of danger the voyage is under way.
E korua i toro. A ra.	And there are two who grieve. *A ra.*
E tagi te tama ki te metua, henua.	The son weeps before the parents, land.

II

Te henua tagi na Rua ko Vaerota	A land weeping under god Rua, Vaerota
E tagi ana ki te hiki haga o te ra.	Weeping from the rising of the sun.
E ragai e . . .[6]	A voyage of danger . . .

Continued as in Verse I.

III

Te-muri-aroha tia mai Havaiki,	It is the Wind-bearing-love from Havaiki,
Puhapuha mai ana, te mea ka aroha.	Thirsting for the emotion love.
E ragai e . . .	A voyage of danger . . .

Final ending
(Hiave)

| E ko tu e te ipo kino | And the beloved one is established (in our hearts) |
| Mai a rau ui i i e. | *Mai a rau ui i i e.* |

The Fagatau version has a similar final ending:

| E ka tu i te po kino. | And established (exists) in the evil underworld. |
| Mahaga rohi e. | *Mahaga rohi e.* |

These endings illustrate the practice of a final ending without special meaning other than being a proper way to end a *fagu*. Also we can see here how different versions arising through isolation can create different meanings. In the Fagatau version the concept of *ipo*, beloved, is replaced by *po*, the nether-world, but the adjective *kino* is kept. Modifying *ipo* by *kino*, which ordinarily means bad or evil, has a parallel in Hawaii where *aloha 'ino*, instead of meaning "bad love" means a love so intense that it causes pain.

The Napuka version that I recorded lacks the ending found in the Hao-Vahitahi and Fagatau versions, indicating that perhaps this feature had become lost. The importance of these other versions is that they anchor the authenticity of these *fagu*, and in particular there can be no doubt that *kino* at the very end of chanting had been passed down from pre-Christian times.[7]

Another important Tahaki chant recorded in Napuka (wax cylinder 424) is one celebrating the union of Tahaki with his lover Hapai. It was sung at a feast given for a boy after the operation of superincision, or for a girl after the breaking of her hymen by her first lover.

THE SONG OF THE UNION OF TAHAKI WITH HAPAI

| *Pepenu* | First Voice |
| Ko te kura rere ko ru e, | The crimson bird in flight is filled with joy, |

---

[7]And not, as Stimson has claimed, a Christian-introduced concept to disguise esoteric meaning which had him change *po kino* to *Po o Kio*. See Stimson (1933a, pp. 58, 60 1934, pp. 50-100, especially p. 60 where the original text is given, and p. 81 where i will be seen to have been changed; 1935, pp. 66-67); and the refutation of this claim by Emory (1940, pp. 120-121; 1949, pp. 312-316; 1958).

Maro

au ki tua,
ana i (hi) toro,
ua pito raua e.

Second Voice

There is harmony seaward.
He crawls forth,
The two cleave together (literally umbilicus
    to umbilicus).

Rena

au ki tua e
o te kura rere mai o (ho)
ru e,
o te tavake ia o Mahuragi,
ua pito raua e.

Verse 1 (all voices)

There is a fitting together seaward,
It is the sacred red bird flying near,
    filled with bliss,
It is the tropic bird of Mahuragi,
The two are belly to belly.

Rena

au ki tua e,
o te tauri mai o (ho) ru e,
o te tui kau, mata uiui mai Mouru,

ua pito raua e.

Verse 2

They are one, seaward,
They turn toward each other,
It is the threading needle of beautiful point
    from Mouru,
The two have come together.

Rena

au ki tua e,
o te kiri kura ia o Tahaki,
o te rava tua ia o Hapai,
a ieka raua e.

Verse 3

They are joined seaward,
The red skin of Tahaki,[8]
And the glistening back of Hapai,
They are lost in ecstasy.

Our informant Te Mae recalled another chant concerning the marvel-
ous skin of Tahaki:

THE SKIN OF TAHAKI

Pepenu

te kiri o Tahaki.

First Voice

The skin of Tahaki.

Maro

vavegavega e ko te kiri o
Tahaki
te ruga, ko te raro
te kiri o Tahaki.

Second Voice

It is like the flesh of a coconut,
    the skin of Tahaki.
Above and below
The skin of Tahaki.

Rena

vavega vega ko te kiri o
ahiki
ohu, e tohu ara mia ki te
ape o Turuki

Verse (All Voices)

Like the white flesh of the coconut
    is the skin of Tahaki.
A sign, a sign at the side of
    Turuki

---

[8]It was the red skin of Tahaki which convinced Hapai that he was really Tahaki, the
of Hema and Huauri. The use of this chant to celebrate the graduation into heterosexual
gives it the sanction of tradition.

E kato tama tohua rire   . . . .
Ko te ruga, ko te raro   Above, below
Ko te kiri o Tahaki.   The skin of Tahaki.

The following song was also given to us as a *fagu* for Tahaki (wa█
cylinder 417). The name Hapai, Tahaki's ardent lover, supports this attri█
bution. In a Fagatau version of the legend, Tahaki wins Hapai, the█
he is rejected by her because he sleeps with her younger siste█
whereupon he goes off to his certain death, which Hapai then mourn█
(Stimson, 1934, pp. 70-77). References to winds, so frequent in Tuamo█
tuan poetry, seem to indicate they served as omens. The northwest win█
is cold and inhospitable and so could foreshadow sorrow. The Rauak█
in this song may be the name of a local wind, or spirit, or an epithe█
for Tahaki.

SONG FOR TAHAKI AND HIS SWEETHEART HAPAI

Pepenu	First Voice
No hakamate noa Rauaki e (i) ki Faga-te-ru-e.	Rauaki causes fainting at Faga-te-rua-e.
Ka mau ra, ka mau e.	Seize, seize.

Maro	Second Voice
Rere tu o e o (i) te tokerau hoki	Flies off to the northwest
Te metua i rave noa mai koe.	The parent who carries you off.

Rena	Verse (All Voices)
Ki te tua no Toga,	On the back of Toga, the south wind,
Ka mau ra, ka mau e.	Seize, seize.
Rere tu e, o i te tokerau hoki,	Flies to the northwest,
Te metua i rave no mai koe.	The parent who seizes you.
Rere tu o e i ruga,	Flies above,
I ruga Rauaki,	Above Rauaki,
I raro, i raro ake Hapai.	Below, below is Hapai.
He matagi e tokerau.	The wind is a northwest wind.
E titotito noa, e navenave noa	There is pecking, pecking, it is blissful
Ka mau ra, ka mau e.	Seize, seize.

Te Mae also recalled the following fragment of a *fagu* relating
the pursuit of Tahaki by Hapai when she found he had left her:

E horo Tahaki, e aru i Hapai	Tahaki sails off, Hapai pursues,
Ko koe tariga rogo te riri roa.	Yours was an ear hearing which caused great anger.
Tera Mapu, te ipo tagi, ko ei au,	There is Mapu, the mourning sweetheart, that is me,
Kuriri te manu.	The bird has become a wandering tattler.

A favorite *fagu* of the old people of Napuka was the following song
which starts out with "My bird the *tinaku* flies hither" (wax cylinder
407T6). It was explained to me that no one had ever seen a *tinaku*,
its voice was just heard in the night. Its cry was an omen that something
important was about to happen. The name Marutia stands for Maruia,
the woman in the ancient name for Napuka, Te-puka-Maruia, and the
original ancestor and chiefess of Napuka. Te-papa-tagitagi is a flat, bare
bit of land, a *tahora*, on the neighboring island of Tepoto.

A SONG ABOUT THE COMING OF BIRDS

Pepenu	First Voice
'e rere mai nei taku manu e tinaku hoki.	My bird flies hither a *tinaku* indeed

Maro	Second Voice
: ui a tei uta, e vaka tei tai,	There is a questioning inland, a canoe at the shore
, u o Marutia ki tai,	And Maruia is seaward
Jo uta, no uta te vaka Mahae	Inland, inland is the canoe Mahae,
a iku, ta iku ra, te vahia	Signaling, signaling with its hand,
mai hoki.	it works its way in.

Rena	Verse 1 (All Voices)
ui a tei uta e	There is an inquiring inland
e rere mai nei, te rere mai nei	Flies hither, flies hither
aku manu ko te kura-hope-nui-a-tavake	My bird of the long-red-tail, the bos'n bird
a iri ki ruga ia Te-papa-tagitagi,	It alights on the flat Te-papa-tagitagi (The-flat-of-crying [of birds])
autu, tautu ra, te vahia mai hoki.	Bobbing up and down, it works its way inland.

Rena	Verse 2
a potopoto i fano, tagi hia ra koe	The *potopoto* birds soar, calling to you
e tere, te tere i Kanake	The voyage, the voyage to Kanake
noano te keria tuea	Wide is the digging
airi ki ruga ia Te-papa-tagitagi	Alighting in the flat-of-singing
autu, tautu ra, te vahia mai hoki.	Bobbing up and down, it works its way inland.

KOIVI

Songs of endearment or of a topical nature were usually called *koivi*.
Such songs were often informal and dealt with pleasant pastimes. Two
koivi are presented here. The first example (wax cylinder 418, chanted

by Teufi a Te Tohu) was also said to be a *fagu* or a *papa rutu* indicating
that some texts can be used for various purposes.

1.

Tera, tera hoki, i te taetae rekareka ta Ragi-titi,[9] ko te pei, ko te hoperepere	That, that is the pleasant pastime of Ragi-titi, the juggling of balls, the throwing of balls back and forth.

2.

Tera, tera hoki i te taetae rekareka ta Gana-te-haru e, ko te huke.	That, that is the pleasant pastime of Gana-te-haru, surf-riding.

3.

Tera, tera hoki i te taetae rekareka ta Gaki-hara-po-tiki, ko te fatu ia makuono.	That, that is the pleasant pastime of Gaki-hara-po-tiki, the twining of ear-ornaments.

4.

Tera, tera hoki, ko te taetae rekareka ta Te roro ma, ko te uru makuono. Taku arofa.	That, that is the pleasant pastime of Te-roro and company, the insertion of ear ornaments. This is my welcome.

The second chant was given by Teufi, about age 65 (wax cylinder
118). He explained that a man, merely by speaking a magic spell, transferred to an islet the two wells Fararoa and Kerekere, and the sand
spot Takapua-ia-riki. The second part refers to the woman Patea who
had a child which came by magic *(kapua)* to Te-tarefa-purari (the old
name for the east end of Napuka, now called Tefata). These mythic
events inspired this chant.

Te tagata e, te tagata Te reko noa, te reko noa Te fatu noa, te fatu noa E komo ko Fararoa, i kapua mai i Te-mutu E komo ko Kerekere i kapua mai i Te-mutu	The man, the man Just the speaking, just the speaking The owner, the owner Fararoa was the well transferred by magic to Te-mutu (The-islet) Kerekere was a well transferred to Te-mutu

---

[9]Ragi-titi, according to Te Mae, was a deity who presided over pastimes such as juggling

E rari niganiga o Takapua-ia-riki
  i kapua mai i Te-mutu.
E rari toto to Patea i kapua mai
  i roto i Te-tarefa-purari
Taku arofa, te toto o Patea.

A single mixture of sand was
  Takapua-ia-riki transferred to Te-mutu.
A single blood of Patea was
  transferred to within Te-tarefa-purari
My homage to the blood of Patea.

PEHEPEHE

Rhythmic recitations were called *pehepehe* and were often used for
he glorification of places or people. One of the major types was *fakataru-ara*, songs glorifying the land. Each atoll of the Tuamotus has its *faka-aratara*, or glorification chants, and inhabitants seemed never to tire
f composing variations of them to extoll cherished spots and notable
ncestors. To appreciate them more fully it is necessary to know a little
f traditional history. The atolls Pukapuka, Napuka, and Tepoto were
elieved to be occupied by the same people. Maruia, a woman, was
he first *ariki*, chief. It is not known where she came from, whom she
narried, or who were her children, but the three atolls belonged to her.
The ancient name of Pukapuka was Puhaga, and its poetic name (that
s, the name used in chants) was Mahina or Mahina-te-tahora (Mahina-he-whale). The ancient name of Napuka was Te-puka (the *Pisonia grun
is tree*), its poetic name Te-puka-a-Maruia. It was also called Te-puka-uga (The-puka-to-windward), while Tepoto, the adjacent atoll, was
alled Te-puka-raro (The-puka-to-leeward).[10]

The three atolls were thought to resemble a fish and were linked
gether in this way: the head *(omoomo)* was Pukapuka and the belly
(korahi) Napuka (wax cylinders 398, 399), and the tail *(nokonoko)* Tepo-
. An example for each of the three islands is given here.

CHANT EXTOLLING NAPUKA

1.

henua ko Te-puka,
tahua Hirioro,
marae Ragihoa,
tane Mokio
vahine Fagu-taku-ariki

iri te tau e, tautau e.

A land is Te-puka,
Its assembly ground is Hirioro,
Its *marae* is Ragihoa,
Its man (chief) is Mokio,
Its woman (the chief's wife) is
  Fagu-taku-ariki
Close together is the hanging (the words)
  are strung out.

---

[10]The names recorded by Commander Wilkes of the United States Exploring Expedition
838-1842), including Henuake (which means simply "strange land") for Pukapuka and
aitoohee for Napuka—which appear on old maps—seem without local foundation. These
e not place names now known within the atolls.

2.

Fakatupu ruga ahua,	Islets spring up,
Tairi te rau o Tuna,	The leaves of Tuna (the coconut tree) flutter,
Aheahea te rau o te tamanu,	The leaves of the *tamanu* tree glisten,
A topa te maru o Nihu-maru.	Shade falls at Nihu-maru.

3.

Fakatara atu ra vau i te igoa o taku henua	I extol the name of my land
Te-puka ruga, Te-puka raro	The Te-puka windward (Napuka), the Te-puka leeward (Tepoto)
Titau ki te nuku o Hina.	Trying to approach the land of Hina (the moon).
Ka takahuri haga taketake	White terns wheel in flight
Ka tau ki ruga ki ruga Puka rua.	Land upon each of the Puka (gatae trees).
Te vahine teretere Apita	A woman voyaging is Apita
A kuru ei ruga, a kuru ei raro	Applying effort above, applying effort below
Ka ka toki	The adz cuts.
E toki e, te huru a te manava.	An adz is the nature of thought
E ru e te kaiga o Te-puka	May the land of Te-puka enjoy peace.
Eha ra teie ko Te-puka?	What is this about Te-puka?
E vaiho ra e fakatikarea ake no te keiga.	It provides a land of happy living.

CHANT EXTOLLING TEPOTO

O Tepoto nui a Maruia!	O great Tepoto of Maruia!
Noho ranga tapairu ki ruga i Havana.[11]	Lovely young people dwell on Havana.
Takahiga taku vae ki Te-vai-higohigo,[12]	I stamp my foot on Te-vai-higohigo,
Popo-tara kia Noho-ariki.	On Popo-tara belonging to the woman Noho-ariki.
Tu-fara-riki tonaenae, tauraga fakariki ki te aro o Makuru-ruahine.	At Tu-fara-riki the springs well up where the chiefs land before the front of Makuru-ruahine.
Niu-roa, Niu-poto; Tagi-roa, Tagi-poto.	Big Niu, Little Niu; Big Tagi, Little Tagi (the currents between Tepoto and Napuka).
Ka tau, ka topa Ki-manu-taketake;[13]	Land, fall down at Ki-manu-taketake;
E tu Fakahau, e aru a Fakahau	Stand at Fakahau, search at Fakahau.
A aru hoki tapahi.	Search for adz-blades.
E ru a te kaiga.	The land is peaceful.

---

[11]Havana is the place of the main *marae*.
[12]Te-vai-higohigo is the principal well south of the village.
[13]Ki-manu-taketake is the center of the island where there is a cave called *"te pi o te henua* (the navel of the land)."

Ko toku fenua ra i totohi ai o
  Ki-manu-taketake.
O toku fenua ra i totohi ai ko Tepoto
  nui a Maruia te henua.
O toku fenua ra i totohi ai tagi
  hia ra koe.

The place of my birth is Ki-manu-
  taketake.
The land of my birth is great Tepoto
  of Maruia.
The land of my birth sung about by
  you.

CHANT EXTOLLING PUKAPUKA

Ko Mahina-te-tahora te henua.
Ka para te hinano,
Puapua marere fararei te pua
  ruga nei.
Ka hoka ko Te-vai-o-Hiro,
Ka marino ko Te-vai-tahetahe,
Marigirigi ko Te-vai-rupe

Ko Te-kena-horo-taha,

Tanumia e maire ki Tara-te-fare

Taua ra e, Mahina-te-tahora.

Mahina-the-whale is the land.
Let the pandanus blossom mature,
Scattered flowers meet the flowers
  above.
The-pond-of-Hiro reflects light upward,
Calm is the pond The-flowing-water,
Covered with ripples is
  The-pond-of-the-dove.
The-booby-sailing-over-the-beach (is the
  name of the plain).
Let the fragrant *maire* fern be planted at
  End-of-house.
Yours and mine are Mahina-te-tahora.

Taunting chants in *pehepehe* form were a part of Napukan tradition and conveniently channeled the expression of ill feelings.

On a Sunday afternoon after church services at Napuka we witnessed a gathering of disputants presided over by Chief Maono, to discuss grievances. One dispute was over the alleged stealing of a canoe, another over encroachment on another's land to steal coconuts. In the heat of the discussion, conventional taunts and insults, such as the one given here, were shouted back and forth until one side reached such a point of exasperation that nothing remained but *tipou te ohure*, that is, turning one back to the other party, baring the buttocks, then bowing in the opposite direction. At this point, Maono would say, *"Atira teie tama'i 'urutia, ho'i i te fare"* (Enough, is this war with Germany, go back to your homes). The crowd then dispersed, and the disputants went home rather satisfied that they had been able to express their feeling publicly.

The following chant, a *pehepehe*, was given by old Teuriga Vahine (wax cylinder 420). It was called Porutu's taunt to Te Fare-patoa.

1.

Ko tupa, ko tupa, ko tupa vaevae,
Ko kai, ko kai, ko kai maemae,
Ei roto i te mono kautira a
  Te Fare-patoa.

Land-crab, land-crab, legged land-crab,
Eater, eater, eater of filth,
That is what is in the medicine
  bag of Te Fare-patoa.

2.

Ko tupa ake ra,	Acting like a crab,
Ko kohao ana ake ra.	Festering like an ulcer.
O fakeakea kohao ana	A *fakea* crab boring away,
Raheroa e kohao ana	A coconut-crab digging away
Tei roto i te mono kautira o	That is what is in the medicine bag
Te Fare-patoa.	of Te Fare-patoa.

3.

Kirinau ake ra	Acting like a hermit crab
Ka fao ana ake ra	Digging a hole
Tei roto i te moni kautira o	That is what is in the medicine bag
Te Fare-patoa.	of Te Fare-patoa.

4.

Mauga nui, mauga iti, mauga	Big mound, little mound, tiny
korekareka,	mound,
Aka revareva na keiga o tupa roa.	Like dangling rootlets are the bones of the land crab.

The last stanza was then repeated, but with terms for coconut crab *(kaveu)*, a variety of land crab *(fakea)*, and the hermit crab *(kirinau)*. The answer of Te Fare-patoa was:

Porutu ta-gira, porutu a kohi te parira	Sufficient is the firewood, the piling up of cooking stones (of clam shell),
Porutu haere i te kato rahamo	The gathering of ferns (to cover the oven)
Porutu a keri te kopuha, porutu a kapopo a	The digging of the pit, the gathering of kindling
Porutu ta-gira, porutu a tute	Of firewood, the moving in place
Porutu a kai te katiga ki ruga i te rotika	The eating of the food from the oven
Porutu ta-rahamo, porutu a tanu Porutu i hamo rotika.	The covering over with ferns, the burying The piling over of the oven with sand.

It was customary to welcome visitors from another land with a present of food, after they had been comfortably installed in their houses and had an opportunity to bathe and dress for the occasion. The presentation was made by the chief at the village assembly ground in *pehepehe* form. Our Bishop Museum group was thus welcomed at Napuka by Chief Maono. These are the ceremonial words traditionally spoken at such presentations, and dictated to us by Maono himself (wax cylinder 398):

Kotaha, kotaha rurururu,	Frigate bird, frigate bird, of musty smell,
Kariga, kariga hogohogo,	Booby, booby smelling like urine,
Goio, goio parahurahu	Noddy tern, noddy tern so thin,
Kiriri, kiriri muremure,	Small tern, small tern nice and plump,

Hope toretore,	With tails so fat,
Fakauru rigorigo ki te mata keinaga.	To impress nicely the new arrivals.

I interpret the meaning of the recitation as follows: The frigate bird, the booby, and the brown noddy tern (usually *kikiriri* or *kukururu* but here rendered *kiriri*) are not good eating, but the tern is, bringing delight to those of the land. What is being offered is the equivalent of the tern. In recording this chant I was given to understand that *rurururu* meant smelling mustily, a sense we came across through this context. The last sentence translated literally would be "spirits of the deceased *(rigorigo)* enter the *mata keinaga*" (people who possess the land). I was told, however, that *rigorigo* here was a reference to the gentle and pleasing cry which a ghost bird makes at night and that *keinaga* referred to the very small fish that came at times in schools, hence a group of new arrivals. Without these explanations the chant would be unintelligible.

Napukans were also versed in the legend of Maui, which is demonstrated by the following erotic chant. Fariua of Fagatau includes a similar version in the opening of his account as the chant responsible for inciting Ataraga to possess Huahaga, who then conceived Maui (Stimson, 1934, pp. 5-6). The words are intended to excite desire, but they do so as much by their vigorous and rapid delivery and pattern of sound as by the meanings they have. The category of this chant was not noted but it appears to be a *pehepehe*.

EROTIC CHANT FROM THE LEGEND OF MAUI

Te kiri vi, te kiri vi,	The tight skin, the tight skin!
Tai korau, tai korau,	. . . .
Tu-mimi, tu mimi.	The source of urine, the source of urine!
Takero vahine, te roroua a te hakonokono	The woman Takero, (she is) the circle of the fruit-picker.
Penei e fakarori, penei e fakarori	Thus is the wavering, thus the wavering!
Te mea te vahine	The thing of the woman
Pikitore mai haki!	Climb up upon it!
Ruanuku raua itoito.	The two are like Ruanuku in endurance.
Nako ra tu, nako ra tu	Thus, thus,
A puta to tohe e te kaunauna!	Your vagina is punctured by the red fish!

After the stones laid over the wood for a ground oven were heated, a stick, called a *tute*, was used to level the stones to receive the food to be cooked. While using this stick one would often hear the following chant, which, as with the chant used when making fire by the frictioning method, was also an erotic chant (wax cylinder 420). It, too, appears to be a *pehepehe*.

CHANT WHEN PROBING AN OVEN

1.

E tute aha tena tute,
E tute rotika tena tute.

What kind of a probing is that probing?
It is the probing of an oven, that probing.

2.

E tute aha tena tute,
E tute umauma tena tute.

What kind of a probing is that probing?
A probing of breasts, that probing.

3.

E tute aha tena tute,
E tute ureure tena tute.

What kind of a probing is that probing?
It is a probing of the penis, that probing.

PAPA RUTA

At Napuka we were told that dance songs were called *papa ruta,* but it should be noted that such terms differ from island to island in the Tuamotus.

A great favorite while we were at Napuka was the following chant for a frigate bird dance said to have been introduced from the island of Hikueru in the Western Tuamotus (wax cylinders 400, 415). Because we were not acquainted with the meaning of some of these terms in the local allusions of the time, we could not completely understand them. However, the terms give the chant a very acceptable patter and enable it to be uttered in rapid-fire delivery.

CHANT FOR THE FRIGATE BIRD DANCE

Kotaha taku manu huri e
Te rere, te rere mai nei taua manu ra,
Mai Opatapata, ka hano i te ao marama.

Frigate bird is my bird turning.
It flies, it flies hither that bird.
From Opatapata, it soars into the world of light.

Ka tute hia, ka huri e,
Ka rere i Fagatau.
Tipitipi pahara, tupai marara,
Fatifati to pererau.
Kukina e, gatata he,
Gatata, gatata teia o te moana,
Te okaoka a he, umh!
Te manu ho'i au a Keha (repeat)
Te manu ho'i au a Tu-te-ra.
Tute, rere, tute, rere, te puai
    a Huto.

It dives, it turns,
It flies to Fagatau.
Slicing the air, striking at the flying fish,
Your wings flap.
Exploding, shaking,
Shaking, rumbling this of the ocean,
Is the spear.
I am a bird belonging to Keha
I am a bird belonging to Tu-te-ra.
Dip, fly, dip, fly with the strength
    of Huto.

A huri na te manu tai e,
Teie mai nei taua manu ra,
Tei kori mai nei ki ruga Tutehia.

It turns that sea bird,
Here it is, that bird,
Dancing upon Tutehia.

Hurihuri noa o te otaha, o te
    riaria o Te-mahitio.
Atahi aru iti no Ripo, e piti
    aru iti no Ripo.
Papa te hua o Ripo.
Po ana huri e o te tai e
Taringa piti, taringa toru to wawae.
Hikoko iti, putarau iti, a horo.

The frigate bird reels hither ...

One little wave for Ripo, two little
    waves for Ripo.
The genitals of Ripo strike.
When night comes over the sea
Two ears, three ears are your feet.
Dashing about, penetrating, running away.

LITERATURE CITED

BURROWS, EDWIN G.
    1933. *Native Music of the Tuamotus.* B.P. Bishop Mus. Bull. 109. Honolulu.
EMORY, KENNETH P.
    1932. "The Tuamotu Survey." In H. E. GREGORY, *Report of the Director for 1931*,
        pp. 40-50. B.P. Bishop Mus. Bull. 94. Honolulu.
    1935. "Report of Kenneth P. Emory." In H. E. GREGORY, *Report of the Director for
        1934*, pp. 61-65. B.P. Bishop Mus. Bull. 133. Honolulu.
    1940. "Tuamotuan Concepts of Creation." *J. Polynesian Soc.* **49**(1):69-136.
    1947. *Tuamotuan Religious Ceremonies and Structures.* B.P. Bishop Mus. Bull. 191.
        Honolulu.
    1949. "The Tuamotuan Tale of the Female Spirit Who Assumed the Form of Tu's
        Wife." *J. American Folklore* **62**(245):312-316.
    1958. Review of J. Frank Stimson, *Songs and Tales of the Sea Kings. American Anthro-
        pologist* **60**(4):791-794.
EMORY, KENNETH P., and J. FRANK STIMSON
    [n.d.] Original Manuscript Notes of the Bishop Museum Tuamotuan Expedition, 1929-
        1935. 8 vols. Dept. Anthropology, B.P. Bishop Mus., Honolulu.
GESSLER, CLIFFORD
    1937. *Road My Body Goes.* New York: Reynal and Hitchcock.
SHAPIRO, H. L.
    1930. "The Practice of Incision in the Tuamotus." *Man* **114**:140-143.
STIMSON, J. FRANK
    1933a. *Tuamotuan Religion.* B.P. Bishop Mus. Bull. 103. Honolulu.
    1933b. *The Cult of Kiho-tumu.* B.P. Bishop Mus. Bull. 111. Honolulu.
    1934. *The Legends of Maui and Tahaki.* B.P. Bishop Mus. Bull. 127. Honolulu.
    1935. "Report of J. Frank Stimson." In H. E. GREGORY, *Report of the Director for
        1934*, pp. 66-67. B.P. Bishop Mus. Bull. 133. Honolulu.
    1937. *Tuamotuan Legends (Island of Anaa). Part I, The Demigods.* B.P. Bishop Mus.
        Bull. 148. Honolulu.
    1957. *Songs and Tales of the Sea Kings.* DONALD S. MARSHALL (ed.). Salem: Peabody
        Mus.
STIMSON, J. FRANK, and DONALD S. MARSHALL
    1964. *A Dictionary of Some Tuamotuan Dialects of the Polynesian Language.* Salem:
        Peabody Mus.

DANCE AND THE INTERPRETATION
OF PACIFIC TRADITIONAL LITERATURE

ADRIENNE L. KAEPPLER[1]

B. P. Bishop Museum, Honolulu

D ANCE AS A VISUAL EXTENSION of literature is a striking feature of the traditional cultures of the Pacific area. The association of litera- ture with dance is one of many cultural complexes which relate the cultures of the Oceanic Pacific to those of south and east Asia and sepa- rate them from cultures in which dance does not interpret literature. This visual manifestation in movement gives an additional dimension to literature that creates a complex artistic structure involving aesthetic criteria for creation and performance in literature, music, and dance.[2] The literature-interpreting dance tradition of each cultural group com- bines these elements in a unique artistic form. Because of this diversity, one might be tempted to disregard the not so obvious basic similarity

[1]The Tongan material in this paper is based on 1½ years of field work in the Kingdom of Tonga from 1964 to 1967 supported by the Wenner-Gren Foundation for Anthro- pological Research and Public Health Service Fellowship 5-F1-MH-25984-02 from the National Institute of Mental Health. To both of these agencies I wish to express my apprecia- tion as well as to the Tongan Government under the late Queen Sālote Tupou III and the present King Tāufaʻāhau Tupou IV for permitting me to carry out research in Tonga. I also wish to thank my mentors of the diverse dance traditions studied in the past nine years: Hawaiian, Mary Kawena Pukui and Patience Namakauahoaokawena Bacon; Japa- nese, Bando Mikayoshi, Yamakura Miyumi, Akiyama Takayuki and Togi Hiroshi; Korean, Halla Pai Huhm, Chung Won Kim, and Chun Hung Kim; Chinese, Sophia Delza and Alice Chen; Philippine, Pat Valentin; Balinese, Hazel Chung Hood; Javanese, Hardja Susilo; Malaysian, Kaharudin bin Mo'min; Niuean, Cook Island and Tahitian dance, Mata Smith; as well as the more casual, but none the less important, instruction of many Polyne- sian friends.

[2]See Kaeppler (1971a) for the aesthetic interrelationships of Tongan dance and litera- ture.

of the main function of dance in most of the Pacific area—which is to interpret literature. Many Pacific literary genres are not interpreted with dance. It is the task of this paper to focus on the similarities and differences in those literary genres in which movement is an integral part—first of all in gross terms between some Oceanic Pacific cultures and their counterparts in east and south Asia; second, among the three major Oceanic subareas of Melanesia, Micronesia, and Polynesia; and finally between two specific societies in Polynesia. It will also be seen that this evidence supports current views of the migration of the Polynesians ultimately from Asia, and the differentiation of island Melanesia from the ancestral Oceanic culture by means of a later migration into the area that did not reach as far as Polynesia (see, for example, Green, 1966, 1967, 1968; Golson, 1971).

Dance traditions which interpret literature in the Oceanic Pacific differ from those in east and south Asia in a quite fundamental way that can be said to account for the basic differential use of the legs. In the Asian-Indonesian traditions the dancer becomes a character in a known story which is conveyed by costume, face paint, and stylized gestures which may correspond to words or ideas. Although these traditions are based on literature, they need not have accompanying poetry or dialogue (see Soedarsono, 1969, for Javanese examples). On the other hand, in much of island Oceania the dancer does not become a character in a drama, but is a storyteller *par excellence.* Here the dancer tells a story orally, usually in rhythmic poetry, and accompanies the words with actions. Dance in the Asian area is often an integral part of the great theatrical traditions such as "Chinese opera" or the Japanese Nōh and Kabuki. These, in part, stem from the great Eastern religions of Buddhism and Shinto, but even in their secular forms are concerned with imparting morals. In Indonesia, where performances are not as theatrical in presentation, the dancer often becomes a character in one of the great epics, the Ramayana or the Mahabharata, with many dance movements related to those of puppets.

These Asian traditions do not aim to be realistic (that is, to interpret in a Western, realistic manner) but are, rather, what has been called "theater of presentation." That is, they do not attempt to tell a new story realistically, but to dramatize theatrically part of a story already known to the audience. For example, the character of a Chinese general is conveyed (to the initiated) by the color of his face paint and costume, while the number of flags he carries on his back tells the number of soldiers he commands. In the Japanese Nōh, the dancer might sing or tell why he is dancing. However, the ancient poetic idiom is not intelligible to the ordinary speaker of Japanese. In other words, in order to understand or appreciate Asian dance as interpretation of literature or the enhancement of a story by visual means, one must have read or heard the story beforehand. These Asian and Indonesian dance forms come from cultural traditions with a large body of secular and religious written literature. The stories are presumably known to the viewers before they see the dancers perform the roles. The dancer uses his whole body to convey action and often no verbal description accompanies it.

Contrast this with the nonliterate world of Oceania. Before the coming of the Europeans there was no body of written secular literature or sacred books. Stories of creation were often incorporated into the prologue of genealogies of high chiefs, such as the Hawaiian Kumulipo (Beckwith, 1951). This chant of more than 2,000 lines is a name chant in honor of Lono-i-ka-makahiki (an ancestor of King Kalākaua) which tells not only how he was related to all his forebears, but also how he was related to all things in the universe and thus established a claim upon the care of spirits that animated the material world. Such chants and genealogies were passed from generation to generation in the oral tradition and were often the responsibility of a priestly or ceremonial-attendant class. Stories and traditions of demigods such as Maui were in the public domain and often functioned to explain topographical features of the landscape, such as two mounds of soil in Tongatapu where Maui shook the roots of a tree, or an arch in Eua, Tonga, formed where Maui threw a spear.

In Oceania there were no long epics to teach abstract morals, as in the Ramayana, no dichotomy of good and evil to be dramatized, as Rangda and Barong of Bali, no insistence on filial piety in which a father's death or injury must be revenged at all costs, as in Japan. Here, instead, were stories that explained the familiar world and how it came to be the way it is, and stories that sang the praise of the chiefs and their genesis from the beginning of time. Thus, in contrast to Asia, the literature of Oceania was less extensive, less abstract, did not lend itself to dramatization, and was more concerned with explaining the here and now. This traditional literature was even more well known to the people than its counterpart was in Asia because it was useful and relevant from day to day and gave the time-honored sanction of tradition to ordinary affairs as well as to the stratified sociopolitical system of which it often was a part.

If it is true that in Oceania an individual knows his traditional literature—indeed uses it to explain the world about him—and that the dancer is a storyteller who does not dramatize in the usual sense of the word, how can dancers interest and even excite an audience? The answer lies in the observer's understanding of sophisticated figurative poetry and the subtleties of movement. To the noninitiated observer Asian dance is probably more inviting, for one can appreciate that a story is being enacted, although he may not understand it, and also he can appreciate the virtuosity of bodily movement as pure dance. In Oceania the dancer usually makes less use of his body—the feet are used mainly to keep time, the hands are used to describe, and quite often the dancers are in a seated position. The lack of dramatization makes it impossible to follow a story or even know that one exists. The movements themselves, although certainly graceful and perhaps even erotic, shortly become boring.

It is also enlightening to contrast the two indigenous audiences. An Asian audience comes and goes at any time, talks and even eats during a performance, watching only a certain dancer or part that appeals to him. An audience in Oceania tends to listen to every word, watch every movement, move their heads in concert with the dancers, and shout at intervals. It is obvious that there is something quite different going on in these two dance traditions. In the Asian tradition there is a recognized repertoire passed from teacher to student through many years of training, each time adhering to a specific formalized composition—movement following movement in a recognized sequence. The dancer is judged for the technical perfection of how precisely he follows the traditionally accepted performance for that character or role. In Oceania, on the other hand, the composition may quite likely be a new one. The item is based on traditional stories, legends, or myths, but a story is not told in the usual sense. Traditional literature is referred to, perhaps in a roundabout way, but the poetry is really the vehicle for saying something else, usually something that is relevant for the occasion on which it is being presented. In addition, the order of the dances and the placement of the dancers supplies further information. Thus the basic differences between the dance traditions of Asia and Oceania are *dramatis personae* versus storyteller, and stories already known versus new compositions.

The above characterization of Oceanic dance is most readily apparent in the ethnological manifestation of ancestral Oceanic culture, most easily discernable today in Polynesia. At least some of island Melanesia was at one time inhabited by these ancestral Oceanic people. However, later migrations into the area, perhaps via New Guinea, brought new cultural complexes and physical types that changed the ancestral Oceanic culture into what is now known as Melanesian. New Guinea had been inhabited long before the rest of Oceania and, probably owing to geographic isolation, preserved some very ancient traits. Melanesian dance seems to represent a combination of ancestral Oceanic and New Guinea traditions. Melanesia and New Guinea will be treated here as one sub-area of the Oceanic Pacific.

From the evidence available it seems quite clear that dance in both Polynesia and Micronesia was a visual extension of poetry, while in Melanesia it was aimed more at spectacular display during times of life crises and secret society rituals. Indeed, the differences between Melanesian and Polynesian dance can perhaps be related to prehistoric migration and to the ethnological differentiation of political types reflecting societal differences that have been characterized by Sahlins as "bigman societies" and "chiefdoms" (Sahlins, 1963).

The leader or bigman in many Melanesian-New Guinea societies is often a self-made man—he becomes a leader by creating a followership, succeeding because he possesses to a superior degree skills that command respect in his society, such as oratory, bravery, gardening prowess, and magical powers (Sahlins, 1963, p. 291). He amasses goods and has great public giveaways often in connection with the erection of a bigman's dwelling or a men's-house, the erection and consecration of a slit-gong, the purchase of a higher grade of rank in the secret societies, or the sponsorship of a funeral or other religious ceremony. These ceremonies are the occasions for spectacular displays of the visual and performing arts. There are basically two kinds of dance in these Melanesian ceremonies and we might call them dances of impersonation and dances of participation.

In the dances of impersonation the dancers take the roles of mythical or ancestral beings celebrated in their oral literature. Indeed, the dancer-actor becomes something else, and his attire is usually distinctly nonhuman or supernatural—consisting often of a huge mask and a full otherworldly costume. The dance movements are dictated by these two considerations; that is, that the dancers are not human and that they wear attire in which it is difficult to move. The movements are those of legs and swaying bodies—the arms often being covered and used to steady costume and mask, or perhaps to hold a drum to accompany the dance. The movements do not interpret poetry, for supernatural beings seldom speak in words that can be understood by human beings.

The dances of participation are often extensions of these dramatic ceremonies, for individuals who do not impersonate spirits often join in and dance with them, imitating their steps. In dances celebrating head-hunting, warfare, or funeral rites, in which everyone participates, these same movements are used—often to the accompaniment of drumming. The dances have a character of spontaneity and do not require long and arduous training. They do not aim at simultaneous flawless execution of intricate movements, but rather are intended to create a

mass rhythmic environment, and one might characterize the dance movement as a visual extension of rhythm. If words are associated, they are
repetitious and seem not to tell a story. Although we do not know the
internal structure of a single dance tradition in Melanesia, it seems probable that the kinemes[3] would be primarily those of legs and body.

Contrast this with the entirely different world of Polynesia. Polynesian dance is a visual extension of poetry which sings the praise and
honor of high-ranking chiefs. Whereas in Melanesia prestige comes to
the self-made bigman, in Polynesia power resides in chiefly office and
dance texts tell of a chief's deeds and his descent from the gods. Genealogical rank is a distinctive feature of Polynesian societies and dance pays
allegiance to the rank-based sociopolitical system, in that it reflects and
validates the system of social distinctions and interpersonal relationships.
In these societies where power resides in the office and the regime is
long and enduring, specialists compose poetry, add music and movement,
and rehearse the performers for many months before a public ceremony.
Movements are primarily those of the hands and arms and interpretation
is that of a storyteller rather than an actor. The lack of dramatization
in Polynesian dance may help to account for the absence of dance masks
in Polynesia in pre-European times. We do know the structure of at
least two Polynesian dance traditions (Tonga and Hawaii)[4] and the kinemes are primarily those of the arms.

Micronesian dance, although certainly not identical, is related to
Polynesian dance. Movements are mainly of hands and arms in accompaniment to poetry. On some islands, such as Yap, there is a similar
concern for rank in the placement of dancers, as well as an emphasis
on rehearsed execution of the movements. But, although movements
and types of dance have a superficial similarity to those of Polynesia,
there are differences as well. In the Yap Empire, for example, dances
were given as tribute to Yap by Ulithi, Woleai, and other islands, and
the dance texts were in languages not intelligible to the Yapese dancers—
the function of the movements was not to illustrate a story but to decorate
it. Instead of acknowledging a chief's deeds or genealogy as in Polynesia,
the Yapese Empire dancers demonstrated the overlordship of Yap to
the other islands. Even in Ifaluk where texts were in the indigenous
language, the movements did not interpret poetry but, according to Burrows, were abstractly decorative (1963, p. 57). Thus, although dance
movements in both Polynesia and Micronesia are concerned with poetry,
we might separate the two areas in this respect by characterizing Polyne-

[3]Movement equivalent of a phoneme—see Kaeppler (1967c, 1972).

[4]See Kaeppler (1967c, 1972) for the structure of Tongan dance. A similar study is
in process for Hawaiian dance.

sian dance as illustration of poetry and Micronesian dance as decoration of poetry.

In many parts of Micronesia dance was associated with tattooing, and with the decline of the practice of this art has come the virtual demise of these dances. The importance of and dependence on the sea of the Micronesians is illustrated in dance. In some areas dances were performed on the platforms of canoes, canoelike paddles were used in other dances, and in some areas canoe head-ornaments were worn by the performers. In Ifaluk a large percentage of dance texts deals with the sea (Burrows, 1963). A study of the influence of the sea on Micronesian dance would tell us a great deal about the underlying value systems.

Again, we do not know the structure of any of the Micronesian dance traditions, but it seems likely that the kinemes would be primarily those of hands and arms, and, if we can believe descriptions by early Western observers, the head.

Although, in general, Polynesian dance can be said to illustrate poetry in the form of storytelling, each Polynesian group accomplishes this end differently. Dance-literary traditions in Polynesia use sophisticated poetic devices and levels of interpretation. The movements create a secondary abstraction, in that they refer to selected words of poetry, while the words themselves may refer to a hidden meaning. Examples from Tonga and Hawaii will be analyzed here in order to demonstrate the differences in illustrative movement in the interpretation of Polynesian traditional literature. Dance in Tonga is still a living tradition, in which new dances are still created, and which remains a functioning part of the sociopolitical system. Much of the living Hawaiian dance tradition, however, has so radically departed from the traditional that it has become a kind of "airport art" (tourist attraction) and reference here will be to traditional Hawaiian dance, especially as it was known in the 19th century, which is only occasionally performed today and is seldom created.

In Tonga one of the oldest dance types is 'otu haka, a dance performed by women seated cross-legged in a curved row. The name is descriptive, meaning "a row of arm movements." A pre-Christian example of 'otu haka that incorporates a Tongan view of the universe and uses a minimum of movement is "Lau Langi." The movements of this 'otu haka are particularly important to this discussion, for not only is there no dramatization, there is also a minimum of illustration. The movement used for the first half of each line is pāpātenga and the movement for the second half of each line is pasi, fu, pasi, fu; that is, the alternation of two types of hand clapping. Pāpātenga is a Tongan dance motif in which the knee is struck repeatedly with the open palm and derives from a movement used in everyday life to attract another's attention or for emphasis. Perhaps it is not out of place to speculate that the origin of Polynesian dance might be attributed to an effort to hold the attention of listeners while giving an oral narration. Elaboration of movements would occur over time, with hand actions interpreting words of poetry, and eventually becoming an aesthetic element in their own right—the allusive quality of the basic poetry being extended by the allusive quality of the movements. As Polynesians moved to far-flung islands, each group would elaborate selected parts of the basic proto-Polynesian movement vocabulary in much the same way as they elaborated selected parts of the proto-Polynesian sound system. Invariably, in Polynesian dance there is not much moving about, the leg movements are mainly to keep time and are basically stepping in place. In each Polynesian group this has evolved into a distinctive stylistic feature of their dance. This is also true with arm movements. For example, the distinctive Tongan movements are the rotation of the lower arm and the flexion and extension of the wrist. Distinctive features of Samoan dance include the flexion and extension of the wrist in conjunction with flexion and extension at the elbow. In eastern Polynesia the movements have become more narrative, the greatest elaboration in this direction having evolved in Hawaii.

The poetry of the *'otu haka* to be examined here, "Lau Langi," tells of creation of the land and of various levels of the sky. It is addressed to "you composers," implying that they shall pay heed to traditional Tongan cosmology, and appropriately uses the *pāpātenga* attention-attracting motif. The poetry incorporates a Tongan explanation for why the sky has different appearances on different occasions and where the thunder, stars, clouds, and other celestial phenomena are to be found.

LAU LANGI	THE SKIES[5]
1 Ke fanongo mai ho'o pulotu na, Tulituli tuli ē	Listen to us you composers
2 Kae fai 'emau talatupu'a, Tulituli tuli ē	While we tell you a tale from long ago
3 Koe talanoa talu mei mu'a, Tulituli tuli ē	The story from the beginning
4 Mei he 'etau 'uluaki matu'a, Tulituli tuli ē	From our first old men
5 Na'e fakatupu hotau fonua, Tulituli tuli ē	Our land was created
6 'O fakapulonga mei 'olunga, Tulituli tuli ē	Shrouded from above

[5]Translation with the help of Sister 'Okostino, a Tongan Catholic Sister who is a descendant of one of the high chiefs of Tonga.

7 Pea tau totolo hangē ha unga,　　　And we crawled as crabs.
　Tulituli tuli ē
8 Langi tu'o taha langi tu'o ua,　　　The first and second skies
　Tulituli tuli ē
9 Tala ange kia Maui Motu'a,　　　Tell to Maui Motu'a
　Tulituli tuli ē
10 Ke ne teketeke ke ma'olunga,　　　To push them high
　Tulituli tuli ē
11 Ke havilivili he 'oku pupuha,　　　So the breeze can come in, for it is hot
　Tulituli tuli ē
12 Pea fakamaama e fanua,　　　And bring light to the land
　Tulituli tuli ē
13 Pea tau tu'u hake ki 'olunga,　　　And then we stood up
　Tulituli tuli ē
14 'O 'eve'eva fakamafutofuta,　　　And walked about proudly
　Tulituli tuli ē

15 Langi tu'o taha langi tu'o ua,　　　The first and second skies
　Tulituli tuli ē
16 Ko e langi pe 'a Maui Motu'a,　　　Are the skies of Maui Motu'a
　Tulituli tuli ē
17 Langi tu'o tolu langi tu'o fā,　　　The third and fourth skies
　Tulituli tuli ē
18 Nofo ai 'a 'Ūfia mo Latā,　　　Are the living place of 'Ūfia and
　Tulituli tuli ē　　　　　Latā — the covered and enclouded
19 Ko e langi kehe, Langi 'uha　　　These are separate skies — a sky that
　na 'ufia e langi ma'a,　　　rains and covers the cloudless sky
　Tulituli tuli ē
20 Pea lilo ai Tapukitea,　　　There is hidden the star Tapukitea
　Tulituli tuli ē　　　　　(Venus — the morning star)

21 'Ikai ha mai ki tu'a,　　　And it can't appear outside
　Tulituli tuli ē
22 Langi tu'o nima langi tu'o ono,　　　The fifth and sixth skies
　Tulituli tuli ē
23 Nofo ai e la'ā mate toto,　　　Are the living place of the blood
　Tulituli tuli ē　　　　　red sunset
24 Ne hangē ha tui ngahomohomo,　　　There, resembling a loosely made
　Tulituli tuli ē　　　　　flower girdle or necklace
25 Ae fetu'u 'ene fakaholo　　　Are the stars that stand in rows
　Tulituli tuli ē　　　　　(the milky way)

26 Langi tu'o fitū langi tu'o valu,　　　The seventh and eighth skies
　Tulituli tuli ē
27 Ko e langi pe 'a Tamutamu,　　　Are the skies of Tamutamu (the
　Tulituli tuli ē　　　　　reddish cloudy sky)
28 Toki me'a lahi ange fau,　　　It is a tremendous thing
　Tulituli tuli ē
29 'Ene ita 'oka longolongotau,　　　Like anger that is silent before
　Tulituli tuli ē　　　　　the burst
30 Langi tu'o hiva tu'o hongofulu,　　　The ninth and tenth skies
　Tulituli tuli ē

31 Ko e langi 'ape 'oku 'u'ulu, Tulituli tuli ē	Are the skies of thunder (the noise that ends in little or nothing)
32 Kae fēfē 'a e talatuku, Tulituli tuli ē	But what about the last
33 Mo e langi ne fulufulumotuku, Tulituli tuli ē	And the sky of clouds of fleece — like feathers of birds
34 Ke fanongo mai 'a e pulotu na, Tulituli tuli ē	Listen to us you composers
35 Kae fai 'emau talatupu'a, Tulituli tuli ē	While we tell you a tale from long ago.

The skies and heavenly bodies are important symbols to the Tongans, especially in poetry and in visual arts, such as tapa design and the incising of war clubs. These celestial phenomena symbolize the highest chiefs — the sun being the symbol of the king or queen. Thus, for example, when the monarch dies, it is said that the "sun has fallen." The highest line of chiefs, the Tu'i Tonga line, were descendants of the Tongan sky god Tangaloa, and were considered not only chiefs, but sacred. The Tu'i Tonga were buried in large stone tombs that were known symbolically as *langi*, the word also meaning sky. Queen Sālote, who descended from the Tu'i Tonga line through her mother, was a prolific composer of dance texts and in one of her last compositions she takes the theme of the enumeration of the skies from the above *'otu haka* (Lau Langi) and applies it to the enumeration of the stone graves of past Tu'i Tonga. This dance, of the *lakalaka* type, is called " 'Otu Langi," or series of *langi* tombs. The text lists the names of the *langi* and enumerates the large named stones that are found in the walls. Ideally, this naming of the graves and large stones should recall to the listener the traditional tales associated with each, as well as the genealogy of those buried there and their living descendants. One six-line stanza of this *lakalaka* makes reference to four *langi*, two large named stones, and an old story about Tamatou. This story is about a child who succeeded to the Tu'i Tonga title upon the death of his brother. The child had a carved wooden doll which he decreed should be the Tu'i Tonga instead of himself and no one dared to object for the Tu'i Tonga was sacred. Several years later when the child was old enough to rule, he declared that his doll Tamatou was dead and accordingly was buried in a two-terraced stone tomb called Langi Tamatou (McKern, 1929, p. 55). In the dance text the story is not told — for it is supposed that simply to mention Tamatou is all that is necessary.

Although *lakalaka* is a relatively modern dance type, it would appear to be an evolved form of the pre-European *me'elaufola* (Kaeppler, 1967b, 1970). The poetry of a *lakalaka* is a series of concepts and references rather than a story, and it is usually composed to commemorate a specific event. Specific words are alluded to with hand actions. Poetic allusions are often to mythology and genealogy — often in quite a roundabout or indirect way — which illustrates the Tongan ideal of "not going straight." Some of the allusions are understood by everyone, but many are understood only by other poets. The desire is to take something old and transform it into something new. To understand the poetic transformation one must "work from his own knowledge" that he has gained through the study of genealogy, mythology, and history. For example the third stanza of the *lakalaka* " 'Otu Langi" begins:

Langi tu'o nima langi tu'o ono	The fifth and sixth skies
Hopo ai ae la'ā mate toto	Raises there the blood red sunset

This is only a slight change from verses 22 and 23 of the "Lau Langi" *'otu haka* above; however, there are no other references to this *'otu haka* prototype anywhere else in the *lakalaka*. Thus, in order to make the poetic transformation one must recognize that these two lines came from the old *'otu haka* and realize that it depends on two meanings of the same word *langi*. One must also know the symbolic association of the sky with the Tu'i Tonga and that Queen Sālote (who composed the poetry) is descended from the Tu'i Tonga line (through her mother). Much of this is common knowledge but one must make the association instantaneously in order to go on to an understanding of the next allusion. One must listen to every word. The poetry in figurative language elevates the king and chiefs in this stratified society, and such a performance pays them the highest possible honor that can be accorded.

A *lakalaka* in honor of Prince Tungī (now King Tāufa'āhau Tupou IV) will be used here in order to analyze the allusive quality of the complex poetry and movement. This *lakalaka* is from the village of Lapaha, a section of Mu'a on the island of Tongatapu. *Lakalaka* of Lapaha are known collectively as "Lomipeau" the name of the legendary double canoe which is said to have brought the stones for the *langi* of the Tu'i Tonga. Many of the *langi* are in this area. Lapaha was the former "capital" of Tonga and is the seat of the Tu'i Tonga line of kings. This line is no longer in power, but the descendants of this line and their high rank are acknowledged on state occasions as well as during day-to-day interpersonal relations (Kaeppler, 1971b). The poetry *(ta'anga)* was composed by Queen Sālote in the 1930's to be performed when Prince Tungī went away to school. The music was composed by Vili Pusiaki (to whom was entrusted the leading part), Tungī Mailefihi (the prince consort), and Setone Hopoate (a cousin of the royal family).

The movements *(haka)* were composed by Vili Pusiaki, the outstanding
pulotu haka (choreographer) of that time.
The poetry *(ta'anga)* of this *lakalaka* and its translation are as follows:

LAKALAKA 'AE LOMIPEAU[6]

I. *Fakatapu*

1 Tapu mo e Kalauni e Fonua	Permit me to speak, oh Crown of the Land
2 'Oku fakamalu 'a Lalo mo 'Uta	Embodiment of Kauhalalalo and Kauhala'uta
3 Laukau'anga 'o Tonga ki tu'a	The people of Tonga are proud
4 He ai 'etau fatungamotu'a	Of the existence of our old customs that bind us together
5 'O tuk unga tonu 'ete fiefia	And it is right that we should rejoice
6 Kei tangitangi 'ae mo'onia	For our royal house still flourishes
7 'O moto 'a 'ofa 'i he maheni	The buds of love spring from kinship
8 Ko hoto kahoa fakataukei	And becomes as my familiar floral necklace
9 Ne 'ine'i ā taka ē matangi	Little wonder the wind arose and became unsettled
10 'O fakahoha'asi e 'Otu Langi	Disturbing the *langi* (tombs of the Tu'i Tonga)
11 He mafola 'a hono ongoongo	When news of him (Tungī) spread
12 Lea 'a e toa Vaha'a-kolo	Broadcast by the *toa* trees of Vaha'akolo

II. *Lakalaka*

13 'Uoi 'Uoi 'Uoi he koe folau	Sigh, sigh, sigh, for the boat is sailing
14 'Oku hua liliu 'i Hakau-tapu	And it turns at Hakau-tapu (reef sacred to the King)
15 'Oku 'ai lā fakamanumanu	Its sails spreading like streamers
16 Angina he afu 'o e Tokelau	Sailing fast before the fine sea spray blown by the north wind
17 Mapaki e Hea tongi 'e he Manu	The Hea blossoms fell pecked by the birds
18 Lu'ia 'i Longolongofolau	Scattered on the expectant voyagers (The going away of Tungī)

III

19 Kulukona 'o Tavake-fai'ana	Beloved one of Tavake-fai'ana (place name at Ulukalala's lands at Vava'u)
20 Na'e toli he matangi mafana	Plucked by the warm breeze
21 Kohai 'e Ofo he 'ene ngangatu	Who is surprised at his fragrance
22 Fakatoukatea 'i Monotapu	Double canoe of Monotapu (old Tu'ipelehake's burial ground at Foa Island at Ha'apai Group)
23 He 'oiaue fakatoukatea 'i Monotapu	Oh yes, double canoe of Monotapu

IV

24 He 'Oku 'ilo 'e ha fine Fuoloa	The old knowledgeable ladies know
25 'A e fā he liku 'o Maluhola	The Fa (pandanus) of the rocky shores of Maluhola (place name in Vava'u)

[6] Translation with the help of the Honorable Ve'ehala and Tupou Pulu.

26 Fio heilala Tatakamotonga	Mixed with the *heilala* of Tatakamotonga (village of the Ha'a Takalaua line of chiefs)
27 He kaloni 'o e Manu launoa	Perfume of the frivolous bird
28 He fakama'unga 'o Nuku'alofa	Becomes the mainstay of Nuku'alofa
29 Ta'ahine tu'u hake 'o teu	Young woman arise and adorn yourself
30 Kae tuku ke u luva 'e au	Let me take off
31 'A e faka'ilonga Tuitu'u	The symbol of the Tuitu'u (chiefly necklace)
32 Metali e pitoi ngalau	The medal (heart) of *pitoi ngalau* (garland)
33 He teunga ki ha po fetau	The uniform for a repartee
34 Lafitani 'o e Lomipeau	Lieutenant of the ship of state

V

35 'Isa 'oku hanu 'a 'Anamatangi	Alas, 'Anamatangi (the royal residence at Kauvai) is complaining
36 Mo Kolongahau hono li'aki	And Kolongahau (Lapaha) for being forsaken

VI

37 Ta kuo ngalo 'apē kinaua	They are being forgotten perhaps
38 He naua 'o e Uafu ko Vuna	Because of the billows of Vuna Wharf?

VII

39 Launoa pe he'ena 'ofa	Though spoiled by their love
40 Ka he puli e Kava 'i Atatā	They will not be forgotten, just as one does not forget the kava of Atatā (a proverb)
41 'Oku Fotu 'o hangē koe la'ā	An appearance as natural as the emergence of the sun
42 Fai'anga 'oe Pātapata	An occasion for jubilation

VIII *Tatau*

43 Pe'i 'eva he funga 'o māmani	Even if traveling to the ends of the earth
44 Ka ko 'ofa te tau fehokotaki	Love will keep us in contact.

The poetry is in the usual form of a *lakalaka* text with three major sections. The first section, *fakatapu*, is a sung version of a stylized speech prelude which recognizes the king and chiefs and asks their permission to speak. By mentioning Kauhalalalo and Kauhalauta, the two major societal divisions of Tonga from which all chiefly lines derive, the queen acknowledges all the ranking lines of Tonga without mentioning them individually, and by implication recognizes and supports the traditional social system. Thus, the *fakatapu* is really in praise of Tongan society and points out that only Tonga has managed to retain its kings and social system in spite of the encroachment of Western civilization, and of this they are proud. A second important concept in this stanza is that the people of Tonga love and understand each other because of their principles of relationship by which they descend from the kings of old and their present kinship ties. These are worn as proudly as a floral necklace. On another level the whole *fakatapu* can be seen as the queen speaking to Prince Tungī, for he is the embodiment of the Kauhalalalo and Kauhalauta, having descended from the three major societal lines of Tonga. Because of these kinship ties he should be familiar with his people and be instrumental in creating love and friendship. Yet Tungī is exalted enough to influence natural phenomena as reported in lines 9 to 12. These lines also say that Tungī is as much a part of Lapaha (the place of the *'otu langi*) as he is of the present capital, Nuku'alofa, as a reminder that he descends both from the Tu'i Tonga line (highest ranking line of chiefs) and the Tu'i Kanokupolu line (the present ruling line of chiefs). This is neatly accomplished by means of a Tongan poetic device which equates people with places and by making reference to geographic areas by famous landmarks, such as *'otu langi* and *toa* Vaha'akolo, These symbolize Lapaha and Nuku'alofa, respectively, and ultimately refer to the Tu'i Tonga and Tu'i Kanokupolu lines of Tungī's genealogy.

Stanzas 2 through 7 are the *lakalaka* section of the poetry which tell the story. Stanza 2 elaborates the reason for the composition and performance, that is, the going away of Tungī. Stanza 3 praises Tungī by referring to his genealogical relationships. Tungī is referred to as *kulukona* (a flowering bush) of Tavake-fai'ana, emphasizing the kin ties with the chief Ulukalala of Vava'u using a poetic device which refers to chiefs by uncommon flowers and the tropic bird *(tavake)*. The nature symbolism continues with Tungī being plucked by the warm breeze. "Warm breeze" is equated with Tonga (especially Vava'u) and the line says that Tonga, the land of warm breezes, has picked Tungī for its next king. Line 21 states that no one is surprised at Tungī's greatness (fragrance because of the *kulukona*) because he is of double chiefly parentage. *Fakatoukatea*, a double canoe with both sides equal, poetically refers to chiefly descent on both sides. That Tungī is also sacred (having descended from the sky god Tangaloa through his mother) is suggested by the place name Monotapu, which in addition brings in his kin ties with the Ha'apai chiefs. In stanza 4, flowers and place names are combined to refer to Tungī's genealogy, implying that it is the mixture of his ancestral lines that make him outstanding just as a mixture of flowers makes the best scent. Lines 33 and 34 are again a reference to the performance occasion − Tungī going away to school is part of his grooming to be the next king. In stanzas 5 and 6 Tungī's hereditary lands at Kauva and Lapaha complain because the king has shifted his residence to Nuku'alofa (symbolized by the Vuna wharf). But stanza 7 answers that although he has moved, he cannot forget their love just as one does not forget the proverb about the kava on the island of Atatā in line 40.

The last stanza, here comprising only two lines, is the third major section in the structure of a *lakalaka*, the *tatau*. This is the closing counterpart of the *fakatapu* opening. Ordinarily this section would again acknowledge the chiefs. Here, however, because it is written by the queen there is no need to do so. Thus, in keeping with the story it tells of a Tongan's love for Tonga and refers here to the queen and Tungī, Tungī and Tonga, and in a generalized way to all Tongans, wherever they may be, and Tonga — for Tonga, although it is a small place, is the best place for Tongans.

Although the poetry can be interpreted on several different levels, this text is relatively straightforward. In dance texts that take mythological or historical subjects as their theme it is much more difficult to find the hidden meanings (see for example, Kaeppler, 1967a). Many more references and subtleties could be pointed out but enough has been said in order to compare it with a Hawaiian counterpart.

The performers of such a *lakalaka* are both men and women, often two-hundred or more. They are arranged in two or more rows facing the audience. The men stand on the right side (from the observer's point of view), and the women stand on the left. Each sex performs a different set of movements that are consistent with the Tongan view of what is suitable and appropriate for each sex. The arm movements allude to words of the poetry which often are themselves allusions. For example, stanza 3 would be interpreted in movement as follows. *Kulukona* (flowering bush) is choreographed with a beautiful, but not interpretive movement. The line is completed with a rotating-circling movement of the hands around each other at chest level. The same movement is used for the interpretive words of the next two lines, that is, breeze and fragrance. These concepts are conveyed here by the agitation of air which his rotating-circling movement creates. *Toli*, to pick, at the beginning of the second line of this stanza, is interpreted by a picking movement, the most obviously narrative movement in this group. *Tavake* is given an added interpretation by a quick side movement of the head *(fakateki)*, which recreates the head movement of the bird *(tavake)*. Fakatoukatea, double canoe, which refers to Tungī's double chiefly parentage, is interpreted by a repetition of side arm movements and with movements of the dancers. In the arm movements the right arm makes a lateral movement to the right side and then into the center to touch the left hand. Following this the left arm repeats the movement to the left side and the whole line is repeated in poetry and movement. Further, this important concept is interpreted throughout the stanza by changes in the dance formation. Instead of the more usual foot movements of a series of side steps nearly in place, the men and women walk toward each other and the usual two lines become four. The men then move to the front of the women. During the repetition of the stanza the men and women move back to their original two lines. This intermixes the men and women and then re-emphasizes the two groups, in an additional reference to Tungi's chiefly ancestry on both male and female sides.[7]

In order to point out differences in movement interpretation we can hypothesize how this stanza would be interpreted in Hawaiian dance. *Kulukona* would no doubt be interpreted by shaping the hands to resemble a flower; *tavake* by moving the arms to resemble a bird in flight; *matangi,* wind, by moving the arms alternately over the head; and double canoe by forming the hands to look like a canoe prow that moves on the waves. The Hawaiian interpretation would be more literal and narrative in nature and would be more likely to interpret nouns, in contrast to the Tongan interpretation of verbs.

To compare this similar, yet different, approach to interpretation of dance poetry in Polynesia, a series of dances for Hawaii's last king Kalākaua (1836-1891), will be used. Hawaiian dances are relatively short compared to the 25- to 35-minute productions of the Tongans. Thus in order to make the comparison, several dances of different categories will be used. Hawaiian sung poetry *(mele)* was of two main types – *oli,* which included all kinds of *mele* not intended for dancing, and *mele hula,* which had dance accompaniment. *Mele hula* were classified according to the accompanying musical instrument which was usually one of untuned percussion (Kaeppler, 1973a, 1973b). The Hawaiian *hula,* like the Tongan *faiva,* were stylized visual accompaniments to sung poetry and the movements were intended to enhance the meaning of the poetry. In contrast to the usual Western idea that music accompanies dance – in Polynesia it is poetry that is basic and most important.

In Hawaii, as in Tonga, dance without poetry did not exist, except for the very short rhythmic introductions, interludes between stanzas and closing phrases. Each *mele hula* had a melodic pattern, but this might differ from school to school or from individual to individual. In addition the dance might be accompanied by a different percussion instrument, depending on the choreographer. The poetry for five *mele hula* in honor of King Kalākaua follows. These songs and dances are among those preserved by Mary Kawena Pukui, who also made the English translations.

---

[7] For a more detailed description of the choreography of this stanza see Kaeppler (1972, pp. 212-213).

KAULILUA I KE ANU WAI'ALE'ALE (HULA PAHU)

1 Kaulilua i ke anu Wai'ale'ale	Bitterly cold stands Wai'ale'ale
2 He maka halalo ka lehua makanoe	The lehua blossoms, soaked with fog, hang drooping
3 He lihilihi kuku ia no 'Aipo	Around 'Aipo swamp the thorny shrubs grow
4 O ka hulu a'a ia no Hau-a-'iliki	Pinched and made cold by the frosty dew
5 Ua pehia a 'eha ka nahele	Pelted and bruised by the beating rain
6 Maui e ka pua, uwe 'eha i ke anu	Bruised are the flowers that moan in the cold
7 I ke kukuna la wai o Mokihana	Touched by Mokihana's sunlight that shines thru the mist
8 Ua hana 'ia a pono a pololei	I can act in good faith and honor
9 Ha'ina ia aku no ia 'oe	As I declare this fact to you
10 O ke ola no ia o kia'i loko eia	That a pond keeper must receive his living from the pond
11 Kia'i Ka'ula nana i ka makani	Ka'ula looks on and observes the wind
12 Ho'olono i ka halulu o ka Maluakele	Hearkening to the roar of the Maluakele
13 Ki'ci, halo ia Makaike'ole	Peering and peeping at Maka-ike-ole
14 Kamau ka ea i ka Halau-a-ola	Keeping the breath of life in Halau-a-ola
15 He kula lima ia no Wawae-noho	A place loved and caressed is Wawae-noho
16 Me he puko'a hakahaka la i Wa'ahila	Like branchy corals standing at Wa'ahila
17 Ka momoku a ka unu, Unulau o Lehua	Torn and broken by the Unu-lau gale of Lehua
18 A lehulehu ka pono, le'a ka ha'awina	So come the many little blessings that one enjoys to share
19 Ke 'ala mai nei ka puka o ka hale la-cia	For the door of the house is fragrant with humanity

HE ALOHA NO NA PUA (HULA PĀ IPU)

1 He aloha no na pua	I am fond of the flowers
2 Na pua ohelohelo	Flowers with rosy cheeks
3 Ohelo ai a ka manu	The berries picked by birds
4 Ka lehua ula i ka uka	And the red lehua of the upland
5 Nani wale hoi ka ikena	What a joy it is to see
6 I ka ua nui a o Hilo	The heavy rains of Hilo
7 A nui mai ke aloha	It makes love gush forth
8 Ua like me ka wai puna	Like a bubbling spring
9 He ihona no a he alu	Going down an incline
10 Hakalia i ka piina	Then up over a rise
11 Ka piina a o Poulua	The rise of Poulua
12 Elua o'u makemake	Where there are two things I admire
13 Ka wali a o ko kino	The suppleness of your body
14 Ka nahe a o ko maka	And the sparkle in your eyes
15 Haina mai ka inoa	The end of my song I sing
16 O Kalanikaulilua	In honor of the chief

EIA NO KĀWIKA (HULA PĀ IPU)

1 Eia no Kāwika ʻehe	Here is David
2 Ka heke a o na pua ʻehe	The greatest of descendants
3 Ka uwila ma ka hikina ʻehe	Like the lightning in the east
4 Malamalama Hawaii ʻehe	Brightening Hawaii
5 Kuʻi e ka lono i Pelekane ʻehe	Report of him reached Great Britain
6 A lohe ke kuini o Palani ʻehe	And was heard by the Queen of France
7 Nawai ka pua iluna ʻehe	Whose offspring is this so high above
8 Na Kapaʻakea he makua ʻehe	Kapaʻakea was the name of his sire
9 Haʻina ia mai ka puana ʻehe	This is the conclusion of our praise
10 No Kalani Kāwika he inoa ʻehe	In honor of King David

HOLO ANA O KALĀKAUA (HULA KĀʻEKEʻEKE)

1 Holo ana o Kalākaua	Kalākaua sails away
2 E imi i ka pono na moku	To seek prosperity for the islands
3 I Kahiki a hoʻi mai	To Kahiki and return
4 I Kahiki a o pelekane	To Kahiki, land of the whites
5 Mai Kahiki a Wawae-pahu	From Kahiki to Wawae-pahu
6 I ka ohe kāʻekeʻeke	With the bamboo *kāʻekeʻeke* (stamping tubes)
7 I ka pahu kani a Lono	And the drum of the chief, Lono
8 O Lono-i-ka-makahiki	Lono-i-ka-makahiki
9 Hoʻoheihei kani moana	It is beaten out at sea
10 Kani Hawea pahu aliʻi	Hawea the royal drum
11 E o mai o kalani	Answer us O Chief
12 (O) Kalākaua no he inoa	To your name chant, O Kalākaua

LILIKOʻI (MELE MAʻI)

1 Ka ua i Lilikoʻi, Lilikoʻi e	The rain at Lilikoʻi, Lilikoʻi
2 Oheohe i luna la	It gathers high above
3 Puhaʻu i lalo e	Tumbles down below
4 Ku aku la ʻoe i ka uwehewehe kui kela la	You are pierced by the needle shuttling back and forth
5 Aia ihea? (Eia no ia la)	Where is it? It is here
6 Aia mahea? (Eia maʻanei la)	In what place? Right here
7 Eia nei, o kuli o lohe i neia la e-maumau e.	Say whether you are deaf or do hear this — Hold on!
8 Hana kui kele ka ua i ʻOpae-ʻula la	Like a piercing needle is the rain of ʻOpae-ʻula
9 Mahiki i luna la	It leaves the sky
10 Haʻule i lalo e	And falls below
11. Ku aku la ʻoe i ka uwehewehe kui kela la	You are pierced by the needle shuttling back and forth
12 Aia ihea? (Eia no ia la)	Where is it? It is here
13 Aia mahea? (Eia maʻanei la)	In what place? Right here
14 E ia nei, o kuli o lohe neia la e-maumau e.	Say, whether you are deaf or do hear this — hold on!

This series of dance texts can be seen to honor Kalākaua in much the same way that the long Tongan text honors Tungī. The first dance, "Kaulilua i ke Anu Wai'ale'ale," is a *hula pahu*, which is the most elevated of all Hawaiian dance types because it is accompanied by a *pahu* drum. This type of drum was originally a sacred temple drum brought from Kahiki (the homeland) by Laka the goddess (or god) of the *hula* and not many chiefs of the historic period have *hula pahu* composed in their honor. Mary Kawena Pukui (pers. comm.) has informed me that this particular dance was composed for Kaumealani, a Waialua chiefess, by her mother. Indeed, the poetry refers to a passionate, yet disdainful woman. With the passing of time the chant was inherited by Kalākaua and demonstrates not only that he descends from this woman, but also that, because of his elevated genealogy, he is entitled to be honored with this sacred dance type. Much like Tongan poetry, this song text appeals to genealogy to honor the living. Although the movements interpret the words in a more realistic manner than the Tongan, one has to know the background of the inheritance of this composition to understand how the poetry and movements can refer to Kalākaua.

The second dance, "He aloha no na pua," a dance accompanied by the double gourd drum, *ipu*, is relatively straightforward. It praises Kalākaua with nature symbolism, comparing him to flowers and birds in much the same way as the Tongan text honored Tungī. There is a surprising similarity in some of the poetic imagery, for example, the Tongan lines 17 and 19

The Hea blossoms fell pecked by the birds
Scattered on the expectant voyagers

and the Hawaiian lines 3 and 4

The berries picked by birds
And the red lehua of the upland.

The Hawaiian text in general, however, uses more explicit body imagery such as "rosy cheeks," "sparkle in your eyes," and the "suppleness of your body." The movements, too, are much more explicit — the hands form flower shapes, the cheeks are touched, two fingers held up to interpret "two," and movements made at eye level interpret "eyes."

The third text, also accompanied by *ipu*, states that the fame of Kalākaua has reached Great Britain and France, but the most important implications are genealogical—he is the son of the great chief Kapa'akea, which is the reason that he should be so highly honored. Line 2, translated here as the "greatest of descendants," in literal translation means the "highest of all flowers" and is similar to stanza 3 of the Tongan *lakalaka*. The interpretation with movement does not refer to the genealogy itself but rather to the words that poetically allude to the genealogy (usually flowers). The literal translation of lines 9 and 10 is "this is in honor of this flower, Heavenly David is his name." The last line of the previous text, "He aloha no na pua," also adds Kalani (heavenly) to Kalākaua's inherited name, Kaulilua, and is comparable to the heavenly symbolism in Tongan poetry.

In the fourth dance, "Holo Ana o Kalākaua," the performer accompanies himself with bamboo stamping tubes *(kā'eke'eke)*. The text tells of Kalākaua's trips away from the islands but in a much more direct way than the Tongan text in stanza 2, and refers to Kalākaua's trip to the United States to work for a reciprocity treaty. The reference to Lono-i-ka-makahiki is genealogical and refers to Kalākaua's great ancestor, in whose honor the Kumulipo was composed. This chant tells of the creation of plants, animals, and men, and establishes Kalākaua's relationship to nature as well as to man. Lono-i-ka-makahiki in another manifestation was god of peace and agriculture and thus, in addition to establishing Kalākaua's relationship with the gods, this may be a reference to the peacefulness of his reign.

The last text is a *mele ma'i*. This kind of dance is traditionally performed last of a group of dances. *Mele ma'i* was a special kind of name chant composed in honor of a chief's sexual parts and alluded to these physical necessities for perpetuating the royal lines with nature symbolism. Movements often allude to the nature symbols rather than to the body parts. Faster in tempo and quite rhythmic, *mele ma'i* were probably conducive to the aesthetic exhilaration ideally created by Polynesian dance (see Kaeppler, 1971a).

This group of Hawaiian dances is arranged in the order in which they would be presented; that is, the sacred and more formal dances preceding the less formal and secular. Only the first dance of the group retains the subtleness of ancient Hawaiian *hula* in the allusive quality of poetry and movement. The other dances are 19th-century compositions in which the narrative potential of Hawaiian dance has been exploited to make the dance easier to understand to those who no longer understood the poetic subtlety of the Hawaiian language, for by Kalākaua's time English had become the medium of communication. (In Tonga this change was not necessary because there was never a large element in the population which could not speak Tongan.) Kalākaua's genealogy, his physical person, and his fame are recounted, as well as what he has done for Hawaii to deserve its praise and honor, and perhaps a wish is expressed for offspring to continue this elevated genealogical line. In addition, the texts pay allegiance to the sociopolitical system of the 19th century—a combination of indigenous Hawaiian concepts intertwined with ideals adapted from English monarchy. The movements, as aesthetic elements in themselves, enhanced the text and invited the watcher to admire how the movements interpreted concrete things and yet referred to deeper meanings and more abstract concepts.

Poetry for a Hawaiian dance was probably composed in honor of a chief for a specific occasion and then became part of the repertoire of chants in honor of that person. In the hands of different choreographers the movements might be quite different, since each might interpret different words of the text, or a different meaning of the same line, or a different line entirely if the poetry had been incorrectly heard or remembered (for most poetry existed only in the oral tradition). In fact, there was no one "correct" movement sequence for a text and part of the excitement of watching was to discover how skillfully the choreographer had interpreted the text in a culturally satisfying way.

Dance and its poetry in Hawaii, in Tonga, and in other parts of Polynesia do not tell an integrated story for an uninformed listener. Instead, the dancer tells a story, orally and visually, that is intended for those who know the poetic references and the cultural context of the performance. Traditional literature, and especially dance texts, may appear to the uninformed listener to be fragmentary and inconclusive, while to a member of the society the moral or purpose is readily apparent. Only if one knows the cultural background will the danced story emerge in all its dimensions. Indeed, in all of the Pacific area one must know the traditional literary background before one can fully appreciate or understand the phenomena of dance. For example, without knowledge of the Ramayana and Mahabharata, Javanese dance becomes a series of difficult movements, or without the literary background of Kabuki and Nōh, Japanese dance becomes a series of decorative and restrained movements between static poses.

Dance movements give to all these Pacific and East Asian literary forms an added dimension that can be enjoyed for itself or as an extension of the literature. This dance-literature, because of its double impact, is not only enjoyable but is a culturally acceptable milieu for imparting moral values and cultural ideals. Ways of thinking about dance and literature in the Pacific are qualitatively different from those of the West, and we should not look at them only through the eyes of a Westerner. How these cultural forms are perceived by those who originated them can be illuminating, not only for their own sake as a study of artistic forms, but also as a vehicle for understanding human behavior.

LITERATURE CITED

BECKWITH, MARTHA WARREN
  1951. *The Kumulipo: A Hawaiian Creation Chant.* Chicago: Univ. Chicago Press.
BURROWS, EDWIN GRANT
  1963. *Flower in My Ear: Arts and Ethos of Ifaluk Atoll.* Seattle: Univ. Washington
     Press.
GREEN, ROGER C.
  1966. "Linguistic Subgrouping within Polynesia: The Implications for Prehistoric Se
     tlement." *J. Polynesian Soc.* **75**:6-38.
  1967. "The Immediate Origins of the Polynesians." In G.A. HIGHLAND and OTHER
     (eds.), *Polynesian Culture History: Essays in Honor of Kenneth P. Emory*,
     pp.215-240. B.P. Bishop Mus. Spec. Publ. 56. Honolulu: Bishop Mus. Pres
  1968. "West Polynesian Prehistory." In I. YAWATA and Y.H. SINOTO (eds.), *Prehistor
     Culture in Oceania*, pp. 99-109. Honolulu: Bishop Mus. Press.
GOLSON, J.
  1971. "Lapita Ware and Its Transformations." In R.C. GREEN and M. KELLY (eds
     Studies in Oceanic Culture History, Vol. 2, pp. 67-76. Pacific Anthropologic
     Rec. 12. Honolulu: Dept. Anthropology, Bishop Mus.
KAEPPLER, ADRIENNE L.
  1967a. "Folklore as Expressed in the Dance of Tonga." *J. American Folklo.*
     80(316):160-168.
  1967b. "Preservation and Evolution of Form and Function in Two Types of Tonga
     Dance." In G.A. HIGHLAND and OTHERS (eds.), *Polynesian Culture Histor*
     Essays in Honor of Kenneth P. Emory, pp. 503-536. B.P. Bishop Mus. Spe
     Publ. 56. Honolulu: Bishop Mus. Press.
  1967c. The Structure of Tongan Dance. Ph.D. Dissertation, Univ. Hawaii.
  1970. "Tongan Dance: A Study in Cultural Change." *Ethnomusicology* **14**(2):266-27
  1971a. "Aesthetics of Tongan Dance." *Ethnomusicology* **15**(2):175-185.
  1971b. "Rank in Tonga." *Ethnology* **10**(2):174-193.
  1972. "Method and Theory in Analyzing Dance Structure with an Analysis of Tonga
     Dance." *Ethnomusicology* **16**(2):173-217.
  1973a. "Acculturation in Hawaiian Dance." *Yearbook of the International Folk Mus*
     Council for 1972, Vol. 4, pp. 38-46.
  1973b. "Music in Hawaii in the Nineteenth Century." In *Die Musikkulturen Asier*
     Afrikas and Ozeaniens im 19 Jahrhundert, pp. 311-338. Regensburg: Bosse
McKERN, W.C.
  1929. *Archaeology of Tonga.* B.P. Bishop Mus. Bull. 60. Honolulu.
SAHLINS, MARSHALL D.
  1963. "Poor Man, Rich Man, Big Man, Chief: Political Types in Melanesia and Polyr
     sia." *Comparative Studies in Society and History* **5**(3):285-303.
SOEDARSONO
  1969. "Classical Javanese Dance: History and Characterization." *Ethnomusicolc*
     8(3):498-506.

SOME EXTRA-OCEANIC AFFINITIES
OF POLYNESIAN NARRATIVES

BACIL F. KIRTLEY

University of Hawaii, Honolulu

T HIS STUDY WILL DISCUSS, under four categories, the thematic affinities which Polynesian narratives share with tales from other areas of the world. I, Presumably Recent Influences—Biblical; II, Presumably Recent influences—Animal-tale and Folktale; III, Traditional General Motifs; and IV, Traditional Indicative or Denotive Motifs.[1] Since the amount of relevant material is extensive, the present survey will focus upon motifs which typify the relationships of Polynesian tales to those of the world at large, or which, by raising questions of origin and diffusion, invite systematic investigation.

I. RECENT BIBLICAL INFLUENCES

Though scholars like Dixon (1916a, pp. 24, 40), Williamson (1933, p. 68-69, 94-95), and Beckwith (1940, pp. 43-46, 60, 493), have indicated repeatedly that Polynesian converts to Christianity introduced Biblical

---

[1] "General" is used here to refer to motifs which, since they occur in many geographical areas and since they are not sufficiently distinctive or complex that their polygenesis must be ruled out completely, cannot prove genetic relationships between narratives. "Indicative" motifs are those which, because of their highly distinctive cast, strongly suggest genetic relationships between narratives, but they cannot prove finally their common ancestry without exhaustive study. "Denotive" motifs are those which are complex or strikingly singular, which have a lurid unexpectedness and originality, and which strongly suggest, if they do not ultimately prove, genetic affiliations of narratives. Several of these are Oceanic extensions of clearly revealed distribution patterns. Their relationships to extraterritorial themes, consequently, can be in little doubt. The three adjectives contain an element of subjectivity, of course, but as relative terms, perhaps they will be of some convenience in the following discussion. By "recent," the time since European contact is meant.

elements into their inherited mythology, Barrère (1967, pp. 103-119), by concentrating upon this redactional activity itself, suggests the prevalence of the phenomenon. Perhaps the most audacious improvisations on Mosaic legendry were those created from 1865 to 1870 by the Hawaiians Kepelino and Kamakau, and naively perpetuated by Abraham Fornander (1878, pp. 59-100) in the "Kumuhonua legends" (Barrère, 1967, pp. 109-110). In these plagiarisms, a triad of deities (Kane, Ku, and Lono) create the first man from red clay and the first female from his rib (Fornander, 1878, pp. 61-62). A *moʻo,* or reptile, contrives the primal couple's downfall (p. 81), and "the large white bird of Kane" ejects them from Paradise (p. 82). Led by the marplot Kanaloa, a band of angels revolts against the ruling powers and is banished to "uttermost darkness" (p. 83), and Kanaloa's futile attempt to create a human being introduces death into the world. A world flood is caused by mankind's wickedness, but the patriarch Nuu survives this catastrophe (p. 87). Further, the Abraham-Isaac story is imitated (p. 97), as are accounts of the Hebrew escape across "the Red Sea of Kane" (p. 99, note 1) and of the career of Joseph—his abandonment in a pit, and his later successes in a foreign land (pp. 100-101).[2]

Other informants from the Society Islands, New Zealand, the Tuamotus, and the Marquesas, Barrère demonstrates (1967, pp. 104-117), ingeniously revised their putative mythology to approximate more closely Biblical passages.

II. PRESUMABLY RECENT ANIMAL-TALE AND FOLKTALE INFLUENCES

One infers from the distribution of beast-fable type stories—that is narratives treating zoomorphic humans performing in a simplified and self-contained fictive world—that these either have been introduced, or else have been reintroduced, in fairly recent times. The entirety of Polynesia, like most regions of the world, has furnished myriads of folktales containing animals with human traits (see Ky., 1971, Chapter B).[3] Stories coming from most groups of this area, however, depict animals playing

---

[2]The author has not seen Mrs. Barrère's book on the Kumuhonua legends, published by the Bishop Museum Department of Anthropology in 1969, but the reader will doubtless find there a detailed treatment of the Hawaiian pseudo-myths. A popular article on the subject once appeared in *The Paradise of the Pacific* (Anonymous, 1915, p. 10).

[3]Ky. refers to Kirtley, 1971 or 1955. Check the explanation given at the end of the article, just before the Literature Cited. References to Ky., 1955, to Ky., 1971, or to T will cite specific motif numbers or, as here, chapters, rather than volumes and page For convenience, motif-indexes usually will be cited rather than individual works whe the former's entries list several references or survey articles, or when the motif-referenc seems important.

incidental or supporting roles in plots which center around human heroes. Western Polynesia and the Outliers, in contrast, possess a vital animal-tale tradition, which seems to derive primarily from Melanesia and Micronesia (though in a few tales from these areas, as well as in a few from the Central-Marginal groups, transplants from Aesop, doubtless inspired by European pedagogy, can be detected).

"The Landcrab and the Rat" illustrates Polynesian animal-story affiliations with this kind of narrative in more westerly divisions of Oceania. The tale in Samoa (where it has inspired a well-known proverb, a fact suggesting a certain venerability) relates that a crab, a snipe, and a rat build a boat and go to sea. When the boat upsets, the crab sinks safely to the sea bottom, the snipe flies away, and the rat is left struggling in the water. An octopus carries the rat to shore, but during the voyage, the ungrateful passenger gnaws upon the neck of the octopus—hence the latter's tubercles (Turner, 1884, pp. 218-219). The incident in many versions provides an etiology for the enmity between the two species and explains the effectiveness of a rat-shaped fishing-lure in octopus angling (Beasley, 1921, pp. 100-114). With slight variations of plot and characters, the same basic tale has been noted in the Western Polynesian groups of Uvea, the Ellice Islands, Tonga, Samoa, Niue, Pukapuka, and in the Outlier islands of Kapingamarangi, Nukumanu, Ontong Java Lessa, 1961, pp. 263-264), and Rennell and Bellona (Elbert, n.d.). Pukapuka is the tale's eastern limit. To the westward, Lessa (1961. pp. 263-264), who has made a searching comparative study of its Oceanic forms, uncovered 12 printed versions from Micronesia, 24 from Melanesia, and 82 from Malaysia (in which he includes Indonesia and Madagascar).

"The Landcrab and the Rat" is an attenuated form of a tale which in its oral form can be traced back to India (Dixon 1916a, pp. 334, notes 20-25) and as a written text can be found in Sanskrit classics like the *Panchatantra* (written between A.D. 200 and A.D. 500) and the *Jātakas* (composed by at least 270 B.C.) (Adriani, 1893, p. 349; Kirtley, 960, p. 32). The Sanskrit version, entitled "The Monkey and the Crocodile," appears repeatedly in the fable literature of the Orient, and by way of Persian, Arabic, and Hebrew intermediate translations, it entered into the literature of medieval Europe (Kirtley, 1960, pp. 32-33). The scholarly studies and bibliography centering upon the tale are extensive pp. 36-37).

Polynesia possesses other animal-tales with extra-Oceanic origins. The almost universal "Tortoise and Hare" (Th., K11.3.), Aesop's fable which dramatized the racing victory of a slow but persistent animal over a speedy but sleeping opponent, is recorded in Niue (Loeb, 1926,

p. 201), Uvea (Burrows, 1937, pp. 166-167), and Samoa (Turner, 1884 p. 218). Another form of the tale in which the slower animal contestan deceptively wins the racing contest by stationing its relatives, who have its identical appearance, along the track to be run (Th., K11.1.), appears among Polynesians in Rennell Island (Bradley, 1956, p. 334; Elbert n.d.). The story probably diffused from Micronesia, for it has been report ed from the Mortlock Islands, Truk District (Grey, 1951, pp. 7-9), and Ponape (Hambruch, 1936, p. 180). Other Oceanic examples have beer gathered in abundance from Indonesia (de Vries, 1925-1928, pp. 46-47 359-360, 404 and notes; Dixon, 1916a, pp. 192, 334, note 18). And beyond Oceania the story is almost ubiquitous (Thompson, 1961, Type 1074).

Another example of internationally occurring fable literature which probably reached Polynesia during late precontact times is the Niuean tale of the flying fox and its treacherous behavior during a war between the birds and the quadrupeds. Because of its ambiguous nature, thi animal can plausibly join whichever side is winning. At last, when it treachery is discovered, it is disowned by both groups and in shame assumes a nocturnal existence (Loeb, 1926, pp. 194-195). In two Samoar stories, a sea cucumber is the creature which, during a war betweer the fishes and the birds, repeatedly vacillates (Ky., *B261.1.0.2.). The widely distributed Eurasian prototype of the story has a bat, rather thar a flying fox, as the opportunistic animal (Th., B261 and B261.1).[4]

Another category of animal story which belongs to a broad, almos world-wide tradition, is one which explains the characteristics of a specie by the adventures of a prototypical representative of the species (Th A2200-A2299.). Stories in which one animal causes another's body alter ations—changes of color, shape, size, or loss or gain of a member—are found almost exclusively in Western Polynesia and the Outliers (Ky A2200 to A2299.), a circumstance reflecting their relatively late diffusion from more westerly Oceanic regions.

Compared with Africa or North America, for instance, Polynesia ha adopted a negligible amount of exotic narrative material of the ordinar wonder-tale variety, and most of that borrowed was transmuted so thoroughly into the native vein as to be unrecognizable. The postcontact erosion of indigenous tradition, it seems, did not create among the Poly nesians any noticeable thirst for an alien one. A few examples of clea borrowing, however, did occur, and are interesting as curiosities, if fo no weightier reason.

The Polynesians' own long-existing traditions about ogres and spirit

---

[4]Tales of animal warfare are fairly common in Oceania. See Ky., Mts. B263.5. (betwee groups of birds: Marquesas, New Zealand), *B263.9. (between dog and lizards: New Zea land), *B263.10. (between groups of fishes: Nukumanu).

doubtless made them receptive to European tales about the Devil. A New Zealand story, for instance, is a close adaptation of the popular European legend of the "Black School" (Th., G303.19. and S241.2.).[5] It recounts that the female ruler of the lower world takes mortals for an apprenticeship in magic. At the end of their tutelage, the pupils dash frantically from her house, for the goddess exacts the lives of the last two persons to leave the house as the price of her instruction (Kararehe, 1898, p. 50; Ky., M218.+). Again, in a Bellona tale, an ogre's name is uttered and he mysteriously materializes (Elbert and Monberg, 1964, Nos. 185A, 185B; Ky., C21), a motif reflecting the European notion that the Devil may appear if his name is spoken. A Maori story about a sinister card player who invariably wins (Grace, 1907, pp. 108-110) is actually a popular European legend of the Devil as a card player, the climax of which is the Devil's vanishment in a puff of sulfurous smoke after his cleft feet are noticed (Th., G303.4.5.3.1.).

Another ogre motif in Polynesia, the origin of insects from the body of a slain monster, exists in at least one Hawaiian example (Green, 1923, p. 43). Hatt (1949, pp. 89-90) considers this idea to be a "special" motif—that is, one which is sufficiently distinct as to require diffusion. Since the Green example seems to be unique in Polynesia, the story probably arrived recently and via ship-borne visitors or immigrants.

Another New Zealand tale bears strong traces of European origin. When an enraged wizard invokes a spell to kill the first female who comes along a particular path, the victim ironically proves to be his own sweetheart. Numerous parallels to the story are found elsewhere (Th., M10ff., M415, S240 and S241).

A legend which in Europe has been attached to heroes such as King Alfred (Th., B523.1.) is associated in Niue with a chief named Foufou. Like his European prototypes, the Niuean ruler is a fugitive and hotly pursued. After he takes refuge within a cave, a spider (his god) at once spins a web across the mouth of the grotto and this deception spares the cave from search (Loeb, 1926, p. 218).

Polynesian examples of the far-distributed "transformation-combat" motif, in which two adversaries repeatedly change their shapes in an effort to gain a decisive advantage, occur in the Tuamotus, Societies, and Hawaii (Ky., D615). The motif possibly is not a recent acquisition, however, for it is found also in tales from the Mountain Arapesh of New Guinea and in stories from the Mariana Islands (Ky., 1955, D615). Frobenius (1938-1940, pp. 14-17, Map 17, p. 16) claims that the trans-

---

[5]Amusing is the frequency with which these stories (particularly in Norway) present a minister as their protagonist.

formation-combat motif quintessentializes somehow the *Stil* of the European *Märchenwelt*. The existence of the theme in Oceania, as well as in North and South America, would seem to blunt the thrust of his argument, however.

III. TRADITIONAL GENERAL MOTIFS

The traditional general motifs that will be discussed in this study, while they may not be taken as *a priori* clues of genetic relationships between different areas, are narrative ideas that appear to have a limited or unusual distribution and seem to reveal curious similarities of mythic conceptualization between far-separated regions.[6] Several of the themes, moreover, have figured in the theoretical speculations of well-known scholars and their Polynesian occurrence is perhaps significant.

Several Polynesian motifs associated with the gods and their possessions seem to be recorded from a rather limited number of regions. The idea that the creators of the world were male and female is a conception which the Hawaiians (Henry, 1928, p. 342) share with the Japanese (Th., A12.1.). Some peoples of the ancient Near East conceived of one of their gods as being in form partially human and partially fish, and the identical notion occurs in texts from the Tuamotus, Tahiti, the Cooks, Samoa, and Niue (Ky., A131.1.). Indic myth describes a many colored god (Th., A123.7.1.), and a Niuean narrative (Loeb, 1926, pp. 159, 161) describes a red-and-white god and a god with a striped body. In the New World, the Kato Indians tell that a dog accompanies the Creator, just as the Hawaiians relate that a dog goes with Lono (Beckwith, 1940, p. 347). A bird is the Creator's companion in some Indic and Indonesian myths (Th., A33.2.), as he is in Tongan and Samoan accounts (Ky., A33.2.).

Though an abnormal manner of birth is a feature commonly found in culture-hero biography, Polynesia shares several specific variations of the theme with rather limited areas. According to a distribution map of the *Forschungsinstitut für Kulturmorphologie* presented by Frobenius (1938-1940, Map 1, p. 8), the motif of the hero's posthumous birth (Th., A511.1.6.) is reported from Southeast Asia, North and South America, Indonesia, Melanesia, and from New Zealand in Polynesia.[7] Tonga also furnishes an example of this motif (Gifford, 1924, 124). The rebirth or

---

[6]The writer is aware of the risk of generalization upon the occurrence and the nonoccurrence of folklore themes. His statements about distribution patterns are all highly provisional and based upon the assumption that the current type and motif indexes and special monographs have uncovered, at the least, representatively pertinent data.

[7]Since Frobenius's article is loftily undocumented, his maps — somewhat blurred and unfocused — derive authority from his reputation alone.

double birth of the culture hero has a more restricted distribution: Ireland (Th., A510.2.), Melanesia, and the Marquesas (Ky., A510.2. and *A511.1.7.1.). The hero is abandoned at birth in myths from the Tuamotus, Marquesas, Societies, Cooks, Hawaii, and New Zealand (Ky., A511.2.1.), as he is in the Bible (Moses), and in narratives from elsewhere (Th., A511.2.1.). His growth is described as miraculously swift in myths from several Polynesian groups (Ky., A511.4.1.), as it is in many Melanesian, Micronesian (Ky., 1955, A511.4.1.), and extra-Oceanic areas (Th., A511.4.1.). Polynesian narratives repeatedly describe the hero's being reared in seclusion (Ky., A511.3.1.), a biographical touch found, according to Thompson (A511.3.1.), in medieval Irish literature.

Though Polynesian etiological stories correspond in their general content, emphasis, and dramatic structure with those from other areas of the world, these resemblances, owing to the inherent simplicity of plot, are usually too dim to offer persuasive evidence for specific extraterritorial kinships. The story of the coconut's origin from the head of a slain monster, eel, or human (Ky., A2611.3., *A2611.3.1., A2681.5.1.), for instance, is not only an often recorded Polynesian folktale-type (Kirtley, 1967, pp. 89-107), but is also a localized adaptation of a widespread mode of mythic explanation, and the formula is used in myriads of plant etiologies (Roosman, 1970, pp. 219-232; Frobenius, 1938-1940, pp. 10, 11, Map 7; Th., A2610ff.). Its degree of affiliation with parallel extraterritorial narratives is difficult to estimate, however. The story of a bird acquiring its color at the time it steals fire from a primeval sole possessor, which occurs in New Zealand and the Cooks (Ky., A2218.3., *A2218.3.1.), is found also in other parts of the world (Th., A2218.3.). The motif is quite distinct and unlikely to originate polygenetically; yet, its slightness inhibits productive investigation. And Tonga, Bellona, and Rennell mutually furnish texts, which are probably mutually cognate, dealing with the origin of the blood-colored sap in particular trees (Ky., A2755.2.); but the relationship of these stories to analogical ones in distant India (Th., A2755.2.) is again difficult to assess.

Polynesian narratives contain a number of ogre-motifs that are widespread in world folklore. The cosmopolitan theme of killing an ogre by feeding him hot stones (Th., G512.3.1.) appears in tales from the Societies, the Cooks, the Tuamotus, New Zealand, and Bellona (Ky., G512.3.1.),[8] and is also well-known in Melanesia, Micronesia (Ky., 1955. G512.3), and Indonesia (Dixon, 1916a, p. 133 note 6). Wallis (1960, p. 319) conjectures that the motif "suggests the giving of the swaddled stone to Kronos" and finds in its Oceanic occurrence a possible link

---

[8]The Maoris claimed that their ancestors killed *moas* by feeding them hot stones (Heuvelmans, 1959, pp. 236-237).

with Mediterranean mythologies of antiquity. Graebner (1919-1920, p. 1108) suggests that the idea, occurring also in the Sudan, is a survival linked somehow with an ancient Indo-Germanic cattle-herding culture complex (p. 1113). Frobenius (1938-1940, pp. 17-19, and 18, Map 18) interprets the ogre-killing by means of heated stones as a manifestation of an archaic Oriental-Oceanic ethos, and contrasts that form of assault with blinding the ogre by the instrument of an *Eisenstab (ein Objeckt der Eisenindustrie)*, relective of a basically different reality orientation: *"Zwei Zeiten, Zwei Perioden,"* he reflects.[9] The motif's almost universal distribution, however, would seem to support no theory except that it is either fantastically old or polygenetically invented.

Other ogre-motifs with a globe-encircling distribution, not surprisingly, are found in Oceania. Some of these are the "fee-fi-fo-fum" utterance, which occurs in stories from at least ten Polynesian groups (Ky., G84), as well as in tales from Melanesia and Micronesia (Ky., 1955, G84); the task of lousing an ogre, which appears in narratives from six Polynesian groups (Ky., G466), also in Melanesia and Micronesia (Ky., 1955, G466); and the inducement of a magic sleep by lousing, which is reported from seven Polynesian groups (Ky., D1962), as well as from Melanesia and Micronesia (Ky., 1955, D1962).

Various mythical and humanlike races, leading wispy and sinisterly alluring lives just beyond the periphery of everyday mortal experience, figure in Polynesian traditional narratives. These beings, like the *Menehune* of Hawaii or the *Patupaiarehe* of New Zealand, resemble the fairies of European tradition in their general folkloristic image and role; also the narratives concerning them have specific features paralleling European stories. Beckwith (1923, pp. 50-51) has particularized the similarities between Polynesian and European conceptions of the Happy Otherworld —a sunny and lovely paradise where the dwellers lead joyous lives untouched by age, illness or want—and narrations upon the fairy-mistress themes—particularly the idea, recurrent in both regions, that the lover of a fairy or otherworld being must observe rigidly some tabu as a condition of a continuing liaison, or else the mistress returns to her own world (Ky., C31ff., C932). In both areas, as in the folklore from most other parts of the world, food from the otherworld is forbidden to mortals (Th. and Ky., C211).

In the folklore of almost every region, supernatural beings of many species—ogres, fairies, trolls, giants, dwarfs, elves, demons, spirits, ghosts, and even gods—are imagined to shun daylight, either because some inscrutable metaphysical law constrains them (like Hamlet's father's ghost),

---

[9]One recalls, perhaps with bafflement, that Odysseus sharpened and heated a *wooden* stake to blind Polyphemos.

or else because exposure to sunlight is thought to be fatal to them. Graebner (1919-1920, p. 118) indicates that even in remote antiquity the chthonic beings of Babylonian mythology were believed to exhibit this sensitivity to light. Certainly, Polynesian texts from all parts of the Pacific present the idea, in a number of permutations, that supernaturals must avoid daylight (Th. and Ky., C311.8.1., C752.2.1., E452, F383.4., F383.4.3.), a theme with equivalents from numerous geographical regions.

A comparison of the "F Chapters" in the general and in the Polynesian motif-indexes, or a perusal of Luomala's book (1951) on the mythical races of Oceania, will illustrate the large number of correspondences that Polynesian narratives on this theme share with tales from other areas.

IV. TRADITIONAL INDICATIVE OR DENOTIVE MOTIFS

Indicative motifs are sufficiently distinctive that, found in two or more areas, they may suggest genetic affiliations. If comparative study confirms the probability of a historical connection between occurrences, they become denotive motifs. The relative and provisional sense of these terms, however, must be emphasized.

Several curious elements in Polynesian cosmogony have parallels in other areas of the world. The idea that the universe originated from a "cosmic egg" is found in the Society Islands, Hawaii, and New Zealand (Dixon, 1916a, pp. 20-21; Ky., A641). It occurs additionally in the mythologies of Borneo and Burma, and is widespread in other regions of Asia and Europe (Th., A641; Wallis, 1960, p. 318). Myths from the Society Islands and Tonga relate that the oceans originated from the Creator's sweat (Ky., A923), an idea that is found also in ancient Scandinavian literature (Th., A923). And the growth of land masses from a substance like earth, sand, or stone dropped upon the primeval water is described in creation accounts from most Polynesian groups (Ky., A810 to *A833.1.). In a major comparative study, Lessa (1961, pp. 275-289) documents the Oceanic manifestations of this motif, which Hatt (1949, pp. 13-14) believes is the crucial idea underlying the earth-diver myth, a narrative he traces throughout both the Old and New Worlds (pp. 12-36).

Polynesia shares with other areas two ideas about the structure of the world which, owing to their arbitrary singularity, appear to be denotive. The Marquesans believe that the earth rests upon the back of a fish (Christian, 1895, pp. 188, 199), as do tribes in Siberia (Th., A844.3.); and the Ellice Islanders' view that the earth is supported by a turtle is found among the Gilbert Islanders (Ky., 1955: A844.1.), the Indians of Asia, the Siberians, and the Iroquois and Northeast Woodland Indians of North America (Th., A844.1.).

Hatt (1949, p. 61) believes that the Siberian notion of a large number of skies, seven or nine, is "probably of Babylonian origin . . . [and] based upon astronomic observations of the movements of the planets, the sun, and the moon . . . ." Whether the concept of multiple heavens is actually an indicative, rather than a general, motif is debatable. At any rate, Polynesian narratives mention not only nine sky-worlds, but refer to a plurality of sky-worlds ranging in number from three to fourteen, ten being the most common number (Ky., A651 -*A651.1.8.2.).

Three aspects of another commonly reported Polynesian sky-myth have far apart and historically venerable analogues—that of the Sky-Father and Earth-Mother (Th., Ky., A625, A1971), of the raising of the heavens to their present height (Th., Ky., A625.2.), and of the propping or fixing aloft of the sky (Th., Ky., A665ff.). Polynesian accounts of the Sky-Father and Earth-Mother are not, as claimed by Dixon (1916a, p. 35), limited to New Zealand, but occur in most parts of the area. The analogy with ancient Greek myth is inescapable. The sky-raising theme is world-wide in distribution and is probably at least as old as the third millenium B.C. (Kramer, 1944, p. 52). Related to the concept of pillars holding up the sky is that of a world column (Th., Ky., A841), the cosmological and ceremonial importance of which has been emphasized in several ancient and primitive religions (Hatt, 1949, pp. 60-61).

A Polynesian mythological theme which seems to appear quite rarely in other areas is the depiction of heavenly bodies in the role of cannibals, though anthropomorphizations of all manner of objects and phenomena are a common fabric of folk narrative, of course. The specific portrayal of the sun as a man-eater occurs in Samoan and New Zealand tales (Ky., A711.2), as well as in narratives from India, North America (Th., A711.2), and Nauru (Micronesia), where Sun and Moon are portrayed as cannibalistic brothers (Brandeis, 1904, pp. 111-114).

In texts from the Tuamotus, the Marquesas, New Zealand, and the Reef Islands, stars are shown as cannibals (Ky., *F499.1.2., *F499.4., G811.8.1.; Williamson, 1933, Vol. 1, pp. 128-129), a theme occurring also in tales of the Tinguian (Philippines) and Chinese, who recorded a widespread panic caused by a star-demon called the Celestial Dog, which was believed to consume human livers and drink human blood (Willoughby-Meade, 1928, p. 161). In Tahiti comets are thought to be evil spirits (Ky., *F499.4.), if not explicitly cannibals, in which guise myths from the Torres Straits depict them (Ky., G11.8.). Australian tribes around Port Essington similarly believe falling stars are cannibals and mention "Yumbubur, the shooting-star devil that feeds on the entrails of the newly dead" (Hill, 1951, p. 380). Also, several Peninsula tribes of North American Indians believe meteors are cannibals (Th., G11.8.). The theft of the sun (Th., A721.1.), a narrative theme found in numerous areas of both hemispheres, appears sparsely in Polynesia. In a Hawaiian story the rays only are stolen (Beckwith, 1940, p. 437), and in a New Zealand tale the sun itself is taken (Wohlers, 1875, p. 6). The famous Polynesian story of Maui's snaring the sun and regulating its course (Ky., A728.2.; Luomala, 1949) has analogues from Africa and North America. Luomala (1940) analyzed the structure of the tales from each region and concluded that the traditions of the three areas were not related in origin. Later, she examined other examples of the sun-snaring myth and concluded that the Bengali form derives from the same source as does the Oceanic (Luomala, 1964, p. 217).

A Polynesian moon-myth which has far apart non-Oceanic cognates is presented most revealingly in the Maori stories of Rona, summarized by Róheim (1927, pp. 449-451). These narrate that when Rona goes by moonlight to fetch water, the light fails and she stumbles. She scolds the moon, and the orb in reprisal carries her off with her calabash (and sometimes with a tree to which she clings) to live in the sky. She can, the stories generally conclude, be seen there today, along with the tree and the calabash. Narratives with some of these elements have been collected from Tahiti (Leverd, 1912, p. 3), Hawaii (Beckwith, 1940, p. 221), and other Polynesian groups (Ky., A751.8ff.). On the Eurasian continent myths explaining the image upon the moon by Rona-like accounts are found from Iceland to Japan and along the Northwest Pacific Coast of North America (Róheim, 1927, pp. 442-448). The concept apparently was formulated in southern or southeastern Asia, whence it diffused to other regions now possessing it (pp. 457-462).

A New Zealand explanatory myth about the origin of a river's currents (Ky., *A939.1.) relates that two rivers race in order to determine which can first reach their common ancestor the ocean, and in doing this they establish their respective characteristics (Best, 1924, p. 210). The Khasis in India have an analogous tale of contesting rivers (Gurdon, 1907, pp. 178-179), and Russian folklore explains that the present currents of the Volga and Vazuza Rivers originated from their behavior during a race to the sea (Afanas'ev, 1957, Vol. 1, p. 139), a story related in that country of several other pairs of rivers which flow into each other (p. 481, No. 94).

Though Polynesian myths vary widely in their accounts of mankind's origin, the creation processes described nearly all have counterparts in extraterritorial narratives. Oceanic myths from the Marquesas, the Chatham Islands, Samoa, the Fijis, the Solomons, the Admiralties, and the

Massim narrate that human beings originated from eggs (Ky., A1222), a theme with Indic, Chinese, and South American Indian cognates (Th., A1222). Relations from Hawaii, the Marquesas, and the Ellice Islands state that mankind descended from a fish (Beckwith, 1940, p. 129; Ky., A1224.6.), an idea found in South American Indian belief (Th., A1224.6.). Oceanic myths from the Tuamotus, the Societies, Hawaii, Samoa, the Gilberts, and the Marshalls picture the first humans as rudimentary and amorphous beings which only gradually assumed their present form (Ky., A1225), a concept with Indonesian and Australian parallels (Th., A1225). The idea that the first man descended from the sky—which occurs in narratives from Samoa, New Zealand, Rotuma, and Truk (Ky., A1231)—is of world-wide distribution (Th., A1231). Both hemispheres and a number of Oceanic islands possess similar emergence myths, in which primeval humans issue from beneath the ground (Th., and Ky., A1232, A1234), from caves (A1232.3.), from trees (A1236), or from stones (A1245). The myth that mankind originated from the mating of a tree and a vine seems to have been noted only in Samoa and Borneo (Dixon, 1916a, p. 159). A frequent sequel to this account in Western Polynesia (Ky., A1224.2.), however, is that the tree is destroyed, and as it rots worms or larvae emanate from the putrescence, and these gradually evolve into human beings. Elsewhere, mankind's descent is traced from worms, maggots, or larvae by several groups of South American Indians (Th., A1224.2.). Finally, the Morioris of the Chatham Islands, the Samoans, and other Oceanic island groups narrate that the first human was born from a blood clot (Dixon, 1916a, p. 109, note 17; Th., and Ky., 1971: A1263.1.1.).[10]

A number of Polynesian myths upon the origin of death resemble those from other parts of the world. A Samoan story quoted by Williamson (1933, Vol. 2, p. 146) tells that the gods held a council to decide mankind's fate. One god suggests that men should cast their skins as crustaceans do their shells and so renew their lives, or be like torches which, when shaken, blaze alight again. Another god objects, and thus death begins. The connection of immortality with shedding the body's outer covering, as do crabs or lizards, appears also in narratives from Hawaii, the Tuamotus, and Ontong Java (Ky., *A1335.3.1., *A1335.4.1., *A1335.17.). In a related story from Melanesia (New Britain and the Bismarck Archipelago), the serpent, which can change its skin, is given

---

[10]Gudmund Hatt (1949, pp. 80-83) examines the theme of birth from a blood clot in order to assess the possibility of a genetic relationship between the idea in North America and Oceania, but he comes to no conclusion. The blood-clot birth, not associated with human origins, is quite widespread in Oceania, and has been noted in Mangareva, Hawaii, New Zealand, Rotuma, the Loyalties, the New Hebrides, New Britain, and the Admiralties (Ky., T541.1. and T541.1.1.).

immortality instead of man, and the tale in this form is widely distributed and at least as old as the mythology of ancient Babylon (Th., A1335.5.). The World-Tree or Tree-of-Life concept is well known in North America (Hatt, 1949, p. 61). Wassén (1940, pp. 69-70) has pointed out a South American and Palauan version of the theme, and Luomala (1942, pp. 190-191) has indicated the existence of the concept in Hawaiian mythology, where two Trees-of-Food are the equivalent: one tree supplies vegetable food and the other attracts fish (Beckwith, 1940, pp. 286-287; Ky., *A1420.7., F811.5.3.).[11]

Also, indicative motifs which are not cosmological in nature appear in Polynesia. Since the pursuit by a rolling head occurs in a couple of Hawaiian collections (Ky., R261.1.), and apparently nowhere else in Oceania, it may be, therefore, a recent import from the Northwest Pacific coast of North America, where a considerable number of Hawaiians long were employed by fur companies during the 19th century. Though the theme occurs in Europe, Asia, Africa, and South America, its popularity among the North American Indians has been enormous (Th., R261.1.).

Examples of the Orpheus story—the plot of which involves a person's traveling to the underworld in order to acquire the soul of a beloved spouse or relative and his returning with it to the land of the living—have been collected repeatedly in Polynesia from Mangareva to Rennell, and the tale is equally popular in other areas of Oceania (Ky., F81.1.). Only close comparative studies can reveal the relations of the Oceanic versions with extraterritorial examples, found in great abundance (Hatt, 1949, pp. 65-69; Th., F81.1.).

Oceanic narratives mention several means of ascent to the sky which seem adequately curious to raise issues of possible relationships with parallels cited elsewhere. The motif of a hero using a spider web as a ladder to the sky has been noted in the Chatham Islands, New Zealand, Hawaii, the Banks Islands, the New Hebrides, and the Carolines (Dixon, 1916a, p. 166; Ky., F51.1.1.). The same detail is present in tales from Asia, North and South America, Africa, and Indonesia (Hatt, 1949, pp. 49, 51, 53; Th., F51.1.1.). Again, in Marquesan and Hawaiian tales, a person's tongue is used as a pathway to the sky (Ky., F57.2.), as it is in Indian narratives (Th., F57.2.). And the incident of a person's traveling to the upper-world upon rising smoke appears in myths from the

---

[11]Another theme of the Palauan and Choco Indian myths (Wassén, 1940, p. 71), for which Luomala (1942, pp. 190-191) mentions a Hawaiian parallel, is the trick of diverting fierce guardian fish from their task by throwing fruit in the water. The motif occurs in the famous legend of Punia, who tricks a pack of sharks in this way (Beckwith, 1940, p. 443).

following groups: Hawaii, the Ellice Islands, Kapingamarangi (Ky., F61.3.1.), and Samoa (Lessa, 1961, pp. 369-371) in Polynesia; general in Micronesia (Lessa, 1961, p. 370); in the Banks Islands and the New Hebrides in Melanesia (Ky., F61.3.1.); in Roti in Malaysia (Lessa, 1961, p. 371); and in India (Th., F61.3.1.) and Siberia (Hatt, 1949, p. 56) in Asia.

Two Polynesian stories dealing with trick seductions resemble sequences popular in North American Indian tales. In a story from the Marquesas which is much like the "sham doctor" tale (Th., K1315.2.1.), a girl is seduced when she is persuaded to sit on a particular plant (Steinen, 1934-1935, p. 233); and a Tuamotuan narrative presents the "lecherous-father" theme when a man seduces his daughter by hiding beneath the sand (Th., Ky., T411.1.).

Thompson captions a Jamaican motif (G322.) as follows: *"Piercer-of-souls: fishes men."* This basic notion receives some interesting colorations in Oceania. A Marquesan myth speaks of a blind cannibal god who dangles a hook and line from the heavens, jigging for victims (Steinen 1933-1934, pp. 370-372). In a New Zealand tale, when the gods throw down a hook and line from the sky, a man puts the latter into his mouth. The gods set the hook and the victim acquires a painful disease of the jaw (White, 1887-1890, Vol. 1, p. 67). Other stories from the Societies, the Tuamotus, and the Cooks contain the incident of a blind ogress trying to catch the hero by swinging her great hook (Ky., *K525.11.). In a Carolinian myth, a god in the sky-world momentarily hooks the trickster hero in the neck, until the latter can sever the rope with a shell (Dixon, 1916a, p. 261, note 3). Living far to the west of Oceania, the Ainus of Sakhalin Island have furnished a striking cognate of the man-fishing theme in the story of a young bride who awakes in the night to find her groom hooked with an iron ring and being drawn skyward through the roof by an amorous goddess (Pilsudski, 1912, p. 85).

Whether the narrative motifs connected with angling for humans grew simply from a fisherman's ambivalent identification with his prey, or whether they were originally suggested by some custom, like the widely practiced Melanesian funeral ceremony of fishing for the soul of a recently dead person with a pole, line, and croton leaves (Riesenfeld, 1950, pp. 140, 175, 205, 253, 667), is open to speculation. And whether the soul-fisher theme merges with what Frobenius (1938-1940, pp. 10, 11, Map 9) terms the *"Mädchenangel-Sage"*—and shows in his distribution map to occur in eastern and southeastern Asia, Oceania, and much of North America—cannot be stated, since his article lists no sources.

The story of Hina and the marking of fish is actually a folktale-type (in the folkloristic sense of being a recurrent narrative pattern), although a fairly simple one, and has Asian and European parallels which may or may not be genetically related to the Oceanic story. The Polynesian tales, though with varying details, are noted in the Cooks, Niue, the Chatham Islands, the Tuamotus, the Ellice Islands, Uvea, Kapingamarangi, and in the Fijis. The following elements are fairly consistent, however. A young woman, usually Hina (the most popular goddess and the archetypical female of Polynesian myth), is left by her parents to guard some valuables or watch drying clothes. She neglects her duties, and her parents scold or punish her, whereupon she resolves to leave her home and go on a sea voyage. She calls upon different fishes to carry her across the ocean. As each fails her, she punishes it in such a way that the species is changed permanently. Finally, a turtle or shark is able to bear her weight, but during the sea voyage she marks it in some way: for instance, the turtle's head retracts because she cracked a coconut upon it, or the shark smells ammoniac because she urinated upon it (Dixon, 1916a, pp. 71-72; Ky., *A2211.16., *A2211.17., *A2213.5.3., A2412.4., and A2305.1.ff.). A quite similar story is found in India, and a tortoise or crocodile carries the Rice Goddess or other sacred person across a body of water and is physically altered as a reward or punishment (Türer-Haimendorf, 1940, pp. 112-113, Th. A2221.5., A2223.6., A2231.7.2., A2231.7.3., A2239.7.). A European tale with the equivalent plot elements of the Oceanic and Indic narratives is *"Die Sage von Jesu Flussübergang,"* which has been studied comparatively by Dähnhardt (1900, Vol. 2, pp. 87-95). The animal in most European versions punished for its failure to transport Christ is the horse. A Lithuanian version, however, appears in a collection of Jonas Balys (1940, Vol. 1, pp. 96-97) in which Jesus, like Hina, punishes various fishes for their churlishness or inadequacy.

The "open-sesame" motif proliferates in Polynesia (Ky., D1552.2.), as it does in the remainder of Oceania (Lessa, 1961, pp. 334-346), Frobenius's statement and chart notwithstanding (Frobenius, 1938-1940, pp. 14, 16, Map 16).

Polynesia furnishes several examples of what Frobenius (p. 12) calls the west Asian version of the Herakles myth, that highly specialized version of the Jonah legend in which the hero emerges from the swallowing monster's stomach bald-headed (frequently after slicing his way out with a shell or knife), his hair having dropped out because of the intense and protracted heat. Though a satisfactory survey of this theme would require many pages, a brief indication of the motif's distribution is necessary. Polynesian accounts from the Tuamotus, the Marquesas, Tahiti, and Hawaii, contain the bald-headed-emergence incident (Ky., F921), and it turns up in a Melanesian tale from the Torres Straits (Haddon, 1890, pp. 56-58). The Koryak of Siberia know the motif (Jochelson, 1908, pp. 169, 293), as do numerous tribes along the American Northwest Coast (Frobenius, 1904, pp. 81-83; Jochelson, 1908, p. 375, note 38; Th., F921), the Cherokee of the Mid-Atlantic region (Frobenius, 1904, pp. 95-96), and several tribes of South American Indians (Rühle, 1925, pp. 13, 19). Classical myth, of course, relates that Herakles dived down a dragon's throat, spent three days hacking through its viscera, and emerged victorious but hairless (Graves, n.d., Vol. 2, p. 169, No. 137). Jewish legendry embellished the story of Jonah with the baldness aftermath (Ginzberg, 1909-1938, Vol. 4, p. 252; Vol. 6, p. 351). A little known American poet, Robert Frank Jarrett (1916, p. 180), embodied the incident in a romantic narrative poem. However, an Irish Fenian ballad written down in 1627 (Dillon, 1948, pp. 49-50) exploits the motif with an outrageous lack of restraint which confirms that race's notorious reputation for hyperbole. Two hundred warriors of the Fian, says the ballad, are swallowed by a monstrous beast. After they slice it open, one hundred and ninety-nine come forth without hair and one (who had been bald to begin with) without a scalp (ITS, Vol. 28, p. 239).

The singularity of Motif F921 is so extreme that one at first rejects the likelihood it could have been invented more than once. Its distribution, on the other hand, is erratic and suggests no obvious diffusionary history. One explanation for the motif's odd embodiments and manifestations may be that it parallels some process of nature susceptible to anecdotal interpretation by men everywhere, and one can see in the idea the imagistic analogy of the birth process. Babies, that is, generally do issue hairless from the womb.

Wallis (1960, p. 326) remarks that "an Iranian parallel in Indonesia and Oceania is the concept that the soul enters or leaves the body through the big toe." He mentions some other Asian manifestations of this belief and connects it with the motif found in Hawaiian narratives of resuscitating a dead person by forcing his soul into his body through the big toe (Ky., *E38.2.). Additionally, the belief that the big toe is the portal of soul entry has been noted among the Malayan Negritos (Evans, 1923, p. 156).

The motif of the "obstacle flight," in which fugitives toss behind them various objects which become transformed into barriers hindering their pursuers, has been studied by a number of investigators (Hatt, 1949, pp. 92-94; Th., D672), and the residual opinion after debate is that the New World versions diffused from the Old World. The motif occurs in Polynesian narratives from the Marquesas, Samoa, and Niue (Ky., D672). And the "reversed obstacle flight," an obvious variation in which pursuers magically erect obstacles in front of their quarry, has been noted in the Tuamotus, Tonga, and Samoa (Ky., D673). A detailed analysis would reveal perhaps the kind of relationship which the Polynesian motif bears to the theme elsewhere.[12]

Dixon (1916b, pp. 80-87) first studied the Oceanic versions of the swan-maiden story (Th., D361.1.), and his conclusions that it has an extraterritorial origin is supported by Lessa (1961, pp. 120-167), who presents evidence that the tale's basic elements were shaped in India, spread into Southeast Asia, and thence into Oceania to areas as distant as Australia and the Tuamotus (pp. 160-166). The Polynesian swan-maiden theme is therefore conclusively denotive.

The "vagina-dentata" motif–a woman with teeth or fangs in her vagina savages lovers–appears in tales from the Marquesas to Samoa (Ky., F547.1.1.). Since Hatt (1949, pp. 85-87) points out examples of the theme in Siberia and in North and South America, since Penzer (1952, pp. 41-44) cites instances of vagina dentata in Japanese and in Indic folklore, and since ethnologists show occurrences of the motif among the aboriginal Vataan Ami tribe of Taiwan (Eberhard, 1964, p. 51), the Polynesian examples of the fantasy are a plausible extension of the distribution pattern and indicate a diffusion from some eastern Asian matrix.

A Marquesan tale (Steinen, 1933-1934, pp. 347-349, 360-364)–Polynesian analogues have been noted also in the Tuamotus, the Cooks, Hawaii, Samoa, Tonga, Fiji, and Tikopia (Beckwith, 1940, pp. 498-504; Dixon, 1916a, pp. 66, 140-141 and notes; Ky., F112, F112.1.)–relates that, when a hero is abandoned at sea and swallowed by a fish, he cuts his way out and comes ashore at an Isle of Women, where the inhabitants take pandanus roots as husbands. He weds a woman, makes her pregnant, and then teaches the islanders the art of natural childbirth as an alternative to their deadly Caesarean practice (in stories from several Polynesian groups the hero teaches the art of cookery). When his hair eventually begins to gray and his wife shows no signs of age, he leaves the island for his first home. This story occurs also in Melanesia, where a New Guinea version (Riesenfeld, 1950, p. 360) bears an astonishing similarity to the Marquesan tale. It appears in Micronesia also. Outside of Oceania the motif of a journey to a land of amorous women, whose persistent attentions frequently have fatal consequences for the hero, occurs among the Atayal aborigines of Taiwan (Norbeck, 1950, pp. 37-39), in China, India, ancient Greece, Ireland, and North America (Th., F112, F112.1.).

---

[12]Lessa's study (1961, pp. 403-411) concerns only the "Atalanta type," Mt. R231, not the theme involving the magical transformation of objects.

The motif of a hero's introduction of natural childbirth, often entering tales about the Isle of Women, is well known in North America along the Northwest Coast and in the Cumberland Sound region (Hatt, 1949, pp. 83-84). And in Polynesia, island groups other than those mentioned by Hatt possessing the motif are the Marquesas, Tonga, Mangareva, and Kapingamarangi (Ky., *T584.0.7. and T584.3.). The theme is popular also in Melanesia and Micronesia (Riesenfeld, 1950, pp. 128-129, 206, 220-221, 224, 225, 232-233, 247, 360, 405, 479; Hatt, 1949, p. 84).

The motif of the "one-sided man" (Mt. F525) is noted among the Siberian tribes and the native peoples of the New World (Hatt, 1949, pp. 87-89). Polynesia also has the incident in several forms. A Tongan story tells of a man who causes himself to be killed and cut in two pieces, so that his legs and buttocks may be affixed to his murdered king's body, which lacks these features (Gifford, 1924, pp. 31-32), while Samoa and Rotuma furnish tales of a man who splits in two parts (Ky., F525.2.). In a Marquesan story, the hero places together half bodies in order to create whole people (Steinen, 1934-1935, p. 216). The Hawaiian motif of a man whose body is half stone (Ky., F525.1.1.) is perhaps related.

A final Oceanic narrative which appears to have New World cognates has been captioned the "Posthole Murder": a precocious boy trickster offends a band of elder youths, who lure him down a hole into which they are to position a house pillar. The boy escapes the descending log by a ruse (or with the help of animals), and emerges mockingly triumphant at the top of the pole (Mt. K959.6.). Lessa (1961, pp. 393-402) has studied Pacific versions of the story and finds the tale present in several Melanesian areas, though it has been utilized most creatively in Micronesia, where it figures as part of the Olofat or Nareau mythic cycle. He cites two Ellice Island examples from Polynesia proper and an instance each from the Outliers of Nukumamu and Ontong Java (Lessa, 1961, p. 402). Tikopia also furnishes the theme (Firth, 1961, p. 101).

Frobenius (1938-1940, pp. 7, 8, Map 3) indicates an extensive New World distribution—covering the United States, Central America, and northwestern South America—of the Posthole Murder, which he terms *"Der Lausbub im Hauspfeiler."* The mystery of Frobenius's sources has been mentioned. One firm cognate, however, can be indicated in the *Popol Vuh* (Goetz and Morley, 1950, pp. 99-101), a document written shortly after the Spanish conquest by a Quiché Indian of Guatemala and embodying cosmological traditions of a group of ancient Mayans. The *Popol Vuh* version lies quite within the canon of the narrative type as it occurs in Oceania, and the problem raised by this correspondence is related to the larger issue of trans-Pacific contacts. Though the major portion of narrative themes in each Polynesian island group is apparently indigenous and exists only within a relatively limited and contiguous area, considerable numbers of motifs and types are shared between groups, often far removed from one another. A smaller amount of Polynesia's mythic ideas occurs also in other regions of Oceania, and a still slighter quantity of story materials exists in both Polynesia and extra-Oceanic areas. The last category of affiliations has formed the subject of this study, and specific thematic correspondences have been treated under four different categories of thematic affinity. The kinds of exotic influences perceptible in the traditional narratives of Polynesia make it clear that much of the area has participated in an exchange—even if in an attenuated form—of intellectual culture throughout its history. Though few whole complex narratives of Eurasian origin withstood the erosion imposed during their transmission through the cultures lying to the west of Polynesia, certain hardy and viable conceptual elements did survive and take root. This process of transmission and adaptation and its implications require continuing investigation.

ABBREVIATIONS

ITS	Irish Texts Society
Ky.	See Kirtley, Bacil F., 1955, 1971. If no date is given in a Polynesian citation, the reference is to 1971. Melanesian citations are to 1955.
Mt(s).	Motif(s)
Th.	See Thompson, Stith

LITERATURE CITED

ADRIANI, NICOLAS
  1893."Sangireesche teksten met vertaling en aanteekeningen." *Bijdragen tot de Tall-, Land-, en Volkenkunde* 42:321-440.
AFANAS'EV, A.N.
  1957. *Narodnye Russkie Skazki.* V. Ya. Propp (ed.). 3 vols. Moscow: Gosudarstvennoi Izdatel 'stvo Khudozhestvennoie Literatury.
ANONYMOUS
  1915. "Hawaiian Legends Resembling History of Old Testament." *Paradise of the Pacific* 28 (Sept.): 10-16.

BALYS, JONAS
    1940. *Lithuanian Folk Legends.* Kaunas.
BARRÈRE, DOROTHY B.
    1967. "Revisions and Adulterations in Polynesian Creation Myths." In G.A. HIGH-
    LAND and OTHERS, *Polynesian Culture History: Essays in Honor of Kenneth P.
    Emory,* pp. 103-119. B.P. Bishop Mus. Spec. Publ. 56. Honolulu: Bishop Mus.
    Press.
BEASLEY, HARRY G.
    1921. "Some Polynesian Cuttlefish Baits." *J. Royal Anthropological Inst. Great Britain
    and Ireland* **51**:100-114.
BECKWITH, MARTHA WARREN
    1923. "Polynesian Analogues to the Celtic Otherworld and Fairy Mistress Themes."
    In C.F. FISKE (ed.), *Vassar Medieval Studies.* New Haven: Yale Univ. Press.
    1940. *Hawaiian Mythology.* New Haven: Yale Univ. Press.
BEST, ELSDON
    1924. *The Maori.* Polynesian Soc. Mem. 5. 2 vols. Wellington.
BRADLEY, DIANA
    1956. "Notes and Observations from Rennell and Bellona Islands." *J. Polynesian Soc.*
    65:332-341.
BRANDEIS, ANTONIE
    1904. "Das Gesicht im Mond." *Ethnologisches Notizblatt* **3**:111-114.
BURROWS, EDWIN G.
    1937. *Ethnology of Uvea (Wallis Island).* B.P. Bishop Mus. Bull. 145. Honolulu.
CHRISTIAN, F.W.
    1895. "Notes on the Marquesans." *J. Polynesian Soc.* **4**:187-202.
DÄHNHARDT, OSKAR
    1907-1912. *Natursagen.* 4 vols. Leipzig and Berlin: Teubner.
DILLON, MYLES
    1948. *Early Irish Literature.* Chicago: Univ. Chicago Press.
DIXON, ROLAND B.
    1916a. *The Mythology of All Races,* Vol. 9, *Oceanic.* Louis B. Gray (ed.). Boston:
    Jones.
    1916b. "The Swan-Maiden Theme in the Oceanic Area." In S.A. BARRETT and OTHERS
    (eds.), *Holmes Anniversary Volume: Essays Presented to William Henry Holmes,*
    pp. 80-87. Washington: Bryan.
EBERHARD, WOLFRAM
    1964. "Abstract of 'Fairy Tales of the Vataan Ami,' by Wang Sung-hsing." *Abstracts
    of Folklore Studies* **2**:51.
ELBERT, SAMUEL H.
    [n.d.] Animal Stories from Rennell and Bellona. MS.
ELBERT, SAMUEL H., and TORBEN MONBERG
    1964. *From the Two Canoes: Oral Traditions of Rennell and Bellona.* Honolulu-Copen-
    hagen: Univ. Hawaii Press and Danish National Mus.
EVANS, IVOR H.N.
    1923. *Studies in Religion, Folk-lore and Customs in British North Borneo and the Malay
    Peninsula.* Cambridge: Cambridge Univ. Press.
FIRTH, RAYMOND
    1961. *History and Traditions of Tikopia.* Polynesian Soc. Mem. 32. Wellington.

FORNANDER, ABRAHAM
1878-1885. *An Account of the Polynesian Race: Its Origins and Migrations.* 3 vols. London: Trubner.

FROBENIUS, LEO
1904. *Das zeitalter des sonnengottes.* Berlin: Reimer.
1938-1940. "Das Archiv für Folkloristik." *Paideuma: Mitt. Kulturkunde* 8:1-19.

FÜRER-HAIMENDORF, CHRISTOPHE VON
1948. *The Raj Gonds of Abilabad.* Vol. 3 of *The Aboriginal Tribes of Hyderabad.* London: Macmillan.

GIFFORD, EDWARD W.
1924. *Tongan Myths and Tales.* B.P. Bishop Mus. Bull. 8. Honolulu.

GINZBERG, LOUIS
1909-1938. *The Legends of the Jews.* 6 vols. Philadelphia: Jewish Pub. Soc. America.

GOETZ, DELIA, and SYLVANUS G. MORLEY
1950. *Popol Vuh: The Sacred Book of the Ancient Quiché Maya from the Spanish Translation of Adrián Recinos.* Norman: Univ. Oklahoma Press.

GRACE, ARCHDEACON
1907. *Folk-tales of the Maori.* Wellington: Gordon and Gotch.

GRAEBNER, FR.
1919-1920. "Thor und Maui." *Anthropos* 14-15:1099-1119.

GRAVES, ROBERT
[n.d.] *The Greek Myths.* 2 vols. Baltimore: Penguin Books.

GREEN, LAURA S.
1923. *Hawaiian Stories and Wise Sayings.* MARTHA BECKWITH (ed.). Poughkeepsie: Vassar College.

GREY, EVE
1951. *Legends of Micronesia.* 2 vols. High Commissioner Trust Territory of the Pacific Islands. Dept. Education. Micronesian Reader Ser.

GURDON, PHILIP R.T.
1907. *The Khasis.* London: Nutt.

HADDON, ALFRED C.
1890. "Legends from Torres Straits." *Folklore* 1:47-81, 172-196.

HAMBRUCH, PAUL
1936. "Ponape." 3 Teilband, "Die Ruinen. Ponapegeschichten." In G. THILENIUS (ed.), *Ergebnisse der Südsee-Expedition 1908-1910.* II Ethnographie, B Mikronesien, Band 7. Hamburg: Friederichsen, De Gruyter.

HATT, GUDMUND
1949. *Asiatic Influences in American Folklore.* Det Kgl. Danske Viderskabernes Selskab 21, No. 6. Copenhagen: Munksgaard

HENRY, TEUIRA
1928. *Ancient Tahiti.* B.P. Bishop Mus. Bull. 48. Honolulu.

HEUVELMANS, BERNARD
1959. *On the Track of Unknown Animals.* RICHARD GARNETT (trans.). London: Hart-Davis.

HILL, ERNESTINE
1951. *The Territory.* Sydney-London: Angus, Robertson.

JARRETT, ROBERT FRANK
1916. *Occoneechee, the Maid of the Mystic Lake.* New York: Shakespeare Press.

JOCHELSON, WALDEMAR
1908. *The Koryak.* Pub. Jesup North Pacific Exped. 6. New York: Stechert; Leiden: Brill.

KARAREHE, W. TE KAHUI
1898. "Te Tatau-O-Te-Po." *J. Polynesian Soc.* **7**:59-63.

KIRTLEY, BACIL F.
1955. A Motif-Index of Polynesian, Micronesian, and Melanesian Folktales. Ph.D. dissertation, Indiana Univ. (Publ. 14,600 Univ. Microfilms Ann Arbor, Mich.)
1960. "History and Origin of an 'Alphabet of Ben Sira' Fable." In RAPHAEL PATAI, FRANCIS L. UTLEY, and DOV NOY (eds.), *Studies in Biblical and Jewish Folklore,* pp. 29-37. Bloomington: Indiana Univ. Press.
1967. "The Slain Eel-God and the Origin of the Coconut, with Satellite Themes." In D.K. WILGUS (ed.), *Folklore International: Essays in Traditional Literature, Belief, and Custom in Honor of Wayland Debs Hand,* pp. 89-107. Hatboro, Pennsylvania: Folklore Assoc.
1971. *A Motif-Index of Traditional Polynesian Narratives.* Honolulu: Univ. Hawaii Press.

KRAMER, SAMUEL N.
1944. *Sumerian Mythology.* Publ. American Philosophical Soc., Vol. 31.

LESSA, WILLIAM A.
1961. *Tales from Ulithi Atoll.* Folklore Studies 13. Berkeley and Los Angeles: Univ. California Press.

LEVERD, ARMAND
1912. "The Tahitian Version of Tafa'i (or Tawhaki)." *J. Polynesian Soc.* **21**:1-12.

LOEB, EDWIN M.
1926. *History and Traditions of Niue.* B.P. Bishop Mus. Bull. 32. Honolulu.

LUOMALA, KATHARINE
1940. *Oceanic, American Indian, and African Myths of Snaring the Sun.* B.P. Bishop Mus. Bull. 168. Honolulu.
1942. "An Analogy between a South American and Oceanic Myth Motif and Negro Influence in Darien." *J. American Folklore* **55**:190-191.
1949. *Maui-of-a-Thousand-Tricks: His Oceanic and European Biographers.* B.P. Bishop Mus. Bull. 198. Honolulu.
1951. *The Menehune of Polynesia and Other Mythical Little People of Oceania.* B.P. Bishop Mus. Bull. 203. Honolulu.
1964. "Motif A728: Sun Caught in Snare and Certain Related Motifs." *Fabula* **6**:214-252.

NORBECK, EDWARD
1950. *Folklore of the Atayal of Formosa and the Mountain Tribes of Luzon.* Anthropological Pap., Mus. Anthropology 5. Ann Arbor: Univ. Michigan Press.

PENZER, N.M.
1952. *Poison Damsels and Other Essays in Folklore and Anthropology.* London: Sawyer.

PILSUDSKI, BRONISLAS
1912. "Ainu Folklore." *J. American Folklore* **35**:72-87.

RIESENFELD, ALPHONSE
1950. *The Megalithic Culture of Melanesia.* Leiden: Brill.

RÓHEIM, GÉZA
1927. "Mondmythologie und Mondreligion." *Imago* **13**:442-537.

ROOSMAN, RADEN S.
  1970. "Coconut, Breadfruit and Taro in Pacific Oral Literature." *J. Polynesian Soc.* **79**:219-232.
RÜHLE, OSKAR
  1925. "Sonne und mond in primitiven mythus." *Philosophie und Geschichte* 8. Tübingen: Mohn (Siebeck).
STEINEN, KARL VON DEN
  1933-1934. "Marquesanische Mythen." *Zeitschrift Ethnologie* **65**:1-44.
  1934-1935. "Marquesanische Mythen." *Zeitschrift Ethnologie* **66**:191-240.
THOMPSON, STITH
  1955-1958. *Motif-Index of Folk-Literature.* Rev., enl. ed. 6 vols. Bloomington-Copenhagen: Indiana Univ. Press.
  1961. *The Types of the Folktale: Antti Aarne's Verzeichnis der Märchentypen Translated and Enlarged.* 2nd. rev. FF Communications 184. Helsinki.
TURNER, GEORGE
  1884. *Samoa: A Hundred Years Ago and Long Before.* London: Macmillan.
VRIES, JAN DE
  1925-1928. *Voksverhalen uit Oost-Indië.* 2 vols. Zutphen: Thieme.
WALLIS, WILSON D.
  1960. "Classical and Indo-Iranian Analogues in Southeast Asia and the Pacific Islands." In STANLEY DIAMOND (ed.), *Culture in History: Essays in Honor of Paul Radin,* pp. 317-332. New York: Columbia Univ. Press.
WASSÉN, HENRY
  1940. "An Analogy between a South American and Oceanic Myth Motif." *Etnologiska Studier (Göteborg)* **10**: 69-79.
WHITE, JOHN
  1887-1890. *The Ancient History of the Maori: His Mythology and Traditions.* 6 vols. Wellington: Disbury.
WILLIAMSON, ROBERT W.
  1933. *Religious and Cosmic Beliefs of Central Polynesia.* 2 vols. Cambridge: Cambridge Univ. Press.
WILLOUGHBY-MEADE, GERALD
  1928. *Chinese Ghouls and Goblins.* London: Constable.
WOHLERS, J.F.H.
  1875. "The Mythology and Traditions of the Maori of New Zealand." *Trans. New Zealand Inst.* **7**:3-55.

MELANESIA

DUALISM IN TROBRIAND CULTURE

DAVID B. EYDE*

University of Texas at El Paso

M ANY ASPECTS of Trobriand culture are organized in part by the opposition of elements that are symbolically "male" on the one hand, and "female" on the other. The following discussion is devoted to an exploration of these oppositions.

EXPRESSIONS OF AFFINITY

Both Malinowski (n.d., pp. 94-105, 121-133) and Powell (1969a, pp. 196-198; 1969b, pp. 594-595) make clear that relations between Trobriand wife-givers and wife-takers are asymmetric, that wife-givers are sharply differentiated from wife-takers. This asymmetry is the basis for the establishment of political power on the part of successful leaders, who marry matrilaterally.[1] Affinal relations between subclans of equal standing tend to be patrilateral specifically in order to balance out the status implications of any particular marriage.

These asymmetric social relationships are channels for the flow of goods, and the asymmetry is directly related to the fact that two different

*The opportunity to prepare this article was provided, in part, by an Initiation Summer Research Grant from the University of Hawaii. An earlier draft was read to Dr. Raymond Firth's graduate seminar held at the University of Hawaii during the spring of 1969. Another draft was read by Dr. H.A. Powell. My thanks to Dr. Firth and Dr. Powell and to fellow participants in the seminar for helpful comments and discussion. Of course, the end result is my responsibility solely.

[1]Powell's discussion resolves finally the puzzle of the myth (Malinowski, 1927, pp. 103-104) which recounts how Tudava, the most important culture hero of the Trobriand Islands, married his mother's brother's daughter.

classes of goods are involved. The two classes of goods are already apparent in the exchanges which formalize the marriage agreement (Malinowski, n.d., pp. 89-94). In these exchanges, cooked food moves in both directions and may perhaps be seen as some sort of mediator between the classes of goods given by wife-givers and wife-takers, respectively. The goods given, along with the bride, by wife-givers are uncooked vegetables. The wife-takers reciprocate with fish and inedible valuables of various sorts. The pattern of exchanges established at this time persists throughout the marriage, the wife's kin giving uncooked yams, *urigubu,* to the husband at harvest time, and the husband reciprocating with gifts of valuables from time to time (Malinowski, 1935, p. 199).

A fundamental aspect of Trobriand social structure, the relationship between affines, is thus expressed by the contrast between two classes of goods: uncooked vegetables, associated with the wife; and fish and valuables, associated with the husband.

ECONOMIC EXCHANGES

In the exchanges between affines a relationship which is fundamentally one of kinship serves economic and political ends. But there are also economic relationships which appear to be modeled on affinal ones.

Strikingly similar to affinal exchanges are the exchange relationships between trade partners in inland and coastal villages. These partners ceremonially exchange vegetables for fish (Malinowski, 1961, pp. 187-188). Precisely the same classes of goods are involved here as in the affinal exchanges.

The contrast of "male" goods given by the husband and his kin in exchange for "female" goods given by kin of the wife is reminiscent of the *kula* exchanges, which indeed appear to be based upon a kind of "fictitious affinity." The *kula* ring is a system of circulation of valuables in which the districts stand in persisting asymmetric relationships, in that the shell valuables given in one direction differ from those given in the opposite direction (Malinowski, 1961, pp. 81-104). The necklaces *soulava,* which move clockwise, are identified as a male principle, while the armbands, *mwali,* which are exchanged for the necklaces, move counterclockwise and are conceived as a female principle. When the necklaces and armbands are exchanged in the *kula,* they are said to marry (Malinowski, 1961, pp. 81-82).

That the exchanges between *kula* partners and exchanges between affines are, as Malinowski suspected, intimately related is indicated by an informant's remark: "We do not now *kwaypolu* or *pokala* the *mwali*

for they are women, and there is no reason to *kwaypolu* or *pokala* them"
(Malinowski, 1961, p. 356).

Kwaypolu and *pokala* (in this context) are solicitory gifts given in
the *kula*. They are gifts of food, and may include pigs, but also include
uncooked vegetables (Malinowski, 1961, p. 410). It is clearly this aspect
that the informant had in mind. As would be expected from the circulation
of the armbands, Kiriwinans *pokala* Sinaketa, and Sinaketans *pokala*
the Amphletts, but Sinaketans do not *pokala* Kiriwina (Malinowski, 1961,
p. 355). Like the armbands, uncooked vegetables move counterclockwise
around the *kula* ring.

A difficulty lies in the fact that in the context of affinal exchanges
armbands figure among the valuables given by the husband's kin to
the bride's (Malinowski, n.d., p. 90). In the *kula* they function as female.[2]
Without pretending to resolve this difficulty entirely, it can be noted
that uncooked vegetables could not possibly function as enduring items
of value in the *kula* trade. Some hard goods had to be substituted for
them.

Though it is possible that the Trobrianders do not know the full
outline of the *kula* ring (Malinowski, 1961, p. 83), they are certainly
aware that it circulates (Malinowski, 1961, pp. 278, 356, 483). The
evidence is strong that the *kula* ring is on a symbolic level a system
of "circulating connubium" based upon fictitious asymmetric affinal
relationships.[3]

---

[2]Dr. Powell (pers. comm.) writes me:

"It isn't only that *soulava* are male and *mwali* female. The *mwali* themselves are also
divided into males and females, and one of the objects of the adept *kula* seems to have
been to obtain and unite the pairs of "mates" recognized among the more important
armshells. (They are distinguished by the females having in their embellishments miniature
doba — skirts). I don't think the *soulava* were paired in this way."

It is possible that Trobriand conceptual organization involves not simply two contrasting
sets which are symbolically male and female, but rather a more complex system in which
contrasting subsets are also "male" and "female," respectively. But there is no further
evidence on this point.

[3]It may be that the *kula* ring is more than just a symbolic system of circulating
connubium. The *kula* districts with which the Trobrianders are directly concerned are,
moving clockwise, northwest Dobu, the Amphlett Islands, Vakuta, Sinaketa, Kiriwina,
and Kitava (Malinowski, 1961, p. 82). Trobriand men, of the last four named districts,
are forbidden to have sexual relations in the Amphletts (Malinowski, 1961, p. 272) or
in Dobu (Malinowski, 1961, p. 364), but the men of the Amphletts and Dobu are permitted
to have sexual intercourse with Trobriand women (Malinowski, 1961, p. 273). Marriage
between Sinaketans and Kiriwinans are frequent. The rule is, in such cases, that a man
of Sinaketa marries a woman of Kiriwina (Malinowski, 1961, p. 470). Kiriwinan men
are provided with sexual hospitality when they visit Kitava (Malinowski, 1961, p. 487).
A similar sort of hospitality is provided visiting Kitavans in Kiriwina (Malinowski, n.d.,
p. 260), but the Kitavans, unlike the Kiriwinans, bring their women with them (Malinowski,
1961, p. 488), which must at least put a damper on things. The Kiriwinans are generally
district endogamous, but one principal exception lies in marriages between Kiriwina and
Kitava (Malinowski, 1961, p. 83). Malinowski does not tell us which way wives move,
but he was principally observing wives residing with their husbands in Kiriwina. Migrations

MYTH AND RITUAL

Tudava, the great culture hero of the Trobriand Islands, is recognized throughout the Massim as the originator of gardening and garden ritual (Malinowski, 1935, pp. 68-75). The myths about him vary to some extent, but it is clear that he emerged from the ground at the most famous hole of emergence in the Trobriands, at a place called Obukula, near Laba'i on the northwest shore of the district of Kiriwina (Malinowski, 1927, p. 102; 1935, pp. 2, 68; n.d., pp. 496-499). In one version of the myth, Tudava himself was the first to emerge. In another, he was preceded by another male figure, Gere'u. After Tudava, other men came out, and Tudava gave each his totem. Tudava moved to the southeast from Kiriwina, creating the islands of Kitava, the Marshall Bennett group, and Murua by throwing stones in front of him as he went. He also took garden plants, garden techniques, and garden ritual to these islands, which were settled from Kiriwina. Tudava himself disappeared to an island to the east of the Laughlin Islands, but on Murua he taught his garden ritual to Gere'u and the latter's sister, Marita. This pair carried the crops and ritual to Misima and the D'Entrecasteaux Islands. There, they were shipwrecked, but some of the yams in their canoe drifted on to the Trobriands, closing the circuit commenced by Tudava (Malinowski, 1935, pp. 68-75). Thus garden ritual is associated primarily with males and moves clockwise around the *kula* ring.

One of the principal varieties of fishing ritual in the Trobriands is the ritual used in the construction of canoes (Malinowski, 1918, pp. 90-91). Canoes are associated, mythologically, with the *mulukwausi,* female familiars of the canoes, who move in mythology from Kitava to Dobu thus counterclockwise around the *kula* ring (Malinowski, 1961, pp 311-321). In all other cases, as well (Malinowski, 1918, pp. 90-91; 1935 p. 17; 1961, pp. 367-368), fishing ritual moves counterclockwise and is to some degree associated with females.

This evidence from mythology indicates that the formula, fish is to vegetable as male is to female, can be expanded to the following: the ritual of gardening (male) is to the earth (female) as the ritual of fishing (female) is to the sea (male).

Something similar to the formula is also reflected in Trobriand ritual itself. Garden ritual in the Trobriands involves the transmission of sacred

---

of people in the entire area show a marked tendency to move counterclockwise (Malinowski, 1961, pp. 288-289). Some of these migrations involve the movement of matrilineal subclans from community to community (Malinowski, 1961, p. 289). Such a movement can only occur when a woman of high rank marries into a lower-ranking community and her sons remain there (Malinowski, 1935, pp. 362-364). All this evidence very strongly suggests that the *kula* ring is really a connubial ring asymmetrically governing sexuality and marriage between *kula* districts.

potency to the earth and growing vegetables through various implements and structures (Malinowski, 1935, pp. 95-99, 102, 129-132). Margot-Duclot and Vernant (1946) have demonstrated convincingly that there are close parallels between Trobriand beliefs about the propagation of garden plants and Trobriand beliefs about the propagation of human beings. They point out (pp. 23-33) that the earth is conceived as female, while the implements used on the garden, and the superstructure of poles built over it, on which Tudava is said to seat himself (Malinowski, 1935, p. 129), are conceived as male.[4]

Just as the sacred potency of gardening is primarily associated with garden implements and the superstructure over the gardens, so the sacred potency of fishing is primarily associated with fishing implements and the canoe which sails over the sea (Malinowski, 1918, pp. 90-92). In a number of contexts, in fact (Malinowski, 1935, pp. 129, 149, 249), the superstructure over the garden is specifically compared to a canoe. The former is urged in spells to be firmly anchored (Malinowski, 1935, p. 129), the latter are urged to move swiftly (Malinowski, 1961, p. 132). But, while the garden superstructure is conceptually male, the canoe is conceptually female (Malinowski, 1961, pp. 132, 138, 320). Given the masculine potential of sea water in Trobriand belief (Malinowski, n.d., pp. 175-176), the general scheme of Trobriand ritual appears to involve the notion that the superstructure, which is the conductor of male potency to the female earth in garden ritual, is comparable to the canoe which is the conductor of female potency to the male sea in fishing ritual.

Fishing ritual is limited to two villages in northwest Kiriwina (Malinowski, 1918, pp. 90-92). It might appear, then, that the rest of the Trobriands lack rituals which "balance" those of the gardens. But this is not the case. It will be recalled that valuables are equated with fish. Kula valuables, in fact, are made of shell. The ritual devoted to valuables, kula ritual, is thus the equivalent of fishing magic. Not surprisingly, kula ritual is also devoted in large part to canoes (Malinowski, 1961, pp. 124-266).

---

[4]Margot-Duclot and Vernant (1946, pp. 30-33) also note the frequency with which, in Melanesia, the superstructure of poles over the garden is related to aspects of social structure. It is interesting, therefore, that the Trobriand garden is a system of rectangles within which there is a hierarchy of magical corners (Malinowski, 1935, pp. 89-91, 99-100, 14-115, 121-128, 430-434). There is a close parallel here to the areal structure of Trobriand society: hamlets, villages, clusters, and districts linked to one another by a hierarchy of leaders from traditionally ranked clans and subclans (Malinowski, 1935, pp. 346-347; Powell, 1960, pp. 121-124, 135). In view of the way harvest ritual performed in the village parallels that performed over the gardens (Malinowski, 1935, p. 224), and in view of the fact that the term for the early harvest, isunapulo (Malinowski, 1935, p. 165), is also the term for the "spots of emergence" of the subclan ancestresses (Malinowski, 1935, pp. 341-342), it is probable that the Trobriand rituals of the gardens are also a recapitulation of the origins of Trobriand society and a renewal of it.

It is striking that one important part of the latter rites is a set of spells, *kayga'u,* which is divided into the *"kayga'u* of the Underneath and the *"kayga'u* of the Above." The former is directed toward the creatures of the sea; the latter toward the *mulukwausi,* female familia of the canoe (Malinowski, 1961, pp. 246-247). This structure appea to reflect a conception of *kula* ritual like that suggested.

The Trobriand gardening cycle lasts all year but culminates in t rites of harvest in the season of the southeast trade wind. Can construction culminates in fishing and overseas *kula* expeditions duri the northwest monsoon (Malinowski, 1935, pp. 50-51). The dualis organization of ritual may well also be tied in to the division of t year into two principal seasons separated by brief periods of calm: tl southeast trade wind season and the northwest monsoon season. Eac season is associated with a different system of wind magic, owned t inhabitants of Kitava to the southeast and the Lousancay Islands the northwest, respectively (Malinowski, 1935, pp. 50-51; 1961, p 224-225).

CONCLUSION

Much of Trobriand thought appears to involve notions of th asymmetric circulation of persons, goods, and services belonging t contrasting classes. Membership in these classes is arranged approxi mately as follows:

Female	Male
Wife-givers	Wife-takers
Vegetables	Fish and valuables
Mwali	*Soulava*
Land (Earth)	Sea
Fishing and *kula* rites	Gardening rites
Canoe	Garden superstructure
Counterclockwise	Clockwise
Southeast	Northwest
Trade wind	Monsoon

LITERATURE CITED

MALINOWSKI, BRONISLAW

1918. "Fishing in the Trobriand Islands." *Man* **18**(53):87-92.

1927. *Sex and Repression in Savage Society.* London: Kegan Paul. New York: Harcourt, Brace.

1935. *Coral Gardens and Their Magic: A Study of the Methods of Tilling the Soil and of Agricultural Rites in the Trobriand Islands.* Vol 1: *The Description of Gardening.* New York: American Book Co.

1961. *Argonauts of the Western Pacific.* New York: Dutton. (First published in 1922. London: Routledge. New York: Dutton.)

n.d. *The Sexual Life of Savages in North-Western Melanesia.* Harvest Paperback. New York: Harcourt, Brace and World. (First published in 1929. London: Routledge.)

ARGOT-DUCLOT, J., and J. VERNANT

1946. "La terre et la categorie du sexe en Melanesie." *J. Soc. Océanistes* **2**(2):5-53.

OWELL, H. A.

1960. "Competitive Leadership in Trobriand Political Organization." *J. Royal Anthropological Inst. Great Britain, Ireland* **90**:118-145.

1969a. "Genealogy, Residence and Kinship in Kiriwina." *Man* **4**(2):177-202.

1969b. "Territory, Hierarchy and Kinship in Kiriwina." *Man* **4**(4):580-604.

HORATIO ALGER IN NEW GUINEA

BEN R. FINNEY

University of Hawaii, Honolulu
and
Center for Cultural and Technical Interchange
Between East and West, Honolulu

Hᴏʀᴀᴛɪᴏ Aʟɢᴇʀ sᴛᴏʀɪᴇs are, in American popular thinking, tales of worldly success based on a rags-to-riches theme. They stem from a late 19th-century author, Horatio Alger, Jr., who was himself a great success; some 120 books which sold an estimated 17 million copies flowed from his pen (Falk, 1963, p. 151). But Alger's life is not the model for the genre of tales that bear his name. Rather, the model is derived from the simple formula that appears in all his books. Most of these are boys' stories, fictional biographies bearing titles like *Ragged Dick, Risen from the Ranks*, and *Struggling Upward* in which Alger preached that boys, no matter how poor and humble their origins, can, if they work hard, live clean, and save their money, achieve wealth and success. The message is pure Americana, a late 19th-century affirmation of faith in equality of opportunity and the self-made man, and an exhortation for the youth of America to get on with the job.

The original Horatio Alger stories have been the subject of much criticism and ridicule as exemplifying the worst aspects of American character. According to Falk (1963, p. 152), by the 1930's their author had come to be regarded as a "kind of villain of private enterprise, a wet-nurse of Wall Street, providing moral pap for a generation of would-be business tycoons," and was blamed by such literary commentators as Van Wyck Brooks for corrupting New England values of idealism and self-reliance into worship of the "bitch-goddess" of success. Yet, despite this criticism, a dispassionate observer would probably be forced to agree with the most recent commentator on Alger and his works, Richard Huber (1971), who has analyzed the American idea of success, and its promoters, from Colonial times to today. To Huber, Alger was not a villain, but merely one of a chain of writers who expressed American popular thinking on the necessary relationship of individual effort, wealth, and social status, and provided in their writings the models after which the ambitious could mold their behavior.

Although the youth of today's "post industrial" America would probably laugh at Horatio Alger stories and find their message to be, at best, quaint, this does not mean that biographical tales illustrating the merits of hard work, thriftiness, and a determination to reach long-term goals are dated elsewhere in the world. Even the leaders of the People's Republic of China apparently find stories featuring these themes to be an essential part of their country's literature, although, of course, public good, not private gain, is the main objective of their stories' heroes. That other developing countries might find, as did late 19th-century America and contemporary China, that their own national versions of Horatio Alger stories would help promote development goals is a suggestion that Whyte and Braun (1966) have recently put forward. Citing the work of McClelland (1961) on the relationship between achievement themes in children's textbooks and subsequent development records of the countries concerned, they argue that the heroes presented in textbooks and popular literature should be congruent with a country's development goals. For example, a poor country bent on rapid economic development would do well to feature entrepreneurs as heroes, instead—as Whyte and Braun maintain is common—of military leaders, politicians or other men with little or no direct role in economic growth. They do not propose, however, that "development heroes" be wholly invented, but rather urge "that educators and writers of children's literature be encouraged to re-examine the country's history to find men who might serve as models for the kinds of achievements and ambitions that need to be fostered" (Whyte and Braun, 1966, p. 56).

In New Guinea, or at least in the eastern half of that island which is now the independent country of Papua New Guinea, there is plenty of biographical raw material on indigenous entrepreneurs who, in areas where economic conditions have been favorable, have pioneered the growing of cash crops and the establishment of business enterprises among their people. Little of this material can, however, be found in the historical record since, save for the work of a few anthropologists,

---

[1]See, for example, Epstein (1964), Maher (1961), and Salisbury (1970).

the accomplishments of these men have been largely ignored by the chroniclers of modern New Guinea. The purpose of this essay is to illustrate the type of biographical material that is available by citing some "Horatio Alger stories" that I collected in New Guinea, and to urge that an intensive effort be made to collect more material of this kind to include in textbooks and other forms of literature intended for New Guinea's youth.

The locale for the stories presented here is the Goroka region of the Eastern Highlands District of Papua New Guinea. This is a fertile, well watered but subtropical highland area which is the home of some 60,000 New Guineans who, although divided into five main cultural-linguistic groups, share enough features to be referred to by the common name of Gorokans. The Gorokans, like the other groups of the New Guinea Highlands, lived in Stone Age isolation until European prospectors and patrol officers penetrated the region in the early 1930's. They did not come fully under the control of the Australian administration until the late 1940's. In the early 1950's, within a generation of their "discovery" by the outside world, the Gorokans began growing coffee commercially, and since then their economic growth has been impressive. They have not been content to be mere growers; as soon as they began to earn money from their coffee harvests they started pooling their cash to start retail stores, trucking ventures, and even restaurants and garages. Although they still grow much of their own food and carry out other subsistence tasks, in terms of the rapid rate at which they have taken up cash cropping and then small business activities, the Gorokans stand out as one of the most economically dynamic groups in contemporary New Guinea.

Leading the Gorokan entry into the cash economy were a number of pioneering entrepreneurs—men who first saw the opportunities presented by the introduction of coffee and the later need for retail, transport, and other services, and who first organized land, labor, and capital to exploit these opportunities. In so doing, they led their fellow Gorokans into the cash economy. In 1967-1968 I had an opportunity to investigate Gorokan economic growth and to interview prominent Gorokan entrepreneurs. The latter, it is important to emphasize, were not at all adverse to talking about their commercial success. Indeed, they were proud of their personal accomplishments as well as the role they had played in promoting overall economic growth among their people. Almost all, in fact, had their own Horatio Alger story which they loved to tell, particularly to Europeans like myself curious about how men literally "out of the Stone Age" could become successful entrepreneurs in the 20th century. Below are brief summaries of the success stories of three leading

Gorokan entrepreneurs: Apo Yeharigie, Sinake Giregire, and Hari Gotaha.

Apo Yeharigie is the oldest of the Gorokan entrepreneurs, having been born in about 1915. He also has the longest continuous experience with Europeans. As a teen-aged youth, Apo attached himself to the first prospecting party to work in Goroka, and after that he served as a personal servant to Australian patrol officers from the mid-1930's to the end of World War II. During that time he traveled throughout New Guinea and had a variety of experiences unusual, if not unique, for a Gorokan of that day. After the war Apo returned to Goroka and made, in comparison to other Gorokans who at that time had little or no money, a modest fortune growing vegetables commercially, prospecting for gold, and operating a coffee plantation. When I arrived in Goroka in 1967, Apo's reputation seemed more legendary than real. I was told that he had just retired, leased his plantation to a European, and had gone off to the seashore to live at ease on a small island in the harbor of Madang on New Guinea's north coast. Conflicting tales were then circulating around Goroka on just how Apo achieved success; most knowledgeable observers knew that Apo had done well in vegetable farming, gold prospecting, and coffee growing, but none were sure how he first managed to succeed in these enterprises.

To try to straighten out the details of his career I flew to Madang and rented a canoe to take me out to Apo's island retreat. There I found him, relaxing in an attractive thatched-roof house that served as a combination bar and dining room for him and his associates. Even though I was a stranger, Apo was willing to talk about his career. However, he touched only lightly on his experiences during the 1930's and the wartime years, and emphasized only what he felt were the essential highlights of his commercial career. However brief and selected his remarks were, they are nonetheless revealing, for they show how Apo, like most other Gorokan entrepreneurs, conceptualizes the road to success to be one of investment, hard work, profit making, and then reinvestment of profits in a series of successively larger enterprises.

Apo started his tale by saying that he returned to Goroka after the war with $14 in savings.[2] (This is much more than a New Guinea laborer could earn in a year at that time.) This money he used to buy seeds and garden tools, and then he started to cultivate tomatoes and other "exotic" vegetables for sale to European personnel stationed in Goroka. He also began to grow large quantities of sweet potatoes for sale to the administration for provisioning their workers, hospital patients, and

---

[2]Amounts cited in this essay are in Australian dollars ($A 1.00 = $U.S. 1.12) and shillings (1 shilling = $A .10).

prisoners. After a few years his profits amounted to $238, a figure he unhesitatingly quoted as he did all the other figures mentioned in his narrative. He used these savings to fly to Kainantu, a gold-mining center some 50 miles east of Goroka, to purchase picks, shovels, and other prospecting equipment and to hire and provision a crew of workers to prospect for gold in the streams and river banks throughout the Eastern Highlands District. After a few years of working alluvial deposits Apo says that he came back to Goroka with accumulated savings of $1,060. He acquired land in his home village, and, following technical advice obtained from an administration extension worker, set about laying out a coffee plantation. He used his savings from gold prospecting to buy tools and equipment, as well as to hire workers to clear and plant the 9,923 coffee trees he said made up his holding. Although Apo experimented with commercial trucking and some other ventures, coffee growing remained his main commercial activity until declining health and labor problems led him to retire.

While Apo's commercial activities were virtually phased out when I made my inquiries in Goroka, those of other, younger, entrepreneurs were on the rise. Perhaps the most dynamic of these men was Sinake Giregire who, with a plantation of some 30,000 trees, was the biggest indigenous coffee grower in Goroka and all of New Guinea as well. In his narrative Sinake, like Apo, emphasized investment, profit making, saving, and then reinvestment of profits, but was more open than Apo had been about the obstacles he faced in his youth, and also about his early experience working for Europeans.

At the end of World War II, when Sinake was about eight years old, he enrolled in a Lutheran Mission School located near his village. Because of his academic promise, two years later he was sent to the Lutheran Mission headquarters on the coast to continue his schooling in the more advanced schools there. When he was 13 years old, however, a near fatal attack of malaria forced him to drop out of school and return home to Goroka (which, at an elevation of 5,000 feet, was relatively free of malaria). Sinake never did return to school. After convalescing at home for a year or two he decided to get a job instead, and first took a position as a mechanic's helper with a small airline based at the Goroka airfield. He remained with the airline for several years before quitting to take a job at an agricultural experiment station near Kainantu. Sinake stayed there only briefly, for, even though he was only about 20 years old, he was anxious to go into business for himself.

His first venture was a pit saw which he set up near Kainantu to make timber planks for sale to the administration. He was fairly successful in organizing this business, and at one time employed 10 or so workers to cut down the trees and saw them into rough planks. However, Sinake could not compete easily with power-operated European sawmills, and after a year or so he switched his attentions to gold prospecting. With a crew of about a half a dozen workers Sinake began panning for gold in stream beds throughout the Eastern Highlands District and was able to accumulate enough money to return to his home village and start growing coffee on a large scale.

In 1955, before he left Goroka for Kainantu, Sinake had tried to get into coffee growing, but because he was only an inexperienced teen-ager without money or status he could gain access to only a small amount of land and could recruit little in the way of help. In 1958, however, after winding up his business ventures in Kainantu, Sinake was able to return home as a man who, although still young, had proven his commercial ability. He had some $1,800 in savings to invest in building up a coffee plantation. His clansmen were therefore impressed enough with his accomplishments to allocate to him a large tract of land, and Sinake went ahead to buy tools and equipment and hire the laborers needed to clear and plant the land. As Sinake's coffee trees began to bear and furnish him with a cash flow, his status in his home area increased. In the early 1960's, he was elected as the first president of the newly organized local government council, an unusual honor for so young a man. Since then his economic and political fortunes have continued to rise; his coffee holdings now extend over 40 acres, he operates a coffee-buying business with a fleet of six trucks, has a wholesale—retail store, and represents the western half of Goroka in the Papua New Guinea House of Assembly as well as being a cabinet member within the national government.

The Gorokan entrepreneur who seemed most to enjoy telling his Horatio Alger story was Hari Gotaha, a genial young man who controlled one of the largest Gorokan "commercial empires." This was a mini-con-glomerate composed of a retail store, restaurant, and service station, all strategically located on prime commercial land adjacent to the town market, as well as a small coffee plantation, some cattle, and a trucking business. "It all started with 30 cents worth of self-rising flour" was the way Hari began his story. In 1959, when Hari was a youth employed as a personal servant in a European household, he decided to go into business for himself. So he went out, bought some flour, and returned to his employer's kitchen (the lady of the house was then away at work) and used the stove to cook up a batch of scones. These he took to a nearby village and quickly sold for a modest profit. He then immediately re-invested the proceeds into more flour and other ingredients and soon had a flourishing business of baking scones and selling them at the town market in Goroka. So flourishing, in fact, was his business that Hari's employer suggested that he leave her employ and devote himself full time to his baking trade (and with his own equipment). Using a wood-burning stove that he purchased with his accumulated profits, Hari went immediately to work and soon built up a bank account of $600, a large amount for a young man who had no significant holdings in coffee, the chief source of wealth for the Gorokans.

Out of this amount he invested $200 for shares in a European company, and put the other $400 into a small restaurant where he could make scones, meat pies, and other goods, and prepare and serve meals as well. This restaurant was so successful that within a short time he was able to build a small retail store and stock it with trade goods.

Hari's business empire grew from these small beginnings with but a single hitch. Public health officials closed his restaurant because of substandard hygienic conditions and construction. Hari responded to this setback by hiring a carpenter and putting some $5,000 into a restaurant, built in accordance with the building code, and equipped with a refrigerator—freezer, large stove, and running water. Later, as more profits accumulated, he bought his first truck to inaugurate a local hauling business. In 1968 he tore down his old retail store, a modest thatched-roof structure, and replaced it with a large, modern structure which, including display cases and a full inventory, he says cost him $25,000 in cash. Later, after I left Goroka, Hari purchased some cattle and opened a service station.[3]

When I first met and interviewed him, Hari maintained that he made all his investments out of accumulated profits that he had banked, and had not relied on external sources of credit. After a survey of the credit practices of local firms and banks (all European controlled and wary of lending to New Guineans) I concluded that this was substantially correct as far as the use of credit from sources outside the community was concerned. Save for a small loan for restaurant equipment, Hari had indeed been independent of credit from banks and other institutions. I also learned that in 1968 Hari had even turned down an offer of a large loan from the newly organized Papua-New Guinea Development Bank, an institution organized by the Australian administration and mandated to make loans freely available to New Guineans. The bank director earnestly wanted to lend Hari the money since he knew from Hari's record that the store would be successful and that the loan would be promptly repaid (and, hence, that his institution would have a shining example of its effectiveness to display to Europeans in New Guinea

[3]See Anonymous (1971) for a recently published version of Hari's career and his latest business accomplishments.

skeptical about the wisdom of lending money to New Guineans). He was much chagrined when Hari turned down the offer of the loan with the reply that he wanted to do everything "by myself."

These stories—as told to me and summarized here—might appear to be the proud boastings of individualistic entrepreneurs who have broken out of their society to pioneer new and inherently alien commercial practices. Nothing could be farther from the truth. These men, and other Gorokan entrepeneurs whom I studied, are not men who have broken out of their society; they are ambitious Gorokans whose actions, however "modern" they might seem, are entirely congruent with traditional Gorokan values, and their efforts are appreciated and supported by the majority of their fellow clansmen and tribesmen.

Traditional Gorokan society, like most other New Guinean societies, was one in which there were no hereditary privileges. A man's status depended primarily on what he did, not who he was. A man who became a successful warrior or a skilled orator was honored, but the most important avenue to high status was in the economic sphere. An ambitious youth who wanted to get ahead could do so by working his way up from a mere subsistence farmer to a wealthy and renowned "financier." A youth might start, for example, with nothing more in the way of assets than the right to plant sweet potatoes on vacant clan land. He would then indebt himself to established men by borrowing a sow and taking a wife (for whose brideprice he would further indebt himself) who would tend the sweet potatoes needed to feed the sow. If the sow were fertile and he and his wife were hard working, this would-be financier could begin to build up his own herd of pigs, the prime source of wealth in traditional Gorokan society. After using some pigs to pay off debts incurred in getting started, the next step for him would be to begin to expand his financial position by using surplus pigs. He would lend them to other would-be pig raisers, trade them for mother-of-pearl shell, bird-of-paradise plumes, and other valuables, and contribute to and help promote large exchange ceremonies in which up to a hundred or more pigs might be slaughtered. If successful in these banking, trading, and exchange activities, he would gain followers among those who benefited from them, and be generally acclaimed as a successful financier. He would then have achieved status as a leader in Gorokan society—as a "big-man" or a "man with a name," as Gorokans referred to the leaders who worked their way to the top of the society.

From this simplified model of traditional Gorokan economic behavior,[4] it can be seen that modern Gorokan entrepreneurs follow the same

---

[4]See Strathern (1969) for a full treatment of the role of production and finance in Highlands societies.

style of upward mobility through economic effort, even though the focus of this is now in the cash economy rather than the subsistence economy. They start small, without inherited status or wealth, build up their holdings through hard work and astute management, and then emerge as wealthy and respected men. They are, in fact, known as a new type of "big-man," a "big-man of business," and are among the most honored men of their day.

Not only do their fellow Gorokans honor these modern entrepreneurs, but they also provide them with tangible support for their economic efforts. For example, if clansmen see that one of their number seems to have the drive and knowledge required to pioneer new activities successfully in the cash economy, they are much more likely to get behind him—even to the extent of donating their labor or cash to help him build up his enterprises—than they are of jealously working against him. Such donations are not, however, "free gifts"; they are transactions that create or affirm ties of mutual obligation between leaders and supporters. While leaders gain much material support in this way, they, in turn, must serve their followers lest that support be cut off. A successful entrepreneur is, for example, expected to be generous to his followers by giving them food, cash, and also traditional valuables like pigs when needed, although, of course, the skillful financier must make sure that this reciprocity does not bankrupt him. In addition, less tangible but probably more important benefits are expected to flow from the entrepreneur to his followers. The latter gain a measure of pride—still a key element in a society like Goroka where clan solidarity and interclan rivalry is still strong—by being associated with a successful business leader, and they also learn through his example, and oftentimes his direct aid, how they themselves can participate in the cash economy as producers and small businessmen.

The three Horatio Alger stories that I have related do not touch on this question of aid to an entrepreneur that supporters may furnish to help him build up his commercial holdings. I have told these stories much as they were told to me by the entrepreneurs in question when I first interviewed them, and I suspect that the entrepreneurs may have avoided this question more for one or both of the following reasons than plain egotism. First, they know that most Europeans are totally ignorant of the nature of Gorokan society and, hence, they tend to tell their tales in terms which they know are within the realm of European experience. Second, they are aware that many Europeans, particularly administration officials, agricultural officers, and others concerned with their economic progress, frown upon group involvement in cash cropping and other commercial ventures; thus they probably have learned to boast only of their individual efforts and to avoid mentioning support received from the group. Whatever the motivation, it became clear to me as my researches in Goroka continued that these seemingly individualistic entrepreneurs were as much dependent on group support as on their own individual efforts in building up their business holdings. In each case, including that of Hari who was at first most emphatic about doing everything "by myself," I discovered in subsequent interviews, and from other sources, that these men had all received considerable aid from their clansmen and others. Indeed, it became obvious that one of their main entrepreneurial skills was soliciting resources from many individuals and combining these to form productive enterprises.[5]

The story of the late Bimai Noimbano's commercial career is worth telling here to demonstrate how Gorokan entrepreneurs use resources provided by the group to build enterprises which, although ostensibly theirs alone, can in fact be considered to be as much clan (or whatever the relevant social group) as personal property. I was able to learn more about the nature of Bimai's enterprises because the estate of Bimai, who died in 1966, was in dispute when I was in Goroka in 1967-1968. Consequently the investigation then under way revealed details which—to the outside observer at least—would not otherwise have come to light.

Bimai's childhood, like that of the heroes in the original Horatio Alger stories, was filled with misfortune. He was born in about 1920, the son of a famous warrior. But he was not born in his father's village, for his mother was banished from there and her husband when it was discovered that she had become pregnant too soon after the birth of her previous child and had therefore broken her culture's *post-partum* sex taboo. Bimai's mother sought refuge with the Yamei clan, into which her sister had married, and Bimai was born and reared there. A second tragedy for Bimai occurred in the early 1930's when his father was shot and killed when he challenged the first European patrol to penetrate his region. Bimai did, however, have the good fortune to be adopted by a man of Yamei clan who looked after his welfare as he grew up.

Bimai first became interested in cash crops in 1949 when he went to Manus, an island off the north coast of New Guinea, as a plantation laborer. From there Bimai moved back to the Highlands to the same agricultural experiment station where Sinake later worked. There Bimai learned a bit about coffee growing, and left in 1951 with a load of coffee seed and seedlings to plant in his home village. His first attempt to grow coffee failed, however, because he planted the coffee on too

---

[5]Finney (1973) presents a more complete analysis of the careers of these and other Gorokan entrepreneurs, as well as an historical analysis of Gorokan economic growth.

steep a slope and at too high an elevation. Undaunted, he sent some young boys to pick up more seed (a 140-mile round-trip hike over mountain trails and rough dirt tracks), and tried growing coffee again. His second try failed also, although this did not apparently discourage Bimai. Soon after this second failure an agricultural extension team visited the Watabung region, Bimai's home area, and Bimai seized upon this opportunity to get professional help firsthand. With the aid of team members Bimai was able to establish a proper nursery for coffee seedlings, and then, a year later, to transplant them to start the first plantation in Watabung.

Bimai soon had a flourishing coffee plantation, one of the largest in Goroka. He also raised pigs and chickens for sale and even experimented with a commercial fishpond. As his coffee began to bear well, and receipts from it and chicken and pig sales began to create a considerable cash surplus, Bimai started investing in other enterprises: a retail store, a small cattle herd, and a coffee-buying business that eventually grew to include a fleet of four trucks. He also became a major stockholder and a director in a coffee-buying and processing cooperative society that was organized to serve the neighboring district of Chimbu along with Watabung. When he died Bimai was without a doubt one of the leading Gorokan businessmen, and the undisputed economic and political leader of Watabung.

But, however hard working and thrifty Bimai was, it cannot be said that he built up his business holdings without any assistance. When he first got started, for example, his adoptive clansmen, particularly the younger men in his own age group, helped him clear, lay out, and plant his coffee plantation, and then later helped him tend and harvest his trees. He was also able to obtain from his clansmen a steady supply of sweet potatoes to feed his pigs and, in addition, was even able to prevail on some households to take care of his pigs on their land and feed the pigs with their crops until they were ready to be sold. Later, as he began to branch out into other enterprises, Bimai received considerable financial aid from Yamei clansmen and others throughout Watabung. The extent of this aid was not realized (at least not by European observers) until after Bimai's death when his creditors stepped forth to claim a return of their contributions from his estate. In an open meeting of his close relatives, Yamei clansmen, and local government councilors of Watabung, more than $6,000 of such claims were approved and registered for payment. Among the claimants were those who had only contributed a few shillings toward the purchase of a truck, as well as some major contributors, including one close business associate of Bimai who submitted a claim for some $1,049 which he said he had given

Bimai over a period of 12 years. These cash claims, which were to be paid from Bimai's cash reserves as well as money realized from the sale of his movable property, were not the only claims. The Yamei people vigorously opposed the attempt of Bimai's older brother (born and raised in Bimai's father's clan) to take over his deceased brother's coffee plantation, and asserted that since the plantation had been built upon Yamei land, and largely with the labor of Yamei clansmen, it belonged to the people of Yamei.

When I pressed Bimai's associates for an answer as to why they and others were willing freely to give Bimai labor, goods, and cash, most of their answers indicated one primary reason: Bimai offered them economic leadership. He was a man who seemed to know something about the mysteries of the cash economy, and he was willing to experiment and lead the way in growing coffee, operating a coffee-buying business, and other activities that promised to benefit everyone, not just Bimai. From all that I could learn about Bimai it appears that he accepted that, in addition to helping his supporters with gifts of cash, pigs, or other goods, his major obligation was to aid them to participate in the cash economy. He, for example, apparently was generous with technical advice on how to grow coffee and with coffee seeds and seedlings. On some occasions he even lent some of his key workers to help his supporters start or operate their coffee holdings. Similarly, when it came to his coffee-buying business it is apparent that this enterprise was as beneficial to the people of Watabung as it was to Bimai. Before Bimai began buying coffee the Watabung people apparently found it difficult to sell their coffee because few buyers (who at this time were all Europeans) bothered to extend their buying trips into remote and mountainous Watabung. Simply by organizing a coffee-buying business which would regularly purchase Watabung coffee, Bimai was, therefore, performing a service crucial to the development of Watabung and the welfare of the people who were trying to grow coffee there. Considering these benefits, as well as more minor ones that accrued to the people of Watabung because of Bimai's entrepreneurial activities, it is no wonder that Bimai received virtually every vote cast by the people of Watabung in the 1964 elections for the House of Assembly.[6]

The significant level of group participation in Bimai's enterprises should serve as a warning to anyone tempted to take a New Guinean entrepreneur's tale of strictly individual enterprise as the complete story. Those who might wish to collect such Horatio Alger stories for textbook or literary use must, therefore, be willing to dig deeply into the social

---

[6]Watabung, however, is only one part of Goroka; and Sinake Giregire, who is more widely popular throughout Goroka, won the election.

context so that the nature and extent of, among other things, the entrepreneur's relationship with his supporters can be told as an integral part of the history of his enterprise. Anthropologists who, because of their long residence in and intensive study of a society, may be well acquainted with the nature of New Guinean enterprise, could perhaps be requested to gather and publish material on New Guinean development heroes. But, I suspect that their talents may not be entirely satisfactory for the job. Few of them are interested in development, and of those who are (I include myself here) it must be remembered that, however much they may strive for an "insider's view" of the development process in general, or of entrepreneurship in particular, they remain outsiders whose need to explain and translate what they see in New Guinea in the idiom of their discipline and for an audience based primarily in affluent, industrial nations must inevitably involve the imposition of ideas and concepts alien to the New Guinea experience. My plea, therefore, is for the appearance of one or more New Guinean Horatio Algers—men (or women) fully cognizant of the nature of New Guinean societies—who would be willing and able to search out the success stories of modern New Guinean commercial leaders, and then formulate these, in textbook case study or fictional forms, for young New Guineans to read and ponder.[7]

LITERATURE CITED

ANONYMOUS
  1971. "And He Built His Business on Scones." *Pacific Islands Monthly* **42**(3):112.
EPSTEIN, T. SCARLETT
  1964. "Personal Capital Formation among the Tolai of New Britain." In R. FIRTH
    and B. S. YAMEY (eds.), *Capital, Saving and Credit in Peasant Societies*, pp.
    53-68. Chicago: Aldine.
FALK, ROBERT
  1963. "Notes on the 'Higher Criticism' of Horatio Alger, Jr." *Arizona Quart.* **19**(2):151-
    167.
FINNEY, BEN R.
  1973. *Big-Men and Business: Entrepreneurship and Economic Growth in the New Guinea
    Highlands.* Honolulu: Univ. Press Hawaii.

---

[7]While Leo Hannett, a young New Guinean political scientist, might not appreciate having his name associated with that of Horatio Alger, his analysis of the seemingly bizarre circumstances that gave rise to one particular New Guinean venture provides a case in point, illustrating how a New Guinean observer can easily and quickly comprehend those aspects of New Guinean commercial behavior alien to the experience of most foreign observers (Hannett, 1969).

HANNETT, LEO
  1969. A Successful Small Business Born from a Thunderclap. Unpublished paper presented at Third Waigani Seminar, May. Port Moresby.
HUBER, RICHARD M.
  1971. *The American Idea of Success*. New York: McGraw-Hill.
MCCLELLAND, DAVID C.
  1961. *The Achieving Society*. Princeton: Van Nostrand.
MAHER, ROBERT
  1961. *New Men of Papua*. Madison: Univ. Wisconsin Press.
SALISBURY, RICHARD F.
  1970. *Vunamami*. Berkeley: Univ. California Press.
STRATHERN, ANDREW J.
  1969. "Finance and Production: Two Strategies in New Guinea Highlands Exchange Systems." *Oceania* **40**(1):42-67.
WHYTE, WILLIAM F., and R. R. BRAUN
  1966. "Heroes, Homework, and Industrial Growth." *Columbia J. World Business* **1**(2):51-57.

INDONESIA

I WATU GUNUNG

A BALINESE CALENDRICAL MYTH

JACK H. WARD*

University of Hawaii, Honolulu

ALL SOCIETIES seem to have means of scheduling events. The Balinese have a very complicated calendar system which is of central importance for scheduling all sorts of activities. Anniversaries of temples and shrines are occasions for the regular observance of festivals which are calendrically determined. Families determine the best days for teeth filing and other rites of passage through the advice of someone well informed in calendrical calculation. Individuals decide on the appropriate days to begin various undertakings by consulting the calendar. One of my informants would not begin the task of transcribing a *topeng* play with me until an investigation revealed the proper day for beginning such work. In short, the daily lives of individuals and groups, both large and small, are directly involved with their calendar.

In view of the significance of the calendar to the Balinese, it is not surprising to observe that the calendrical system is a highly elaborate one involving a large number of linguistic terms for various units in the system and understood only by certain individual experts.[1] Actually two calendars are used in Bali. One may be called the Hindu-Balinese calendar and the other is often called by scholars the Javanese-Balinese calendar. One might expect that the latter system would be purely native and without Indian influence. However, that is not the case since many

---

*Research for this article was made possible by funds granted by the Carnegie Corporation of New York, through the London-Cornell Project at Cornell University.

[1]In Tabanan, for example, such an expert would often be referred to as a *siwa*, from Sanskrit for the god Shiva.

Indic elements are evident in addition to a large number of features which do, indeed, seem to have no origin in the Indian subcontinent.

The Hindu-Balinese calendar is similar to that used in the Western world. Both are solar-lunar systems. As in the West the Hindu-Balinese year consists of twelve months. All these periods of time still retain Sanskrit names as well as a Balinese language identification for each of the first ten months. The year begins in the spring about the time of the equinox, with the *saka* dates being 78 years behind those of the Western calendar. (For details of both systems see Goris, 1960, pp. 115-118; Covarrubias, 1937, pp. 313-316.) Certain communities use the Hindu-Balinese system more commonly than do other communities. Generally speaking, the greatest use of this calendar is found in the northeastern and central mountainous areas, with secondary use being given it in the north coastal area of Buleleng (Goris, 1960, p. 118). One holiday, that of Nyepi, is determined by the Hindu-Balinese calendar.

The Javanese-Balinese calendar was probably brought into Bali under the influence of the kingdoms of Majapait in Java and Gelgel in Bali. At least the areas in which this system receives strongest emphasis (that is, the south central regions of Klungkung, Gianyar, Badung, and Tabanan) are those in which the influence of these kingdoms has been the greatest.[2] It will be this calendar, rather than the Hindu-Balinese one, which will occupy most of our attention in the following discussion.

The Javanese-Balinese system is considerably more complicated and involved than the Hindu-Balinese, and has many more variables.

This calendar is composed basically of a set of ten simultaneously running weeks of different duration. The weeks range in length from one day (the name for the week being *ekawara* and that of the day being *luang)* to ten days in duration *(dasawara* being the name for the week).[3] Each type of week is identified by a Sanskrit number (except for nine) which indicates the number of days in that week. This is followed by the form *wara* (Sanskrit for day, as in a series). Each day of any specific week has its particular name. Since all ten weeks run concurrently, any twenty-four hour period may be identified by ten names. Most days will be identified by the average Balinese with the day-name taken from the seven-day week followed by the name for that day taken from the five-day week. The co-occurrence of particular

---

[2] It is speculated that this calendar was originally an agricultural calendar connected with the cultivation of rice. This would also correlate well with its distribution because south central Bali is the area of greatest rice cultivation. The more mountainous areas raise little if any rice. See Pigeaud, 1967, for his classification of the Watu Gunung myth.

[3] In Java, where this calendrical tradition is basically much the same as in Bali, there is no one-day week. Furthermore the day-name *luang* itself means "empty."

days of certain weeks is considered to be auspicious or dangerous depending upon the combination. The days of the five-, six-, and seven-day weeks are particularly prominent in such calculations. The three-day week is important because village markets are regulated on this basis. It is not too surprising that the name of the day in the one-day week is not heard very much since all days bear this name. Probably for a similar reason the names from the two-day week are not often heard. Although any and all days have their own significance, those for the four-, eight-, nine-, and ten-day weeks are not much used by the average Balinese. A calendrical expert would, of course, be familiar with their potency. In this connection, it might be significant that neither the four-, eight-, nor nine-day weeks go evenly into the 210-day period which is the duration of the year as determined by the Javanese-Balinese calendar.

While the Hindu-Balinese calendar has twelve months, each of which is named, the Javanese-Balinese calendar gives names only to the seven-day weeks *(saptawara)*. Any *saptawara* is called *wuku* or *uku*.[4]

There are thirty such individually named *uku* in the year, and the year therefore is 210 days long. The series of weeks begins with the weeks *Sinta* and *Landep* and ends with the 30th week, *Watu Gunung*. With such an array of 10 types of weeks, 53 names for days and 30 names for weeks (as well as still other variables not mentioned) it is easy to imagine that learning such a system could present real problems. The myth of I Watu Gunung addresses itself to this matter and presents a rationale for the origin of the names as well as a frame within which the order of the names may be retained.

It might be claimed that the story of I Watu Gunung presents much more of Balinese culture and tradition than just its calendar. This is undoubtedly true, especially with any single version of the story. However, if one examines more than a single version it becomes evident that there is considerable variability in this folktale *(satua)*.[6]

---

[4]The days of the *uku* are dedicated to the celestial bodies, not unlike the names of the days in the Western calendar. Equally significant, the names occur in the same order in both systems (Goris, 1960, p. 117). This surely reveals an Indic influence, as does the fact that the names for the days in the eight-day week are derived from the principal gods of the Hindu pantheon. The naming process for the other days has not been systematically presented.

[5]The day name *sri* occurs three times, as the first day of *triwara*, first day of *astawara* and as the fifth day of *dasawara. Dewi sri* is the goddess of agriculture (especially rice) and is the wife of *Wisnu*, god of water, fertility, and the underworld.

[6]A *satua* is prose literature. It might be written down, as many folktales have been, on palm-leaf manuscripts. These are almost invariably without an author, scribe, or date being identified. For a discussion of various types of literature in Bali, see Pigeaud, 1967; J. Hooykaas, 1955, p. 236 f.; C. Hooykaas, 1963.

The calendrical elements are among the more stable features of the tale, although they may be presented differently in various accounts. The actual story line will not be the only aspect of the tale which varies. Previously published tales in Balinese have usually come from hand-written manuscripts and rate rather high in terms of literary style, elegance of arrangement, completeness of story line, and consistency in the use of speech levels. The following story was recorded on tape in Ubud, Bali, in 1965. The informant was an elderly Anak Agung from the village of Pedjeng. He was considered by some to be expert in story telling, although the *tjokorda* (prince), in whose *puri* (palace) I lived, did not feel that he had full control of the folklore. Whether this is because the particular story told was not the version known to the *tjokorda*, I was not able to determine. It can be observed that the storyteller did take shortcuts which reportedly would not be done in a written version of the tale. Also, he was not absolutely consistent in his use of speech levels. Some of these features of the tale will be pointed out in the transcription and translation portions.

In order to provide an overview of this tale as well as to give a basis for placing this version within a larger context, a synopsis of an earlier version of the tale is presented. This version was obtained by Miguel Covarrubias in the early 1930's and published in his book, *Island of Bali* (1937, pp. 314-315) in connection with his treatment of the Balinese *uku*.

The origin of the names of these weeks is told in the legend of Sinta, a woman who became pregnant after she dreamed she slept with a holy man, giving birth to a beautiful child. One day Sinta lost her temper when the boy became unruly and struck him, wounding him on the head. The boy ran away and his grieved mother searched for him in vain for years afterwards. The grown boy had in time become the powerful ruler of the country of Giling Wesi, where he was known as Watu Gunung, "Stone Mountain," because he was supposed to have obtained his powerful magic from the mountain where he had undergone penance.

One day the wandering mother, always in search of him, came to Giling Wesi accompanied by her sister Landap. The two women were still beautiful and Watu Gunung became so impressed by the strangers that he married both, having in due time twenty-seven children by his mother and aunt. By a scar on the head of Watu Gunung, one day Sinta became aware of the incest committed, and to avert disaster it was decided that Watu Gunung had to marry the goddess Sri, wife of Wisnu, thus becoming himself like a god, free of the curse on incest. He had the audacity to request her in marriage, but was naturally refused, causing Watu Gunung to declare war on the gods. Wisnu took personal command of the armies sent to punish his arrogance and finally defeated Watu Gunung after obtaining the secret of the magic that gave him his powers. To celebrate the victory it was decreed that his twenty-seven sons be killed, one every seven days. Sinta wept for seven days and was received into heaven, so Wisnu added her name as well as that of her sister Landap and of Watu Gunung to the twenty-seven and established the thirty weeks as everlasting signs of his victory.

As one reads the following version of the tale of *I Watu Gunung*
and compares it with the one summarized above, it will be observed
that the stories differ in several respects. For one thing, the pregnancy
is not the result of a dream. For another, the child is not at all beautiful.
In both versions, however, Sinta wounds her child on the head. The
origin of the name Watu Gunung shares certain elements in both tales,
but the ways in which the women and child meet again are vastly different. The names of the 27 other weeks occur in both accounts but
rather than being the children of the incestuous union they are the
princedoms which I Watu Gunung has conquered during his rise to
power. I Watu Gunung does ask for the wife of Wisnu in both versions,
but in the above summary the motive seems to be to save him from
retribution, whereas in the following version the wives (mothers) seem
to be steering him toward his doom. In the above version, the struggle
between I Watu Gunung and Wisnu is a matter of armies and general-
ship, whereas in the following account I Watu Gunung seems to do
all his own fighting for himself. In the 1930 version, the establishment
of the week names and their order in the calendar are overtly dealt
with. In the 1965 recording, the order is presented but the connection
with the calendar is left to inference. Finally, the comparison of both
versions reveals that one account seems to end with full resolution while
in the oral version the final resolution of the conflict is not part of the
story. This is not an uncommon aspect of Balinese tales as witnessed
in such theatricals as the fight between the witch *Rangda* and the dragon
Barong (Belo, 1949). The same aspect is, incidentally, seen in interpersonal relationships between parent (mother) and child by Bateson and Mead
(1942).

One would, of course, expect to find in a full story more elements
than could be set forth in a summary. Naturally, aspects of the tale
missing in the summary can not be compared. However, it is worth
pointing out that the recorded version also accounts for the ten types
of weeks. One might suppose that, if the storyteller had not been interested in taking shortcuts he would have recited all of the names for all
of the days in the various weeks instead of stopping short of this goal.
I had unfortunately induced him to give me the tale by suggesting that
I could take care of the thirst which would surely ensue from all of
that talking. In short, I had promised him a glass of *brem*.

All shortcuts, however, cannot be attributed to the Anak Agung's
thirst, for much of the shortening adds to the impact of the tale, especially
when the action moves fast or the audience might become bored. Finally,
he made much use of dialogue and greatly reduced descriptive or explanatory passages. The barest essentials of these descriptive portions have

been added in the English translation in order that the reader may identify the persons speaking.

NOTES ON ORTHOGRAPHY

The tale is presented in a modified phonemic transcription. The Balinese phonological system consists of the following segmental units. Vocoids: /i, e, ə, a, o, u; w, y/. Consonants: /p, t, c, k, ?; b, d, j, g; m, n, ñ, ŋ ; s, h; l, r/.

The /ə/ is represented in this transcription by two letters. It is written as the letter *e* in all locations except in word final open syllables where the letter *a* is written. /a/ does not occur in word final position. But since the underlying form of morphemes may have final /a/ but not final /ə/, such forms are written with *a* in final position. This simplifies, visually, the morphophonemics of stems plus suffixes.

Standard romanized Balinese has *a* written following many consonants (especially in prefixes) where the actual spoken form contains the /ə/ in such positions. This *a* is a transliteration of the unmodified syllabic symbol of the traditional script. The syllabic symbol stands for a specific consonant followed by the inherent vowel *a* unless otherwise specified. Since the Balinese pronounce these vowels as /ə/ in colloquial speech but in most cases may pronounce them as /a/ in the careful literary speech style, it is less effort to write these forms with the basic syllabic sign. This traditional orthographic practice may have in fact been largely responsible for the acceptability of forms with /a/. Where medial /ə/ was spoken in the colloquial speech recording, *e* will be written in the transcription.

E stands for the vowel /e/ and, since /ə/ never occurs initially, this capital letter is always recognizable as standing for /e/.

The /c and j/ are affricates and in standard romanized Balinese would be written *tj* and *dj* respectively. /?/ is an aspect of juncture. Since juncture occurs at some, but not all, grammatical word boundaries, and since word boundaries are indicated as spaces, the glottal catch is thus not used as a symbol in this tale.

/ñ/ will be written as *ny* except when, in the spoken record, it is followed by /c/ or /j/, in which case only *n* will be written. Since neither */nc/ nor */nj/ are permissible sequences in Balinese, the foregoing convention is unambiguous. The /ŋ/ is written as *ng* for similar reasons.

I WATU GUNUNG*

Inggih, iratu sareng sami pirengang puniki. Kadi gegatran titiang,

---

*Numbered footnotes to this folktale begin on page 283.

titiang nguningang mangkin indik wEntenE ipun si Watu Gunung. Me-
kawit sangkaning ida, pranda sang yang kulogiri. Ida ngardi pisan. Ida
medrewE rabi kekalih. Mewasta I[1] Diah Sinta ketekEn I Diah Landep.
KEnginan mobot rabin ida I Diah Sinta punika. Sampun mobot, wEnten
pewecanan ida ring I Diah[2] punika kekalih. "Adi![3] I Diah Sinta kelawan
Diah Landep! Jani beli[4] anak nanggung yasa. Keneng-kenengin ragan
adinE jumah. SemekelonE beli tuah petang dasa lemeng, beli ninggalin
adi luas." Sapunika ugi pengandikan ida keh begawan kulogiri kedadosan keiringang antuk i rabi sareng kalih. Memarga yakti[5] ida raris merika
ring pesraman nanggung kerti uyakti ida ring pesraman. Kepuputang
nanggung ida kerti, puput budal[6] raris ida merika ring swargan.

1-A

Very well, for all of you (princes), listen to this! As I have said,
I will inform you about the matters which pertain to Si Watu Gunung.
(It) all actually begins with the august Holy man, Sang Yang Kulogiri.
He was very devout. He had two wives who were named I Diah Sinta
and I Diah Landep. Now it happened that I Diah Sinta had become
pregnant. After she had become pregnant, he spoke to them both. "Sis!
Say, Sinta and Landep, now I must go to meditate. Take care of your-
selves (here) at home. I will only be going off and leaving you for just
40 days (nights) at the most." Thereupon the two wives agreed to follow
the instructions from the holy one of Kulogiri. Then he went off to
the bathing place.[7] He offered his prayers at the bathing place, and
when the worship was finished, he then returned to heaven.

2

NEnten uning i rabi ring ida sampun mantuk[6] ring swarganE. Kedadosan wEnten bebaosan i rabi sareng kalih I Diah Sinta ketekEn I Diah
Landep. "Mbok,[8] Diah Sinta, yEn amonE suba wayah bobot mbokE.
Yan peranda liwat pesan. Suba semayan ida nE rauh. Nah, yEn mbok
ngugu itungan tiang, jalan mbok kema jani ka pesraman. Tilikin Ida
Peranda yEn kEngkEn kepida yEn kapa kari nyeneng yan kapa sampun
sEda. Ah, apang beneh ben mbok tiang ngenehang." "Nah, yEn kEto
je pepineh adi beneh. Pepineh adi kekeneh ban mbok, lamun kEto jalan
adi kema ke pesraman."

2-A

The wives did not know that He had already returned to heaven.
Then the wives I Diah Sinta and I Diah Landep conversed. "Sister Sinta,
you are certainly far along in your pregnancy. My but the priest[9] is
very late. He should have arrived by now. Well, if you agree with my

view, you should go there now to the bathing place. Check on Ida Peranda (to see) if he might still be alive or dead. I hope you will agree with me" (said Landep). "Well, I do agree with your idea" (replied Sinta). "Therefore (let's) go to the bathing place!"

3

Pemuput memargi merika ring pesraman. A rauh irika ring pesraman, ten wEnten ida pranda kari irika. Kedadosan merarian sareng kalih ring duur batunE lumbang.[10] Wawu merarian irika, dados nyakit I Diah Sinta. Medal okan ida, lanang. Wawu medal, belah batu punika. Raris ring ngkagan batunE anakE alit punika mecelep. Wawu kecingak anakE alit kantun nyalig, dados nangis Ni Diah Sinta ketekEning Ni Diah Landep. Auwinan nangis, seantukan ragenE jegEg makakekalih, meduwE oka asapunika ageng semalih nyalig. Punika auwinan sungkang pekayun ida.

3-A

Now they have finished going there to the bathing place. When they reached the bathing place Ida Pranda was no longer there. As it happened they both stopped on top of a wide and flat boulder. They no sooner stopped there than (Sinta) went into labor. I Diah Sinta gave birth to her child, a boy. No sooner had (the infant) come out than the boulder split. Therefore the small child (fell) into the hole in the boulder. When it was seen that the infant was still bald, Ni Diah Sinta began crying along with Ni Diah Landep. The reason for crying was that they who were both beautiful should have had a child which was so gross and bald. That was the reason why their thoughts were so distraught.[11]

4

Sampun rekE banget tangis ida, turun[12] ida betara Brahma. WEnten pengandikan ida Sang Yang Brahma. "Eh, duh, cening I Diah Sinta kelawan Ni Diah Landep! To Dadi to sebetanga dEwa ban idEwenE jegEg, ngelah panak bocok? Da dEwa sebet. Jani bapa nyupat panak i dEwa. Bapa ngadanin panak i dEwa. Adanin bapa Yabang Bai. Kerana madan Yabang Bai ben kasal papas ai, ia barak. Kerana madan Yabang Bai. Wastu panak idEwa nE apang kelih." Sapunika pangandikan ida Betara Brahma. Kedadosan duur okan ida para mangkin dados munggah saking belahan batu. Sampun asapunika wEnten wecanan[13] ida Betara Brahma. "Cening Diah Sinta Landep! Ajak panak idEwa nE mulih!" Sapunika pangandikan ida. Kedadosan keajak jakti budal merika ring Kulogiri.

4-A

(Since) they had been weeping so hard, the god Brahma descended. (Here) are the words of the Lord Brahma. "Oh, my children I Diah Sinta and Diah Landep! Why do you bewail for having had an ugly child? Don't feel bad! Now I will change your child with my magic. I, your father, will give a name to your child. I will call your child I Abang Bai. He will have the name I Abang Bai because when the sun hits him he turns red. Grant that your child will quickly grow up!" Thus spoke the God Brahma. Thereupon their child immediately grew up and came out from within the fissure in the rock. As soon as that happened the God Brahma spoke again. "(My) children Sinta (and) Landep, take this child of yours and return home!" Such were his words. And thereupon they dutifully returned (with the child) to Kulogiri.

5

Sampun rauh ring gria[14] Kulogiri, telas antuka[15] keaemaeman asiki. Mauwinan wEnten mewasta dina[16] luang. BEnjangan telas antuka keacmaeman kekalih. Mauwinan wEnten Menga Pepet. BEnjangan telas tetiga.[17] Mauwinan wEnten tri wara.[17] BEnjangan telah[18] patpat. Mauwinan wEnten catur wara. Telas lelima wEnten panca wara. Telas nemnem wEnten sada wara. Telas pepitu wEnten sapta wara. Telas akutus wEnten asta wara. Telas asia wEnten sanga wara. Telas adasa wEnten dasa wara. Sampun puput amunika, kedadosan akuskusan dados asopan.[19] [20]

5-A

As soon as they arrived at the Kulogiri residence (I Abang Bai ate) one rice cake. That is why (the day of the one-day week) is called *dina luang*. The next day (he finished off) two rice cakes. That is why there are (the days) *Menga* (and) *Pepet* (for *duwiwara*). The following day (he) finished three. That is why there is the three-day week.[21] The next day four were eaten up. That is why there is the four-day week. (When) five were eaten (we got) the five-day week. (When) six were consumed, there was the six-day week. When seven, the seven-day week. When eight, the eight-day week. When nine, the nine-day week. When ten, then the ten-day week. After finishing off all that much, a whole rice cooker (full of rice) became as a (mere) mouthful[19] of rice (to him).

6

Napi sedek biang ida ngerateng, mereretu raris Yabang Bai aminta bujana.[22] "Uduh cening, apan bujanan mEmEnE tondEn rateng, anti ndEn malu! Yan suba lebeng, anak cening, gaEnang mEmE ajengajengan." Taler ngereretu. Pungkad ajeng ring kukusanE. Jeg, arayunan dados asopan. Napi duka biang ida! Kepanteg antuk siyut! Dados kanin yuakti prabun ida. Metu rah mekupah-kupahan. Raris ngumbang.

6-A

Once when (his) mother was still in the process of cooking, I Abang Bai was whining and nagging for a *bujana*. "Goodness child, mother's bujanas are not yet cooked (done), just wait for a while! When (this) is cooked, child, mother will prepare a meal (for you)." But (he kept) playing around anyway (and) the food in the *kukusan* was overturned. Would you believe, the whole meal became as a single mouthful (to him). Was his mother ever angry! (He) was pummelled with a long wooden ladle! His head was thoroughly battered! Blood gushed out endlessly. At which point he fled.

7

Sampun rauh ring margi, tedun[12] Ida Betara Brahma. "Ning[23] Yabang Bai, To ngudiang idEwa ngambul[24] dadi idEwa? Nah. Jani bapa ngesEhin idEwa adan. Jani idEwa madan I Watu Gunung. Ben idEwa lekaad di batunE di gunungE, dEwa madan I Watu Gunung.[25] Buin bapa ngemaang dEwa penugraan[26] jani. Wastu idEwa apang jaya wijaya." Sapunika pengenugraan[26] Ida Betara Brahma.

7-A

When (he) arrived in the road, the Lord Brahma descended. "(My) child, I Abang Bai! Why are you running away? Now, I am going to change your name. Now you will be called *I Watu Gunung*. Because you came forth (were born) on a boulder in the mountains, you will now have the name *I Watu Gunung*. And in addition I will give you a great gift. Let it be that you will be undefeatable." Such was the blessing of the Lord Brahma.

8

Wus asamunika raris memargi I Watu Gunung. Rauh ring panegara Ukir. Dados ngarantuh irika ring panegara Ukir. Saluwiring wang meratengan kejeg, prokosa ajengan nakE[27] sami. Mauwinan raris kepraangin antuk jagatE irika ring Ukir. Pemuput kaon para ratu ring Ukir. Raris kanggon pepatih. Malih ngerereh jagat. Ratu ring Kulantir raris kerereh Taler kaon iratu Kulantir. Wawu kalih meduwE[28] panjak. Malih ngerereh ratu. Ratu ring Taulu raris kererereh. Taler kaon. Ngaturang raga sami. Tiga medrewE[28] panjak.

8-A

After all of that I Watu Gunung then went away. He came to a country called Ukir. He laid waste the land of Ukir. All of the people who were cooking their rice had been ordered to give up their food (to I Watu Gunung). That is why (I Watu Gunung) was fought by all the countryside at Ukir. In the end the princedom of Ukir was defeated. Therefore it was taken as a vassal (by I Watu Gunung). (I Watu Gunung) again sought (more) land. Subsequently the prince at Kulantir was sought out. What is more, the Kulantir prince was defeated. Therefore (I Watu Gunung) obtained a second servant. He again searched out more princes. And finally the Leader of Taulu was attacked and defeated. (They) all surrendered themselves. Thus (I Watu Gunung) had three slaves.

9

Malih ngerereh ratu ring Gumbreg. Taler kaon. Ratu ring Weriga rereh taler kaon. Ratu ring Weregadian ngerereh, taler kaon.[29] Ratu ring Julung Wangi rereh, taler kaon. Ratu ring Sungsang rereh, taler kaon Ratu ring Dungulang, taler kaon. Ratu ring Kuningan taler kaon. Ring Langkir taler kaon. Ring Medangsia taler sami kaon. Ring Pujut kaon. Ring Paang kaon. Ring Kereulut kaon. Ring Marakih kaon Ring Tambir kaon. Ring Medangkungan kaon. Ring Matal kaon. Ring UyE taler kaon. Ring Menail taler kaon. Ring Prangbakat kaon. Ring Bala kaon. Ring Ugu kaon.[30] Ring Kelau kaon. Ring Dukut taler kaon. Maka pitu likur para ratu sami kaon.

9-A

He continued by seeking out the prince at Gumbreg who also was defeated. The prince of Weriga was also attacked and defeated. (He) sought out the prince of Weregadian who was then defeated.[29] The prince at Julung Wangi was sought and defeated. The prince at Sungsang was attacked and defeated. The prince at Dungulang was also defeated. Also the prince at Kuningan was defeated. The Langkir (prince) was defeated. At Medangsia (the prince) was defeated also. At Pujut (he) was defeated. At Paang (he) was defeated. At Kerulut — defeated. At Marakih — defeated. At Tambir — defeated. At Medangkungan — defeated. At Matal — defeated. Also at Uye — defeated. Also at Menail — defeated. Also at Prangbakat — defeated. (They) were defeated at Bala. (They) were defeated at Ugu.[30] (They) were defeated at Kelau. (They) were defeated also at Dukut. A total of 27 princes were all defeated.

10

Kali nika raris paom kenikiin[31] para ratu sane kaonang sami. Ke-akEnin. "DEwa pararatu mekejang! Dija buin ada pararatu sakti? YEn

ada buin pararatu sakti, bakal siatin." Raris matur pararatu sami. "Inggih, ratu dEwa agung. Puniki wEnten rerengan titiang pararatu istri
irika ring jagat Kulogiri. Pararatu istri kekalih. Yan[32] punika nyidayang,
iratu ngaonang. Nyandaang iratu raris ngambil nganggEn rabi." "Beh.
YEn kEto, jalan jani kema gebug gumi Kulogiri." Raris megebug irika
ring Kulogiri. WirEh satru istri, prabu istri punika nEnten nyidayang.
Puput ngaturang raga jakti sareng kalih. Raris kehambil kehanggEn[33]
rabi.

10-A

At that time a meeting was called of all the princes who had been
defeated. (The following) was asked of them. "All you princes! Where
are there other worthy princes? If there are other skilled princes, they
will be fought." Thereupon all the princes responded, "Yes, oh august
one, we can tell you this. There are some female rulers in the land
of Kulogiri. There are two princesses (there). Those are the ones you
could defeat. Afterwards, you could then take them for your wives."
"Brag! Well if that is the case, let's go over there now and raise hell
at Kulogiri!" Thereupon war came to Kulogiri. Because the enemies
were female, the female rulers were not able (to prevail). In the end
they both gave themselves up. They were then taken as wives (by I
Watu Gunung).

11

Sampun ida merabi, wEnten cihna raris ring swargan. Abulan pitung
dina yuakti sabehE tan pepegatan. Kedadosan wEnten pewecanan ida,
Sang Yang Indra ring ida Yang Nerada. "DEwa Yang Nerada! Indayang
idEwa kebali. Tilikin di Bali kerana ada ujanE amonE abulan pitung
dina. Mirib ada manusa salah ukur di Bali. Nah, idEwa nilikin!" Raris
tedun kebali ida Yang Nerada. Keucapan mangkin I Watu Gunung
sedek kejukin[34] kutu ring undag metEn. Sedek kejukin kutu punika,
kepanggih antuk I Diah Sinta biketa[35] ring prabu. Dados Eling I Diah
Sinta ring indikE ngebug oka sanE dumun. Kapikayun Oka punika,
Auwinan nangis. Eling ida ring mesomah ring oka.

11-A

When he had become married, there were then signs in heaven. For
one month and seven days the rains poured down without stopping
Therefore Sang Yang Indra spoke to Yang Nerada. "God Nerada! You
should go to Bali. Investigate in Bali the reason for this much rain of
one month and seven days duration. Perhaps there is some human who
has done wrong in Bali. Now be sure that you check on that (for me)."

Then Yang Nerada descended to Bali. It is said that at that very moment I Watu Gunung was in the process of being cleaned of head lice on the stoop of the main sleeping house.[36] In the process of searching for head lice I Diah Sinta happened upon a large scar on the scalp (of I Watu Gunung). I Diah Sinta then remembered the incident in which (she) had long ago pummeled her child (on the head). She (then) recognized (her) child. This caused her to start crying, (because) she then realized that she had become married to her own son.

12

Wawu sapunika, kecingak antuk Yang Nerada. I Watu Gunung salah ukur nyuwang i mEmE. Kepastu irika raris, "dEwa Watu Gunung, mapan i dEwa salah ukur, dumadak[37] apang kalaang[38] i Wisnu." Sapunika pastun ida Yang Nerada. Kepireng antuk i Diah Sinta. "Nah nE, panakE bakal kalaang Wisnu."[39]

12-A

All of this was seen by Yang Nerada. I Watu Gunung had done wrong in taking his mother (as wife). Thereupon the following curse was uttered. "Watu Gunung, since you have sinned, let it be willed that you will be defeated by Wisnu!" Such was the curse of Ida Yang Nerada. (The curse) happened to have been overheard by Ni Diah Sinta. "Well, so it appears that (my) child will be defeated by Wisnu!"[39]

13

Wawu amunika dados nolih I Watu Gunung ring I Diah Sinta Landep. "YEh, to, adi jeg sedih adi ajaka dadua. Apa nE sebetang adi sanget? Apa adi kowangan? Kwala oraang tekEning beli, nyidaang beli ngalihang adi!" "Yah, sapuniki beli, sanE banget sebetang titiang, lud pisan menah titiang. Ngidam manah titiangE. Memadu ring rabin ida Betara Wisnu. YEn nyidayang beli ngerereh rabin Ida Betara Wisnu apang tiang maan memadu tekEn rabin Betara Wisnu. Mara ada keneh tiang liang." "Beh. YEn kEto ben adi Elah beli. "Dija tongos nE WisnuE?" "YEn linggih Ida Betara Wisnu irika weluya ring Sapta Petala." "Nah, lamun kEto, antosang beli."

13-A

After that I Watu Gunung happened to look in on I Dia Sinta (and) Landep. "Say, my but you two are certainly distressed! What is causing you so much grief? What do you need? Just tell me what I can get for you." "Well, it's this way, dear, I am ashamed (to say) what is really troubling me but I have a great need (for something). I greatly crave having as a co-wife the wife of the Lord Wisnu" (Sinta said). "If only you would be able to ask for the wife of the Lord Wisnu, so that I can be a co-wife (to you) along with the wife of the Lord Wisnu. Then my mind would be at ease." "Well, if that is all, that is easy enough for me!" (said I Watu Gunung). "Just where is the place of this Wisnu?" "The Lord Wisnu might be staying there in Sapta Petala" (she said). "O.K. If that is the case. Just wait for me."

14

Paramangkin memurti I Watu Gunung. Belah sek jagatE! Nyungsak raris I Watu Gunung tedun ka Sapta Petala. Mauwinan wEnten mewasta uku Sungsang Carik,[40] Sapunika indikE. Sampun rauh ring Sapta Petala kepanggih Ida Betara Wisnu. Sedek Ida ngabin rabi[41] weluya ring Sapta Petala. Raris tangkil I Watu Gunung. Kenikiin antuk Ida Betara Wisnu. "DEwa Watu Gunung, dadi DEwa laksana? Gemisukan rasanE dEwa teka. Apa anE ada buatan idEwa?"

14-A

All of a sudden I Watu Gunung summoned up all his powers and the earth was split open! I Watu Gunung dashed in headlong and descended to Sapta Petala. This is why there is the week name of *Sungsang Carik*. That was the event (for the naming of the week). Having arrived in Sapta Petala, he met with Ida Betara Wisnu. Wisnu happened to be visiting his wife in Sapta Petala.[41] Then I Watu Gunung was received by the Lord Wisnu who spoke, "DEwa Watu Gunung, why have you made this journey? I suspect that you must have come for something. Is there something that is so important to you?"

15

"Inggih, ratu Betara wEnten. WEnten kapisarat[42] manah titiang ngelungsur ring Betara. Auwinan sapunika rEh[43] dingeh titiang Betara sadu darma. Asing tunasa anakE Betara ten dados tara ngicEn. WEnten wuyakti asapunika?" "Beh, yEn to takonang i dEwa saja. Saja mula tiang sing dadi tara ngemaang asing tunasa. Sing dadi tara ngemaang anE patut."

15-A

"Yes, my Lord, there is. There is an important matter which I want to ask of you. The reason for that is that I have heard that my Lord is truly generous. What-so-ever is asked of my Lord you are not able to deny. Is that really true?" "Well, as far as that goes just go ahead and ask me" (said the Lord Wisnu). "It is true I am not able to refuse to give something which has been asked of me. I am not able to refuse giving anything which is proper."

16

"Inggih yan sapunika titiang wEnten tunas titiang ring Betara." "Nah, apa tunas idEwa, kala oraang." "Tiang nunas rabin paduka Betara pacang anggEn titiang kuranan." "Beh, yEn kEto ben i dEwa, sing beneh. kerana sing? I dEwa anak ratu luwih tengalih kuranan rarangan. Sing ada patuta.[44] AnE bajang, tagih tekEning tiang ncEn ja keneh i dEwa. Tiang ngemaang to i dEwa." "Ten wEnten, titiang weluya puniki rabi deruwEnE manahang titiang nunas pacang anggEn titiang kuranan. SwEca Betara pacang anggEn titiang kuranan, Ten wEnten, taler anggEn titiang kuranan." Sapunika atur I Watu Gunung.

16-A

"All right, in that case I have a request of you," said Watu Gunung. "Well then whatever your request is just ask," answered the Lord Wisnu. "I ask to be given your lordship's wife to be used as my own wife," was I Watu Gunung's request. The Lord Wisnu replied, "Well, if that is what you really intend to ask for, it is not right. Do you know why not? Because you as one of nobility should not make an improper marriage. This is not proper. Now there are some who are not married. Ask me for whichever one you want. I will give her to you." "No sire, I only intend to ask for this wife of yours which I will take as my wife. If you are willing I will take her for my wife. If you are not (willing) I will take her anyway for my wife." So responded I Watu Gunung.

17

Dados duka Ida Betara Wisnu. Mauwinan dados yuda. KEngin yuda punika swEEn nyanE wantah pitung tiban.[45] Yuda punika taler durung wEnten kaon. Irika duka raris Ida Betara Wisnu. Memurti Ida dados wuyakti Ida Kurma. Kurma punika mewasta mpas. Mpas punika meco-co besi wresani, meilat cakra.[46] Malih raris meyuda. Kala meyuda, keni ketambil I Watu Gunung antuk ilat cakra punika. Raris leketik I Watu Gunung. Taler kari urip, nanging kesampun kaon.

17-A

The Lord Wisnu became irate. That is why the war started. What s more the battle went on and on for seven years. Still there was no defeat (for either side). That enraged the Lord Wisnu again. (This time) he transformed himself and became Ida Kurma. That particular *kurma* had the name of *mpas* (the turtle). The turtle had a pointed beak of magnetic iron that gave off a brilliant light. Then they began to fight again. During the fight, I Watu Gunung was struck by the glare from the potent beak. Even with this he was spun down like a spark struck from a flint. He was still alive, but he had been beaten.

18

Kala irika mewangwang I Watu Gunung ring ida Betara Wisnu. "DEwa Betara Wisnu, kalah tiang. Jani kalah tiang, Tiang numadi buin ka Bali. Sing liang anggon tiang rama. Begawan Kesawa[47] anggon tiang rama. Tiang dadi Sang Rewana. Tiang nak[48] sing ja suud mekumo musuh tekEn i dEwa."

18-A

Then I Watu Gunung conceded to the Lord Wisnu. "Lord Wisnu, I have lost. I am defeated for now. However I will be reborn again in Bali. I am not willing to be your friend. I will side with Begawan Kesawa. (By damn) I'll even become Sang Rewana! I am in no way finished being your enemy!"

19

Dados irika Ida Betara Wisnu. "DEwa I Watu Gunung, nah yEn kEto ben idEwa, i dEwa sing suud mekumo musuh tekEning tiang. Tiang anak sing suud memusuh kEn[49] idEwa. Jani i dEwa ka Lengka numadi dadi Sang Rewana. Nah, tiang ka Yodia kal[50] numadi, sing lEn anggon tiang rama Ida Sang Dasa Rata. Tiang dadi Sang Dasa Rati."

19-A

The Lord Wisnu responded. "I Watu Gunung, well, if that is what you are going to do, all right then, so you are not finished being my enemy. Well I am not through opposing you (either). Go, then, to Lengka and be reborn as Sang Rewana. I will go to Yodia and be reborn as a brother to none other than Ida Sang Dasa Rata. I will thus become Sang Dasa Rati."

20

"Beh, yEn kEto ben i dEwa, tiang bin numadi ka Bali. Tiang ka Perejoti. Kal numadi tiang dadi Sang Bomo." "Bah, yEn kEto ben i dEwa, tiang buin masih numadi. Tiang nak sing suud memusuh. Tiang ka Derewati, kal numadi. Tiang dadi Sang Kresna. Elingang yEn raos i dEwa puput ring lengka nu inda kekaonang antuk Wisnu. Ring Perejoti nu inda taler kekaonang[51] antuk Wisnu." REh patin Ida Sang Yang Brahma mastu I Watu Gunung. NgicEn penugran jaya wijaya. Jaya wiyakti ipun polih. Wijaya Wisnu wiakti pacang ngaonang. Puput rekE sampun seindikan I Watu Gunung nunda.

20-A

"Well then I will be reborn on Bali. (Better yet) I'll go to Perejoti. I'll become transformed into Sang Bomo," declared Watu Gunung. (Wisnu's answer was) "Well if you do that I will only do the same. (For) I am certainly not going to stop opposing you. I would go to Derewati and be reborn. I would become Sang Kersna. Don't forget that although you say you would finish it all in Lengka you will still be defeated by Wisnu. Even in Perejoti you would still be beaten by Wisnu." Because that is an essential part of the blessing with which Sang Yang Brahma had ordained I Watu Gunung. (He had) given him the magic gift of super power, *jaya wijaya*. He (Watu Gunung) had in fact received great victories, *jaya*. (But) the true noble power, *wijaya*, of Wisnu would always be supreme. Thus ends the account of the misdeeds of I Watu Gunung.

NOTES TO THE TEXT AND TRANSLATION

1. *I:* Actually a male title but also used for females. The proper female title is *Ni*. The storyteller was not always particular about the distinction.

2. *Diah:* "Princess," also a title for females of a certain rank. For more discussion of titles see Geertz (1966, p. 28+).

3. *Adi:* "Younger sibling." This is also a term of endearment for a wife by a husband.

4. *beli:* "Older brother," also a term of endearment for a husband which may be used in addressing someone or in referring to oneself.

5. *yakti:* "Actually, truly." South central Bali abounds with competing forms for many words. Some are the result of the morphophonemic process of dropping initial syllables in colloquial speech. Others are undoubtedly doublets which originate from other dialect areas, other languages or from literary sources which may perpetuate older forms. This particular word also occurs as *(uyakti), (wuyakti), (wiakti), (wyakti),* and *(jakti)*.

6. *budal, mantuk:* Both mean "return." They are both polite level words but *mantuk* is considered to be more honorific than *budal*. It is therefore generally used when referring to others. Here, however, they are both used in describing action by another in the polite speech level.

7. *bathing place:* Bathing and water in general hold a ritualistic and religious, indeed magical position in the traditions of the Balinese.

8. *mbok:* "Older sister" may also be used in speaking to most any familiar female.

9. *peranda:* As an alternate form of *pedanda*. Actually means a particular type of priest. Used here as an honorific term of reference.

10. *batu nE lumbang:* A shortened form for *batu anE lumbang.* "Stone which (was) flat."

11. *distraught: Sungsang* actually means "upside down."

12. *tedun* and *turun:* Doublets meaning "descend." While both are polite forms, *turun* is considered more honorific.

13. *wecanan:* Shortened form of *pewecanan,* "words, speech."

14. *gria:* The home of a member of the Brahmana caste. A Sanskrit loan.

15. *telas antuka:* A shortened form of *telas antuk ia,* "Finished by him."

16. *dina:* "Day." A Sanskrit loan.

17. Notice the numbers. The native Malayo-Polynesian term is usually used to count the number of rice cakes consumed but the Sanskrit derived numbers are used to designate the weeks of the given duration of days *(wara).*

18. *telas* and *telah:* These forms are similar to *budal* and *mantuk,* in that the storyteller seems to be mixing forms when a strict adherence to the prescriptions of speech level would seem to militate against this.

19 *sopan:* Actually means "handful," that amount of food which is cradled in the four fingers and backed by the thumb nail.

20. The numbering sequence shows the following interesting distributional aspects. Numbers 1, 2, and 3 each has a special polite form which is in keeping with the general level of discourse. The numbers 4, 5, 6, 7, 8, 9, and 10 do not have different level forms. Numbers 2, 3, 4, 5, 6, and 7 all show reduplication (partial or complete) of the number morpheme. The numbers 1, 8, 9, and 10 are unreduplicated number morphemes but are always preceded by the morpheme /a/ which itself means "one." The latter forms are used as counters. See their use with the forms for "rice" and "handful."

21. Identifying the various weeks by naming the days in the weeks is used only for the one day week *(Ekawara)* and the two day week *(Dwiwara).* Beginning with the three day week *(Triwara),* the names of the days are omitted and the week designations are given instead.

22. *bujana:* A kind of food.

23. *ning:* A reduction from the full form *cening.* The habit of elimination of first syllables is quite common in colloquial speech. However where observed it is not with all forms but rather a select few. Classes of forms commonly reduced include forms of address, demonstratives, certain grammatical particles.

24. *ngambul:* "Withdraw in silent revolt."

25. *Watu:* This is a literary (Kawi) form of *batu* "Stone." *Gunung* means "mountain."

26. *penugraan:* Shortened form of *pengenugrahan.* "The giving of a blessed gift, holy gift, from the grace of god." The root is *anugrah* "gift."

27. *nakE:* Short for *anakE* "the people."

28. *medrewE* and *meduwE:* Derived verbs both meaning "to have, own." They are both used here in the same speech level although the former word is considered to be more honorific than the latter. The corresponding familiar form is *ngelah.*

29. As the list of conquered lands is recited the sentence surface structure becomes progressively truncated leaving only the barest semantic and structural essentials.

30. Here the storyteller takes the ultimate shortcut and skips the 25th in the series *Wayang.* This is the name of the 27th week because the weeks *Sinta* and *Landep* begin the series.

31. *kenikiin:* "To be addressed, spoken to." This is an assimilation for *kenikain.* The root is *nika.*

32. *kehambil, kehanggEn:* Both of these forms are structurally and stylistically alike in that both are compound forms built on a stem preceded by the affix *ke-* and both

reveal the pedantic "retention" of an orthographic /h/ at the beginning of the stem. They are literary style variants and are probably more common in the polite vocabulary than in the familiar speech level.

33. *yan:* "If" is largely untranslatable in this type of environment. When it precedes a substantive it serves mainly as an emphatic particle.

34. *kejukin:* Short for *keejukin.* The root is *ejuk* "Search, hunt."

35. *biketa:* Short for *biketE,* "The scar."

36. *metEn:* This is one of several structures in the Balinese household compound. This building consists of an enclosed room set on a raised platform. See Covarrubias (1937, pp. 88-96), for details of the Balinese residential complex.

37. *dumadak:* "Hopefully, let it be that. . . ." This is subject to two interpretations from a structural point of view. Most Balinese would probably (and at least one of my informants specifically did) interpret this as the stem *madak* "Hope, intention," preceded by the intensifier *du* for emphasis. *Du* is not a recurring form. It is more likely that this word represents a rare retention of the Old Balinese infix, *um,* in a literary context, but should now be considered unitary.

38. *kalaang:* Short for *kalahang,* "be defeated," from the root *kalah,* "defeat."

39. Note the verb morphology and the word order restrictions. The English order of subject–transitive verb–object is followed also in Balinese, but with some differences. In such a case, if the verb is derivable it must have the active verbal prefix to indicate that the subject is the actor of the transitive verb. The verb in this sentence lacks such a prefix which indicates that Wisnu is the agent of the verbal action.

40. *Sungsung Curik. Sungsung* (sometimes Julung Sungsang) is the tenth week in the calendar and earlier in this story was the eighth princedom conquered by Watu Gunung.

41. *ngabin rabi:* More completely, this means "to hold (one's) wife on one's lap while cradling her in one's arms."

42. *kapisarat:* "Indication." This sentence would be grammatical without this form. However it is a fancy word that renders the whole sentence more polite and deferential.

43. *rEh:* "Because" is the reduced form of *wirEh.*

44. *patuta:* A reduced form of *patutan,* "a proper thing, deed."

45. *tiban:* "Year." Actually 420 days, that is, 2 *uku* years. One 210-day year is called *oton.*

46. *cakra:* Refers particularly to the fiery wheel which is a Visnuite symbol.

47. *Kesawa:* By becoming the brother of the brother of Rewana, Watu Gunung will thus become Rewana himself. Wisnu employs the same circumlocution at the end of the next paragraph.

48. *nak:* "Person." The reduced form of *anak.* Here the form is largely untranslatable as it is used to give emphasis to the sentence generally and particularly to the preceding noun.

49. *kEn:* "With to." This is the reduced form of *tekEn.*

50. *kal:* Short for *bakal,* "will, intend" (future marker of verbs).

51. *kekaonang.* "Be defeated." The root is *kaon* "defeat." Generally the ka- passives indicate an unintentional passivity or a passive without emphasis on an agent. Here it seems to carry the implication that Wisnu's inevitable victory over Watu Gunung is not so much his doing but is just as much, if not more, the product of the will of Brahma.

LITERATURE CITED

Bali: Studies in Life, Thought and Ritual
     1960. [Selected Studies on Indonesia. Vol. 5.] The Hague: Van Hoeve.

BATESON, GREGORY, and MARGARET MEAD
     1942. *Balinese Character: A Photographic Analysis.* New York: New York Acad. Sci.

BELO, JANE
     1949. *Bali: Rangda and Barong.* Monogr. American Ethnological Soc. Seattle: Univ.
     Washington Press.

COVARRUBIAS, MIGUEL
     1937. *The Island of Bali.* New York: Knopf.

GEERTZ, CLIFFORD
     1966. *Person, Time, and Conduct in Bali: An Essay in Cultural Analysis.* Southeast
     Asia Studies Cultural Rep. Ser. 14. New Haven: Yale Univ. Press.

GORIS, ROELOF
     1932. "Overeenkomst tusschen Javaansche en Balische feestkalender." *Djawa.* **12**:310-
     312.
     1960. "Holidays and Holy Days." In *Bali: Studies in Life, Thought, and Ritual,* pp.
     115-129.

HOOYKAAS, C.
     1963. "Books Made in Bali." *Bijdragen tot de Taal-, Land- en Volkenkunde* **119**:371-
     386.

HOOYKAAS-VAN LEEUWEN BOOMKAMP, JACOBA HINDRIKA
     1955. "A Journey into the Realm of Death." *Bijdragen tot de Taal-, Land- en Volken-
     kunde* **111**:236-273.

NIEUWENKAMP, W. O. J.
     1914. "Een Balineesch Kalender." *Bijdragen tot de Taal-, Land- en Volkenkunde*
     69:112-126.

PIGEAUD, THEODORE G. TH.
     1967. *Literature of Java.* Vol. 1, *Synopsis of Javanese Literature: 900-1900 A.D.* The
     Hague: Nyhoff.

PHILIPPINES

A FUNCTIONAL INTERPRETATION
OF BAJAU SONGS

H. ARLO NIMMO*
California State University, Hayward

A NTHROPOLOGY TEXTBOOKS often conclude discussions of the concept of culture with a list of so-called universals of culture. The list is always general and usually not too long since invariably a society or two does not conform to the "universal" pattern. But on such lists, music always appears—either as "music" or under the more general category of "art." Music of some sort is found in all human societies. And if we believe certain anthropologists (notably Malinowski), universal culture elements occur because they are derived from basic biological needs of the human condition. Music, then, we must conclude is found cross-culturally because it serves needs of biological man.

Such may be the case, but it is difficult to sift through the aeons of culture history to discover whatever basic biological needs resulted in man's first music. Rather, for the purpose of this paper, it is acknowledged that music, specifically song, performs important functions in human societies. These functions vary from society to society, and perhaps can be ultimately traced to biological needs, but of primary interest here are the cultural needs. Specifically, what functions do Bajau songs serve within their cultural context? This paper is addressed to that question.

*This paper is based on two years of field research in Sulu Province, Philippines, from 1965-1967, sponsored by the National Science Foundation, Washington, D.C.; the Wenner-Gren Foundation for Anthropological Research, New York; and the Carnegie Corporation, New York. The author gratefully acknowledges the support of these foundations.

For some years now, anthropologists have used the functional model to explain and interpret human behavior. A. R. Radcliffe-Brown (1935) and Bronislaw Malinowski (1939, 1948) were among the first to suggest that all elements of a sociocultural system are interrelated and contribute to the maintenance of the total system. That is, each element of culture performs a function within the sociocultural system and is related to all other elements. Radcliffe-Brown maintained that just as a living body is an interrelated system of functioning parts, so is a social system. Later anthropologists rejected his analogy as extreme and misleading, but nonetheless the functionalist view has survived the fads and fashions of anthropological theory to be still a legitimate view of human societies. Societies may not operate like living organisms, but their behavior patterns are interrelated and have a *raison d'etre*.

Functionalist theory has been used to interpret many facets of human behavior, but of special relevance to this volume are the functional interpretations of oral literature. Malinowski early noted that magical chants, songs, and other ritual are most commonly used in those realms of human endeavor surrounded by the greatest uncertainty and serve the important function of allaying the anxieties that otherwise add further hazards to such endeavors (1948). Some years later, William Bascom isolated several general functions which folklore performs in all societies. Among these are the validation of cultural norms, the education of youth, and the maintenance of cultural conformity to accepted patterns of behavior (1954). More relevant to this paper, Alan Merriam discusses ten different functions, ranging from aesthetic enjoyment to the integration of society, which he feels music and songs fulfill cross-culturally. He concludes that "Music is clearly indispensable to the proper promulgation of the activities that constitute a society; it is a universal human behavior—without it, it is questionable that man could truly be called man, with all that implies" (1964, p. 227). As this brief survey reveals, functional interpretations of oral traditions are not new in the anthropological literature. Thus, this paper offers no new theoretical interpretation, but rather submits a body of oral literature, namely the songs of the Bajau, to a somewhat traditional anthropological analysis. The data are new, the theory is not.

The Bajau, traditionally known as a nomadic, boat-dwelling people, inhabit the Sulu Islands of the southern Philippines. The Sulu Bajau are one of several boat-dwelling groups scattered throughout Southeast Asia; others have been reported in the Celebes, southern Malaya, and the Mergui Islands of Burma. Although the historical relationship of these different groups is still unknown, little doubt exists concerning the close relationship of the several groups of Bajau within the Sulu Islands;

these people all speak dialects of the Samal language, share many culture
traits, and were until recent times predominantly boat-dwellers. Today,
most of the Sulu Bajau have abandoned their boats as living quarters
for land- or reef-based dwellings. The most confirmed boat-dwellers are
found in the Tawi-Tawi Islands where they number some 1,600 individuals, while the most confirmed house-dwellers live in the Sibutu Islands,
especially in Sitangkai, and comprise a population of about 2,400.
Wherever the Bajau are found, they represent a minority of the total
population. For example, they constitute only about 4 percent of the
total population of the Tawi-Tawi Islands, and in the Sibutu Islands
they form about 23 percent of the total population. Within Sulu, the
Bajau have always been viewed as an outcast group by the land-dwelling
Moslems, but in recent years many of these sea folk have abandoned
boat-dwelling, embraced Islam, and have become incorporated into the
Islamic community of Sulu. Those of Tawi-Tawi, however, are still
predominantly boat-dwelling, subsistence fishermen who continue to
follow their traditional life styles. These are the Bajau who have most
successfully retained their oral traditions, and the songs discussed in
this paper were collected among them.

Although extremely mobile, the Tawi-Tawi Bajau limit their movements to a fairly well defined sea area, about 250 square miles, southwest
of the large island of Tawi-Tawi. Within this area are located the five
main Bajau moorages and the two small cemetery islands where the
sea people bury their dead. These seas are characterized by extensive
coral reefs as well as numerous small islands which are farmed by the
land-dwelling Moslem peoples, upon whom most Bajau are dependent
for the vegetable portion of their diet.

The Bajau houseboat typically houses a single nuclear family. Although this family does a great deal of traveling among the various
houseboat moorages, it always identifies one moorage as its home; or,
if the husband and wife are from different moorages, the family divides
its allegiance and time between the two moorages. Frequently, the nuclear
family fishes and travels with married siblings of either the husband
or wife to form the second important social unit in Bajau society, the
family alliance unit. This unit reveals great structural variation and is
very ephemeral since houseboats regularly join and leave the unit. Its
primary function is that of mutual aid for fishing, ceremonies, and any
other activities that require group assistance. Each moorage consists of
several of these family alliance units to comprise a group of cognatically
related persons, or a localized kindred, with an older man acting as
headman. At the larger moorages, several such localized kindreds may
be found, and the headman of the kindred which first began mooring

there serves as headman for the entire moorage. No formal political organization exists beyond the moorage level to unite the several moorages, but because of the many kin ties and frequent movements among them, the moorages constitute a single, albeit dispersed, Tawi-Tawi community (Nimmo, 1972).

Bajau culture has songs for almost every occasion. The birth of the Bajau infant is heralded by the magical chants of the assisting shaman. The lullabies of the Bajau mother early become part of the child's daily routine, and when he has mastered the rudiments of his language, he, too, becomes a singer of the several songs sung by Bajau children. Adolescents compose ballads to court would-be lovers or to while away the empty hours of youth. Later, in adulthood, wind and fishing songs are added to the Bajau's musical repertoire, and his more mature mind turns with new interest to the night-long chants which a few of the village elders know. And when he dies, his death is mourned with chants by surviving kinsmen and friends as funeral boats transport his body to the traditional burial islands.

Each Bajau song-type can be recognized by its distinctive melody; for example, all Bajau mothers sing their lullabies to the same basic melody, all shark fishermen sing shark songs to the same melody, and so on. However, within this traditional musical framework, each singer does some improvisation which, of course, varies with the creativity of the singer. The lyrics are, for the most part, original and are not sung from memory. Certain stock images and phrases recur in the songs, but each song has the individual stamp of its singer. The originality of the lyrics obviously varies with the artistry of the singer.

Lullabies, or binua, are sung at any time of the day when needed to soothe the sleepy or fussy baby, but they are most commonly heard in the moorage during the darkening hours of evening. The Bajau baby normally sleeps in a hammocklike cradle suspended from the roof of the houseboat, and as the mother sings, she swings the hammock. Consequently, the creaking sound of the swinging cradle accompanies the song; otherwise, there is no accompaniment. To the Western ear, the songs have a mournful, plaintive quality, and to the Bajau ear, also, the songs recall bittersweet, half-pleasant, half-sad images—a melancholy sound that drifts over the moorage waters to prick the sympathies and memories of its listeners. The song is addressed to the child, and his name is usually mentioned in the first line or so, but the general text more often consists of the mother's personal thoughts and reminiscences. If she wishes the moorage dwellers to know of some event, she may sing it loudly so that all can hear. The lullaby gives the singer a license to speak of people and events she would not mention in normal conversation. If someone wishes to respond to a musical statement, he should do so through the same medium. As a result, occasionally a repartee of musical comment may drift back and forth across the waters between two boats. More often, however, the mother sings the song to herself, of things personal which she wishes the moorage to know. She bares a part of herself normally concealed, and her neighbors are sensitive enough to listen quietly, perhaps sympathize, but not mention it in the vulgarities of everyday speech. The following are examples of the Bajau *binua:*

> My daughter I sing a song of sleep to you.
> I am weary, but still I swing your cradle.
> When the moon came out tonight, it shone like a bright coin.
> The mountain on Siasi is very small —
>   there, the Chinese are flying kites.
> Siasi is very, very far.
> Sleep soundly like a bird, my child.

> I sing a lullaby.
> We sail all our lives and our bodies become weary.
> It is to you I am singing, my daughter.
> We suffer from great poverty.
>   but it is our fate to lead this kind of life.
> We do not have fine mats to sleep on, nor robes to wear,
>   we sleep with nothing.
> You are a beautiful child, but you are also a fickle child;
> If I should die, you probably would not cry for me.
> Mount Bongao is very small, and atop it is a tree that gives
>   eternal youth.
> Should I die while you are still young, I hope you have a good life.

Songs called *lia-lia* are commonly sung by small children. The Bajau offer no further definition of *lia-lia* other than a name for this type of song sung by children. It might be called a "spite song" or an "anger song," since it is usually sung during these moods. If a child becomes angry at a playmate, parent, or anyone, he sometimes retires to a secluded spot to give vent to his displeasure through song. One day I was in the houseboat of a young Bajau father, interviewing him about a particular fishing technique. He was repairing a fish net as he patiently answered my questions while his son sat at the prow of the boat. As we were talking, a group of children waded past the boat through the low tide waters and shouted to the boy that they were going to the land village to buy some candy. The child asked his father if he could have some money to join his friends. His father replied negatively. Several times the child asked for money, but consistently got a negative response and finally told his friends to go on without him. We continued our interview while the boy sat at the prow of the boat watching his playmates go to land as tears welled in his eyes. Then with muffled sobs, he began to sing a *lia-lia.* I did not record his exact words, but the song scolded his father for failing to give him money for candy. He sang that other children in the moorage were given money by their fathers, but he was not. Furthermore, he was very angry at his father and did not like him when he was unkind to him. The musical admonishment went on in such tones for about five minutes, until the child's attention was caught by something else and he left the boat. The song was sung quietly, but loud enough for us to hear. When the boy began his song, the father smiled at me and nodded toward his son to call my attention to his words. He continued to talk to me about fishing, but I am certain that he heard all of his son's words.

As the mother who sings lullabies, the child who sings *lia-lia* has a license denied him in speech. He may sing comments about his friends, his parents, or anyone in the moorage which he would say only at the risk of punishment. Although a Bajau child has much freedom, it is early instilled in him that he should not speak disrespectfully to his parents or elders. But there are times in the business of being a child when these adults frustrate one's desires. Since one cannot hit them or speak badly about them without punishment, a way to retaliate is through song. And Bajau children use their unique song tradition in this way. Parents usually pretend they are not listening to the songs, indeed sometimes children seek lonely spots where no one can hear them, but if they are within listening range, the adults usually hear each word the child has to say.

The following two examples illustrate the *lia-lia* song type. Unlike most of the other Bajau songs I collected, these were not recorded. An angry child was usually not willing to accommodate an inquisitive anthropologist with his strange gadgets, so I wrote down the *lia-lia* as I heard them, and consequently will not vouch for their perfect accuracy. Nonetheless, the following translations convey the general tenor of the songs.

> Lia, lia, lia.
> I am angry at you, mother.
> You will not let me play on the beach.
> Other children have good mothers who let them play there.
> But my mother does not like me.
> I wish I had another mother.
> I wish I could go away.

> Lia, lia, lia.
> I don't like the children at this moorage.

> Tomorrow I will go away from this moorage to Luuk Tulai.
> My father is a handsome man;
> He is better than the fathers of the other children here.
> Tomorrow he will take me to Luuk Tulai,
>   because I do not like the children here.

Tenes-tenes is another song-type widely sung by Bajau children, although it is not exclusively theirs, being sung also by teen-agers, young adults, and occasionally older adults. It is a very versatile song-type and is sung on many occasions. While at play, a child may burst into a *tenes-tenes*, singing about whatever comes to his mind or eye. While fishing, sailing, or paddling, a young man (or woman) may use the same song tradition to sing about the travels he has made, the fish he has caught, or the scenery he sees. At evening in the moorage, a teen-age boy or girl may sing *tenes-tenes* to tell his or her love for someone.

The name *tenes-tenes* has no meaning to the Bajau other than a name for a song-type. "Ballad" would perhaps be the nearest English equivalent. The length and tempo of the song depend upon the mood or message of the singer, but all *tenes-tenes* follow the same general musical pattern and each begins by announcing a color for the song, for example, "This song is of blue colors," "This song is of green and red stripes like the snail," or "My song is of the colors of the sunset." The colors have no particular symbolism, nor are they consistent images throughout the song. Rather, they are a pleasant image within the mind of the singer which he attempts to convey to the listener.

The *tenes-tenes* sung by young children is most commonly simply a series of remembrances or images which come to his mind as he plays. One day as I wandered about the exposed moorage reef, I came upon a Bajau girl, about eight years old, playing by herself as she loudly sang a *tenes-tenes*. No other children were around, so I asked if she would sing into my recorder. She replied affirmatively, so I hurried to get my recorder before any other children came, having learned that a group of children at a recorder tend to shout and giggle more than anything else. The following is one of her songs, and although the presence of the recorder introduced an artificial aspect to her singing, the song nonetheless well represents the sort which children frequently sing.

> My song is of blue colors.
> Yesterday my father went fishing, and caught many fish.
> Tomorrow we will sail to Lioboran, and my father and brother
>   will fish there.
> The trees on the island are very tall.
> I often remember my friends who live in Luuk Tulai.
> I hope you are enjoying my song.

> My mother has wavy hair and yesterday she bought a new sarong.
> When I grow up I shall have a lover and be married.
> This is the end of my song.

The *tenes-tenes* sung by teen-agers are the most colorful. During paddling or sailing, teen-agers often sing duets back and forth to one another, or one person may sing while others interject musical comments to his song. Young people sometimes sing to themselves when fishing alone to help pass the lonely hours. Some of the best musical improvisation I heard, however, was during the song fests which Bajau youth periodically arrange. These fests are impromptu affairs which occur when several young people gather in a houseboat, usually during the evening hours. One begins to sing, others join in, and soon young people in neighboring boats come to join them. At such occasions, someone usually furnishes a *gabbang*, a xylophone-type instrument made of bamboo slats and played with two rubber-tipped hammers. While someone plays the *gabbang*, usually a girl, the others take turns singing—never in unison, since each song is the original creation of its singer. Songs at such fests usually have a romantic flavor, since it is a time when a youth may appropriately tell of his love for someone to his peers. The following song by a young man, about 16, is an example of this type of *tenes-tenes*.

> My song is of the many colors of the sail.
> As I left home this morning, I was talking to a certain girl.
> We have been in love since we were small, and now she is
>   almost a woman.
> Once I lay next to her, and lay my legs over hers.
> I told my mother that she should go to the headman, so
>   that we could be married.
> My sister is wearing a sarong as she is playing the *gabbang*.
> My sister and I were invited to sing and play at a wedding.
> This will be my last time to sing, because I am very tired.
> I will even go to the spirit world with my lover after we die.
> I have given much food to my lover.
> Someday I will marry her.
> My lover is almost crazy in her love for me.
> The home of my lover is far away, but I will sail there.

Although this particular singer's girl friend was not present when the song was sung, it is not uncommon for a young man or woman to sing of his or her love for someone present. The name of the individual is not mentioned and often the sentiments are expressed in stereotyped images and phrases, but nonetheless everyone knows what is being said and to whom. Not only does the song allow the singer to express his amorous feelings, but it also serves to announce his infatuation to his peers. As with other Bajau song traditions, the words of the musical statement would never be said so publicly in speech.

Young people often sing *tenes-tenes* while at work. One evening while torch fishing with a group of Bajau, I heard a teen-aged boy and girl sing *tenes-tenes* to one another as we paddled the shallow waters. Their songs consisted of stock phrases and images of love and romance. Personal names were never mentioned, but everyone knew the young people were expressing their love for one another. On another occasion, I was paddling with some teen-aged boys in four different boats to a neighboring island. During the entire trip the boys sang *tenes-tenes* which ranged from love affairs to fishing experiences. Some of the songs were solos while others were musical repartees with the entire group participating. And on a more tragic occasion, I listened to an imprisoned young Bajau man, accused of killing his mother- and brother-in-law, sing *tenes-tenes* throughout an entire night to tell the community of his remorse for his dreadful deed.

Sometimes, *tenes-tenes* occurs as a long narrative ballad in which the singer relates an actual incident which has happened in Sulu. This particular type of *tenes-tenes* is most highly developed among the land dwelling Samal of Sulu, the most talented of whom travel up and down the archipelago performing at weddings, circumcisions, and other celebrations. These balladeers are for the most part young people, in their late teens or early twenties, male and female. Their songs are based upon actual Sulu events which have sparked their creative minds to musical expression. The listeners realize that the singer has altered the event somewhat for the sake of art, but nonetheless much of the ballads is taken for fact and they serve as an important news media in a society which has few newspapers, radios, or other disseminators of current events. This particular type of *tenes-tenes* is not highly developed among the Bajau, although a few of their youths sing the musical stories.

During my first trip to Sulu in 1963, a pirate named Amak was captured after having harassed southern Sulu for almost two years. A young Bajau man, about 15, saw Amak's body after a shoot-out with the Philippine Constabulary officers, and with other stories he had heard about the pirate, composed the following *tenes-tenes*. He is one of only three Bajau I met who sang this particular type of *tenes-tenes*. This song is short compared to some of the songs of the professional, land-dwelling balladeers, who may keep an audience's attention for one, two, or even three hours.

> My song is of the many colors of the sail.
> The home place of Amak, the pirate, is at Paranang in the
>   forest.

On his way home from Bilatan, Tahanan was robbed by Amak.
Amak took money only from the home of Tahanan, and not from
    the other houses in the village.
Tahanan gave Amak more than 100 pesos, but he wanted more.
Tahanan said that he had no more money.
Amak put his gun in the window and shot Tahanan while he was
    in the doorway.
Amak then went to his own house in the forest and slept
    peacefully with his companions.
While Amak was sleeping, the Philippine Constabulary rangers
    surrounded him.
A sergeant and a captain were the leaders of the troop.
All the rangers from Batu-Batu had gone to Paranang to kill
    Amak if they could find him.
In all, there were nineteen rangers who attacked Amak.
As the rangers approached the camp of Amak, they walked very
    quietly.
Amak heard a barking dog, so he slowly came out of the house.
He did not know the Philippine Constabulary rangers were near.
Amak's brother saw the rangers and told Amak they should run
    away.
However, Amak told his brother that the rangers were only
    American soldiers who would not harm them.
Then Amak saw that they were Philippine Constabulary rangers.
He was naked and took cover in the house and began to fire at
    the rangers.
Captain Tanang was the leader of the rangers.
Captain Tanang sneaked up to the house of Amak;
He was so close to Amak that Amak almost stepped on his
    hands.
But the Captain did not move.
Amak loaded his rifle and began firing at the rangers.
Amak was killed and taken by the rangers to the jeep and
    then taken to Batu-Batu.
The body of Amak was very white.
He had curly hair and was blind in one eye.
At about 2 A.M., the rangers threw Amak's body on the wharf
    at Batu-Batu.
The body was then placed outside the Philippine Constabulary
    camp.
Dew fell on the body since it was not covered.
At nine the following morning, a picture was taken of his
    body.
Before taking the picture, the Philippine Constabulary officer
    placed Amak's rifle, kris, and bullet belt next to his body.
In the afternoon the body of Amak was carried by Tinah on
    his shoulders.
But Amak was so heavy that he was dropped in the middle of
    the road.
Amak was taken to his home place at Paranang.

No one likes to pass Paranang Island because it is the home
  of pirates.
The body of Amak was beginning to rot, so the imam bathed
  him and buried him.
Amak smelled like a dried fish.
The imam did not offer prayers for him because he was afraid
  the Philippine Constabulary rangers would not like it.
He only bathed him.
Amak's two widows were crying in the door of the house.
They sang mourning songs all night long.
When Amak was alive, he did not eat and became thin like an
  American's son.
He wore Cutex on his finger nails.
One time Amak went to Borneo with his companions.
They met some Chinese at sea.
Amak and his gang robbed the launch of the Chinese.
They also pirated some goods from a Malayan ship.
They went on further and met an Indonesian boat.
The smoke of the boat was like the smoke of incense.
They fired machine guns at the Indonesian boat, but it outran
  them and went to Borneo.
Later the Indonesian navy caught some pirates and took them.
  to Borneo where they cut off their hands and ears to
  mark them as pirates.
The British cut off the heads of pirates to warn others
The punishment was for offenses these men had committed against
  the Chinese and Malayans.

Kalangan balu, or "songs of the wind," are almost the exclusive
reserve of Bajau men, although occasionally a woman may sing this
song-type. They are sung during the idle or lonely hours of fishing and
sailing trips, usually at night. When heard over the dark waters, the
songs have a lonely, melancholy air to the Western ear. Most often
a man sings his songs alone to the night and the sea, but sometimes
he may sing duets with a sailing companion or a friend within hearing
distance in another boat. Although the singer frequently uses stock
phrases and images, the songs are not sung from memory, but rather
are creations of a mood. Despite their appellation they are not sung
to call the wind, and I met no Bajau who seriously believed that the
songs could bring the wind. Invariably brief, they consist of a single
image or a series of small vignettes, usually unconnected except in the
subconscious of the singer. Themes and images all reflect the sea home
of the singer.

> Changing, shifting winds,
> Tell Salamdulila,
> Do not forget me.

White sails.
Sailing from Kangan.
A smooth sea.

The whirling wind strikes the prow;
The flying wind.

If there is illness in my body, it leaves when I remember
    my lover.
But it is sometimes painful to remember.

White sails.
Sailing to Sitangkai.
Single file.

O south wind,
You bring the dark clouds.
Like a ripe jackfruit are you: on the surface alike and
    smooth, but inside, varied and many.

Now comes the east wind.
It is a good wind.

O wind,
You blow the waves— and my heart —
    into a thousand pieces.

Another song-type sung even more exclusively by men is the *kalangan kalitan,* or "song of the shark." During certain seasons of the year, Bajau fishermen, alone or in pairs, seek sharks in the waters of the open sea. After having baited large iron hooks, the men shake coconut shell-rattles in the water as they murmur a dirgelike song to attract the shark. The songs are usually brief and tend to flatter the shark in order to attract it to the hook. Most Bajau claim that the songs have no magical qualities and are used only because it is traditional to do so. Nonetheless, few if any Bajau would fish for shark without using the songs. It is significant that musical, magical fishing aids of this sort are used only in shark fishing, the most dangerous of all Bajau fishing. The following are examples of the *kalangan kalitan.*

Datu Shark,
Your fin is handsome and looks like a flag in the sea.
I have thrown my baited hook into the deep sea especially for
    you.
Come and take my gift.

I am shaking my rattle to call you.
I know you are under my boat,

> waiting to take my bait.
> Come now and take my bait and hook.

One of the most delicious of Sulu's sea foods is a reef-dwelling crustacean (*Squilla* sp.), called *kamun*. Light pink in color, it is about five to ten inches in length, with large front claws and numerous smaller legs on either side of its body. Certain reefs are known as the habitat of the *kamun*, and Bajau fishermen, especially boys, periodically visit the reefs at low tide to catch the animal. The *kamun* lives in the natural holes of the reef floor, and almost always a male and female are found together. Bajau fishermen prepare a special baited noose which they slip into the *kamun* hole. When the *kamun* takes the bait, the noose springs to catch its head and claws. It is then pulled out by the fisherman. The male is always the first to be caught, and usually the female is reluctant to take the proffered bait after her mate has disappeared. While the fisherman is waiting for the female to take the bait, he sings comic songs, called *kalangan kamun*, to entice her.

> Kamun, I give you food.
> You catch my bait as it comes inside.
> Kamun, I am giving you food, so why don't you take it?
>
> Kamun, tell your mate: "Do not talk anymore. Here is
>   our food. We will go together through our door."
> Kamun, I have given you all kinds of food—even cassava.
> Many of your friends already have nice white rattan around
>   their necks.
> I brought this rattan all the way from Palawan for you.
>
> Kamun, come and take my bait.
> Your husband has already taken it and likes it.
> You take it, too, and join your husband.

Illness is a crisis which also calls upon Bajau musical traditions. Several curers know Arabic chants which came to Sulu with Islam, but a more ancient tradition of chants in Samal, the Bajau language, is also used by curers. These chants, called *kata-kata* and known by only a few of the older men of the community, are reserved for cases of critical illness or crisis. Some of them are extremely long, sometimes lasting three hours a night for a three night period, and unlike the lyrics of other Bajau songs, they are sung from memory rather than improvised. Furthermore, the chants are performed only by specialists who must be paid for their services in order that they be effective. The singers pay to learn the chants and in turn sell them to apprentices.

One of my personal friends among the Bajau was Sarbayani, a renowned chanter of *kata-kata*. Because of our friendship, he promised that I could record his *kata-kata* the next time he was called upon to chant. Several weeks after his promise, a man of the moorage became critically ill. All of the traditional curing methods were tried on him to no avail. As a final attempt to dispel his illness, Sarbayani was asked to chant *kata-kata*. I knew the ill man's family well and they were not averse to my recording the session.

The atmosphere was hushed when I arrived at the houseboat of Sarbayani where the curing session was to be held. Sarbayani was dressed in his best clothes. Sitting next to him on the household's finest mat was the ill man, and sitting around them in circular fashion were kinsmen of the patient. Sarbayani lighted incense and placed it in a small bowl between himself and the patient. He spread his arms with palms upward on his crossed legs, and for several minutes asked the spirits to acknowledge the power of the *kata-kata*, to take pity on the ill man, and to allow his recovery. Then he began to chant.

Each word was stretched to great lengths and the stanzas displayed a wide tonal range. Because the words were so distorted and my knowledge of the Bajau language still somewhat limited, I could understand only a few words. Only later, after many laborious hours of transcribing my tapes with Sarbayani, did I understand the story. Sarbayani chanted for about two hours, stopping only twice for a drink of water. When he stopped for the night, another petition was made to the spirits believed responsible for the illness, and the small group disbanded. For two more nights this procedure was followed, each night being a continuation of the chant which Sarbayani began the first night. Space does not allow for reproduction of the entire text, but the following excerpt conveys the general tenor of the *kata-kata* chants.

> Datu Amilebangsa ordered his followers to prepare food
>   in preparation for a long journey.
> The followers asked: "Where are we going?"
> Datu Amilebangsa said: "We are going to visit a place.
>   Even if we are drifted, we will be able to locate
>   the place. You prepare the food while I go to my
>   mother and father to ask their permission to make
>   the voyage. If they give me permission, we shall
>   leave; if not, we shall not leave."
> The followers finished preparing the food.
> The name of their boat was "Galila."
> Datu Amilebangsa went to his parents' house to ask their
>   permission to leave.
> He said to them: "As you know, the female child usually
>   stays at home, but the male child often travels and
>   leaves home. I want to travel."

His full name was Amilebangsa Sahaia.

His parents said: "If you are seeking a wife, you cannot
leave since you already have a betrothed in this place.
Her name is Gimbaiansampaka-Tapanggamban-Mpaka."

Amilebangsa said: "I am not seeking a wife since I already
have a fiance here."

Amilebangsa's followers came to him and asked: "When will
we leave?"

Amilebangsa said: "We shall leave now. My parents have
given me permission to do so, so long as I am not seeking a wife."

After they began to sail, Amilebangsa said to his followers:
"To which place do you prefer to go, the nearest place
or the farthest place?"

His followers said: "Let us go to the farthest place. If
we are going to a very near place, we do not want to go."

Amilebangsa said: "If we leave now, there is no wind. If
you want to leave now, put up the mast."

Amilebangsa then spoke to the wind and asked it to blow.
He said: "If my mother and father have power, the
strong winds will now blow."

After he spoke the winds began to blow immediately. His
boat went swiftly through the sea, it was like a
sword cutting the water.

Amilebangsa told his followers that he would sleep. He
said: "When we reach our destination, do not go near
the shore because a woman there will use her magic to
cast a spell on you."

Amilebangsa then went to sleep. The boat sailed for three
days and three nights until it finally reached its
destination.

When Amilebangsa awakened, they had reached their destination. They saw many people on shore, men and women,
picking up shells.

Eva-Eva Denda and Misa-hela, two women, were surprised to
see the boat and said: "Whose boat is that? It looks
like the boat of Amilebangsa."

Misa-hela said: "Oh you, in that boat. Who is the owner?"

Amilebangsa's followers said "The owner is inside the boat."

The two women said: "That is the boat of Amilebangsa."

The followers of Amilebangsa said: "You are right. This
is the boat of Amilebangsa, but he is not here."

Eva-Eva Denda told Misa-hela to go into the boat to see if
the men were telling the truth.

The two women then went into the boat without an invitation from the men.

On the deck, they did not see Amilebangsa. Eva-Eva Denda
told her companion to go below deck to see if there
were anyone there.

When Misa-hela went below deck, she saw Amilebangsa sleeping.

Eva-Eva Denda and Misa-hela said: "Why are you sleeping?"
When Amilebangsa awakened and saw the two women he was
surprised and said: "Why did we anchor at this shore?"
The two women said: "Why do you speak like that? If your
reason for coming here is to seek women, you will find
no other women like us."
Amilebangsa said: "Since the time I left the stomach of
my mother, I have never seen such greedy women. I hope
you will not be angry with me, but my reason for coming
here is not to seek women. I already have a fiance in
my home place. The name of my fiance is Gimbaiansampaka-
Tapanggamban-Mpaka."
The two women said: "You cannot fool us with such talk.
We know that your reason for coming here is to find
women. You will find no other women around here like us."
Amilebangsa said: "You are very wanton women. Do you want
to live or die?"
The two women said: "You make it very difficult for us
to entice you."
Amilebangsa said to his followers: "Give me my kris."
After he got his kris, the two women left the boat crying.
They said: "It is very difficult to tempt Amilebangsa."
After sailing for three nights and three days, the boat
reached another island. The people on this island saw
the boat approach and were very curious as to whose
boat it may be.

The story continues in this Odyssey-like fashion to recount the adventures of Amilebangsa and his crew. The text itself deals essentially with
secular events, and has little religious reference although Bajau cultural
values are imparted throughout it. Nonetheless, *kata-kata* are the most
sacred of all Bajau oral traditions.

Death calls upon Bajau song traditions also. As soon as a death
is learned, the women of the moorage break into a wailing, dirgelike
chant. With other members of the moorage, they crowd around and
within the death boat while the deceased is wrapped in a shroud of
white cloth. Normally, the corpse is kept at the moorage the night following death and is transported to the burial islands the following morning.
From the time of death until burial, women wail their mournful refrain
while men attend to the other funeral business. Almost everyone in the
moorage visits the funeral boat to pay respects to the corpse before
its interment, and it is during these visits that songs are addressed to
the spirit of the deceased.

The songs almost always flatter the deceased and express great sorrow
over the death. Usually they are short statements which punctuate the
wail which most persons maintain in the presence of the corpse. Most

of the songs spring from genuine grief, but some are inspired by the belief that if one does not show proper sorrow at death, the spirit of the deceased will return to haunt the offender. Consequently, even if an individual openly disliked the deceased during his lifetime, he will mourn dramatically at his death. In fact, the loudest mourners—excepting the immediate family of the deceased—are usually those who were not on friendly terms with the deceased during his lifetime.

I recorded the following songs in my notes as I heard them. I never attempted to tape-record funeral songs. Some of the Bajau probably would not have minded, but I could never completely throw off my own cultural cloak and impose a tape recorder into these sessions of sorrow and pain. The following songs were all written down during the funeral of a man, about 35, whose sudden death was attributed to the anger of offended spirits.

His brother-in-law who sincerely loved him:

> You were my brother-in-law, my best friend.
> When you were alive, we often fished together.
> You were always generous and always gave away more fish
>   than you kept.
> How shall we continue to live now that you are gone?

His wife:

> My father is dead.
> My mother is dead.
> My sister is dead.
> My brother is dead.
> And now my husband is dead.
> How, then, can I live?

A cousin with whom the deceased never got along:

> You were the best fisherman.
> Everyone in the moorage loved you.
> I respected you more than any man I know.
> You were a good father and husband.
> Now you are gone, but I will see that your wife and
>   children are fed.
> You and I were like brothers.

His aged mother:

> You are gone now, and I am alone.
> But you are not alone.
> With you in your grave are your father, brothers, and
>   sisters.
> And soon I, too, shall join you.

As the preceding discussion demonstrates, Bajau songs serve important functions within their cultural context. A more systematic statement of these functions is presently in order.

1. The most obvious overt function of the songs is in the realm of entertainment. All Bajau acknowledge that they enjoy listening to singers because it is entertaining to do so. And many singers admit that they sing because they derive an aesthetic pleasure from doing so. In a society which has no radios, books, television, or movies, entertainment is sought in other channels and singing is one of the most important. Not surprisingly, much Bajau singing is done during hours of leisure, when work does not occupy one's time, or during tedious work when singing offers a welcome diversion from the tedium of the job. The sheer aesthetic pleasure, then, of listening to songs or singing them is an important function of songs in Bajau culture.

2. Most importantly to the Bajau, the songs serve their stated function; that is, the songs serve the functions for which the Bajau consciously use them. For example, the lullabies do soothe babies to sleep and the *tenes-tenes* ballads do entertain. And to many Bajau, the shark songs do often bring success in shark fishing, the *kata-kata* chants do assist in curing, the *kamun* songs do attract the reluctant crustacean, and the funeral songs do placate the deceased's spirit. To the outside observer, the songs may appear as secondary appendages to the more serious situations which call upon them, but the Bajau can tell of innumerable incidents when the songs have fulfilled their overt cultural function, and their claims cannot be summarily discounted. The greater security which the shark songs provide to the fisherman of this dangerous fish no doubt does contribute to his success in fishing. Similarly, the patient who knows that the most sacred of all ceremonies, the *kata-kata*, is being performed for him is more psychologically prepared for recovery than one who feels nothing is being done for his illness. And the survivor who has sung proper songs to the spirit of the deceased is less likely to become ill than one who has not properly mourned—whether the illness is psychosomatic is irrelevant, since the illness that may result from this neglect is real enough to the afflicted Bajau. The point is that the songs often serve the functions for which the Bajau consciously use them. In addition, the songs have several covert functions which are more apparent to an anthropological observer than to most Bajau. The remaining functions discussed here are of that nature.

3. Songs serve as an important medium for the dissemination of news. Because the Bajau are illiterate and have no access to audio mass communication, they learn of all news — local, national, and international—through word of mouth. This may be through simple conversation

or gossip, or through song. Through any of the song types, excepting the more rigid *kata-kata,* the singer may choose to sing of some current event — most likely a personal event, such as a quarrel with his wife or perhaps a big catch of fish, but in the case of the longer *tenes-tenes* ballads, he may tell of some recent significant local or even national event, such as the capture of Indonesian smugglers or the election of a president.

4. Some song-types, especially the *binua, tenes-tenes,* and *lia-lia,* serve the important psychological function of providing a socially approved channel for the expression of feelings which are normally tabued. A child may sing of his anger and momentary dislike of his parents through *lia-lia* without fear of punishment, but he would never voice such thoughts through everyday speech. While singing to her baby, a mother may tell of her hard life with her husband's parents, but she would be breaking rules of Bajau etiquette if she made the same complaints to her neighbor during their everyday conversations. A youth may sing a *tenes-tenes* of his infatuation for a particular young woman of the moorage, but he would never publicly announce such feelings through speech. The songs, then, provide a safety valve, an approved channel for the expression of the hostilities and emotions engendered in the everyday business of living which are otherwise repressed by the mores of Bajau culture.

5. Bajau songs are also important agents of social control. It is not uncommon for a Bajau who feels that he has been maltreated to sing his case to the moorage. One evening, I heard a young wife loudly sing to the entire moorage about the injustices which her in-laws had heaped upon her. The moorage listeners were sympathetic to her plea and censured her in-laws for their behavior. Within days, her in-laws recitified their behavior, partly because of the discrimination they were receiving from other mooragers. No one cares to hear his sins sung to the moorage, and partly because of this possibility, one is a bit more careful not to offend another.

6. The songs of the Bajau also have educational, or enculturational, functions. Most of the songs are laden with Bajau cultural values, such as the proper way to behave toward parents, siblings, and other kinsmen; the proper courage that befits a man when confronted with danger; the proper way of courting; the proper way to behave toward land-dwellers and other outsiders. The same values, of course, permeate all aspects of Bajau culture, and the songs are simply another reminder of the correct way to behave.

7. The magical and religious functions of the songs are apparent also. The *kalangan kalitan* are sung only when fishing for shark, the

most dangerous type of fishing practiced by the Bajau, and are believed by many Bajau to be essential for successful fishing. Less dangerous types of fishing require no magic, musical or otherwise. The *kata-kata* chants are the most sacred of all Bajau music and are used only for healing critical illnesses. The funeral songs are reserved for occasions of death, and are sung to the spirit of the deceased to insure that his spirit will not harm the survivors. Obviously, these three song-types provide their singers greater security in times which are otherwise fraught with dangers.

The song traditions of the Tawi-Tawi Bajau were still intact when I left Sulu in 1967. However, they are being altered and will continue to be altered—perhaps eventually replaced—by intruding traditions. These Bajau were in the process of abandoning their nomadic boat lives for a more sedentary existence in reef-based pile dwellings. And, as the sea-dwellers become sedentary, they will be incorporated into the Islamic culture of Sulu's land dwellers—as other Bajau have in other parts of Sulu. The prestige of Islamic music traditions will no doubt undermine some of their own, and perhaps ultimately lead to their disappearance. In addition, some Bajau children are being exposed to Western musical traditions through the missionary work of the Oblates of Mary Immaculate Catholic order which has established a school at one of the Bajau moorages. Already some children regularly sing Western songs they have learned at school, and doubtlessly such songs will become increasingly widespread as more children attend school. The transistor radio is beginning to make inroads among the Bajau, and it, too, is introducing new song traditions.

But for the present, Bajau songs continue to serve important cultural functions. And until other songs or other cultural behavior are found to better serve these functions, the songs will be sung.

LITERATURE CITED

BASCOM, WILLIAM R.
1954. "Four Functions of Folklore." *J. American Folklore* **67**:333-349.
MALINOWSKI, BRONISLAW
1939. "The Group and the Individual in Functional Analysis." *American J. Sociology* **44**:938-964.
1948. *Magic, Science and Religion.* Glencoe: Free Press.
MERRIAM, ALAN P.
1964. *The Anthropology of Music.* Evanston: Northwestern Univ. Press.
NIMMO, H. ARLO
1968. "Songs of the Sulu Sea." *Etc.* **25**:489-494.
1972. *The Sea People of Sulu.* San Francisco: Chandler Press.
RADCLIFFE-BROWN, A. R.
1935. "On the Concept of Function in Social Science." *American Anthropologist* **37**:394-402.

GOSSIP AMONG THE PHILIPPINE OLIGARCHY

SOME TENDER HYPOTHESES

RICHARD L. STONE
California State University, Los Angeles

A PATTERN OF BEHAVIOR among elites in the Philippines is examined in this paper: namely, the role of gossip in its intrasegmental unitive functions. I offer some tentative hypotheses concerning such behavior, and suggest that the area of gossip in social relations is of extreme importance in marking off the boundaries of permissible behavior.

THE FOLKLORE OF CORRUPTION

Folklore, according to Bascom (1954, pp. 343-346), fulfills four functions. Briefly, it allows members of a society: (a) a means of psychological escape from the daily round; (b) a means of validating cultural experience and rituals to those who perform them; (c) a means of educating members into traditions of the group; and finally (d) a means of enforcing conformity to the moral norms of the society—that is, it is used to "express social approval of those who conform." I should like, in this discussion, to examine briefly some recurring behavior in the Philippines which seems to me connected with "folklore" of a type. The "folklore" to which I refer is that of "corruption" pointed to by Myrdal (1968) in his discussion of Asian poverty and politics.

In an earlier paper (Stone, 1971), I noted that Myrdal's generalizations about corruption in Asia seemed to apply well to the situation in the Philippines. Myrdal (1968, p. 944) defines the folklore of corruption as "those beliefs about corruption and emotions attached to those beliefs as disclosed in public debate (political campaigns and news media) and in gossip." It is the gossip aspect that interests me here. Whether gossip can be considered as folklore is, of course, debatable. However, if the gossip is ritualized, and the object of the same gossip changes over time, then it may approach folklore status (in a loose sense) and may, I believe, fulfill at least the validating function of folklore.

The importance of gossip in human interaction has been pointed out by Gluckman (1963). He notes (p. 307) that the development of anthropological interest in small group process serves to place gossip and scandal in proper perspective. Citing various pioneering efforts at the analysis of this universal phenomenon (Radin, 1927; Herskovits, 1937, 1947; West, 1945), he stresses the fact that gossip is important not only for its disruptive effects on groups, but, perhaps more importantly, for its unitive functions. Following from this, Gluckman offers a working hypothesis: "The more exclusive the group, the greater will be the amount of gossip within it" (1963, p. 309).

Gluckman goes on to define three social groups which he maintains bear out his hypothesis: the profession; the high status group bent on excluding the parvenu; and the group which carries ascribed exclusiveness. The second of these, the high status group, is the one which is important to this discussion. This kind of group, according to Gluckman (p. 309):

tends to become hereditary; and once they are, it means that each group comprises not only the present members of the group, but also the past dead members. And here is the great scope for gossip as a social weapon. To be able to gossip properly a member has to know not only about the present membership, but also about their forebears. For members can hit at one another through their ancestors, and if you cannot use this attack because you are ignorant, then you are in a weak position. Gossip here is a two-edged weapon; for it also means that you have no ancestors in the group to be attacked through—in short that you have no ancestors. And, each time that someone in your presence refers to a scandal about another's ancestors, or even his own ancestors, he is gently rubbing in the fact that you have no ancestors and do not properly belong to the group and are a parvenu.

Further,

The more exclusive a social group is, the more its members indulge in gossip and scandal about one another. And the more persistently will they repeat the same gossip again and again without getting bored (p. 315).

GOSSIP AMONG THE PHILIPPINE OLIGARCHY

Commentators on the Philippines (see Corpuz, 1965; Bulatao, 1967;

Lynch, 1959; Lynch and Hollnsteiner, 1965; Jocano, 1967) indicate that the colonial experience in the Philippines was one which reinforced and legitimized, in a nominally democratic framework, the hierarchical structure found in its nascent stages by the Spaniards when they arrived. It was nourished for three centuries under Spanish tutelage, and for fifty years under American occupation. The end result is a consolidation of power in the hands of a wealthy few, whose ranks are occasionally broadened by the wily parvenu whose value system is no different from that of the elite. National politics are personality politics, and issues and principles are of little moment. The strong political lobbies are those built around the various commercial agricultural products. Shifting alliances among these groups tend to effectively limit any government action.

There are two major parties, the Nacionalistas and the Liberals. They are ideologically indistinguishable. Indeed, the Philippines has been said to have a "one-and-a-half party system" (Buckley, 1972, p. 34). Elections are held somewhere every two years, but the main function appears to be little more than an occasion for members of the oligarchy to change positions within the power structure. Political allegiance is purchased from the lower strata; among the upper it is determined by private, group, or family interests, by patronage of some sort dispensed in a spoils system which has been brought to the level of high art.

Politics is the national avocation (some say the national vocation), and at all levels of society it is indulged in with a zeal which approaches fanaticism. There is tremendous freedom of political expression; indeed campaigns are arenas of combat in which the most vituperative charges are lodged by opposing candidates against one another. Such charges occurring, for example, in Great Britain, would bring libel and slander suits, and immediate charges of dirty politics. But what appears to occur in the Philippines is simply that members of the same group are gossiping publicly about one another. This is not to say that Philippine elections are free of violence. The violence that surrounds the elections is enormous. In view of the Filipino personality and Filipino social structure, it is surprising that there is not more.[1] The fact that such freedom of expression

---

[1]Hollnsteiner (1965, p. 23) analyzes Filipino group solidarity in the following manner: "The Filipino sees himself as a member of a group and channels his behavior in terms of that group. If he is to remain a part of it, he cannot exhibit independence of it. His first membership is his kin group, more specifically his nuclear family. As he grows older, he begins to align himself with members of his peer group, who see themselves as a unit against all other groups of that nature. The price of membership is intense loyalty to that group and its interests while the benefits are support from other group members. One's interests are the group's interests and vice-versa. Hence, if a co-member has been insulted by an outgroup member, it is the ingroup's responsibility to revenge that collective insult."

is not stifled would seem to indicate that the elite do not feel threatened. I would attribute this to the fact that the political process is not one of opposing segments, but rather of intragroup competition.

Charges of malfeasance, illegitimate assumption of authority, may eventually end up in court, but after elaborate and lengthy court rituals, the defendants usually win. Like the end result of a purification ceremony, the individual is returned to the elite fold, ready to share again in the spoils. A classic case occurred in a recent national election. One of the contenders had been accused of murder and brought to trial, arguing his case successfully to the supreme court; the other had been accused of collaboration with the Japanese during World War II, and the charges were dropped after some litigation.

Gossip is rife about power holders in all groups at all levels, about the elite among the masses, and about the elite among the elite. What is noteworthy about the intragroup gossip is that so much of it is directed at women, particularly wives of office holders. The reasons for this are not completely clear, but I would suggest that it is related to the total role of women in Philippine society, about which I will comment below.

Among the forms gossip takes, two are important for this discussion: (1) gossip concerning the ancestry of the gossip object; and (2) gossip concerning the acquisition of material wealth by the gossip object.

A few examples may illustrate this behavior:

1. During an election in Sulu Province, one of the major items of gossip, kept alive during the campaign, was the charge that the incumbent's wife was part Samal. In many parts of Sulu, this is akin to charging a Mississippi white candidate's wife with being part black. The prevailing mythology surrounding the power structure in Sulu maintains the fiction that no one of Samal identity may ascend to the power structure. Frequent references to Samal origins, in fact, may indicate that this is not the case.[2]

2. In a squatter community in a Manila suburb, gossip among the politically active centered on the incumbent mayor's mistress, accusing her of high-handedness in dispensing patronage and collecting graft. Notable also were references to her origins and her previous occupations.

3. On the national level, the wives of chief executives and highly placed government officials, both appointed and elected, are accused of immediately acquiring material wealth once the husband is in office.

---

[2]See Stone (1962). The Samal are a group ranked in prestige below the Taosug who consider themselves the old nobility of the Sulu area. The Samal can pass as Taosug by adopting Taosug mannerisms, the Taosug language, and joining the mainstream of Taosug life. It is a fiction which all participate in, and it does allow for social mobility among the lower ranked group.

Generally, this is thought to be in the form of precious jewelry. The same stories have circulated among the elite concerning the wives of the president for as long as I can recall. The remarks are inevitably: "Well, _____ is buying her diamonds already," or " _____ has already gotten her land," or "_____ has already opened her Swiss bank account," or " _____ has already made six shopping trips to Hong Kong." The accounts are embellished, the exploits compared with former office-holders' wives, and the stories gain in alleged authenticity.

In part, such behavior can be explained by relating it to the leveling mechanisms of Filipino society. Lynch and Hollnsteiner (1965) refer to the *sociostat,* the function of which is to maintain equality within segments of the ranked society. Gossip and barbed joking serve to remind an individual that he is rising above his segment-mates, and he should be cognizant of this fact. The behavior is culturally acceptable within segments; across segments, it can lead to violence.

Beyond this function, there is another, which may, in the long run, be more important. I would offer the hypothesis that such gossip validates expected behavior, not only on the part of the individual being gossiped about, but also behavior either engaged in by the gossiper, or behavior which the gossiper anticipates she would engage in, given the same situation herself. In other words, the object of gossip becomes the standard of behavior, and validates the behavior of the gossiper and members of her segment.

This follows from what I feel is a general asociality which allows such behavior to go unpunished and inevitably leads people to view an office-holder and his immediate family as individuals who simply exploit power in self-, family, or group interest. The folklore of corruption manifested in the gossip about power holders or those close to power holders reflects what the individual would herself do, placed in the same position. The fact that it is the woman who is both the object of gossip and the gossiper is related to the fact that such behavior on the part of men would be subject, in many instances, to physical retaliation. The woman in the Philippines is, by and large, not the object of violence, and she is thus allowed a wider latitude of behavior which might in the case of the male be of a kind which would produce a violent reaction. In validating the behavior of the wife of the office-holder, she fulfills with impunity the latent function of validating the behavior of the office-holder himself. Thus, to find the limits of behavior that are set upon an individual in the political realm, one must look to the behavior which gossip claims his wife indulges in.

Admittedly, these are tender hypotheses, and there is much work needed before they can be considered testable. I do feel, however, that the above discussion points out some areas for further research. Properly investigated in depth, they may prove fruitful, not only in the study of political process, but in the area of gossip and scandal as both integrative and disruptive aspects of social life everywhere. By viewing gossip as folklore of a kind, we can broaden the area that has been rather specialized in the past, and use the study of folklore as a tool to ferret out the regularities of all aspects of social life.

LITERATURE CITED

BASCOM, W. R.

    1954. "Four Functions of Folklore." *J. American Folklore* **67**(266):333-349.

BUCKLEY, T.

    1972. "Corks in the Pacific. Letter from Manila." *Harpers Mag.* **244**(1461, Feb.):30-37.

BULATAO, J.

    1964. Westernization and the Split-Level Personality in the Filipino. Paper read at the Conference on Mental Health in Asia and the Pacific, East-West Center, Honolulu. (Typescript.)

    1967. "Split-Level Christianity." In A. MANUUD (ed.), *Brown Heritage: Essays on Philippine Cultural Tradition and Literature*, pp. 16-33. Quezon City: Ateneo de Manila Univ. Press.

CORPUZ, O. D.

    1965. *The Philippines.* Englewood Cliffs, New Jersey: Prentice Hall.

GLUCKMAN, M.

    1963. "Gossip and Scandal." *Current Anthropology* 4(3):307-316.

HERSKOVITS, M. J.

    1937. *Life in a Haitian Valley.* New York: Knopf.

    1947. *Trinidad Village.* New York: Knopf.

HOLLNSTEINER, M.

    1965. "Social Control and the Filipino Personality." In *Symposium on the Filipino Personality*, pp. 22-26. Manila: Psychological Assoc. Philippines.

JACANO, F. L.

    1967. "The Philippines at Spanish Contact: An Essay in Ethnohistory." In A. MANUUD (ed.), *Brown Heritage: Essays on Philippine Cultural Tradition and Literature*, pp. 49-89. Quezon City: Ateneo de Manila Univ. Press.

LYNCH, F.
   1959. *Social Class in a Bikol Town*. Research Studies No. 1. Chicago: Univ. Chicago
      Philippine Studies Program.
LYNCH, F., and M. HOLLNSTEINER
   1965. *Understanding the Philippines and America: A Study of Cultural Themes*. Quezon
      City: Ateneo de Manila Univ. Press.
MYRDAL, G.
   1968. *Asian Drama: An Inquiry into the Poverty of Nations*. 3 vols. New York: Pantheon
      Press.
RADIN, P.
   1927. *Primitive Man as Philosopher*. New York: Appleton.
STONE, R. L.
   1962. "Intergroup Relations among the Taosug, Samal and Badjaw of Sulu." *Philippine
      Sociological Rev.* **10**:107-133.
   1971. "*Lagay* and the Policeman: A Study of Private, Transitory Ownership of Public
      Property." In F. LYNCH and A. DE GUZMAN II (eds.), *Modernization: Its
      Impact in the Philippines V.* IPC Pap. **10**:142-166. Quezon City: Ateneo de
      Manila Univ. Press.
WEST, J.
   1945. *Plainsville, U.S.A.* New York: Columbia Univ. Press.

FOLK TRADITIONS AND INTERETHNIC RELATIONS IN NORTHEASTERN LUZON, PHILIPPINES

JEAN TRELOGGEN PETERSON*

University of Illinois, Urbana

IT IS WIDELY ACCEPTED in anthropology that the integrated realms of economic, social, and symbolic behavior provide a system of checks and balances that serves to maintain a functioning society. This paper is intended to examine in some detail the way in which these checks and balances operate in two societies, namely the Agta and Palanan of northeastern Luzon. In particular, it is suggested that symbolic behavior such as folktale, myth, music, and art may provide a people a means for coping with an adverse social environment. This attribute of the symbolic realm is exemplified not only by the psychological benefits, but by the acquisition or expansion of a sense of group cohesion. These suggestions may be illustrated with reference to data on interethnic relations in northeastern Luzon, Philippines.

THE PHYSICAL WORLD

Two racially and ethnically distinct populations inhabit the area surrounding the small bay of Palanan on the northeast coast of Luzon. These are the Palanan, a farming peasant people with a population of about 10,000, and the Agta, Negrito hunter-gatherers, who number about 800.

*This paper is based on field research in Isabella Province, Philippines, from May, 1968, to March, 1970, partially supported by a National Defense Educational Act Title IV fellowship.

The Palanan, who were converted to Christianity in the 17th century, practice permanent field agriculture, raising predominantly corn and root crops, and some rice. From time to time as families grow, or soil is exhausted, or rivers wash out fields, the Palanan find it necessary to move along the coast or upriver where they face the laborious task of claiming new land from the forest and establishing homes on the frontier. There, lacking close Palanan neighbors, they often become socially dependent on Agta to a degree unprecedented elsewhere in Palanan. The Palanan raise relatively little livestock and what pigs or chickens they do have are butchered only for ceremonial occasions or when the family needs cash and wishes to sell the meat. In addition to their agricultural activities the Palanan make hats and mats, which they carry, usually once a year, across the Sierra Madre Mountains to market towns in the Cagayan Valley where they sell these goods for money used to buy enameled metal plates, cast aluminum cooking pots, fabrics, clothing, shoes, and other factory-made items, as well as tobacco which is grown in the Cagayan Valley.

The Agta, who have avoided all contact with missionaries, live by hunting deer and boar in the surrounding forests, fishing in the rivers and on the reefs, and gathering shellfish and forest products such as roots, wild fruits, honey, and eggs. Some Agta practice swiddening as well, but this activity is confined almost exclusively to the old men, and accounts for no more than 30 percent of their staple food supply in the area of maximum swiddening and as little as 1 percent or less in other areas. Agta live in temporary camps along the peripheries of Palanan settlements, thus avoiding areas where agriculture is practiced intensively.

It is the relations between these populations that are of interest to this paper. The Palanan and the Agta are materially dependent on each other. Agta provide as much as 50 percent of the protein consumed by Palanan. In exchange they receive corn or roots which represent at least 70 percent of the staple foods eaten by Agta. In addition to these food exchanges, the Palanan hire Agta to clear new land and to help in their fields during planting and harvest. Finally, the Agta are employed as guides and bearers in the annual treks made by the Palanan across the mountains.

The medium for most of these transactions is the *ibay* (special friend) relationship. Nearly every young Agta man, and the majority of young Palanan men, seek to establish at least one such relationship about the time they marry. The relationship is usually established with an exchange of gifts or favors. *Ibay* regularly exchange appropriate goods, they may request special services from each other, and they may extend credit so that the reciprocal transaction may be completed at a later date. The best *ibay*, according to Agta, are those who are always willing and able to trade. Palanan prefer an *ibay* who is able to provide plentiful protein, but does not make too great a demand for staple foods, and who is willing to labor in his fields.

Certainly the ethnic and racial boundaries which exist in Palanan serve to maintain this viable economic system. It is a kind of ethnic specialization in which each group performs those subsistence tasks at which it is most skilled, relying on the other group to provide alternate food items. Because of this specialization, it is difficult to calculate population density or carrying capacity for the Palanan area, but it is quite probable that both groups would have poorer diets and might in addition experience significant social and economic restructuring without benefit of this specialization.

While economic relations between Agta and Palanan are reciprocal, they are not truly symmetrical. The resource areas relevant to Agta subsistence, that is, the forest, reefs, and rivers, offer food sources which are comparatively less limited than those of the Palanan. In addition to the relative plentitude of fish and game, Agta benefit from the diversity of their subsistence activities, which allow them options in the event of any food shortage. Furthermore, an Agta working an estimated average of five hours a day can daily provide his family with adequate food, and also gain a surplus to share and trade. Palanan production is limited from the outset by the amount of land a farmer owns, and this limitation is acutely felt. A Palanan working about twice as many hours as an Agta feels the need to ration his staple food supply in order to meet his family's needs and grudgingly parts with staples for trade.

Seasonality affects both groups, but again it is the Palanan who is most affected. Generally speaking, the food supply drops off during the rainy season which begins in late September and tapers off in January. For the Agta the diminished returns from fishing during this period are offset by increased rewards from hunting. Any food shortage they experience is largely the result of their reluctance to hunt or fish on rainy days and the Palanan's unwillingness to trade during the rainy season. Corn, the major staple, is harvested in July, which means that near the end of the rainy season Palanan reserves may be running low. More important, however, is the fact that frequent flooding may effectively isolate a family indefinitely. Palanan are desperately afraid of running low on food and being cut off from kinsmen who might lend them some. Furthermore, the Agta value system is such that they may legitimately ask for food from virtually anyone; Palanan, on the other hand, may ask for food only under the most extreme circumstances and would approach only one or two close kinsmen for such a favor.

Another factor tending toward imbalance is that the corn that the Agta receive may be stored, while the protein the Palanan receive must be consumed immediately. Thus, Agta have no check, other than their own preference, on how much food they may wish to obtain in trade, while Palanan do. Finally, demographic factors place further pressure on Palanan food resources. Agta population is so distributed that in the circumscribed areas where they live, on the periphery of Palanan settlement, the ratio of Agta to Palanan is relatively high. This means that the Palanan receive many requests for trade; more, in fact, than they feel they can meet. This fosters the attitude among Palanan that Agta are always asking for too much food, a condition which they resent and find threatening.

The preceding discussion illustrates the nature of economic imbalance in Palanan. In a reciprocal trade situation the Agta are able to provide more goods in trade than the Palanan are willing or able to exchange.

The imbalance of the economic situation is reversed in the social realm. Agta are regarded by Palanan as their social inferiors. The Agta are well aware of this evaluation and some rather indifferently agree with it, recognizing that by Palanan standards they are inferior. They wear little clothing, they are illiterate, they have few material possessions, do not aspire to material wealth, do not work hard, and ask for food when they need it. In short, as seen by Palanan, Agta "have no shame" *(awan ti masanki)*. The Agta, then, recognize that Palanan have standards different from their own; most Palanan fail to recognize this about the Agta. This one-sided ethnocentrism is in itself an indicator of the inferior status of the Agta.

Daily interaction also illustrates this status differential. Agta are pointedly deferential in the presence of Palanan. They tend to dress in their best if they are going into Palanan settlements, keep their eyes downcast in intercourse with many Palanan, maintain stiff and polite postures in Palanan homes, and use Palanan dialect rather than Agta dialect in conversation with Palanan. The Palanan not only fail to show these mutually acknowledged courtesies to Agta, but directly affront them in diverse ways, such as commanding them to do Palanan bidding, making them the butt of jokes, making lewd and sometimes forceful sexual advances toward Agta women, and occasionally beating or otherwise physically abusing Agta men. None of this behavior is unnoticed by Agta, but they have virtually no physical recourse except to leave the area if the offense is too great.

They are, then, willing to accept the role, if not the fact, of their inferiority. Conversely, the Palanan have access to the larger Philippine social and political system, which the Agta do not understand and use only rarely. They thus have legal means of taking over Agta land and unjustly defending themselves from Agta accusations of "land-grabbing." Only one case of Agta retaliation for unfair treatment is known. In spite of this social imbalance the Agta continue to call Palanan friends because the Palanan provide them with staple foods, and many Palanan, recognizing their dependence on Agta, refer to them as friends and brothers.

THE SPIRITUAL WORLD

The social and economic relations of Palanan and Agta are paralleled in the spiritual realm by relations between the *anito* or *hayup*[1] and the *dumindez,* spirits in which both groups believe. The *anito* or *hayup* live exclusively in the forest, although from time to time, particularly at dusk, they approach human habitations, both Palanan and Agta. Not all Agta have had extensive experience with the *anito* and information obtained about them varies with the experience of the individual. The most experienced are shamans who have acquired special friends among the spirits and speak the spirit language *(magablon)* [2] while in trance. These shamans initially meet their spirit friends in a dream and may be told to wear special sweet-smelling herbs in their ear ornaments in order that they may be easily identified by the *anito.* Some shamans have participated in *anito* feasts and report that *anito* food is identical with Agta food, except that it is unsalted. Other individuals have been invited to such gatherings but have been afraid to participate, feeling that it might be dangerous to eat *anito* food. All Agta agree that there are two types of *anito:* those which are eternal and those which come into being when an Agta dies. Some of the former inhabit specific trees, caves, and rocks, others live in shelters like Agta lean-tos. All are known to be avid hunters preying on *anito* boar and deer and gathering *anito* forest products. They also enjoy betel nut and tobacco, but are able to obtain them only from the Agta because these items do not naturally grow in the forest.

---

[1]Some Agta use these two terms interchangeably to refer to all spirits. Others distinguish between *anito* and *hayup,* saying the former are spirits who live much as Agta live, while the latter live in hollow trees, caves, and under the earth. Judging from the fact that older persons prefer to use the latter term exclusively and that *anito* is a term used for spirits in many Philippine languages, including Palanan, I would suggest that *anito* may be a term borrowed from the Palanan.

[2]*Ablon,* the spirit language is glossolalia unintelligible to all but the shaman who is in trance. *Magablon* is "to speak the spirit language," or "one who speaks the spirit language."

Dumindez are the ghosts of dead Palanan who inhabit only the areas where the Palanan population is densest, and are found in particularly large numbers around the cemetery in town. Since these are places where Agta seldom go they have little direct knowledge of *dumindez*. It is known, however, that *dumindez* plant spirit corn and rice and live generally very much as their Palanan counterparts do.

Relations between *anito* and *dumindez* again parallel the physical world. *Anito* protein is traded for *dumindez* corn, *anito* work in *dumindez* fields and carry out other menial tasks for the *dumindez*, all through the medium of a spirit *ibay* relationship. The only difference lies in the fact that in the spirit world negative relations are de-emphasized. *Dumindez* have little opportunity to exploit or abuse the *anito*, who avoid all but trade relations with *dumindez*. Some claim that *anito* dislike *dumindez*. *Dumindez* fear to venture from familiar ground, since *anito* are threatening even to other spirits.

Agta relations with the *anito* are largely dictated by the nature of the *anito*. These spirits are invisible, fearsome, and a bit slow-witted. Invisibility and fearsomeness are definite advantages for the *anito*, which are offset by their limited mental abilities. Nearly every Agta man, woman, or child, can recall some unpleasant experience with *anito*. Commonly they place invisible sticks on the trail which make a loud snap when stepped on, thereby frightening game; they lay invisible vines on foot paths to trip passersby, and they attack unwary and exhausted travelers, and attempt to choke them. As a precaution Agta may wear herbs in their ears, the odor of which fends off *anito*, or they trail a vine behind them while walking through the forest and the ingenuous *anito* mistake it for a snake.

If *anito* behavior were confined to pranks of the sort described there would be relatively little to fear from them, but repercussions of encounters with *anito* are often much more serious. One account tells of how an Agta child became critically ill with stomach troubles. A shaman agreed to intervene with the spirits. At dusk he produced his ceramic plate, which his *anito* friend had commanded him to obtain, and tapped on it to call his friend.[3] The *anito* responded to the sound and came to the shaman, entering his body and speaking to him. In their conversa-

---

[3] Of seven shamans I questioned on the matter, five owned or had owned a ceramic plate for the purposes of summoning their spirit friends. The plates and the spirit relationship may be passed on to the eldest child, or the plate and the ability may be acquired when a spirit first appears to an individual in a dream, telling them, among other things, to obtain such a plate. Most of the plates are of recent origin, but one I saw was a Chinese ceramic, probably of the Ching Dynasty, acquired from a Chinese merchant in Cauayan, Isabela, approximately 75 years ago. The power of the plates is so great that should a nonshaman touch one he becomes ill. Special baskets are woven to hold them to prevent laymen from accidentally touching them.

tion the shaman learned that the Agta child had inadvertently injured an *anito* child while playing with it and the mother was retaliating by pulling at the offender's stomach to make him ill. The *anito* mother agreed to relinquish her hold, realizing that the offense was unintentional and agreeing to accept betel nut, which was to be left in the forest, by way of apology. Many such stories are told of physical or mental illness caused by *anito* in retaliation for harm to them, or to their kinsmen, game, or belongings.

Events such as these may be handled with careful diplomacy. More critical are the cases of evil or simply lonely *anito* who seek to harm living persons without provocation. In some such cases intervention through a shaman may be helpful because the spirit friend of the shaman may be able to take direct action against the threatening *anito* by driving it away or persuading it to leave. At other times the only recourse open to Agta is to leave the area. *Anito* are, some say, unable to cross water, and thus the Agta may escape them. This situation occurs when an Agta dies. Death presents a double danger to the Agta. It means, on the one hand, that malicious *anito* may be nearby and may have caused the death. At the same time the *anito* of the recently deceased person may be suffering acute loneliness and thus may seek to obtain the company of a friend or relative in death. Bereaved Agta are extremely reluctant to admit this characteristic of their dead relatives, but they never fail to take precautions against it and will later acknowledge the paradox of their fear and love of dead friends and kinsmen.

At the time of death several measures are enacted to insure the welfare of the deceased and the safety of the living. Burial occurs within twenty-four hours and the dead are buried with grave goods that will offer them comfort in the afterlife. These include bow and arrow, cooking utensils, food, water, betel, tobacco, and fire-making implements. A small shelter is erected over the grave. On a path leading from the grave the mourners erect a fence of palm frond spines fashioned to resemble crocodile tongues. This will frighten the *anito* should it try to follow them. They then cross water as further insurance against pursuit. On the fourth day following death they return to the grave to mourn. This is a demonstration of love intended to comfort the deceased. On leaving the grave this time they erect another fence, this one a string adorned with the mourning cloths they have worn around their necks and arms. This serves as a reminder to the dead that he is loved and should not cause unhappiness to the living. On subsequent occasions relatives leave gifts of food, betel, and tobacco at the grave in order to show affection and insure good fortune. Such gifts are also left whenever *anito* have been causing unprovoked serious difficulties, such as illness and death.

Should these friendly gestures fail to improve relations the Agta will abandon the area.

The Palanan are at a great disadvantage in dealing with the spirit world. Like the Agta they are frequently victims of pranks, retaliatory action, and unprovoked attacks. Unlike the Agta, they have no members of their community who can intercede for them, and they face the additional difficulty of occasionally suffering the ire of *anito* acting on behalf of Agta who have been wronged. When illness or an unusual death occurs the Palanan may turn to an Agta shaman, asking him to serve as an intermediary. One shaman recounts how she assisted a Palanan on such an occasion. The sick man asked for her help and, in trance, she learned that an *anito* was causing the illness, but could not be persuaded to relinquish its hold. It happened that the shaman's *anito* friend was a warrior. At her request he drove the stubborn *anito* out of the area in a spectacularly noisy battle. Another shaman relates how a Palanan came to him for help when his child was dying. The shaman's inquiries among his spirit friends uncovered the information that the Palanan had greatly offended the *anito*. He had taken over land formerly used by Agta and still inhabited by *anito*, and in clearing the tract had destroyed *anito* lean-tos. The Palanan refused to give credence to this account and soon thereafter his child died.

One case of Agta-*anito* alliance was reported to me by a Palanan. He had gone to an Agta camp to visit and, finding everyone gone, had made himself at home in one of the lean-tos. Almost immediately his stomach bloated painfully. He blamed food he had eaten earlier for this, until the Agta returned and affirmed that his *anito* friend was causing the condition. The *anito* had seen the Palanan enter the unoccupied lean-to and was offended at such brashness. When the Agta told him he would forgive the Palanan, the bloat subsided. Clearly, the Palanan are dependent on the Agta for intercession with the spirit world and must, as well, in some measure check their transgressions against Agta for fear of spirit retaliation.

CONCLUSIONS

In addition to the parallels illustrated by these descriptions, other points may be made which relate this symbolic realm to Agta-Palanan relations in the physical world. The spiritual world as understood by Agta provides a metalanguage in which they can state the nature of their social and political relations with Palanan, and can express the frustrations they experience as a result of the inferior status ascribed to them. An Agta who has been cheated, assaulted, robbed, or abused by a Palanan, whose land has been taken, or whose wife or children have been abused, cannot overtly express his anger toward the individual who wronged him. He can, however, openly tell stories of social injustice and retaliation in the spiritual world. He can, furthermore, symbolically warn or threaten Palanan in this manner, and the Palanan, fearing the spirits and depending on the Agta as spiritual mediums, will be attentive to these tales. Given the integration of economic, social, and symbolic activity, and the shared belief and concern with spirits, the Agta have an effective means of keeping Palanan behavior in check, and of assuring themselves ultimate justice.

In further examining the integrated roles of social, economic, and symbolic behavior in Palanan it is useful to recognize the schismogenic nature of these various activities (Bateson, 1935, 1958). Bateson (1935, p. 175) defines schismogenesis as "a process of differentiation in the norms of individual behaviour resulting from cumulative interaction between individuals," and points out in his epilogue to *Naven* (1958, pp. 287-290) that schismogenesis can be more clearly understood in terms of cybernetics, or feedback mechanisms. Each of the realms of behavior described exemplifies a complementary schismogenesis (1935, p. 181; 1958, pp. 171-187). In the economic realm a reciprocal relationship must be maintained. This reciprocal relationship may be expressed as: A _____ B (1935, pp. 181-182). Furthermore, each potentially schismogenic realm of behavior may be restrained by other behavioral realms through a feedback mechanism.

What may actually occur, however, in any given *ibay* relationship is that the Agta partner offers a quantity of protein, say, once a week to his Palanan friend who reciprocates with adequate staple foods. Pleased with this reciprocity the Agta either initiates trades more frequently or offers a greater quantity of protein with each trade, expecting more staples in return. If the Palanan continues to reciprocate, the Agta will continue to accelerate his trading. Ultimately this would lead to the Palanan's withdrawing from the trading partnership, thus destroying a mutually beneficial relationship. This does, in fact, occur from time to time, and this accelerated trading is a common complaint of Palanan against Agta. The potential acceleration of this trading activity may be represented as: A *(trade)* B *(reciprocate)* A *(trade)* B. . .N.

However, integrated with this potentially destructive imbalance in economic activity is the social imbalance I have already described. Here again schismogenesis is potentially disruptive of relations between Agta and Palanan. Palanan are superordinate in their social relations with Agta, who accept their subordinate role submissively. This is a type of schismogenesis already described by Bateson (1958, p. 179) and represented as follows: A*(dominant)* B *(submissive)* A *(dominant)* . . . N. Should this trend continue to its extreme, it, too, would result in restructuring or breakdown. Either a Palanan might commit murder or an Agta, too greatly abused, would himself resort to violence or would at least abandon relations with that Palanan and leave the immediate area.

Both the economic and the social realms offer certain internal restraints and they serve to restrain each other. That is, weighed against his desire for active trade an Agta must consider the possibility of the ultimate breakdown of a trade relationship if he presses a Palanan too far. Many Agta, however, are unaware of this possibility or unconcerned. They are aware, however, of their social and political inferiority and know that Palanan may be increasingly abusive should they make too many economic demands. This possibility and the inferior role which they accept prevents them from trading too aggressively. Similarly, a Palanan recognizes that, should he become too abusive toward an Agta, that Agta may threaten him economically, either by demanding more trade than the Palanan can afford, or by completely cutting him off from his protein supply. This interaction of the social and economic realms may be diagrammed thus:

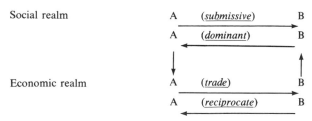

The role of the symbolic realm relative to these schismogeneses is complex. Relations in the symbolic realm are potentially schismogenic. Agta could endlessly threaten Palanan both through the telling of stories and through withholding of shamanistic services. While they do quite pointedly use these stories to communicate their offense at Palanan behavior in specific cases, the possible acceleration does not occur. Apparently Agta satisfaction at simply communicating their dissatisfaction is sufficient to them, at the same time that Palanan fear of possible Agta manipulation of the spirit world serves as a restraint on Palanan social and political excesses. It is interesting that none of these schismogeneses is completely restrained. Each serves a role and thus is only kept in check.

Bateson (1958, p. 194) notes that mutual threat serves to restrain the fissioning which might otherwise result from schismogenesis. The shared acceptance of the power of the spiritual world provides such a mutual threat, thus drawing Agta and Palanan closer together.

It would appear that schismogenesis in these three realms of activity provides an integrated network of checks and balances which enables the continued, mutually beneficial relations of two populations with different value systems, differential access to resources, and competitive behavior in some realms. The symbolic realm of folk tradition thus may serve as a "fail-safe" mechanism in these potentially disruptive relations, should other internal checks fail to prevent difficulties.

In addition to maintaining this dynamic equilibrium these related schismogeneses operate to maintain ingroup cohesion for both the Agta and the Palanan. Palanan cohere in the face of mutual threat of Agta economic superiority; Agta share the common threat of social dominance by Palanan and thus in their subordination they find a restraint to possible internal schismogeneses.

This latter point has significant implications for the positive value of discrimination. It follows that by maximizing outside threat or domination, a people may find great internal cohesion. Actual physical maximization, that is, provoking dominance or threat would be at least uncomfortable, possibly dangerous, and probably dysfunctional. Man, however, has the unique ability to symbolize. Thus, Agta in their stories of relations between *anito* and *dumindez* are able metaphorically to maximize the threat which they share and from it draw a greater sense of cultural cohesion. They symbolically exaggerate the external schismogenesis in order to minimize internal fission, or in other words, they are able to turn a detriment into an asset through the use of the symbolic realm of culture.

The similar ability of turning stereotypic discrimination into a positive force through the manipulation of symbols is characteristic of Afro-American folk traditions (Abrahams, 1970, pp. 7, 56, 60, 85; Keil, 1966). Certainly no one would deny the schismogenic nature of relations between Euro-Americans and Afro-Americans, whether it be the succoring-dependency type manifested during slavery or the dominance-submission type characteristic of most such relations today. Many writers have noted that characteristically Afro-Americans elaborate on this relationship, symbolically maximizing external threat and internal cohesion, as well as symbolically stating aggression against Whites. Abrahams (1970, p. 62), for example, citing this characteristic, ascribes a psychological function to it:

> The use of these (negative) traits for aggressive purposes has a certain irony to it, and does permit hostility directed toward the very source of the group's frustrations. But the ego-gains derived from such activities are small and short-lived because they generally do not register any reaction in the white world

While certainly this psychological mechanism may be operating, it seems fruitful to consider the possibility that this symbolic reminder of discrimination serves as well as a statement of common identity for Afro-Americans as it does for Agta in Palanan (compare Keil, 1966, pp. 164-190).

This would seem particularly important to Afro-Americans who, as Abrahams (1970) describes them, lack a sense of group identity (p. 74) and any sense of identity with a locale (pp. 77-78). Having suffered destruction of many means of cultural identity (Elkins, 1959), this metaphorical statement in folk tradition of shared abuse, suffering, and discrimination affords an important kernel of unity, an opportunity to safely maximize their common heritage without in fact maximizing negative behavior toward them. Hannerz (1968; compare Abrahams, 1970, p. 60) notes that "soul" is such a statement of a common culture and pride in that culture in spite of discrimination. This consideration might be fruitful in the study of any group that is the subject of discrimination. Perhaps hippies, transvestites, drug users, and other deviant groups are opting for discrimination in order to gain an important sense of group identity. An examination of the oral traditions and other symbolic aspects of the culture of such groups might prove interesting.

LITERATURE CITED

ABRAHAMS, ROGER D.
  1970. *Positively Black*. Englewood Cliffs, New Jersey: Prentice-Hall.
BATESON, GREGORY
  1935. "Culture Contact and Schismogenesis." *Man* **35**(Art. 199):178-183.
  1958. *Naven*. Stanford, California: Stanford Univ. Press.
ELKINS, STANLEY M.
  1959. *Slavery: A Problem in American Institutional and Intellectual Life*. Chicago: Univ. Chicago Press.
HANNERZ, ULF
  1968. "What Negroes Mean by Soul." *Trans-action*, July-August, pp. 57-61.
KEIL, CHARLES
  1966. *Urban Blues*. Chicago: Univ. Chicago Press.

JAPAN

TYPE INDEXING THE FOLK NARRATIVE

HIROKO IKEDA*

University of Hawaii, Honolulu

A type-index implies that all versions of a type have a generic relationship
— *Stith Thompson*

THE FIRST SYSTEM of folk narrative classification was compiled by a Finnish scholar, Antti Aarne. It was written in German, and was published in 1910 in Helsinki. The task of doing this was entrusted to him by Kaarle Krohn, his teacher, who was Professor of Folklore at the University of Helsinki. Until his death in 1933 at the age of seventy, Krohn was one of the most influential scholars in the field of folklore, both nationally and internationally. He served as chairman of the Finnish Literary Society from 1917 to 1933, and was a founding member of the Finnish Academy of Science and Letters. He was also instrumental in establishing important academic periodicals, including the Folklore Fellows Communications, a prestigious series of folklore monographs. Its first volume was published in 1910, and the latest, No. 209, by this writer came out in 1971. Every issue in the series has been kept in print, and revenue from the sale supports the Finnish Academy.

The immediate purpose of Aarne's *Verzeichnis* (1910) was the practical necessity of systematizing the great Finnish collection, with other possible target areas, but limited to northern Europe. Nevertheless, his volume marked an epoch in the study of comparative folk literature, since it provided for the first time a common basis for an international comparison of folk narratives.

*Research on which this paper is based was done with the help of grants from the American Council of Learned Societies in 1962 and 1963, and from the American Philosophical Society in 1965, for which grateful acknowledgement is made.

This classification system eventually gained recognition among scholars of neighboring countries, and eight ethnic indices were published before the death of Aarne in 1925. These included the folktale materials of Finland and of Finnish-Swedish people in Finland, of Estonia, Norway, Lapland, Flanders, Bohemia, and Livonia. Because of the many additions suggested by those scholars who compiled the above indices, Krohn by then was planning an expansion of Aarne's *Verzeichnis*.

The concept of an index of narrative motifs (a motif is the smallest element in a tale) occurred to Stith Thompson in the summer of 1922, and he worked on this project during the following two summers. Archer Taylor, Thompson's classmate at Harvard, was teaching at Chicago then, and one day came for a visit. He was shown what Thompson was working on, and "immediately saw the significance of it" (Thompson, 1956, p. 91). He encouraged Thompson to expand the scope of the index. The first draft of the motif index was completed by the end of the university year 1924-1925. (This was later published in six volumes from 1932 to 1936 and a revised edition came out in 1955-1958.)

That summer Taylor went to Finland to see Krohn. He took this 400-page manuscript with him and showed it to Krohn, who at once recognized its value. He wished to apply Thompson's taxonomical skill to the revision and enlargement of Aarne's *Verzeichnis*, and inquired, through Taylor, if Thompson would undertake the task. Thompson agreed.

Thompson spent the academic year 1926-1927 in Europe, and worked on this project mostly in Paris, keeping in close touch with Krohn and many other leading figures in folklore studies. His revision was published in 1928. Since that time this classification system has been widely known as the "Aarne-Thompson Index."

As the title shows, the original work by Aarne, which was in German, was translated into English, without disturbing Aarne's general scheme. The book consisted of two sections, main and supplementary portions. New tale-types created in the preceding eight ethnic indices were all added to this revision, either in the main classification or in the supplement. Types brought together in the supplement had been judged by Thompson (1928, p. 4) to be "of local significance." They were arranged by the original type-numbers given in the ethnic indices, with asterisks added. This dual arrangement was the result of Thompson's scholarly conscience, but was not popular with some users. The types placed in the supplement were too numerous, and sometimes too important to be in the supplement. As a result, users of the book had to be constantly turning back and forth from the main section to the supplement. This was remedied later, in the second revision.

Some of the type descriptions were elaborated in Thompson's 1928 volume, when the originals were too brief, and the bibliographical information on each tale-type was much expanded. The important feature in this version was the inclusion of motif-numbers in the descriptive text. The relationship between the type and the motif in an analytical study has become inseparable since.

In 1935 the Congress for the Study of the Folktale was held in Lund, Sweden, and the further revision of the 1928 Index was one of the problems discussed. Thompson agreed to undertake the further revision, in due time. After the publication of the 1928 volume, many ethnic indices appeared, including volumes from Russia, Spain, Iceland, Lithuania, Latvia, Sweden, Germany, Italy, Turkey, France, India, Czechoslovakia, Hungary, Rumania, and Spanish America. For a further revision, extreme discriminations would be required in the screening of suggested new type-numbers in the above indices. It would involve critical examination of dozens of ethnic indices which have been prepared by various scholars over the years, each with his own interpretations. This is because a narrative might have been interpreted as Type 100, or Type 90, depending on the taxonomists' viewpoint and insight. In some cases a taxonomist might not have recognized a standard tale-type in his material, and would have suggested a new type-number for it.

To my mind there seem to be two different avenues toward making a revision and enlargement of a classification system of narratives, the material for which is growing rapidly. One is to round up and incorporate all the subsequently published ethnic material into one, showing an over-all summary of each type. The outcome, the total summary of already systematized various ethnic data in one volume, would be an indispensable reference tool for future studies. It would be a synthetic register of all the available records to date.

The second avenue would be the compilation of a practical handbook for identification and classification of the folk narrative. Such a list of tale-types is actually needed by folklorists in general, by students, local collectors, and archivists. This handbook should not be bulky but consist of a list of types in the standard classification order, with their descriptions containing motif numbers. It need not include bibliographical notes and location data. Functionally speaking, the above two would complement each other.

Originally Aarne's *Verzeichnis* (1910) was just a simple system of classification. When Thompson revised it in 1928, he added the materials which had come to be available then. What his revision accomplished was to combine the above two avenues into one volume, the classification system and a synthesized register of materials.

Because of the vast accumulation of material since 1928, compilation of the further revision required five years for a crew of trained workers to handle the mechanical task of extracting the data from individual ethnic surveys and arranging them into proper places. In 1961, Thompson's second revision of the *Types of the Folktale* was published. Some forty ethnic groups were covered, with bibliographical sources numbering more than two hundred. The types with asterisks in the supplement section of Thompson (1928) were all incorporated into the principal list with many more added. It is now a fundamental tool for research, a bulky, comprehensive register of folktale material that had been made available up to 1961. It is no longer a simple list of tale-types.

Yet the book is still expected to, and is trying to serve both purposes—first of being a data register, and second of being a classification system. One cannot expect students in an introductory folklore course to be able to handle this tool, but as they are indoctrinated in the study of folklore, they will increasingly appreciate its value.

In order to regain the original function of the type-index, one solution might be to edit the Thompson (1961) volume, and compile a handbook of the Aarne-Thompson classification system of narratives for general use. In fact some years ago I started compiling such a type-list in Japanese, translating Thompson (1961). The Aarne-Thompson classification system is not known among Japanese folklore students except to the few who can use English. I am hoping to provide the others with a basic tool for comparison, in order to widen the horizon of folklore studies in that country. Once it is available in Japanese, the book will also reach the people who read Chinese characters, that is, Koreans and Chinese.

For this project, the basic research of checking the original material in the Finnish and other Scandinavian archives was done in 1965, and in 1966 I had occasion to discuss this project with Thompson in Bloomington. He told me that for my particular purpose, I should feel free to take or leave any types, subtypes and parts of type descriptions. The same could be done if the compilation of an English handbook of the Aarne-Thompson system for general use were to be attempted. It goes without saying that this simplified type-list is to serve the practical purpose of field collecting and classification of the material. Any further research will require consulting the original, Thompson (1961).

When I was working on my doctoral dissertation in the early 1950's, the type-index available was Thompson's 1928 version. My dissertation, "A Type and Motif Index of Japanese Folk Literature," was completed in 1955, including some two hundred types which had European analogues. *The Motif-Index of Folk Literature* by Thompson which I made use of for the dissertation was the first edition, published in 1932-1936.

In 1955, soon after I had completed my dissertation, the new edition of Thompson's motif-index had begun to appear, and the sixth and last volume came out in 1958. Also in 1961 Thompson's new edition of *The Types of the Folktale* was published, as mentioned earlier. A revision and enlargement of my dissertation was undertaken soon after its completion, making use of these newly revised tools. The final draft of my work was finished by the end of 1967, and was published in 1971, bearing the same title as the dissertation. This edition included 439 types (Ikeda, 1971).

The increase from 200 types in 1955 to 439 in 1967 should be accounted for. All the types in my dissertation were the analogues of European types, bearing established Aarne-Thompson type-numbers, and certain types that were known in Japan in only one version were not included. In my 1971 publication, however, I established an analogous type, even if only one oral version had been recorded. Furthermore, even though no oral narrative is on record, if the tale-type is known in Japan by such written sources as literature, historical documents, and other forms of narrative including myths and legends, I considered that these should be included also. Written sources are the surest proof that certain narratives were current at the time of documentation. As for forms of narrative other than the folktale, such as the epic, the legend, and the myth, they were included, because analytically they could be equally classified by their types and motifs. As a matter of fact, Franz Boas took a stand to minimize the distinction between myth and folktale. He says (1940a, p. 405):

> The facts that are brought out most clearly from a careful analysis of myths and folktales of an area like the northwest coast of America are that the contents of folk-tales and myths are largely the same, that the data show a continual flow of material from mythology to folk-tale and *vice-versa*, and that neither group can claim priority. We furthermore observe that contents and form of mythology and folk-tales are determined by the conditions that determined early literary art.

Certain tale-types that are told as folktales in Europe are found in Japan as myths, legends, or in various forms of literature. Literary sources, especially of early dates, are important in determining the age of particular tale-types. The earliest literature in Japan dates back to the 8th century. *Kojiki* and the *Nihongi* are records compiled in A.D. 712 and A.D. 720, respectively. Their purpose was to provide a history of the imperial reign in Japan from the time of the mythological creation of the country. The *Fudoki*, also compiled about that time, covers local records and history, including legends. It was prepared under imperial decree by the officials of various provinces. Records of five provinces exist in their original form. These earliest documents faithfully preserve the oral tradition up to that time.

The *Nippon Ryooiki,* compiled by a Buddhist priest named Kyookai in A.D. 822, contains 116 Buddhist anecdotes relating incidents that were supposed to have taken place in Japan about that time. It is the oldest existing collection of Buddhist tales in Japan, and has had an immense influence on tale collections of later periods. One is the *Konjaku Monogatari,* a collection of more than one thousand existing short stories, put together by an undetermined compiler about the middle of the 11th century. There are 31 volumes, each containing approximately 30 to 40 tales and anecdotes. Volumes 8, 18, and 21 are lost. The first five volumes are tales translated or adopted from Indian sources. Volumes 6 to 10 are from Chinese sources, and the rest, Volumes 11 to 31, concern Japanese events. The first half of the Japanese section covers religious tales, including those adopted from the *Ryooiki.* In the last half are miscellaneous secular tales. Unlike the other works of literature of the same period, which are centered around court life, the *Konjaku* depicts the daily life of such folk as Buddhist priests, robbers, bandits, wrestlers, doctors, students, and diviners. Or it concerns supernatural incidents involving ghosts and ogres. Down the centuries, even to this day, the work has been a source of inspiration to many writers. An example is found in "Yabu no Naka (1922)," a work by R. Akutagawa, from which the famous movie "Rashomon" was derived. The more striking stories in the *Konjaku* have been repeatedly discussed by scholars of Japanese literature, but the rest have remained obscure. In my notes are some 240 tales on traditional themes, which either belong to some 60 different types or include established literary motifs. A remarkable fact is that among the 240 tales are 84 versions of Type 470: "A Journey to Hell or Paradise." From the standpoint of literary appreciation these versions might seem to be a tedious repetition, but when in 1962 I started my research on the *Konjaku* and discovered their existence, scattered in several volumes, I was overwhelmed. I wrote a paper on this, published in 1964. It will be discussed in detail later.

One other genre of literature included in my notes is the Kyoogen, a farcical interlude play, presented as a companion to the Noh drama. Kyoogen are enacted in the spoken languages of the 16th and 17th centuries. About 300 pieces are currently known, but only a much smaller number are usually staged. Each piece is about half an hour in length. With only a few exceptions, types and motifs appearing in the Kyoogen plays are different from those found in the earlier literature mentioned above. Sources other than the early literature must have had influence on this folk drama, which originated in the Middle Ages. Chinese culture, perpetual source of influence on Japan, was undergoing considerable quality change, for the dynasties shifted from Sung to Yuan about that time.

I started taking notes on the above documentary sources soon after the completion of my dissertation. These notes grew rapidly during 1962 to 1963. With enriched notes on hand, careful examination of the enlarged Thompson (1961) index and his 1955-1958 *Motif Index* led to the uncovering of many new Japanese analogues, which had not been recognized by me ten years earlier. This was partly because the versions in Japan had undergone marked changes from the standard plots over the course of time and through acculturation.

The merit of the Thompson, 1961, publication, with its detailed type description, motif analysis, and abundant listing of related types or subtypes to the principal type, should be cited here. If I had been using Thompson (1928), I would never have spotted so many analogues. By being able to identify a few motifs, or even a single motif, of a tale, it very often becomes possible to identify the tale-type, or even the prototype of the tale. Such is the importance of motif analysis. Careful study of the motif in question, by checking it against the *Motif Index* and following up its related motifs often produced fruitful results. Of course a good type description is of fundamental importance in the identification of analogues. However, decisive clues are often found in the short descriptions of subtypes or related types. Therefore one must think twice before eliminating subtypes from a type index.

Another reason for the increase of the number of types in Ikeda (1971) is the inclusion of many Japanese subtypes. When variants unique to Japan had developed, they were included as subtypes. Very often in Japan a well-established tale-type has developed into a "cycle," with the type as nucleus and a cluster of subtypes forming around it. Some subtypes were the result of a variation in the main character. Other subtypes would start out the same as the original type, but proceeded to vary into further plots and endings; compare the clusters of Types 9, 408, 413, 470, 480, 503, 612, 930. There will be a further discussion on the "cycle" below.

Some tales do not have European equivalents, but are established types in Asia, the New World, and the Pacific. The addition to Thompson (1961) of types derived from India was a help in classifying a group of Japanese tales that had generic relations with southern and eastern parts of Asia; compare Types 58, 176, 177, and 225A, for example.

A group of tales that seems uniquely developed in Japan were also placed in appropriate slots in the type-index system as best as I could. They are stories of ghosts and weird beings, which are closely connected with folk beliefs and primitive religion. As to the fox stories Japan is known to possess, the tricks played by the animal are almost the same as those of the Western fairies, brownies, and elves. Many of the motifs F200-399 that are attributed to them exist in Japan in the fox stories. Even jokes based on wordplay in the Japanese language frequently are built on universal basic plots and types.

Until quite recently it has been generally considered that Japanese folk narratives were not closely related to the traditional area of the Western folk literature, which encompasses the expanse of India through Ireland. As late as 1960, Thompson (1961) states in the preface: "Strictly this work might be called *The Types of the Folktale of Europe, West Asia and the Lands Settled by These Peoples,*" thus excluding Japan, among others, from successful application of this classification system.

When I was writing my dissertation more than twenty years ago, I was convinced that Japanese narratives were classifiable by the Aarne-Thompson index system. I maintained in the introductory remark that as high as 80 percent of them could be matched with the Aa-Th numbers. I feel this even more strongly today, and hope that I have proved it with my publication (1971).

In order to clarify my argument with specific examples, I would like to take up Type 470 and its subtypes, on which I published a contribution in 1964 in Japanese. To begin with, Thompson's description of this type will be listed as it appears in his 1961 publication. The original references and the motif analysis are omitted:

Type 470 Friends in Life and Death. The deceased friend followed into the other world.
I. The Visit to the Other World. (a) Two friends pledge themselves never to part. One of them dies. (b) The living friend invites the dead to visit him on Christmas and goes with him when he returns; or (c) a man in a churchyard invites a skull and then goes off with the skull.
II. The Journey. (a) On the way they see many strange sights; among them: (b) fat and lean kine; (c) a broad and a narrow road . . . .
III. The Return. When the living man returns he finds he has been away many centuries; all is changed and he knows no one.
IV. Death. (a) He dies the next day by falling from a tree (or high place). (b) He vanishes after prayer.

Type 470A The Offended Skull (Statue). Festin de Pierre.
A skull is invited to dinner. He attends the dinner and takes the host off to the other world (C13). (Type 470 Ic as independent tale.)

Type 470B (Formerly 825*) *The Land Where No One Dies* (F116).

Type 470* The Hero Visits the Land of the Immortals and marries its queen. He is allowed to visit his home. He must not get off his horse. He breaks the prohibition and dies (F116).

The above description of Type 470 is reproduced by Thompson as it was given in his 1928 publication, although a detailed motif analysis with 15 motifs is appended in the 1961 version, and the three subtypes are new additions. The theme of a man visiting another world led by a guide has been repeated in many famous literary works: Dante's *Divine Comedy*, Bunyan's *Pilgrim's Progress*, Dickens' *Christmas Carol*, and Maeterlinck's *Blue Bird* are examples.

The Japanese analogue in my Index (1971) follows:

I. The Visit. A Buddhist priest (courtier, layman) who during his life has done some good and some evil deeds, dies suddenly. The body is not cremated, but is attended and a watch kept by the family or friends (F2).

II. The Journey. Two (five to ten) messengers come to take him to Hell (Paradise) (ZIII.6). (1) On the way a deep river has to be crossed (F162.2). (2) At one point the road divides into three: one is wide and straight, another passable with some weeds, and the last is overgrown with weeds (F171.2). He is made to take the first or the second depending on how good or bad he has been. (3) He sees a tall golden palace, which is explained as being the future dwelling of his friend (wife), a devout Buddhist.

III. Mediator. At the court of judgment, a Buddha appears and acts as a mediator, making him promise to make amends for his evil deeds, or to finish his uncompleted good deeds.

IV. The Return. He comes back by the same road and revives after one, three, or nine days, and finds he has been away that many years (D2011).

V. Death. He tells people what he has seen, fulfills what he has promised to do (for instance, copying the Lotus Sutra), and dies at the end of the allotted time (E166).

The above is the analysis of 90 versions in the *Ryooiki*, A.D. 822 (12 versions) and the *Konjaku*, A.D. 1077 (84 versions), with 6 versions overlapping in both. These early versions appear time and again in later Buddhist literature, but are unknown in oral tradition. This raises an interesting question regarding the tales disseminated in writing. Ordinarily they are considered to flow into and mingle freely with the stream of oral tradition.

Recently it has occurred to me that in my Japanese analogue analysis above, an explanation was necessary as to the relationship of the Buddhists and the Buddha in Part I. When a man has religious faith in the Buddha, he has entered into a religious pact, committing himself to the Buddha. Therefore the episode of the hero's devotion to the Buddha while still living, causing the Buddha to appear at the Court of Judgment to mediate for him (470-III), can be considered analogous to the "Death Pact Between Two Friends" (Aa-Th 470-Iab). What I should like to do is to revise Part I to read in a more convincing way close to that analysis, as follows: "I. Religious Pact. A Buddhist priest leads a life of devotion to the Buddha and dies suddenly. His devout faith has been recognized by the Buddha, but he also, being human, has done some misdeeds. The body is not cremated, but is attended and a watch kept by the family or friends (F2)."

Independent representation of Type 470-Ic, which is the "Double Invitation" motif, is made into a subtype in Thompson (1961) as *470A The Offended Skull (Statue)*. For this analogue I referred the reader to my Type 780, "The Singing Skull," for in Japan the "Double Invitation" motif does not stand by itself but is combined with the motifs of the "Singing Bones," or "Return from Death to Reveal Murder (E231)." Before proceeding into detail, I shall present the relevant part of my Type 780:

Type 780 The Singing Bone

I. Murder. A man kills his friend (relative) in a lonely mountain pass and steals his money.

II. The Singing Skull (1) Later the murderer passes the spot and finds a skull on a tree, singing. The skull persuades the man to take it along, allow it to sing and thus make money. (2) The skull is found by a passer-by, who treats it with respect, offering it food (E341.2) and praying for its well-being (E341.3).

III. Murder Revealed. (1) The skull will not sing when a bet is made with a life at stake as to whether the skull really sings or not. (2) The skull tells the passer-by whose skull it is, or how the murder was committed.

IV. The Grateful Dead. (1) The murdered man's ghost leads the passer-by home on New Year's Eve, where a memorial feast is being held. The ghost offers him food. They are invisible to the guests. When the father of the dead man scolds a maid for breaking a dish, the dead man is disgusted and leaves, so that the passer-by becomes visible. His explanation clarifies the fate of the missing son, and he is given a reward.

The description of this type in Thompson (1961) is:

Type 780 The Singing Bone. A man kills his brother (sister) and buries him in the earth. From the bones a shepherd makes a flute which brings the secret to light.

The introductory part of the Japanese analogue is an exact match to the above Aarne-Thompson plot, the murder and the singing by the skull or the bones. When I was writing my dissertation, research on this type was done in connection with Type 720: "My Mother Slew Me." The Japanese analogue of Type 720 takes on the "Flute" element of the Aa-Th Type 780. The following is the plot of my Type 720:

Children are murdered by a cruel stepmother during their father's absence. Where the bodies are buried a bamboo grows. A wandering flute-playing monk asks for a piece of the bamboo to make a flute. When he plays on it, the sound travels far and alerts the father, revealing the murder. Or, when the father comes home a bird sings of the murder.

In short, the "Double Invitation" motif, which is attributed to Type

470 in Thompson (1928 and 1961), is found in Japan as an essential element in my Type 780. The "Flute" motif originally found in the Aa-Th Type 780 appears in Japan compounded with Type 720.

My Type 780 was finished early in the 1950's; I wrote my analogues of Type 470 and its subtypes in the winter of 1963, revising them the following year. I established the Japanese analogue of Type 470 only after extensive reading of the early literature, and also after careful study of the motif analysis and the subtypes in Thompson (1961). The two types were linked together by making references to each other in August of 1964. In the *Nippon Ryooiki*, A.D. 822, two versions of Type 780 are found, and, as mentioned earlier, there are twelve versions of Type 470 also included. It seems to me to be a significant fact that both of these tale-types were well established in multiple versions and found concurrently in this Buddhist literature of the 9th century.

As I worked on various tale-types for my publication (1971), I began to conceive a theory that a firmly established type would develop many variants, often borrowing motifs from other tale-types, or combining together other tale-types, thus creating new subtypes. The main type and its satellite subtypes form a "Cycle." (This was discussed earlier.) It is important to point out here that this borrowing seems to occur only among concurrent tale-types. Interrelationships of Types 470, 780, and 720, as presented above, point to their being contemporaneous. Among the types which came to Japan at different times, the borrowing of motifs seems not to have occurred.

This assumption is based on my visualizing several diffusion waves of narrative literature coming into Japan from various directions, the earlier waves dating back beyond the written records.

What I picture as the oldest dissemination route of culture leading to Japan, including oral literature, involves the circumpolar migration course of Mongoloids to the New World (see Boas, 1940c, pp. 344-355). In this circumpolar progression thousands of years ago, it was possible for some migrations to turn southward off the course and go inland, along the coast of Asia, or down the Kamchatka Peninsula, and thus to have reached northern Japan. Northern Japan shares with northern Eurasia and the circumpolar regions such features as mat ceramics, bear ceremonials, and animal tales, especially the bear-fox cycle. My paper (1960) was an attempt to prove the existence of these prehistoric circumpolar cultural traits in Japan. The fact that the "Earth-Diver" motif, which is well established among the the American Indians, is found in *Kojiki* (A.D. 712) may be another proof. I could also supplement my point by citing the existence in northern Japan of house-spirit worship, a well-known practice in Russia (Dorson, 1962, p. 89).

Cultural features which are found encircling the Pacific and moving up along the Japan Current seem equally as old as those of circumpolar distribution. Leo Frobenius (1938) shows by charts a number of motifs of this circum-Pacific distribution pattern. Among them are: "A baby born of a dead mother in her grave (T584.2.1)," "Trick feeding of hot stones (K951.1)," "Origin of food from the body of the slain food goddess (A1420.1)" and "Recovering the lost fish hook (H1132.1.5)," which is to be discussed as Type 470C below. Some of these motifs in his charts were not known by Frobenius to exist in Japan at the time of his writing.

From about 300 B.C. an entirely new type of culture complex known as the Yayoi culture started to come into Japan from the southern part of Korea. A considerable number of people came pouring in with such cultural traits as rice cultivation, weaving, iron tools, bronze weapons, dolmens, pot coffins and Yayoi ceramics. The Yayoi period extended from ca. 300 B.C. to A.D. 200, its culture flourishing in northern Kyushu for some time, and then spreading toward the south and east to cover the western half of Japan. Later developments of the Yayoi culture eventually spread still farther east (Ishida, 1958). This is a possible third wave of the diffusion of oral narratives. Toward the end of the Yayoi period, from about the 3rd to the 5th centuries, the present emperor's ancestors established their power in the central part of Honshu, the main island of Japan. Some Japanese anthropologists maintain that the ruling power of Japan originated in northern Korea, probably Puyo or Koguryo. They point out the close resemblance between foundation myths of Korea and Japan. Many narrative motifs of the myths and legends of Japan show agreement in detail with Korean material.

Coming into the historical period, during the reign of the early emperors, Chinese characters and writing were introduced to Japan from Korea, as was Buddhism. In China the civilization of the T'ang dynasty was in full bloom during the Nara period, which covers most of the 7th and 8th centuries. By this time Japan was sending ambassadors, Buddhist priests, and students directly to China. The introduction of writing and Buddhism into Japan opened a new route for the documentary transmission of folk literature, mostly through Buddhist sources, by way of China and Korea, and from countries beyond. Tales recorded in the *Ryooiki,* A.D. 822, and the *Konjaku,* A.D. 1077, belong to this group, among which is Type 470 under discussion.

Culture of a different quality, because of the domination of the Yuan dynasty, seems to have had an influence on Japanese folk narratives in the 13th and 14th centuries. As mentioned earlier, this could be the explanation of the uniqueness of the subject matter of Kyoogen, the folk drama originated about this time.

The last stratum of narratives in Japan I want to mention seems to bear the mark of Chinese literary tradition of the Ming dynasty, which covers the next two centuries, the 15th and 16th. They are humorous tales of stupid men and women. Many of these tales are also known in Europe. Those belonging to this category bear Aarne-Thompson type-numbers above 1,000.

I shall return to the discussion of the "cycle" of Type 470, which illustrates the co-existence of literary and oral traditions within a cycle.

Type 470 was introduced to Japan through the propagation of Buddhism in the Buddhist literature, and the Legend of Urashima existed in Japanese oral tradition long before the introduction of Buddhism. The last of Thompson's three subtypes, Type 470*, gave me a start when I read its short description for the first time. This 470*, reported in small print and in a handful of versions from Poland, Hungary, and among the Finnish-Swedish group, turned out to be the analogue of the legend of Urashima, or Ura-no-Shimako, a fisherman visiting the Sea World, one of the best known narratives in Japan from the oldest times to the present. Although so well-known, I had to omit it from my dissertation, because I was unable to find the European equivalent in Thompson (1928) at the time of writing. The following is the oldest recorded version found in the local records of Tango Province written in the 8th century:

> One day in the year 478, Ura-no-Shimako, a fisherman, after three days of futile fishing in the ocean, caught a five-colored turtle. Right before his eyes in the boat the turtle turned into a beautiful girl, and she was the daughter of the Sea-God. She took him to her submarine world. While he was kept waiting outside the gate of her palace, he saw seven and then eight children come together. She later explained they were two constellations, the Pleiades group and the Bull. He was introduced to her family, married her, and lived a happy, carefree life. However, after three years he became hopelessly homesick. His wife consented to his going back and gave him a little bejeweled box to take along on his journey home. She warned him never to open it if he ever wished to come back to her again. He was sent back to his home village, but everything was changed and he knew no one. He was told by a villager that three hundred years ago a fisherman named Ura-no-Shimako had gone out to the sea and never returned. Bewildered, he opened the forbidden box, and a mysterious orchidlike fragrance wafted out into the sky.

The Urashima legend ends with instant aging of the hero. In the above version, all the elements of the analysis of Type 470 are there, the visit to the other world, the extraordinary sights witnessed (F171), which are explained to him by the guide, the return and death of the hero. The homesickness is not clearly stated in the Aa-Th 470* description, but it is usual in the case of a human sojourning in the other world, that he or she becomes very homesick (F374).

In my eagerness in 1964 to set up this ancient legend 470* after the pattern of 470, I neglected to have a closer look at the difference between the two, the ending. What I began to suspect some time afterward was that in the ending of this Urashima legend, the motif of the "Forgotten Fiancee (D2003)" might be compounded, borrowed from Type 313.

Type 313 as described in Thompson (1961) is:

I. The hero for various reasons comes into an ogre's power.

II. Tasks. The ogre assigns the hero impossible tasks, such as cutting down a forest or planting a vineyard in one day, which are performed with the magic help of the ogre's daughter.

III. The Flight. The hero escapes with the girl. When pursued closely by the ogre, they throw objects behind them, which miraculously turn into obstacles. They escape and get married.

IV. The Forgotten Fiancee (D2003). The hero forgets his bride when, against her warning, he breaks a tabu on his visit home.

Motifs of the Type 313 are found in the *Kojiki*, which was compiled in A.D. 712, and this type in Japan is interrelated with such similarly ancient types as 328, 400, 465, and 554.

When I was preparing the outline of this paper, I realized that the ending of the Urashima legend (Type 470*) had such elements as the hero's desire to visit his home, the wife's warning against a tabu, and the broken tabu, which altogether constituted the "Forgotten Fiancee (D2003)," and which was Part IV of the Aa-Th Type 313. This suspicion was followed up, and I became convinced that indeed the Urashima legend ended with the "Forgotten Fiancee" motif.

Now that the close relationship between Types 470* and 313 had been established, other ancient types that were already known to be close to Type 313 needed to be re-examined in comparison with 470*, particularly the "Forgotten Fiancee" element. When I was compiling my type list (1971), I thought this motif existed in Japan only at the ending of Type 314, but now there is the Urashima legend that shares the same ending. In addition, the ending of Type 400 has turned out to be another "Forgotten Fiancee" variant which was indeed an exciting further discovery. Japanese Type 400 is as follows:

Type 400 The Man on a Quest for his Lost Celestial Wife

I. The hero is directed to a lake in answer to his prayer for a wife, by divine revelation because he is honest, or by a deer whose life he has saved.

II. He sees celestial maidens bathing in the lake. By stealing the flying feather garment of one of them, she is forced to marry him. They have children.

III. The wife recovers her flying garment by getting information of its whereabouts from her children. She returns to the Sky-world, leaving instructions as to how her husband can follow her there.

IV. The husband visits this other world by following her instructions.

V. Tasks (Compare Type 313-II). There his father-in-law assigns impossible tasks, which are performed with the magic help of his wife.

VI. Tabu on Melons. The husband is warned by his wife against eating melons. While he is performing the task of harvesting an enormous quantity of melons, he is overcome with a desire to eat one and cuts it in two. Water gushes out from inside, and he and his wife are swept apart by the torrent, finally finding themselves on either side of the Milky Way. They are allowed to meet only once a year on the eve of July 7, which is the Festival of Stars.

Some sixty oral versions have been collected in Japan, many stopping at the end of Part IV, without going into the sequel of the father-in-law's tasks. The type is rich in literary sources, the earliest being the *Fudoki*, local records compiled in the 8th century. The tale is often told as legends of ponds and lakes.

In the above the tabu is against the husband eating melons, whereas in the Urashima legend (470*) it is against opening a box. However different the two stories may seem, the underlying basic plot is the same.

There still remain three more Japanese variants within the cycle, which I have casually named 470A, 470B, and 470C. The first two seem to be derivations from earlier prototypes. These two tales begin in the same way. The hero pleases the Sea-God, and is invited to be his guest in the submarine palace. The messenger instructs him on what to ask before they get to the palace. The hero picks a gift as instructed, which is an ugly child, a dog, other magic objects, or the hand of the Sea-God's daughter. Unlike the Urashima legend, the hero comes home soon after the gifts are received, and leads a prosperous life because these gifts provide riches. However, in the end, the magic gifts are abused, and the hero loses them (470A). In Type 470B, the hero comes home with his supernatural wife and they live happily together. She brings prosperity; but then the feudal lord of the province covets her (Type 465), and in order to take her away from the husband, assigns the man impossible tasks (compare 313-II). With the help of his wife, the man accomplishes the tasks, and the lord is punished in the end.

What I call Type 470C in my type list (1971) is the famous "Lost Fish Hook" story of the circum-Pacific distribution. Strictly, it should have been called 470X or 470Y to indicate that the tale was concurrent with the Urashima legend (470*), being recorded in the *Kojiki*, A.D. 712. The story goes as follows:

Type 470C The Lost Fish Hook . . . . *Umisachi Yamasachi*

I. Fisher and Hunter. A fisherman and hunter are brothers. They exchange their tools one day just for a change, but are not successful in using them. The hunter loses the fish hook and attempts to make a substitute. The fisherman demands that the original hook be returned.

II. Visit to the Submarine World. The hunter goes about this according to the instruction of an old man whom he has met on the beach. He is to climb on a tree by a well near the palace gate. The princess's maid comes to draw water from the well, sees his reflection in water and reports it to her mistress. The princess comes out and falls in love with the hunter. They are married.

III. Fish Hook Recovered. After three years the hunter heaves a sigh and is asked by the Dragon King for the reason. Learning of the lost fish hook, the king summons all the fish of the sea, and recovers the hook from an ailing *tai* fish (B548.2.3).

IV. Brother Conquered. The hunter and his wife go home with a gift from the king—jewels to control the tide. He returns the hook and chants a curse as instructed by the king. His brother becomes unlucky in everything and resentful against the hunter. Whenever the fisher stages an attack, he nearly drowns in a sudden rush of the tide: he becomes his brother's subject.

V. Loss of the Supernatural Wife. The wife tells him not to look into the place where she is giving birth. He breaks this tabu and finds she has changed into a huge *wani*. (Currently the translation for this is "crocodile.") She leaves him (D2003).

The main theme is the "Lost Fish Hook," but the structure is the visit to the other world, winning a supernatural wife, her warning against a tabu, the tabu broken, and loss of the wife, the same as other tale-types discussed above, compounding Type 313.

Gudmund Hatt (1949, p. 90) says:

The story of the lost fishing-hook (B548.2.3) is spread over Japan, Indonesia and Micronesia, and closely related forms are found in America, especially on the North Pacific Coast. This has been pointed out long ago by Boas. Dixon has also been interested in this motif: he quotes it from Kei Island, Halmahera, Soemba, Celebes, and Sumatra. In Micronesia, it is recorded by Kubary on the Pelew Islands. It is also known from Yap (Müller, Wilhelm). The most famous version is the old Japanese one, which is recorded in *Nihongi* and *Kojiki.*

The "Lost Fish Hook" is mentioned by Boas (1940b, p. 444):

Another very curious coincidence is found between a myth from the Pelew Islands and several from the North Pacific Coast. J. Kubary (A. Bastian: *Allerlei aus Volks- und Menschenkunde,* Berlin, 1888, Vol. 1, p. 63) tells the following: "A young man had lost his fish-hook, the line having been broken by a fish. He dived after it, and, on reaching the bottom of the sea, reached a pond, at which he sat down. A girl came out of a house to fetch some water for a sick woman. He was called in and cured her, while all her friends did not know what ailed her." In British Columbia we find the same story, an arrow being substituted for the hook, a land animal for the fish.

In the above 19th-century version from the Palau Islands, the plot does not extend into matrimony: the hero meets a girl by a pond who leads him to the ailing woman (fish) who has evidently swallowed the fish hook.

Whether this simplified plot, without the elements of Type 313, is through deterioration, or is an archetype, a comparison of available versions of the area will determine. A question can be raised here regarding the diffusion of a motif. Would a motif disseminate by itself, or when a motif is found in an area, is it a result of the deterioration of a type that once existed there? Further, could a tale-type travel alone, or do different types of tales disseminate together as a group?

Through the study of the "cycle" of Type 470, I have attempted to point out the problems involved in type-indexing. Identification of motifs and tale-types will be achieved through the analytical examination of the source material, both oral and written. Thus I have discovered a number of analogues which have not been known to exist in Japan.

Theories concerning the "cycle," its behavior, the interrelations of the component types and motifs within a cycle, its age and various diffusion routes in connection with time and space these theories were formulated as a result of my work of twenty years, type-indexing Japanese folk literature.

LITERATURE CITED

AARNE, ANTTI
   1910. *Verzeichnis der Märchentypen*. FF Communications 3. Helsinki.
BOAS, FRANZ
   1940a "The Development of Folk-Tales and Myths." In *Race, Language and Culture*, pp. 397-406. New York: Macmillan. (First published in *Scientific Monthly*, 1916, **3**:335-343.)
   1940b. "Dissemination of Tales among the Natives of North America." In *Race, Language and Culture*, pp. 437-445. New York: Macmillan. (First published in *J. American Folklore* 1891, **4**:13-20.)
   1940c. "Relationship between North-West America and North-East Asia." In *Race, Language and Culture*, pp. 344-355. New York: Macmillan. (First published in D. JENNESS (ed.), *The American Aborigines: Their Origin and Antiquity*. Toronto: Toronto Univ. Press, 1933.)
   1940d. *Race, Language and Culture*. New York: Macmillan. (Reprinted, 1966, by The Free Press.)
DORSON, RICHARD M.
   1962. *Folk Legends of Japan*. Tokyo: Tuttle.
FROBENIUS, LEO
   1938. "Das Archiv für Folkloristik." *Paideuma* **1**(1):1-19.
HATT, GUDMUND
   1949. *Asiatic Influences in American Folklore*. Copenhagen.
HAUTALA, JOUKO
   1964. "Kaarle Krohn as a Folklorist." *Studia Fennica* **11**(3):1-72.

HOLBEK, BENGT, and OTHERS
1971. *Biographica: Nordic Folklorists of the Past.* Copenhagen.
IKEDA, HIROKO
1958. "Amerika ni okeru Minwa Kenkyuu no Dentoo to Genzai." [Folktale Studies in the U.S.: Past and Present.] *Bungaku* **26**(8):109-117.
1960. "Kachi-kachi Mountain: A Japanese Animal Tale Cycle." In *Humaniora: Archer Taylor Festschrift*, pp. 229-238. Garden City: Augustin.
1964. "Ura no Shima-ko" [The Urashima Legend and the Don Juan Legend]. In *Ishida Eiichiro Kanreki Kinen Rombun Shuu*, pp. 33-44. Tokyo: Kadokawa.
1971. *A Type and Motif Index of Japanese Folk Literature.* FF Communications 209. Helsinki.
ISHIDA, EIICHIRO
1958. *Nippon Minzoku no Kigen* [Japanese Cultural Origins]. Tokyo: Heibonsha.
1962. "Nature of the Problem of Japanese Cultural Origins." In *Japanese Culture: Its Development and Characteristics*, pp. 1-6. Chicago: Aldine.
KIRTLEY, BACIL F.
1971. *A Motif-Index of Traditional Polynesian Narratives.* Honolulu: Univ. Hawaii Press.
LOWIE, ROBERT H.
1937. *The History of Ethnological Theory.* New York: Rinehart.
OLRIK, AXEL
1965. "Epic Laws of Folk Narrative." In *The Study of Folklore*, pp. 129-141. Englewood Cliffs: Prentice-Hall. (First published in 1909.)
ROBERTS, WARREN E., and STITH THOMPSON
1960. *Types of Indic Oral Tales.* FF Communications 180. Helsinki.
THOMPSON, STITH
1928. *The Types of the Folktale.* FF Communications 74. Helsinki.
1946. *The Folktale.* New York: Dryden.
1955-1958. *Motif-Index of Folk-Literature.* 6 vols. Copenhagen and Bloomington.
1956. Folklorist's Progress. (Mimeo., privately circulated.)
1961. *The Types of the Folktale.* FF Communications 184. Helsinki.

INDEX

114

77 01693 224